The Collected Works
of
J. Krishnamurti

Volume II

1934–1935

What Is Right Action?

KENDALL/HUNT PUBLISHING COMPANY
2460 Kerper Boulevard   P.O. Box 539   Dubuque, Iowa 52004-0539

Contents

Preface

Jiddu Krishnamurti was born in 1895 of Brahmin parents in south India. At the age of fourteen he was proclaimed the coming World Teacher by Annie Besant, then president of the Theosophical Society, an international organization that emphasized the unity of world religions. Mrs. Besant adopted the boy and took him to England, where he was educated and prepared for his coming role. In 1911 a new worldwide organization was formed with Krishnamurti as its head, solely to prepare its members for his advent as World Teacher. In 1929, after many years of questioning himself and the destiny imposed upon him, Krishnamurti disbanded this organization, saying:

Truth is a pathless land, and you cannot approach it by any path whatsoever, by any religion, by any sect. Truth, being limitless, unconditioned, unapproachable by any path whatsoever, cannot be organized; nor should any organization be formed to lead or to coerce people along any particular path. My only concern is to set men absolutely, unconditionally free.

Until the end of his life at the age of ninety, Krishnamurti traveled the world speaking as a private person. The rejection of all spiritual and psychological authority, including his own, is a fundamental theme. A major concern is the social structure and how it conditions the individual. The emphasis in his talks and writings is on the psychological barriers that prevent clarity of perception. In the mirror of relationship, each of us can come to understand the content of his own consciousness, which is common to all humanity. We can do this, not analytically, but directly in a manner Krishnamurti describes at length. In observing this content we discover within ourselves the division of the observer and what is observed. He points out that this division, which prevents direct perception, is the root of human conflict.

His central vision did not waver after 1929, but Krishnamurti strove for the rest of his life to make his language even more simple and clear. There is a development in his exposition. From year to year he used new terms and new approaches to his subject, with different nuances.

Because his subject is all-embracing, the *Collected Works* are of compelling interest. Within his talks in any one year, Krishnamurti was not able to cover the whole range of his vision, but broad amplifications of particular themes are found throughout these volumes. In them he lays the foundations of many of the concepts he used in later years.

The *Collected Works* contain Krishnamurti's previously published talks, discussions, answers to specific questions, and writings for the years 1933 through 1967. They are an authentic record of his teachings, taken from transcripts of verbatim shorthand reports and tape recordings.

The Krishnamurti Foundation of America, a California charitable trust, has among its purposes the publication and distribution of Krishnamurti books, videocassettes, films and tape recordings. The production of the *Collected Works* is one of these activities.

Auckland, New Zealand, 1934

---------- ✳ ----------

First Talk in Town Hall

Friends,

I think each one is caught up in either a religious problem or a social struggle or an economic conflict. Each one is suffering through the lack of the understanding of these various problems, and we try to solve each one of these problems by itself; that is, if you have a religious problem, you think you are going to solve it by brushing away the economic or the social problem and centering entirely on the religious problem, or you have an economic problem and you think that you are going to solve that economic problem by wholly confining yourself to that one particular conflict. Whereas, I say you cannot solve these problems by themselves; you cannot solve the religious problem by itself, nor the economic nor the social problem, unless you see the inter-relationship between the religious, the social, and the economic problems.

What we call problems are merely symptoms, which increase and multiply because we do not tackle the whole life as one, but divide it as economic, social, or religious problems. If you look at all the various solutions that are offered for the various ailments, you will see that they deal with the problems apart, in water-tight compartments, and do not take the religious, social, and

economic problems comprehensively as a whole. Now it is my intention to show that so long as we deal with these problems apart, separately, we but increase the misunderstanding, and therefore the conflict, and thereby the suffering and the pain; whereas, until we deal with the social problem and the religious and economic problems as a comprehensive whole, not as divided, but rather see the delicate and the subtle connection between what we call religious, social, or economic problems— until you see this real connection, this intimate and subtle connection between these three, whatever problem you may have, you are not going to solve it. You will but increase the struggle. Though we may think we have solved one problem, that problem again arises in a different form, so we go on through life solving problem after problem, struggle after struggle, without fully comprehending the full significance of our living.

So then, to understand the intimate connection between what we call religious, social, and economic problems, there must be a complete reorientation of thought—that is, each individual must no longer be a cog, a machine, either in the social or the religious structure. Look, and you will see that most human beings are slaves, merely cogs in this machine. They are not really human beings, but merely react to a set environment and therefore there is no true individual action, individual thought; and to find out that intimate relationship between all our actions, religious, political, or social, you as an individual must think, not as a group, not as a collective body; and that is one of the most difficult things to do, for individuals to step out of the social structure, or the religious, and examine it critically, to find out what is false and what true in that structure. And then you will see that you are no longer concerned with a symptom, but are trying to find out the cause of the problem itself, and not merely deal with the symptoms.

Perhaps some of you will say at the end of my talk that I have given you nothing positive, nothing on which you can definitely work, a system which you can follow. I have no system. I think systems are pernicious things, because they may for the moment alleviate the problems, but if you merely follow a system you are a slave to it. You merely substitute a new system for the old, which does not bring about comprehension. What brings about comprehension is not to search for a new system, but to discover for yourselves, as individuals, not as a collective machine but as individuals, what is false and what is true in the existing system, not to substitute a new system for the old.

Now, to be able to criticize, to be able to question, is the first essential requirement for any thinking man, so that he will begin to discover what is false and what is true in the existing system, and therefore out of that thought there is action, and not mere acceptance. So during this talk, if you would understand what I am going to say, there must be criticism. Criticism is essential. Questioning is right, but we have been trained not to question, not to criticize, we have been carefully trained to oppose. For instance, if I am going to say anything which you are going to dislike—as I shall, I hope—you will naturally begin to oppose it, because opposition is

easier than to find out if what I am saying has any value. If you discover what I am saying has value, then there is action, and hence you will have to alter your whole attitude towards life. Therefore, as we are not prepared to do that, we have made a clever technique of opposition. That is, if anything I am saying you do not like, you bring up all your deep-rooted prejudices and obstruct, and if I say anything which may hurt you, or which may emotionally upset you, you take shelter behind these prejudices, these traditions, this background; and from that background you react, and that reaction you call criticism. To me it is not criticism. It is merely clever opposition, which has no value.

Now, if you are all Christians—and presumably you are all Christians—perhaps I am going to say something which you may not understand, and instead of trying to find out what I want to convey, you will immediately take shelter behind the traditions, behind the deep-rooted prejudices and authorities of the established order, and from that fortress, on the defensive, attack. To me that is not criticism; that is a clever way of not acting, of avoiding full, complete action.

If you would understand what I am going to say, I would request you to be really critical, not to be clever in your opposition. To be critical demands a great deal of intelligence. Criticism is not skepticism, or acceptance; that would be equally stupid. If you merely said, "Well, I am skeptical about what you say," that would be as stupid as to merely accept. Whereas, true criticism consists not in giving values, but in trying to find out the true values. Is it not so? If you give values to things, if the mind gives values, then you are not finding out the intrinsic merit of the thing, and most of our minds are trained to give values. Take money, for example. Abstractly, money has no value. It has the value we give to it. That is, if you want power which money gives, then you use money to get power, so you are giving a value to something which has inherently no value; so likewise, if you are going to find out and understand what I am going to say, you must have this capacity of criticism, which is really easy if you want to find out, if you want to discover, not if you say, "Well, I don't want to be attacked. I am on the defensive. I have everything I want, I am perfectly satisfied." Then such an attitude is pretty hopeless. Then you are here merely out of curiosity—and the majority probably are—and what I shall say will have no significance, and therefore you will say it is negative, nothing constructive, nothing positive.

So please bear this in mind, that we are going to discover this evening, consider together, what are the false things and the true in the existing social and religious conditions; and to do that please do not bring in continually your prejudices, whether Christian, or of some other sect, but rather have this intelligent, critical attitude, not only with regard to what I am going to say, but with regard to everything in life, which means the cessation of seeking new systems, not the search for a new system which, when found, will again be perverted, corrupted. In the discovery of the false and the true in the social, the religious, and the economic systems—the false and the true which we have created for ourselves—in the discovery of that, we shall keep our minds and hearts from creating false environments in which the mind is likely to be caught again.

Most of you are seeking a new system of thought, a new system of economics, a new system of religious philosophy. Why are you seeking a new system? You say, "I am dissatisfied with the old," that is, if you are seeking. Now I say, don't seek a new system, but rather examine the very system in which you are held, and then you will see that no system of any kind will bring about the crea-

tive intelligence which is essential for the understanding of truth or God or whatever name you like to give to it. That means that by the following of no system you are going to discover that eternal reality; but you are going to find it only when you, as individuals, begin to understand the very system that you have built up through the centuries, and in that system discover what is true and what is false.

So please bear that in mind—that I am not giving a new system of philosophy. I think these systems are cages for the mind to be caught up in. They do not help man, they are merely hindrances. These systems are a means of exploitation. Whereas, if you as individuals begin to question, you will see that in that questioning you create conflict, and out of the conflict you will understand— not in the mere acceptance of a new system which is merely another soporific which puts you to sleep and turns you into another machine.

So let us find out the false and the true in the existing systems—the systems of religion and sociology. To find out what is false and true, we must see what the religions are based on. Now, I am talking of religion as the crystallized form of thought which has become the community's highest ideal. I hope you are following all this. That is, religions as they are, not as you would like them to be. As they are, what are they based on? What is their foundation? When you see, when you examine and really critically think about it—not bring up your hopes and prejudices, but when you really think about it—you will see that they are based on comfort, giving you comfort when you are suffering. That is, the human mind is continually seeking security, a position of certainty, either in a belief or an ideal, or in a concept, and so you are continually seeking a certainty, security, in which the mind takes shelter as comfort. Now what happens when you are continually seeking security, safety, certainty? Naturally that creates fear, and when there is fear there must be conformity. Please, I have not the time to go into details. I will do that in my various talks, but in this talk I want to put it all concisely, and if you are interested you can think it over, and then we can discuss it in question and answer meetings.

So the so-called religions give the pattern of conformity to the mind that is seeking security born of fear, in search of comfort; and where there is the search for comfort, there is no understanding. Our religions throughout the world, in their desire to give comfort, in their desire to lead you to a particular pattern, to mold you, give you various patterns, molds, securities, through what they call faith. That is one of the things they demand—faith. Please do not misunderstand. Do not jump ahead of me. They demand faith, and you accept faith because it gives you a shelter from the conflict of daily existence, from the continual struggle, worries, pains, and sorrows. So out of that faith, which must be a dogmatic faith, churches are born, and out of that are established ideas, beliefs.

Now to me—and please bear this in mind, I want you to criticize, not accept—to me all beliefs, all ideals are a hindrance because they prevent you from understanding the present. You say beliefs, ideals, faith, are necessary as a lighthouse which will direct you through the turmoil of life. That is, you are more interested in beliefs, in tradition, in ideals and faith, than in comprehending the turmoil itself. To understand the turmoil you cannot have a belief, prejudice; you must look at it completely, hold it with a fresh mind, with a mind uninfected, not with a mind which is biased with a particular prejudice which we call an ideal. So where there is a search for comfort, security, there must be a pattern, a mold, in which we take

shelter, and therefore we begin to preconceive what God must be, and what truth must be.

Now to me, there is a living reality. There is something eternally becoming, fundamental, real, lasting, but it cannot be preconceived; it demands no belief, it demands a mind that is not tethered to an ideal as an animal is tied to a post, but on the contrary, demands a mind that is continually moving, experimenting, never staying. I say there is a living reality; call it God, truth, anything you like, which is of very little importance—and to understand that, there needs to be supreme intelligence, and therefore there cannot be any conformity, but rather the questioning of those things false and true in which the mind is caught up. And you will see that most people, most of you who are religiously inclined, are in search of truth, and that very search indicates that you are escaping from the conflict of the present, or you are dissatisfied with the present condition. Therefore you try to find out what is the real; that is, you leave the condition which creates conflict and run away and try to find out what God is, what truth is. Therefore that search is the denial of truth, because you are running away—there is escape, desire for comfort, security. Therefore, when religions are based as they are, on the giving of securities, there must be exploitation; and to me religions as they are exist on nothing but a series of exploitations. What we call the mediators between our present conflict and that supposed reality have become our exploiters, and they are priests, Masters, teachers, saviors; because I say it is only through understanding the present conflict with all its significance, with all its delicate nuances—it is only thus that you can find out what is the real, and no one can lead you to it.

If both the inquirer and the teacher knew what truth is, then you could both go towards it; but the disciple cannot know what truth is.

Therefore his inquiry after truth can only exist in the conflict, not away from conflict, and therefore, to me, any teacher who describes what truth is, what God is, is denying that very thing, that immeasurable thing which cannot be measured by words. The illusion of words cannot hold it, and the bridge of words cannot lead you to it. It is only when you, as an individual, begin to realize in the immense conflict, the cause and therefore the falseness of that conflict, that you will find out what is truth. In that there is everlasting happiness, intelligence; but not in this spurious thing called spirituality which is but a conformity, driven by authority through fear. I say there is something exquisitely real, infinite; but to discover it man must not be an imitative machine, and our religions are nothing but that. And besides, our religions throughout the world keep people apart. That is, you with your particular prejudices, calling yourselves Christians, and the Indians with their particular beliefs, calling themselves Hindus, never meet. Your beliefs are keeping you apart. Your religions are keeping you apart. "But," you say, "if the Hindus could only become Christians, then we would have a unity"; or the Hindus say, "Let them all become Hindus." Even then there is a division, because belief necessitates a division, a distinction, and therefore exploitation and the continual struggle of distinctive classes.

We say religions unify. On the contrary. Look at the world split up into narrow little sects, fighting against each other to increase their membership, their wealth, their positions, their authorities, thinking they are the truth. There is only one truth, but you cannot go to it through any sect, through any religion. To discover what is true in religion, and what is false, you cannot be a machine; you cannot accept things as they are. You will if you are satisfied, and if you are satisfied you won't listen to me, and my talk will be useless. But if you are dissatisfied I will help you to question rightly, and out of the questioning you will find out what is truth, and in that discovery of what is true you will find out how to live richly, completely, ecstatically; not with this constant struggle, battling against everything for your own security, which you call virtue.

Again, this fear which is created through the search for security, this fear seeks shelter in society. Society is nothing else but the expression of the individual multiplied by the thousand. After all, society is not some mysterious thing. It is what you are. It is pressing, controlling, dominating, twisting. Society is the expression of the individual. This society offers security through tradition, which we call public opinion. That is, public opinion says that to possess, to possess property, is perfectly ethical, moral, and gives you distinction in this world, confers honors; you are a great person in this world. That is what, traditionally, is accepted. That is the opinion which you have created as individuals, because you are seeking that. You all want to be somebody in the state, either Sir Somebody or Lord, you know, and all the rest of it, which is based on possessiveness, possessions; and that has become moral, true, good, perfectly Christian, or perfectly Hindu. It is the same thing. Now we call that morality. We call morality adjusting yourself to a pattern. Please, I am not preaching the reverse of it. I am showing you the falseness of it, and if you want to find out you will act, not seek the opposite. That is, you consider possessions, whether your wife, your children, your property, you consider that perfectly moral. Now suppose another society came into being where possessions are evil, where this idea of possessiveness is ethically forbidden—driven into your mentality as possessiveness is now driven in by circumstances, by condition, by education, by opinion. Then morality loses all significance, morality then is merely a convenience. Not the right perception of things, but the clever adjusting to circumstances—that you call morality. Suppose that you want, as individuals, to be not possessive, look what you have to fight! The whole system of society is nothing but possessiveness. If you would understand it and not be driven by circumstances which are not called moral, then you, as individuals, must begin to break away from the system voluntarily, and not be driven like so many sheep to accept the morality of nonpossessiveness.

Now you are driven, whether you like it or not, whether you think it is sane or not; you are driven by conditions, environment, which you have created, because you are still possessive, and now perhaps another system will come along and drive you to the opposite—to be nonpossessive. Surely it is not morality; it is just sheepishness to be driven by environment to be possessive or nonpossessive. Whereas, to me, true morality consists in understanding fully the absurdity of possessiveness and voluntarily fighting it; not being driven either way.

Now, if you look, this society is based on class consciousness which is again the consciousness of security. As beliefs grow into religions, so possessions grow into the expression of nationality. As beliefs separate people, condition people, keep them apart, so possessiveness, expressing itself as class consciousness and growing into nationality, keeps people apart. That is, all nationality is based on the exploitation of the majority by the few for their own benefit through the means of production. That nationality, through the instrument of patriotism, is a means of war. All nationalities, all sovereign governments, must prepare for war; it is their duty, and it is no good your being a pacifist and at the same time talking about patriotism. You cannot talk about brotherhood, and then talk about Christianity, be-

cause that denies it; no more here than in India, or in any other country. In India they can talk about Hinduism and say we are one, all humanity is one. Those are just words— hypocrisy.

So all nationalities are a means of war. When I was speaking in India, they said to me (at present the Hindus are going through that disease of nationalism), "Let us look after our own country first because there are so many starving people; then we can talk about human unity"; which is the same thing you talk about here. "Let us protect ourselves and then we will talk about unity, brotherhood, and all the rest of it." Now, if India is really concerned with the problem of starvation, or if you are really concerned with the problem of unemployment, you cannot deal merely with New Zealand's unemployment problem; it is a human problem, not the problem of one particular group called New Zealand. You cannot solve the problem of starvation as an Indian problem, or a Chinese problem, or the problem of unemployment as an English, or German, or American, or Australasian problem, but you must deal with it as a whole; and you can only deal with it as a whole when you are not nationalistic, and you are not exploited through the means of patriotism. You are not patriotic every morning when you wake up. You are only patriotic when the papers say you must be, because you must conquer your neighbor. We are therefore the barbarians, not the ones invading your country. The barbarian is the patriot. To him, his country is more important than humanity, man; and I say you will not solve your problems, this economic and nationality problem, so long as you are a New Zealander. You will solve it only when you are a real human being, free from all nationalistic prejudices, when you are no longer possessive, and when your mind is not divided by beliefs. Then there can be real human unity, and then the problem of starvation, the problem of unemployment, the problem of war, will disappear, because you consider humanity as a whole and not some particular people who want to exploit other people.

So you see what is dividing men, what is destroying the real glory of living in which alone you can find that living reality, that immortality, that ecstasy; but to find it you must first of all be individuals. That means you must begin to understand, and therefore act, to discover what is false in the existing system, and thereby you will, as individuals, form a nucleus. You cannot alter the mass. What is the mass? Yourselves multiplied. We are waiting for the mass to act, hoping that by some miracle there will be a complete change overnight, because we do not think, we do not want to act. So long as this attitude of waiting exists, there will be greater and greater struggle, more and more suffering, lack of comprehension; life becomes a tragedy, a worthless thing. Whereas if you, as individuals, act voluntarily because you want to understand and discover, then you will become responsible, then you will not become a reformer, then there will be a complete change, not based on possessiveness, on distinctions, but on real humanity in which there is affection, there is thought, and therefore an ecstasy of living.

March 28, 1934

First Talk in Vasanta School Gardens

Friends,

It seems rather a pity that on a fair morning like this we should talk about the various oppressions and cruelty that we every day support, and the various exploitations that are taking place consciously or unconsciously about us; and yet we smile through them all and try to endure them, leading a rather

hideous and ugly life, trying to manage somehow to support the daily ills and the misfortunes that confront each one.

Now if you consider what is taking place, you will see that though there is this oppression, this cruelty, this extraordinary exploitation by individuals of others, yet we continually are seeking satisfaction. Either you as individuals are satisfied in tolerating all these things, or you are going to change them, you are going to alter them. Occasionally, in moments of immediate contact, there is an intense burning desire to change, to uproot, and live decently, humanly, completely, and when that immediate contact is taken away with the sufferings of life, we fall back to satisfaction. So if you are merely satisfied, that is, contented with things as they are in the world, then there is nothing more to be said; and I mean that. If you are really satisfied, happy, contented to go on as you are, with things crumbling, when there is so much corruption, exploitation, and cruelty, real horrors taking place in the world, if you are really satisfied with it, I am afraid my talk will be utterly futile. But if you want to alter it, and if you think that, as human beings, we ought to have a different state, different condition, different environment, not only for the select few, but for the whole of humanity, then let us consider the problem together; not that I want to dogmatize or to push you in one direction or another, influencing you to act in a particular fashion, but rather through considering together we shall come to a natural conclusion from which we must necessarily and naturally act. So there are two things open to each individual, either to do patchwork, to reform, or bring about a complete reorientation of thought, a complete change.

What I call patchwork is this continual alteration in the existing system of thought, but keeping the foundation as it is intact. That is patchwork, isn't it? To keep things fundamentally as they are and alter the superficial difficulties, change about the transient afflictions, but not tackle the fundamental things. Now such work and such thought based upon this idea, I call patchwork or reform. It is like improving the slums of the city. Not that it is bad to improve the slums of the city; but that there should be slums, that there should be people who are exploiting, that there should be this distinction of class division is the problem, not how much improvement you can make. Until we recognize that, and as long as there is not a radical, fundamental change, merely dealing with symptoms is not going to do anything.

So I want this morning to show that so long as thought, and therefore action, is based on this idea of self-aggrandizement, or self-growth, or continually limited self-consciousness, there must be problems arising from this limited consciousness. That is, whether you make any social changes or social reform, so long as the system of thought is based on possessiveness, security, proprietary rights, and so on, there must be problems which can be dealt with only symptomatically, not radically. That is, sirs, suppose there is a reform in possessions; you still think it is perfectly right that you should own your little patch of ground, that everybody else should have patches of ground. That is, you want to cling to your particular possessions and let others have their own possessions; whereas, to me the very idea of possessiveness must lead to conflict with your neighbor, must lead to distinctions as nationalities, class consciousness, snobbery; and if you are reforming how much you shall possess or how much you shall not possess, then you are dealing only symptomatically, not radically. It is like going to a doctor who deals with the symptoms and not with the cause.

Let me take another example. To deal with the symptoms is to consider that you can stick to your particular religion and I can stick to mine, and let us be tolerant. Now, as I explained the other night, to me, the whole process of the foundation of a religion comes through the adherence to a particular belief or dogma. You say you are a religious person, a Christian, because you have certain beliefs, certain ideals, certain dogmas, and you say to yourself that there will be a perfect world when all the people believe as you do, or all the people in the world come to your particular form of thought; and we are trying to patch up, to reform with that attitude towards religions. To me, real reform, real change, real radical change of thought, lies not in the patchwork of reforming religions but in seeing the absurdity of religions. So long as you have beliefs, there must be divisions. So long as you are encaged in a particular form of thought, naturally you are separate from me, and there is no human contact. Then, only prejudices meet, not real human understanding.

So as long as you merely want to reform, that is, to bring about changes in the existing systems of thought, of culture, of possessiveness, though you may momentarily alleviate the suffering, solve the innumerable problems that arise, you are but postponing, putting away for the moment the fundamental question, which is whether a society or a culture shall be based on self-aggrandizement, possessiveness, and exploitation.

So you, as individuals, have to find out what you intend to do, whether you shall belong to a society, to a system of thought, based on this self-aggrandizement, with all its nuances, with its delicate subtleties; or whether you, as individuals, see that so long as that state exists there must be wars, there must be cruelties, there must be exploitation, and therefore you, as individuals, are prepared to change completely and not merely deal symptomatically. As individuals, we are confronted with this problem, with this question, whether we will deal symptomatically, do patchwork, or bring about a complete change of thought, not based on possessiveness and self-importance. Now such an attitude will necessarily bring about by degrees a new society, a new state, a new consciousness, in which there cannot be exploitation, there cannot be this incessant struggle to exist, to merely exist. And you will only deal with this question if you are really considering, if you are concerned, if you are really suffering, not merely sitting down intellectually discussing, theoretically observing. So it is for you to decide by reason, and therefore by action, whether as individuals you will, by your own understanding, bring about a humanity in which there is real understanding, or continue with this ceaseless struggle.

I have been given some questions, and I will answer these. This is what I intend to do every day.

Question: Some of my friends have remarked that although they find your sayings intensely interesting, they prefer service rather than too much thinking about questions of truth. What are your observations on this point?

KRISHNAMURTI: Sir, what do you mean by service? Everybody wants to help. That is the cry of those people who think they are serving the world. They are always talking about helping the world, especially those people who belong to sects. It is their particular form of disease, because they think that by doing something, it does not matter what, they are going to help, by serving people they will help. Who is to say what is service? A man that belongs to the army, prepared to kill the barbarian that enters his country, says he is serving the country. The man that kills, the butcher, says he is serving the community. The exploiter who has the means of production in his hands, monopolized, says he is serving the community. The man who exploits beliefs, the priest, says he is serving the country, community. Who is to decide?

Or shall we look at it quite differently? Do you think a flower, a rose, is ever considering that it is serving humanity, that it is helping the world by its existence because it is beautiful? On the contrary, because it is beautiful, supremely lovely, unconscious of its own magnificence, it is truly helping. Not like a man who goes about shouting that he is serving the world. That is, each one wants to use his means, or his ideas, to exploit the world, not to set the world free. Personally, if you will not misunderstand me, that is not my point of view at all. I do not want to help the world, as you would call it. I cannot help, it naturally happens. That is service. I do not desire to make others come to my particular form of belief or ask them to come into my particular cage of thought, because I hold that to have a belief is a limitation.

To really serve, one must be supremely free from the limited consciousness we call the 'I', the ego, self-centered consciousness; and so long as that exists, you are not really serving the world. Unless you really think, you cannot find out if you are truly helping the world. So let us not first consider whether we are helping the world, but rather find out if we have the capacity to think and to feel. To really think, mind must not be tethered to a belief. That is very simple, is it not? To think really profoundly, frankly, completely, your mind cannot be held by prejudice or a certain belief, or by fear, or by preconceived ideas. To think, the mind must start anew, afresh, and not with a background of tradition. After all, tradition is only valuable when it helps you to think, not when it overpowers you by its weight.

Let me put this thing differently. We all want to help. When you see suffering in the world there is an intense desire to help; but to truly help people you have to go to the fundamental cause of things. You have to discover the cause of suffering, and you can only do that if there is profound thinking. And this thinking is not mere intellectual delight, but it can only take place, this thinking, in action.

Question: It is asserted here that only one or two people in the world can hope to grasp the importance of your message. Therefore the secondary teaching of modern Theosophy is necessary as a substitute for the salvation of the world. What have you to say?

KRISHNAMURTI: Sir, first of all you must find out what I have to say before you can say it is impossible. This is what I want to say. Our whole system of thought and action and living is based on individual aggrandizement and growth at the expense of others. That is a fact, is it not? And so long as that fact in the world exists there must be suffering, there must be exploitation, there must be the division of classes; and no forms of religion can bring about peace, because they are the very creation of human cravings, they are the means of exploitation. That living reality, which I say exists—call it God, truth, or whatever name you like—that supreme intelligence which I say exists, which I say I have realized, is to be found only through freedom from the hindrances which you have created through the search for security and comfort, the security of religions and that artificial security of possessiveness.

Surely, to understand what I am saying is not very difficult. The difficulty lies in putting what I am saying into action. Now, to put it into action does not need courage, but rather comprehension. Most of us are waiting for the world to change, rather than beginning to change ourselves. We are waiting for the world system to alter this attitude with regard to possessiveness, and are not trying to find out if we can, as individuals, be really free from possessiveness. To understand this, this freedom from possessiveness, one must discover intelligently what are one's needs. You know, when you have found out what are your needs, then you are not possessive. Each man will know his needs, very clearly, very simply, if he intelligently approaches it; but there cannot be the discovery of what are his needs so long as mind is caught up in possessiveness, greed, and exploitation. So when you discover what are your needs, you are not making a compromise with your needs and the world's conditions which are based on possessiveness. I hope I am explaining this.

What I want to say is that there cannot be human, vital relationships, or living joyously in the plenitude of life in the present—which to me is the only eternity—so long as mind and heart are crippled through fear; and to overcome that fear we have created innumerable hindrances, such as religions, beliefs, possessiveness, securities. Hence, as individuals, we continually give suffering, continually add to the struggle, to the chaos of the world. Surely that is very simple, really, if you come to think of it.

If you really want to find out what I am saying, please examine one of the ideas I put forward and carry it out in action; then you will see that it does become practical, not vague, theoretical, impossible to grasp. Then you don't want any secondary teaching.

You know, this idea that as people do not understand, therefore you must give them something they will understand, is really a clever way of exploitation. It is the attitude of the capitalist class. It is the attitude of the man who has many possessions. That is, he wants to feed the world, to guide the world, he wants to guide the other man; whereas, I desire to awaken the other man so that he will act for himself. If I can awaken him to his own strength, to his own understanding, to his own responsibility, to his own action, then I destroy class distinction. Then I do not keep him in the nursery to be exploited as a child by one who is supposed to know more. That is the whole attitude of religions, that you can never find out what truth is—only one or two people find out—therefore let me, as a mediator, help you; therefore I become your exploiter. That is the whole process of religion. It is a clever means of exploiting, being ruthless to keep the people in subjection, as the capitalist class does in exactly the same way—one class by spiritual means, one class by mundane. But if you look at it, both are ruthless exploitations. (Hear! Hear!)

Sirs, please don't bother to say, "Hear, hear." What is important is to act, not intellectually agree with me. That has no value. Agreement can only take place in action. That means, when you say, "hear, hear," that you have to stand out alone against society, against your neighbors, against your family, against everything that society for generations has built up. That demands great perception, not courage, not this heroic attitude towards life, but great and direct perception of what is true.

Now, to me, life is not meant to be a school. Life is not a thing from which you learn, it is meant to be lived—to be lived supremely, intelligently, divinely. Whereas, if you make it into a constant battle, struggle, continual effort, then life becomes hideous; and you have made it so because your whole thought is self-growth, self-expansion, self-aggrandizement, and as long as that exists, life becomes a hideous struggle.

So that is what I want to say. Surely that is very easily understood. Easily understood in a sense. One cannot grasp at once all its significance. One can see in what direction it lies, and to change one's attitude there must be great affliction, not contentment, great burning conflict which will force you to dis-

cover; and heaven knows, we have conflicts all day long, but we have trained our mind to be cunning, and so pass over these conflicts lightly, escape from them. Hence we may have conflict after conflict, problem after problem. Our mind has learned to be cunning, and therefore to escape.

Question: Will you please explain in greater detail what you mean by your statement that, "Your teachers are your destroyers." How can a priest, provided he is honest in purpose, be a destroyer?

KRISHNAMURTI: Sir, why do you want a priest; to keep you morally correct? Is that it? Or to lead you to truth? Or to act as your interpreter between God and yourself? Or merely to perform a rite, a ceremony of marriage or death, or of Sunday morning? Why do you want priests? When we find out why we need them, then we shall discover they are destroyers.

If you say a priest is necessary to keep our morality straight, surely then you are no longer moral, even though the priest may force you to be moral; for to me morality is not compulsion; it is a voluntary action. Morality is not born of fear, conditioned by circumstances. True morality is voluntary understanding and therefore action. Therefore to me a priest is unnecessary to uphold your integrity. Or if you say he is necessary to lead you to truth as a mediator, as an interpreter, then I say both you and the priest must know what truth is. To be led somewhere you must know where you are going, and the leader must also know where he is going; and if you know where truth is, you don't want a leader. Please, that is not cleverness. These are just facts.

But now what have we done? We have preconceived what truth is, as contrast, as an opposite from that which we are. We say truth is tranquil, truth is wise, unbounded.

Because we are not that, therefore we have made that into an opposite, and we want someone to help us to get there. What does that mean? Someone to help you to run away from this conflict to something which you suppose must be truth. Therefore, the priest is helping you to run away from realities, from facts.

I was talking to a priest the other day, and he told me that he maintained his church because there was so much unemployment. He said, "You know, the unemployed people have no homes, no beauty, no life, no music, no light, no color, nothing—horror, a hideous life; and if they come once a week to the church, at least there is beauty, there is some quietness, there is some perfume, and they go away pacified for the rest of the week, and come back again." Surely is that not the greatest form of exploitation? That is, this particular priest was trying to pacify them in their conflict, trying to quiet them, in other words dope them from trying to discover the real cause of unemployment.

Now, if you say priests are necessary to perform the rites, the ceremonies of Christianity, then let us inquire whether those rites and ceremonies are necessary. Are they necessary? As I don't attend them, I cannot answer. They have no value to me; but to you who attend them, are they valuable? In what way do you profit by them? You go to them on Sunday morning, feel very devotional, uplifted, whatever it is, and for the rest of the week you are either exploited or are exploiting. There is still cruelty, and all the rest of it. So where is the value, the necessity of the priest?

If you say it is a means of earning money, then we will put it in quite a different category altogether. If you treat it merely as a profession, as that of the law, the navy, the army, or any other profession, then it is quite a different thing, and most religions with their priests are that and nothing else but that—an old profession.

So if you look to a priest for your guidance as a teacher, I say he is your destroyer or exploiter. Please, I have nothing against Christian priests or Hindu priests—to me they are all the same. I say they are unessential to humanity. And please do not accept what I am saying as final authority to you, a dogmatic statement. Look at it, consider it yourself. If you accept what I am saying, I will also become your priest; therefore I will become your exploiter. Whereas, if you really consider the matter all around, not for a passing moment but completely, you will see that religions with all their sectarian teachers, are really keeping humanity apart. They are increasing the horrors of war, class distinctions, nationalities, and therefore all these things lead to war and greater exploitations in which there is no real affection, real love, real thoughtfulness.

Question: Is there a future life?

KRISHNAMURTI: Are you really interested in it? I suppose you must be or you would not have put the question. Now, wait a minute. Why do you inquire if there is a future life; just for amusement or curiosity, or because you are afraid in the present, therefore you want to find out what is the future, or merely for information? Now, you know some of the modern scientists, some of the well-known scientists, are saying that there is a future life. They say that through mediums one can discover for oneself that there is life after death. All right, let us take it for granted there is. What if there is a future life? What have you done in discovering that there is a future life? You are not any happier, any more intelligent, any more human, thoughtful, affectionate. You are back where you were before. All you have learned is another fact—that there is a life hereafter. It may be a consolation; but even then what? You say, "It gives me certainty that I shall live next life." Then what? Even though it gives you certainty that you are going to live, you have precisely the same problem, the same troubles, the same transient joys and pleasures although there is another life. Whereas, to me, though it may be a fact, it is of very little importance. Sir, immortality is not in the future, immortality or eternity, or whatever you like to call it, is now present; and the present you can only understand when the mind is free of time.

Now I am afraid I have to be a little metaphysical, but I hope you do not mind. It is not really metaphysical. As long as the mind is a slave to time, there must be the fear of death, the fear and the hope of a future life, and a constant inquiry into that question. That is, where there is fear there is already a slow decay, a slow death though you may be living. The very inquiry into the future shows that you are already dying. To live completely, to live in that plenitude of the present, in the eternal now, mind must be free of time. Is that not so? Time, I am not using the word as we generally use it, for convenience, to catch a boat or tram, and the next appointment, and so on—I am using the word *time* as memory. If each morning you were born anew, afresh, not with all the memories of yesterday, with all the burdens, with all the encrustations of the past, then each day would be new, fresh, simple; and to be able to live in that, is to be free of time. That is, mind has become a storehouse of memory, afflicted by the past, burdened by the innumerable experiences which we have had.

Please, I hope you will think with me with regard to this, otherwise you will not quite understand it. So, with the burden of the past, the burden of innumerable memories, we confront, we meet every experience—a fresh experience, a fresh thought, a fresh en-

vironment, a fresh day; with the background of the past we meet the present. Is that not so? If you are a Christian, you have the background of a Christian mind, Christian dogmas, beliefs, tradition, and you try to meet life with those ideas. Or if you are a socialist, or any other person, you have certain prejudices, certain ideas, certain well-defined dogmas, and you meet life with that background, with those spectacles. Thus you are meeting the present continually with a background of the past, and therefore you do not understand the present. There is a continual process of misunderstanding, which creates memory; and therefore, there is the accumulation, the accentuation of this memory, and hence the desire to know if I shall live a next life. Whereas, if you were able to meet everything anew, with an uninfected mind, with a mind that is not burdened with possessiveness of the past, or with the memory of a future, then you would see that there is no such thing as death; that there is no fear. Then life is continually becoming an ecstasy, not a fearful, horrible struggle; but that demands great alertness, awareness of thought, of mind and heart in the present.

I am afraid the questioner will be disappointed. He wants to know if there is or if there is not—a categorical reply, "yes" or "no." I am afraid there cannot be a categorical reply. Beware of categorical replies, "yes" and "no." Is it not more important, really, to know how to live than to find out what happens when you die? It is only the dying already who want to know what happens after death—not the living. So let us inquire and find out if we can live richly, humanly, completely, divinely, instead of finding out what lies beyond. Then you will find out what lies beyond, when you know how to live supremely, intelligently. Then you will find out what is beyond. Then, that discovery is not a theoretical thing, it is a fact; then, you will discover that it has very little significance, because there is no such thing as "beyond." Life is one complete whole, without a beginning or an end. Then that ecstasy, that wisdom, brings about a completeness of living in the present.

Question: Will Britain become fascist, and is it a progressive movement?

KRISHNAMURTI: No movement based on possessiveness, keeping class distinctions, encouraging fear, can be a progressive or a true movement. I have read some fascist books, and they talk about the divine right of possessiveness, keeping class distinctions, nationality, the limitations of frontiers. Surely that cannot be a human movement. Whereas, a true movement, which destroys these, which helps people to understand and think, that surely is a real movement, a spiritual movement, a human movement. You know these movements are encouraged or discouraged by individuals like yourselves. If they supply your demands or possessiveness, guarantee your stronghold, your own investments, spiritual or mundane, you encourage them; and you discourage those which are trying to belittle, and help to destroy those that show the falseness of possessiveness. To me, there is no such thing as instinctive human possessiveness. All possessiveness is an artificial thing, created by an artificial, wrong society. Instinctively, human beings are not possessive. They have been trained by circumstances which they have created. So whether fascism is a progressive movement or not is of little importance. What is of importance is whether you, as individuals, see that so long as the world, with its governments, so long as in the world there exists this continual self-aggrandizement, subtly, consciously or unconsciously, this self-importance, spiritually or mundanely, there must be sorrow, there must be continual cries of pain, there must be wars, there must

be exploitation, and there will be no real love. Therefore it is for you as individuals to think anew, to discover, to find out if your whole basis of thought and action is based on this limited self-consciousness.

March 30, 1934

Second Talk in Vasanta School Gardens

Friends,

Most people who are at least thoughtful desire to find out if there is something which is more lasting, in which life is more full, complete, and they describe that reality as God, truth, or life itself. Now, to me, there is such a thing as reality; something that is enduring, complete, eternal, but as I have been saying in my last two talks, the very search for truth is to deny it, because that reality is to be a discovery, not to be followed. I hope you see the difference. If we go after truth, that reality, you must know what it is, you must have a preconception, but if you begin to discover it, then that discovery is real and not the search for truth; so I want in my brief talk this morning to help you rather to discover it, and not to follow it.

First of all truth, or that reality, is not to be found by running after it, because when we seek something, it indicates that our mind, our whole being is trying to escape from that conflict in which mind and heart are caught up. Whereas, if we can become conscious, aware of the many hindrances which we create through fear, and then free the mind from that fear, from those hindrances, we shall discover what that eternal life is. That is, instead of trying to find out what truth is, let us discover what are the hindrances which we have created through fear, and in understanding the cause of fear and its many hindrances then we shall find out what that thing is which is indescribable.

It is no good talking to a prisoner about freedom, to a man who is in prison; he will know what freedom is the moment he is out of prison. But most of us are desirous of finding out what freedom is before we are conscious of what prisons are; and as long as we are merely seeking freedom, reality, richness of life, we cannot understand, it must be imaginative, unreal, shaped out of a limited, conscious mind. Whereas, if we can find out what are the prison walls that enclose the mind and heart, and then free the mind from its hindrances, surely, then, we shall be able to find out that which is.

So what are the hindrances that we have created? Is it not first of all authority, born of fear? Mind is caught up by some authority; driven, shaped, molded by some external authority; either religious authority or social, or you have developed an inner authority. You know, one first of all accepts external authority, because we are incapable of acting, thinking, and feeling for ourselves, so we set up an outside authority, that of religion, that of a teacher, that of a social system; and then we think we reject that external authority and develop an inner authority, an inner law, which is only the reaction from the external. That is, instead of finding out what is this external authority which we have set up to be our guide, we reject that and we think we have to find out a law for ourselves, individually, and thereby live according to that law. That is what most people do. There is an external, objective authority which they reject or understand, and develop an inner authority, a subjective authority.

Now, to me, authority, whether objective or subjective, is the same, because authority implies shaping, an imitation, a control, a conditioning, whether imposed externally or by inward effort and exertion. So that, to me, is the first hindrance. A man that understands does not need authority. There is only per-

ception, and that perception does not demand the imitation of authority. I hope you see all this. First of all, one is a slave to social authority, religious authority, and you gradually develop by conflict, by trouble, what you call a subjective authority, and you say, "It is my understanding. I must obey that law which I have found out for myself." While the mind is merely the instrument of obedience, surely such a mind cannot understand. Understanding is perception, not an imposition, either externally or inwardly.

Again, to repeat the same thing put differently, we have external ideals imposed on us through education, through politics, through social influence, environment. Then we feel they are confining, limiting, controlling, dominating, usurping our individual thought, so we develop our own ideals—we think we develop our own ideals, beliefs, to which we try to conform. That is what we have done; we have rejected the external and are obeying the inward ideal which we have established for ourselves, and we think we have made tremendous progress. What we have done is merely rejected the external, and established our own beliefs, and we are trying to imitate, to follow those beliefs. Now this idea of following, imitating, being guided, controlled, dominated, is, to me, the very first hindrance which prevents the clear perception of any experience, or that fulfillment in perfect understanding, because our whole mind, when it is obeying, being controlled, is dominated by this idea of gain. We think of wisdom, understanding, completeness, in terms of accumulation, not as infinite pliability, therefore eternal. That thing which is pliable is lasting, but that which is burdened, the result of many, many accumulations, therefore capable of resistance, is transient and cannot understand.

I am afraid I see by the faces there is very little understanding of what I am saying. Wait a minute, sirs; I am afraid by listening to one or two talks you are not going to understand what I am saying. What brings about understanding is not listening, merely listening, but rather trying to fulfill in action.

So to put it differently, mind and heart are the result of environment, and then your environment controls the way you think and the way you feel. Do not say, "Is that all—mind? There must be something more, something which is more lasting." I said to discover that, let us begin from things we know, and from that start—not from a mysterious thing which we do not know, about which we can but romance. So mind and heart, thought and feeling, are the result of environment, and so long as you are a slave to that environment, there cannot be understanding; you cannot then master environment, and to master environment is to understand it.

That is, environment is, after all, the social system and that system which we call religion, made up of many doctrines, beliefs, dogmas, innumerable prejudices, and the mind is a slave to this environment. Take for instance, if you depend on mind for your livelihood, as most people do, as everyone must, you are controlled to a great extent by the beliefs that you hold. Suppose that you are a Roman Catholic, and you want to find a job in a Protestant place, or if Protestant, you want to find a job in a Roman Catholic institution or office; if they discover your beliefs, it might not be so easy to find a job, so you put away your beliefs or accept what the other says momentarily, because you desire to earn money, because you must have money. Through external environment, mentally, you are under control, so your beliefs are merely the result of environment, conditioned by the environment; and as long as you do not break down the false environment of society and religion, your beliefs and ideals are worthless, because they are but the result of environment born of fear.

So to understand that which is lasting, eternal, there must be conflict between the individual and the environment, and only in that conflict can you pierce through the walls of limitation. We accept thoughtlessly or unconsciously so many conditions imposed by society or by religion, accept them as being true. Traditionally, our mind is driven into a mold, and we unconsciously accept these things, and therefore we are slaves to these things; and it is only by continually questioning, by constant awareness, that we can free the mind from the environment, and therefore be master of the environment.

Question: Virtue does not appear to be a very prominent feature in your teachings. Why is this? Has the virtuous life so small a part to play in the realization of truth?

KRISHNAMURTI: What do you mean by virtue? Do you mean by virtue, a contrast to vice? That is, do you call courage, bravery, a virtue in contrast to fear? First of all, one is afraid, and you think you must develop the idea of courage, so you pursue courage; that is, you are running away from fear, and this process of running away from fear you call bravery, courage, which becomes virtue. To me, a man who pursues a virtue is no longer virtuous; whereas, if you begin to find out what causes fear, not cover up fear by the idea of what you think is brave, but try to find out what is the fundamental cause of fear, then in the discovery of the cause you are neither courageous nor fearful, you are free of both these opposites.

After all, virtue is merely the result of a false environment, isn't it? To resist the environment, you must have great character nowadays. At least that is what is called character. That is, society has created, or rather we have helped to create a society in which to be nonpossessive is considered a great virtue. Isn't it? We have established a society where possessiveness indicates constant fight with your neighbor, consciously or unconsciously, constant battle, self-assertion, continual cutting out of others; and a man who does not want to do that, you call a virtuous man, a noble man. To me it has nothing to do with nobility or virtue. If the environment is changed, if the social conditions are changed, then to be possessive or nonpossessive is the same thing, then you call possessiveness neither virtue nor an evil thing. Whereas now, as society is constituted, to break away from these false standards is considered either a virtue or a sin. But if we begin to alter the environment in which the mind and heart are held, then this whole idea of virtue and sin have a different meaning altogether; because, to me, virtue is not to be sought after, to be gained, to be possessed, or sin to be abhorred or run away from—whatever is meant by sin.

So to me, to live naturally, that demands a great deal of intelligence, not brutal, savage, unthinking life, primitive life—I do not mean that when I use the word *naturally*. To live a natural life, full, spontaneous life, creative, intelligent life, you can do that only when you understand the false standards and the true standards of society, and have broken away from them because you understand their significance; therefore, you are no longer bound by this pursuit of the opposite which we call virtue.

To put it very briefly, when you are afraid, you are seeking courage, and we call that courage a virtue; whereas, really, what are you doing? You are running away from fear. You are trying to cover up fear by an idea, what you call courage. So momentarily you may cover up fear by an idea of what you call courage, but fear will continue to exist and show itself in different forms; whereas, if you try to find out what is the fundamental cause of fear, then mind is not caught up in the conflict of opposites.

Question: Do you think that the method of psychoanalysis, the bringing of the motives of the unconscious mind into a knowledge of the conscious, will assist the individual to free his mind from the primitive and egotistical complexes and cravings, and will thereby allow his thought to carry him on to that happiness of which you speak?

KRISHNAMURTI: That is, the mind has many complexes, and the question is whether you can free the mind of these by self-analysis. Is that not the question? The mind and heart have many hindrances, impediments which we call complexes—unconscious, hidden. Can we free them; can we uproot them through the processes of self-analysis, and thereby free the mind from the egotistical and limited point of view?

I am afraid you will have to follow this a little bit carefully, because it may be the first time you have heard it, and you may find it rather complicated, but it is not. To me, the mind can be free of those impediments only in full consciousness, when your whole being is active, aware. Now, in the process of self-analysis, your whole being is not functioning; only that part of you which you call mind, thought, intellect. With that one part of the mind you are trying to discover the hidden complexes; whereas, I say, you can bring all these hidden hindrances into full conscious action only when you are fully aware in the present.

I will put it differently. Now suppose you have the complex of snobbishness. Most people have it. How are you going to find out? To find out, to me, does not lie through this process of self-analysis; that is, intellectually to look into the actions that have taken place, and so discover this idea of snobbishness. First of all, you want to discover if you are a snob or not. You don't want to alter it, but to discover it, isn't it so? Wait a minute, please. Just follow this. When you discover it, then you will act one way or the other. First of all, you have to find out if you are a snob, so how are you going to discover it? Only when you are fully conscious, fully aware of that which you are saying and feeling at the moment of saying and feeling—not after you have said and felt. Is that not so? That is, if you are fully conscious of what you are saying and what you are thinking, then in that full awareness you will discover for yourself if you are a snob or not; not by sitting down and intellectually analyzing an event. I know there are innumerable questions arising out of this, but I cannot answer all those. But if you think of it, you will see that by this way of being continually alert, fully conscious in that which you are doing, you will bring the unconscious, hidden, into full consciousness, and thereby you will create the disturbance which is necessary, and by that disturbance you will free the mind of that complex, of that hindrance.

Question: You seem to regard the pursuit of ideals as an escape from life. Is there no substance of truth in the highest ideals?

KRISHNAMURTI: Why do we want ideals? I do not say they are not truths; but why do we want them? We say we need them because we cannot, without a standard, a measure, an ideal, guide our lives through the constant battles and struggles of life. Is that not it? So we want a standard, a continual measurement by which to judge our actions in daily life. What does that indicate? That we are more interested in the ideal, in the measurement, than in the conflicts, the struggles, the sorrows which confront us. So, as they are so large, so conflicting, so immense, these struggles, we establish ideals as a means of escape from them. Whereas, to me, to understand the conflict, the troubles, the sufferings, mind must be free to understand them as they are, not by a measure, not by a standard.

Surely, when you are really in great conflict, great suffering, at that moment you are not thinking of the ideal, of what you should do and what you should not do. You are so consumed by the suffering, you want to find out. Then you are not looking for an ideal to lead you out of that. It is only when suffering diminishes, quietens down, that you turn to an ideal to help you out of that suffering.

To me, all ideas must be the means of alleviation of suffering, and, therefore, cannot possibly explain to you the reason of suffering. Take the average person, and you will see that he has innumerable ideals, many ideals, beliefs, and according to those he is trying to live all day long, if he at all thinks about it: so he makes of life a continual battle between what are facts and what he wants to be. Now, if he realizes, fundamentally, what are facts, and what is real, and recognizes their significance, then he will find out the very root of comfort, and therefore free himself from these false standards, false measurements, which are continually trying to shape his mind to a particular pattern.

Question: Do you believe in communism, as understood by the masses?

KRISHNAMURTI: I don't know what is understood by the masses, so I cannot explain that. So what is it, now? Let us look at it, not from the point of view of any "ism," but from the point of view of the ordinary human state. How can there be real understanding of peoples when you are considering yourself as a New Zealander and I am considering myself as a Hindu? How can we contact each other? How can there be a vital relationship between us, a human understanding between us? Or if we divide ourselves by certain labels, you calling yourselves Christians and I calling myself Hindu, with certain prejudices, dogmas, creeds, how can there be real brotherhood? We can talk about tolerance—which is an intellectual invention to keep you where you are and to keep me where I am—and try to be friendly. This does not mean I am talking of uniformity; now there is uniformity. You are all of one belief, one ideal, one dogma, though you may vary in that prison, painting each bar differently; but it is a prison, and you want to retain your prison with its decorations, and the Hindu wants to keep his prison with its decorations, and they try to be brotherly, and this brotherhood is called tolerance. Whereas, to me, the whole idea is the very negation of real understanding, human unity. So through the process of time, you may be driven like so many slaves to accept communism, as now you accept capitalism; and in that force of being driven, there cannot be voluntary action, as now there cannot be voluntary action. So if you merely accept either, and live in either, surely you are not being creatively individual. You are merely like so many sheep, either capitalistic sheep or communistic sheep, driven by environment, condition, forced to accept. Surely such a thing is not moral; such a thing is not rich, or spiritual, true. And I say the true human state can only come about when you, as individuals, voluntarily do these things, because you see the necessity, the immense profundity in this—not merely superficial excitation. Then there is the possibility of individuals living creatively, fully; not when you are driven.

Question: What do you consider is the cause of unemployment?

KRISHNAMURTI: You know we have built up a structure for many centuries, for many generations, a structure based on individual competitiveness, ruthless self-security, where the most clever, cunning, gets to the top, and gets the whole directive means into his hands. It is obvious. We see this everywhere, and naturally, when the world is divided up into nationalities, which are the culmination of that possessiveness and the greed of individuals, naturally there must be unequal distribution, therefore naturally, unemployment.

You know, to me, it is very simple to see this. Perhaps for you it is very complicated, though you may be more educated than I am, though you may have read a great deal. The cause, to me, is very simple. So what are we going to do? That is, you will tell me, "Why don't you talk about the common conditions of labor, work for the change of economic conditions, then everything will be all right; so why not concentrate your whole mind on that particular subject, and then alter it?" How can I alter the whole of society of which you and I are a part? How can we alter it? By first of all having an intelligent attitude, and therefore action, towards the whole of life. That is, you cannot take up the economic problem by itself and say, "Solve that, and everything else is solved." The economic problem is merely the symptom of the whole human problem, so if we can create an intelligent opinion and therefore intelligent action as a whole, concerning all human beings, then we shall act definitely with regard to the economic conditions. So I feel that what I have to do is to create an opinion, not merely an intellectual opinion, but an opinion born of action; and then, when there is such an opinion, then, being intelligent, you will use any system, any intelligent system to bring about a complete change in the economic system.

Question: You do not believe in possession or exploitation; but without one or the other how could you travel or lecture to the world?

KRISHNAMURTI: I will tell you very simply. To live in the world without exploitation, you must withdraw completely to a desert island. As the system is—as it is now—to live at all, if you live in that system, you must exploit it.

Let us understand what I mean by exploitation. Now, to me, if you do not discover for yourself intelligently what are your needs, then you become an exploiter. If you discover for yourselves, intelligently, what are your needs, then you are not an exploiter; but that demands a great deal of intelligence. We have, first of all, many things because we think by the possession of many things we shall be happy. So in order to possess those many things we must exploit; whereas, if you really thought out what are your essential needs, in that there is no exploitation, really, if you come to think of it. And I have found out for myself what are my needs. With regard to my travel, friends ask me to go to different places, and I go. If they don't ask me, I don't travel; and even if I don't talk or teach—well I can do something else. Now, if I wanted to convert you all to a particular form of thought, and force you, and collect funds to alter it—that I would call exploitation. That which I am talking about is the inevitable, whether you like it or not, and the intelligent man intelligently accepts the inevitable. So I do not feel that I am exploiting, and I know I am not, nor am I possessive.

Again, that sense of possessiveness—to be really free of all that, one has to be so very alert, aware, so as not to deceive oneself, because in the thought that one is free of possessiveness may lie a great deal of self-deception. One so often thinks that one is free, but lives really in the cloak of self-deception. The moment your need is satisfied, you do not cling to it; you do not feel proprietary rights over it.

Question: Would it give you any surprise if the Christ of the Gospels were suddenly to appear, so every eye should see him?

KRISHNAMURTI: You know, mind wants miracles, romantic ideas, extraordinary supernatural phenomena. Not that there are not miracles, not that there are not supernatural phenomena; but we seek them because our minds and hearts are so poor, so empty, so wretched, so ugly, and we think we can overcome that poverty of mind and heart by seeking those miracles, running and chasing after phenomena. And the more you pursue phenomena and miracles, the less you are rich, the less plenitude of mind and heart, the less affection. When there is the plenitude of heart and mind, then whether there are miracles or superphysical phenomena will have very little significance. Now, we create such divisions, such distinctions between the physical and superphysical, because the physical is so intolerable, so ugly. We want to run away, and anyone that can lead you to the superphysical, you follow, and you call that spiritual; but it is nothing else but another form of real, gross materialism. Whereas, true spirituality consists in living harmoniously, with perfect unity in your heart and mind, because there is understanding, and in that understanding there is the delight of living.

March 31, 1934

Talk to Theosophists

Friends,

I will just say a few words before I attempt to answer some of these questions.

First of all, I should like to say that what I am going to say should not be taken in a partisan spirit. Most of you here are probably Theosophists, with certain definite ideals and ideas, with certain definite teachings, and you think I hold contrary views and make out that I belong to another camp with other ideals and beliefs. Let us rather approach the whole thing from the point of view of discovery rather than trying to say, "We believe in this, and you don't; therefore, we are upholders of certain ideas which you are trying to destroy." Now that spirit, that kind of attitude, indicates opposition rather than understanding; that you have something which you desire to protect, and if anyone questions what you have, you immediately will say that he is attacking or I am attacking. It is not at all my intention to attack anything, but rather to help you to discover if what you are upholding is true. If it is true, then no one can attack it, and it does not matter if anyone attacks it, if what you hold is real; and you can only find out what is real by considering it, not protecting it, not being on the defensive.

You know, wherever I go Theosophists ask me, as do other organizations, to speak to them; and Theosophists with whom I have lived for so long have taken up this unfortunate attitude, that I am attacking them, destroying their pet beliefs, which they must protect at all costs, and all the nonsense of it. Whereas, I feel if we can really consider together, reason together, and see what we have in our hands that we want to protect, then instead of belonging to any one particular camp, or particular section of thought, we shall naturally understand what is true; and that which is true has no party. It is neither yours nor mine. So that is my attitude in addressing you, and in talking anywhere: to help you to discover—and I mean this honestly—if what you hold is really lasting, or a thing that you have built up out of conceit, out of self-protection, self-preservation, out of search for security. Such things have no value though they may wear the clothing of surety, of certainty, and of wisdom.

Now, sirs, I would like to say that, to me, truth has no aspects. We are in the habit, especially Theosophists I think, and some others besides, of saying that truth has many aspects: Christianity is one aspect, Buddhism

another, Hinduism another, and so on. This merely indicates that we want to stick to our own particular temperament and our own prejudices, and be tolerant to other people's prejudices. Whereas, to me, truth has no aspects; it is one, and that which is complete, whole, has no aspects. It is not like a light with many colored lamps. That is, you place colored lamps over that light, and then try to be tolerant to a red light if you are a green light, and invent that unfortunate word *tolerance,* which is so artificial, a dry thing that has no value. Surely you are not tolerant to your brother, to your children. When there is real affection there is no tolerance, so, it is only when the heart has withered that we talk about tolerance. I, personally, do not care what you believe or do not believe, as my affection is not based on belief. Belief is an artificial thing; whereas affection is the innateness of things, and when that affection withers, then we try to spread brotherhood through the world and talk about tolerance, the unity of religions. But where there is real understanding there is no talk about tolerance.

Understanding does not lie through books. You can be students of books for many years, but if you do not know how to live, then all your knowledge withers; it has no substance, no value. Whereas, one moment of full awareness, full conscious understanding, brings about real, lasting peace; not a thing that is static, but that peace which is continually in movement, unlimited.

Now I wonder how I am going to answer all these questions.

Question: Can a ceremony be helpful, and yet be not limiting?

KRISHNAMURTI: Do you really want to go into the question, or do you just want to deal with it superficially? How many of you really perform ceremonies? It has become, unfortunately, a subject over which you quarrel in the T. S.

Now what is a ceremony? Not the putting on of a tie, cleaning yourself, eating, or the appreciation of beauty—because I have discussed with people, and they have trotted out all these arguments. They say, "We go to church because there is so much beauty in it. It is our self-expression. Is not putting on a suit and cleaning your teeth, is that not a ceremony?" Surely this is not ceremony. The appreciation of beauty is not ceremony. You do not attend church or attend a ceremony to self-express. So ceremony as you use it has a very definite meaning. A ceremony, as far as I can make out, according to your own usage of that word, is where you either hope to advance spiritually through its efficacy, or you attend it in order to spread in the world spiritual forces. Shall we limit it to that, and not bring in extraneous arguments? Is that not so? Ceremony is only applicable where you are spreading spiritual force, and in which you hope to gain spiritual advancement. Let us examine these two things.

First of all, when you say you are spreading spiritual force in the world, how do you know that you are doing this? Either it must be based on authority, acceptance of someone else's edicts or precepts, or you feel that you are spreading it. So let us put away the authority of another, because that is childish. If someone else merely says, "Do that," and you do it, then there is no value; it does not matter who it is. Then we merely reduce ourselves into children, and become the instruments of authority. Therefore there is no vitality in our actions. We are merely imitative machines.

Now we might think that by attending a church we feel elated, we feel full of vitality and a sense of well-being. I am not insulting when I say that by taking to drink you feel the same, or attending a stimulating lecture; but why do you place ceremony as being much more important, more vital, more essential, than appreciation of something which really stimulates you? If you really examine it, it is much more than appreciation of beauty which stimulates. You hope by attending a ceremony, by some miraculous process your whole being is going to be cleansed. Now to me, such an idea is, if I may say so, really absurd. Such ideas are instruments of true exploitation. Whereas, really being integral, complete within oneself, you cannot look to someone else to cleanse your mind and heart. One has to discover for oneself. So, to me, this whole conception that ceremonies are going to give you spiritual understanding and attainment, is really the very thing which every so-called materialistic person thinks. He wants to be somebody in this world, he wants to have money, so he begins to accumulate, possess, exploit, to be ruthless; and the man who wants to be somebody in the spiritual world does exactly the same thing, only he calls it spiritual. That is, behind it all, there is this idea of gain; and to me such an idea, the desire to attain, is in itself a limitation. And if you perform ceremonies as a means of gain, then all ceremonies are but limitation. Or if you go and perform ceremonies as essential, as necessary, then you are merely accepting it on authority or tradition. Surely such a mind cannot understand what life is, what the whole process of living is.

I am surprised that this question should arise wherever I go, especially among those who are supposed to be a little more advanced, whatever that may mean, who have been students of philosophy for years, who are supposed to be thoughtful. It but indicates that they have really sought substitutes. You are fed up with your old churches and institutions, and you want some new toy to play with, and you accept that new toy without finding out if it has any value; you cannot find out if anything has value so long as you are merely seeking substitutes.

Have I dealt with that question completely, comprehensively? I would really like to discuss this with people, this idea of ceremonies. I have discussed with those who have recently become priests, and they give me, not some valid reason, but some reason based on authority, as, "We have been told," or some kind of excuse for their action.

Now, there is another aspect of it which is completely different. That is this idea that in ceremony lies magic—not white and black magic, I am not talking about that—that the mystery of life is unfolded through a ceremony. You know, I have talked with some Roman Catholics, and they will tell you that that is their reason for going to church. That is not the reason given by any of the ceremonialists of the theosophical bent, so do not use that club against me again. Now life is mystery. There is something immense, magical, about life; but to pierce its veil is not to create spurious, unnatural things to discover the true mystery—and, to me, these sacerdotal ceremonies are unnatural. They are really a means of exploitation.

Question: It has been suggested that the power that speaks through you belongs to the higher planes, and cannot be sent below the intuitional, so that we must listen rather with our intuition if we would get your message. Is that correct?

KRISHNAMURTI: What do you mean by intuition? What does intuition mean to you all? You say it is something which we feel instinctively without going through the process of logical reason: a "hunch," as the Americans would say. Now I really question whether your intuition is real or merely the glorified unconscious hopes; subtle, deceitful longings. You know, when you hear reincarnation spoken of, or you hear a lecturer talk about reincarnation, or you read of it in a book, and you jump to it and say, "I feel it is true, it must be," you call that intuition. Is it really intuition, or is it the hope that you will have another opportunity to live next life; therefore you cling to it, and call it intuition? Wait a minute. I am not denying that there is intuition, but what the average person, what the usual person calls intuition, that is not true, that is something without reason, validity, without understanding behind it.

Now the questioner says that it has been suggested that the power that speaks through me belongs to the higher planes, and cannot be sent below the intuitional. Surely you understand what I am talking about. Don't you? Pretty obvious. Now wait a minute. It is easy to understand what I am talking about, but if you don't pursue it, carry it out in action, there is no understanding; and because you don't carry it out in action, you rather transfer it to the intuitional world, and therefore say it is suggested that I am speaking from the higher plane, and therefore you must go to your higher and try to understand what that means. In other words, although you understand what I am trying to say, fairly well, it is difficult to put it into action; therefore, you say let us rather remove it to a higher plane, and from there we can discuss. Is that not so? If you say, "I do not understand what you are talking about," then there is a possibility of further discussion. I will then try to explain it differently, so that we can discuss it, go into it, consider it together; but to start with the assumption that to understand me you must go to the higher plane—surely there is something radically wrong in that attitude. What is the higher plane, except that which is thought? Why go any further? But do you not see, my point is we are starting with something mysterious, something far away, and from that we try to find out the obvious, the realities, and, therefore, there are bound to be great deceptions, great hypocritical actions, falseness. Whereas, if we start with things that we do know, which are very simple to find out if you give your thought, then you can go really far, infinitely. But it is absurd to start from that mysterious, and then try to relegate life to that mystery, which may be romanticism, false, imaginative. Such an attitude of mind which says, "To understand you we must listen with our intuition," may be false, so that is why I said your intuitions may be utterly false. How can you listen with something which may be false, which may be your hopes, predilections, longings, or dreams? Why not listen with your ears, with your reason? From that, when you know the limitation of reason, then you can go—that is, to climb high you must begin low; but you have already climbed high, and you have no further to go. That is what is the trouble with all of you. You have climbed the heights intellectually; naturally your beings are empty, arrogant. Whereas, if you begin near, then you will know how to climb, how to move infinitely.

You know, all these are means and ways of real exploitation. It is the way of the priests—to complicate matters, when things are infinitely simple. I won't go into what I have to say, I have explained that over and over again; but to make it complicated, to coat it with all kinds of traditions or prejudices and not recognize your prejudices, that is where the hideousness lies.

Question: If a person finds the Theosophical Society a channel through which he can express himself and be of service, why should he leave the Society?

KRISHNAMURTI: First of all, let us find out if it is so. Don't say why he should or should not leave; let us go into the matter.

What do you mean by a channel through which he can express himself? Don't you express yourself through business, through marriage? Do you or don't you express yourself when you are working every day for your livelihood, when you are bringing up children? And as it shows that you do not express yourself there, you want a society in which to express yourself. Is that not it? Please, I hope I am not giving some subtle meaning to all this. So you say, "As I am not expressing myself in the world of action, in the everyday world, where it is impossible to express myself, therefore I use the Society to express myself." Is it so, or not? I mean, as far as I understand the question.

How do you express yourself? Now, as it is, at the expense of others. When you talk about self-expression, it must be at the expense of others. Please, there is true expression, with which we will deal presently, but this idea of self-expression indicates that you have something to give, and therefore the Society must be created for your use. First of all, have you something to give? A painter, or a musician, or an engineer, or any of these fellows, if he is really creative, does not talk about self-expression; he is expressing it all the time; he is at it in the outside world, at home, or in a club. He does not want a particular society so that he can use that society for his self-expression. So when you say "self-expression," you do not mean that you are using the Society for giving forth to the world a particular knowledge or something which you have. If you have something, you give it. You are not conscious of it. A flower is not conscious of its beauty. Its loveliness is ever present.

"Be of service to the world." Are you of service to the world, really? Please, you know, I wish you could really think, honestly, frankly; then if you really think honestly, frankly, you will be of service to the world—not in this extraordinary way. Let us find out if we are of service to the world. What is the world in need of at the present time—or at any time, in the past or in the future? People who have the capacity to be completely human; that is, people who are not bound up by their narrow circles of thoughts and prejudices and the limitations of their self-conscious emotionalism. Surely, if you really want to help the world, you cannot belong to any particular sect or society, any more than you can belong to any particular religion. If you say all religions are one, then why have any religion? Religions and nationalities really encage people, trammel them. This is shown throughout the world, throughout history; and the world has come now to more and more sects, more and more bodies enclosed by walls of beliefs, with their special guides; and yet you talk of brotherhood! How can there be real brotherhood when this possessive instinct is so deep, and so must lead to wars because it is based on nationalism, patriotism. Surely your talk of brotherhood shows that you are not really brotherly. A man who is really brotherly, affectionate, does not talk about brotherhood; you do not talk about brotherhood to your sister, or to your wife, there is a natural affection. And how can there be brotherhood, real unity of humanity, when there is exploitation? So to really help the world—as you do talk about helping the world—if you would really help it to be free of all its commitments, its vested interest, its environments, then you would see that you are never talking about helping the world; then you would not put yourself on a pedestal to help somebody at a distance, lower down.

Question: Do you approve of our invoking the aid of the angels of the angelic kingdom, such as the angel Raphael in sickness, the angel of fire in the ceremony of cremation? Are they props and crutches? (Laughter)

KRISHNAMURTI: Please, some of you laugh at it, but you have your own particular prejudices, superstitions. You may not have this "angelic" superstition. You have some others.

Now, let us not look at it from the point of view of invoking aid. First of all, if you are normal, then there is a normal miracle taking place in the world; but we are so abnormal that we want abnormal actions to take place. I have answered the question so often. All right. First of all, suppose you are suffering, and you are cured, it may be by a doctor, it may be by an angel; if you do not know the cause of suffering, you will again become ill. Personally, I have dabbled a little in healing, but I want to do something else in life, to really heal the mind and heart; that is, to let you discover for yourself the cause of suffering; and I assure you, no calling on angels, continual attendance by the doctor, is ever going to show you the cause of suffering. You may be healed symptomatically for the moment, but unless you really find out for yourselves—nobody else can find out for you—what is the cause of suffering, you will again be ill. In discovering the cause you will become healthy.

Question: Have you sympathy for those who admire your beauty, but ignore your wisdom?

KRISHNAMURTI: It is the same thing as the other question. Let us listen to you intuitively, and ignore your words. Only this is put differently. You know, wisdom is not to be bought. You cannot buy it from books. You cannot get it by listening. You may listen to me for hundreds of years, but you are not going to be wise. What brings wisdom is action. Action is wisdom; it cannot be separated. And because we have divided action from our thought, from our emotions, from our intellectual capacity of reasoning, we are carried away by superficial things, and thereby are exploited.

Question: Do you consider that the Theosophical Society has finished its work in the world, and ought to retire into solitary confinement?

KRISHNAMURTI: What do you think, you who are its members? Is that not a much more apt question, than yours to me? Sirs, may I put it this way? Why do you belong to any society? Why are you Christians, Theosophists, Christian Scientists, and God knows what? Why do you exclude and seclude yourselves? "Because," you say, "This particular form of belief, this particular form of expression, of ideas, appeals to me; therefore I am going to subscribe myself to it." Or you belong to it because you hope to get something out of it: happiness, wisdom, office, position. So instead of asking me if the Society should retire, ask yourselves why you belong to it. Why do you belong to anything? There is this horrible idea that we want to be exclusive—the Western Club, the Eastern Golf Course, and all the rest of it. Exclusive hotels—you know. So likewise, we say we have something special, so do the Hindus, so do Roman Catholics. Every person in the world talks about having something special, so they exclude themselves, and become the owners of that special thing, and so thereby create more divisions, more conflicts, more heartaches. Besides, who am I to tell you if the society should retire into confinement? I wonder how many of you have really asked why you belong to it. If you are really a social body, not a religious body, not an ethical body, then there is some hope for it in the world. If you are really a body of people who are discovering, not who have found, if you are a body of people who are giving information, not giving spiritual distinctions, if you are a body of people that have a really open platform, not for me or for someone special, if you are a body of people among whom there are neither leaders nor followers, then there is some hope. But I am afraid you are followers, and therefore you all have leaders. And such a society, whether it is this or another, is useless. You are merely followers or merely leaders. In true spirituality there is no distinction of the teacher and the pupil, of the man who has knowledge and the man who has not. It is you that are creating it, because it is this that you are seeking—continually to be distinctive. You cannot all of you be Sir Richard Something-or-other, so you want to be somebody in this Society, or in another society, or in heaven. Don't you see, if you really thought about these things and were honest, you could be an extraordinarily useful body in the world. You could then really work for the intrinsic merit of its ideas—not for some fantasy and emotionalism of your leaders. Then you would examine any idea, and find out its true significance and work it out, and not depend on the honors conferred for your services, on the enticement to work. That way leads to narrowness, bigotry, to more divisions and cruelties, and ultimately to utter chaos of thought.

Question: What is your attitude to the early teachings of Theosophy, the Blavatsky type? Do you consider we have deteriorated or advanced?

KRISHNAMURTI: I am afraid I do not know, because I do not know what Madame Blavatsky's teachings are. Why should I? Why should you know of someone else's teachings? You know, there is only one truth, and therefore there is only one way, which is not distant from the truth; there is only one method to that truth, because the means are not distinct from the end.

Now you who have studied Madame Blavatsky's and the latest Theosophy, or whatever it is, why do you want to be students of books instead of students of life? Why do you set up leaders and ask whose teachings are better? Don't you see? Please, I am not being harsh, or anything of that kind. Don't you see? You are Christians; find out what is true and false in Christianity—and you will then find out what is true. Find out what is true and false in your environment with all its oppressions and cruelties, and then you will find out what is true. Why do you want philosophies? Because life is an ugly thing, and you hope to run away from it through philosophy. Life is so empty, dull, stupid, ignominious, and you want something to bring romanticism into your world, some hope, some lingering, haunting feeling; whereas, if you really faced the world as it is, and tackled it, you would find it something much more, infinitely greater than any philosophy, greater than any book in the world, greater than any teaching or greater than any teacher.

We have really lost all sense of feeling, feeling for the oppressed, and feeling for the oppressor. You only feel when you are oppressed. So gradually we have intellectually explained away all our feelings, our sensitiveness, our delicate perceptions, until we are absolutely shallow; and to fill that shallowness, to enrich ourselves, we study books. I read all kinds of books, but never philosophies, thank goodness. You know, I have a kind of shrinking feeling—please, I put it mildly—when you say, "I am a student of philosophy," a student of this, or that; never of everyday action, never really understanding things as they are. I assure you, for your happiness, for your own understanding, for the discovery of that eternal thing, you must really live; then you will find something which no word, no picture, no philosophy, no teacher can give.

Question: Are the teachings which Theosophy gives concerning evolution of any consequence for the purpose of the growth of the soul?

KRISHNAMURTI: What do you mean by evolution, sirs? As far as I can make out, growing from the unessential to the essential. Is it? Growing from ignorance to wisdom. Is that not so? Nobody shakes his head. All right. What do you mean by evolution? Gaining more and more experience, more and more wisdom, more and more knowledge, more and more and more and more; infinitely more and more. That is, you go from the unessential to the essential; and that essential becomes the unessential the moment you have attained, you have reached it. Is that not so?

Are you too tired? Is it too late? Please, you have to think with me. This is my second talk during the day; but if you do not think with me, it will be rather difficult for me. I have to push against a wall.

You consider something as essential today, and go after it, and get it; and tomorrow that thing becomes unessential, and you say, "I have learned that." That which you had thought essential has become the unessential, so you go on and on and on, and you call that growth, evolution; getting more and more, discerning more and more between the essential and the unessential—and yet there is no such thing as the essential and the unessential. Is there? Because that which you think is the essential today becomes the unessential tomorrow, for you want something else.

Let me put it differently. You see some pleasurable object you think you want to possess, and you possess it: then satisfied, you move to another thing. It may be some emotional craving, desire, and you get that. You want an idea, and you pursue that, and get it. And ultimately you want to reach God, truth, happiness; and the man who wants happiness, God, truth, you consider spiritual, and the man who wants a hat or a tie, or whatever it is, you call mundane, materialistic. The unessential is the hat, and the essential is the God or truth. What have we done? We have merely changed the object of our desires. We have said, "Well, I have had enough hats, enough cars, enough houses, and I want something else," and you go after that and get that, and then you finish with it and want something else; so you proceed gradually until you ultimately want something which you call God, and then you think you have reached the ultimate. All you have done is played with your desires, and this process of continual choosing you call evolution. Is it so or not?

Comment: At one time one individual is satisfied with one thing and another individual with another.

KRISHNAMURTI: But surely the desire is the same thing. Desire is the same whether it is the desire for a hat or for God. There is the desire behind it; wanting, until we have gone through the range of our desire; whereas, if we really understood the significance of each object which desire is running after, that it is neither essential nor unessential, we would then understand the true significance of that object; and evolution then has a different meaning—not this perpetual attainment, gaining, all the time succeeding.

Comment: Will we stop desire?

KRISHNAMURTI: Surely not. If you stop desire, then—goodbye! It is death. How can you stop desire? It is not a thing you turn off and on. Why do you want to stop desire? Because it gives you pain. If it gives you pleasure you continue, you don't ask me; but

the moment it gives you pain you say, "I had better stop it." Why do you have pain? Because there is no understanding. If you understand a thing, then there is no pain.

Comment: Can you give an illustration of that point? That pain stops when you understand it.

KRISHNAMURTI: Cannot you think it out? Perhaps I will give it later. Let me put it all differently. We are used to this idea of killing desire, disciplining desire, controlling it, subjugating it. To me, this way of thinking is unhealthy, unnatural. You desire a hat or a coat or something—I do not know what—and you multiply desires because the object which the desire is pursuing does not give you satisfaction. Is that not so? So you pursue it, but you change to another object. Now, why is your desire pursuing one thing after another? Because you do not understand the very object which the desire is pursuing; you do not see the full significance of the desire for an object. You are more concerned with the gain and with the loss, rather than with the significance of this pursuit. Am I explaining? Please, one must think about it.

Question: Does what you wrote in "At the Feet of the Master" still hold good?

KRISHNAMURTI: All right, sirs. What does the question imply? What are the implications in that question? Do I still believe in the Masters, eh? Isn't that so? And naturally, if I believe in them, I must still believe in the teachings, and so on. Let us find out. Let us look at it quite openly, not as if I were attacking your Masters, whom you have to protect.

Now, why do you want a Master? You say we need him for a guide—the same thing which the spiritualists say—the same thing the Roman Catholics say—the same thing everybody says in the world. This applies to everyone, not to you particularly. To guide you to what? That is the next question, obviously, isn't it? You say, "I must have a guide to happiness, to truth, to liberation, to nirvana, to heaven"—you must have somebody to lead you to that. (Please, I am not a clever lawyer trying to browbeat you; I am trying to help you to find out for yourselves. I am not trying to convert you to anything.) Now, if you are interested in the discovery of truth, then guides are of no importance, are they? It does not matter—you would pick anybody. How do you know he is going to help you to truth? It may be that the man who sweeps the road will help you—your sister, neighbor, brother, anybody; so why do you pay particular attention to your guides? Oh, don't shake your heads. I know all about it. You say, "Oh yes, quite right, it is so"; and yet you are all seeking probationary discipleship, distinctions, initiations. So to you what matters is, not truth, but who is the guide who will lead you. Isn't that it? No? Then please tell me what.

Comment: You said in "At the Feet of the Master" we had to be desireless, and now you say we have—

KRISHNAMURTI: Wait a minute sir. Yes, it is a contradiction. I hope there will be lots of contradictions. There is a lady who said "No." She shook her head. I would like to find out.

Comment: I forget exactly what your question was with regard to the Master. I feel it is not the way I personally look to the Master. I feel that just as I look to you to help me to understand and discover, so the Master will help us to understand and discover.

KRISHNAMURTI: That is, to most of you the Master is the guide. You cannot deny that, can you? You cannot say, "No, I do not care who will lead us to it."

Comment: I don't think the important thing is the guide; not the special guide.

KRISHNAMURTI: You don't have special guides?

Comment: That is why we come to hear you.

KRISHNAMURTI: Please, try to find out what I am talking about. Do not say, "We don't want Masters, guides," and all that; let us find out. So don't say, "This does not apply to me." If you really think about the thing I am talking about, it will apply to you, because we are all in the same circle.

So, if you want to find out what truth is, as I said this morning, if you ask a guide, then you must know, and he must know, both of you must know what truth is. But if you know what truth is, and you have a dim perception of it, then you will ask nobody. Then you are not concerned whether you are a probationary pupil, or an initiate with special honors, and all the rest of it. You want truth, not distinctions. What do you say to that?

Comment: I would say that it is with many not the desire for distinction, but the desire for understanding.

KRISHNAMURTI: You are not trying to protect. I am not trying to knock down. Please, let us discuss together with that attitude. How can you have understanding when you are a pupil, a distinguished person, a distinctive entity with more special privileges than someone else?

Comment: I do not feel that I have any special privileges; only what I make myself. I do not feel that anyone confers privileges upon me.

KRISHNAMURTI: I am sorry I am not explaining fully. All right. What is it but distinction, self-aggrandizement, when you are somebody's special pupil? You will say, "No. That will help me to truth. That step is necessary towards truth." Is that not so? So that step is merely the accentuation and exaggeration of self-consciousness. To understand, there must be less and less of the 'I' consciousness, not more and more. Is that not so? To understand anything there must be no prejudice; there must be no consciousness of "my path" and "your path," "my" this and "your" that. Anything that accentuates the "my" idea must be a hindrance. Must it not?

Comment: We are taught there are Masters.

KRISHNAMURTI: Well, I cannot enter into that. If you say, "It is authority; we are told," then there is nothing more to be said; but does that satisfy you all?

Comment: No.

KRISHNAMURTI: For the moment, forget everything you have learned here about the Masters, disciples, initiation. If you were really frank, you would see it. It is merely that everyone wants to be something, and this process of wanting to be somebody is used and exploited.

What is this consciousness which we call the 'I'? When are you conscious of it? (Please, I must be brief, because I must stop.) What is this consciousness? When are you conscious of yourself? When there is this conflict, when there is a hindrance, a frustra-

tion. Remove all frustration, remove all hindrances, then you do not say 'I'. Then you are living. It is only when you are conscious of pain that you are conscious of the body. So when there is pain, emotionally or intellectually, then you are conscious as something separate. Now we have accentuated it, brought about a condition in the mind that we call the 'I', and we take that as a fact and desire to proceed with expansion of that consciousness into truth—enlarge that consciousness more and more, through probation and initiations and all the rest of it, which indicates you have a false cause. That is, the 'I' is not reality. You have a false cause, and you have the false answers, as initiations, as expansion of consciousness of the 'I'; and hence you say somebody is necessary to help you to realize truth, to expand your consciousness; or you say, "The world needs a plan, and there are wiser people than I; therefore I must become their instrument to help the world." Therefore you establish a mediator between them and yourself—somebody who knows and somebody who does not know. And therefore, you merely become an instrument of exploitation. I know you all smile and disagree with me; but please, it does not matter. I am not here to convince you, or you to convince me. If you look at it with reason you will see.

So you establish a plan known to the few, and you merely become an instrument of action, to carry out orders. Take, for instance, if the Master said, "War is right." I am not saying that they have said it. You know in the last war how everybody said, "God is on our side," and we all jumped at it. Now, if you, as an individual, begin to really think, you will see war is a pernicious thing. And if you really thought of it, you could not join a war. But you say, "I do not know. The plan says there must be a war and good will come out of evil, so let me join." In other words, you really cease to think. You are merely instruments to be driven, cannon fodder. Surely that is not spiritual, all those things. So please, with regard to whether I believe in Masters or not, to me it is of very little importance. Whether you believe in a Master or not has nothing to do with spirituality. What is the difference between a medium that gets messages, and you that get messages from the Masters?

Comment: Are we to believe in nothing?

KRISHNAMURTI: Please, just a minute. Please, you see I have been talking about this. Why do you want belief? (Laughter) Please do not laugh, because everybody is in that position. We all want beliefs as props, as something to sustain us. Surely, the more and more you have beliefs, the less and less you have of strength, of inward richness. I am so sorry I cannot go into all this. It is half-past eight, but I would like to say this. Wisdom, or understanding, is not to be got at by holding on to things; holding on to your beliefs or ideas. Wisdom is born when you are really moving, not anchored to any particular form of belief; and then you will discover that it does not matter whether the Masters exist or do not exist, whether your society is essential to the world or not. These things are of very little importance. Then you are bringing about a new civilization, a new culture in the world.

You know, it is most extraordinary! Dr. Besant said to all the members, and I used to hear this very often, "We are preparing for a World Teacher. Keep an open mind. He may contradict everything you think, and say it differently." And you have been preparing, some of you, for twenty years or more; and it does not matter whether I am the teacher or not. No one can tell you, naturally, because no one else can know except myself; and even then I say it does not matter. I have never contradicted it. I say, "Leave it. That

is not the point." You have been preparing for twenty years or more, and very few of you have really an open mind. Very few have said, "Let us find out what you are talking about. Let us go into it. Let us discover if what you say is true or false, irrespective of your label." And after twenty years you are in exactly the same position as you were before. You have innumerable beliefs, you have certainties, and your knowledge, and you are not really willing to examine what I am saying. And it seems such a waste of time, such a pity that these twenty years and more should go wasted, and you find yourselves exactly where you were, only with new sets of beliefs, new sets of dogmas, new sets of conditions. I assure you, you cannot find truth, or liberation, or nirvana, or heaven, or whatever you like to call it, by this process of attachment. That does not mean that you all must become detached, which only means you become withered, but try to find out frankly, honestly, simply, whether what you are holding with such grim possessiveness has any significance, whether it has any value; and to find out if it has any value there cannot be the desire to cling to it. And then when you really look at it in that way, you will find something which is indescribable. Then you will discover something real, lasting, eternal. Then there will be no necessity for a teacher and a pupil. It will be a happy world when there are no pupils and no teachers.

March 31, 1934

Second Talk in Town Hall

Friends,

Probably most of you have come because you are in search of something. At least most of you are here because you hope to find something by attending this meeting, because you are in search of something which you do not know, but hope to discover. You are here because there is a desire to find happiness, because everyone, in some way or another, is suffering; there is a continual gnawing going on in our minds and hearts, we are unsatisfied, incomplete, questioning. Continual explanations are being given for our innumerable sufferings, and so you come here to find out if you can get something in return for your search. By attending this talk, you hope to find an answer to your problems, the cause of your suffering.

Now, generally, what happens when you suffer? You want a remedy. When there is a problem, you want a solution. When there is an ache, you want a remedy. So we go from one remedy to another. We suffer and we want to find out what is the remedy for that suffering, so we go from one lesson, from one experience, to another, from one remedy to another or from one explanation to another, from one system to another or from one belief to another, changing your sects continually—that is, going from one cage to another cage, battering vainly against these bars to find out why there is suffering; and all the time mind and heart are merely seeking a remedy, an explanation. So, you will never find the explanation, because, what happens when you are suffering? Your immediate demand is that suffering should be relieved, that pain should be alleviated, so you accept a remedy which is given, without properly examining it, without properly finding out its true significance. You accept that because, psychologically, you have set up a hope and that hope blinds, and therefore there is no clear understanding of that remedy. If you think over it, you will see that it is a fact. You go to a doctor; he gives you a remedy. You never ask him what it is. All you are concerned with is that the pain should go away.

Now you are here at this meeting with that same attitude of mind, if you are seek-ing. If you are here out of curiosity, well, I have nothing much to say, I am afraid. But if you are here to find out, if you are seeking a remedy, then you will be disappointed, because I do not want to give a remedy, an explanation; but in considering things together, reasoning together, we shall find out what is the cause of suffering.

So, to discover what is the cause of suffering, do not seek a remedy; but rather try to find out what is the cause of the suffering. One can deal superficially, symptomatically; but that way you will not find out the real, basic, fundamental cause; and you can only find out the cause of suffering if you are not creating a barrier by the immediate longing that you shall be freed from that pain. For instance, if you lose somebody whom you love greatly, there is intense suffering. Then a remedy is offered—that he lives on the other side, the idea of reincarnation, and so on. You accept that remedy for your suffering, but that sorrow still remains. That loneliness, that emptiness is still there, only you have covered it over with an explanation, a remedy, a superficial drug. Whereas, if you were really trying to discover what is the cause of that suffering, then you would examine, you would try to find out the full significance of the remedy which is being offered, whether it be the idea that he lives on the other side, or the belief in reincarnation. In that state of mind, when there is suffering, there is acuteness of thought, there is an intense questioning; and this intense questioning is really what causes suffering. Isn't it? If you have lived together with your wife, your brother, or anyone, and that brother, or wife, or friend has died, then you are face to face with your own loneliness, which creates in your mind the questioning attitude—the full consciousness of that loneliness. That moment of acute awareness, of full consciousness, is the moment to find out what is the cause of suffering.

Now, to me, to discover the cause of suffering, there must be that acute state of mind and heart which is seeking, which is trying to discover. In that state, you will see that the mind and heart have become the slave of environment. Mind, with the vast majority of people, is nothing but environment. Mind and heart are environment, depending on their condition; and as long as the mind is a slave to environment, there must be suffering, there must be continual conflict of the individual against society; and the individual will be free of environment only when he, by questioning the environment, conquers the limitation placed on him by environment. That is, it is only when you understand the true significance of each environment, the true worth of the environment which has been placed about you by society, by religions, that you pierce through the limitation imposed, and thereby there is born true intelligence.

After all, one is unhappy because there is no intelligence, which is understanding. When you understand a thing you are no longer in conflict, you are no longer bound by that which has been imposed on you by authority, by tradition, by deep-rooted prejudices. So intelligence is necessary to be supremely happy, and to awaken that intelligence, mind must be free of environment. The innumerable encrustations created by religions and society, throughout the ages, have become our environment. You can be free of environment, which individuals have created, only when you understand its standards, its values, its prejudices, its authorities. And you then begin to find out what is the fundamental cause of suffering, which is the lack of true intelligence, and that intelligence is not to be discovered by some miraculous process, but by being continually aware, therefore continually questioning, trying to discover the false and the true in the environment placed about us.

I have been given some questions, and I am going to try to answer them this evening.

Question: Do you believe in God? Are you an atheist?

KRISHNAMURTI: I presume you all believe in God. It must be so, because you are all Christians, at least you profess to be, so you must believe in God.

Now why do you believe in God? Please, I am going to answer presently, so do not call me an atheist, or a theist. Why do you believe in God? What is a belief? You do not believe in something which is obvious, like the sunshine, like the person sitting next to you; you do not have to believe. Whereas, your belief in God is not real. It is some hope, some idea, some preconceived longing which may have nothing to do with reality. If you do not believe, but really become aware of that reality in your life, as you are aware of sunshine, then your whole conduct of life will be different. At present, your belief has nothing whatever to do with your daily life; so, to me, whether you believe in God or not is immaterial. (Applause) Please do not bother to clap. There are many questions to answer.

So your belief in God, or your disbelief in God, to me are both the same, because they have no reality. If you were really aware of truth, as you are aware of that flower, if you were really conscious of that truth as you are conscious of fresh air and the lack of that fresh air, then your whole life, your whole conduct, your whole behavior, your very affections, your very thoughts, would be different. Whether you call yourselves believers or disbelievers, by your conduct you are not showing it; so whether you believe in God or not is of very little importance. It is merely a superficial idea imposed by conditions and environment, through fear, through authority, through imitation. Therefore, when you say,

"Do you believe? Are you an atheist?" I cannot answer you categorically; because, to you, belief is much more important than reality. I say there is something immense, immeasurable, unfathomable; there is some supreme intelligence, but you cannot describe it. How can you describe the taste of salt if you have never tasted it? And it is the people that have never tasted salt, that are never aware of this immensity in their lives, who begin to question whether I believe or whether I do not believe, because belief to them is much more important than that reality which they can discover if they live rightly, if they live truly; and as they do not want to live truly, they think belief in God is something essential to be truly human.

So, to be a theist or an atheist, to me, are both absurd. If you knew what truth is, what God is, you would neither be a theist nor an atheist, because in that awareness belief is unnecessary. It is the man who is not aware, who only hopes and supposes, that looks to belief or to disbelief, to support him, and to lead him to act in a particular way.

Now, if you approach it quite differently, you will find out for yourselves, as individuals, something real which is beyond all the limitations of beliefs, beyond the illusion of words. But that—the discovery of truth, or God—demands great intelligence, which is not assertion of belief or disbelief, but the recognition of the hindrances created by lack of intelligence. So to discover God or truth— and I say such a thing does exist, I have realized it—to recognize that, to realize that, mind must be free of all the hindrances which have been created throughout the ages, based on self-protection and security. You cannot be free of security by merely saying that you are free. To penetrate the walls of these hindrances, you need to have a great deal of intelligence, not more intellect. Intelligence, to me, is mind and heart in full har-

mony; and then you will find out for yourself without asking anyone, what that reality is.

Now, what is happening in the world? You have a Christian God, Hindu Gods, Mohammedans with their particular conception of God—each little sect with their particular truth; and all these truths are becoming like so many diseases in the world, separating people. These truths, in the hands of the few, are becoming the means of exploitation. You go to each, one after the other, tasting them all, because you begin to lose all sense of discrimination, because you are suffering and you want a remedy, and you accept any remedy that is offered by any sect, whether Christian, Hindu, or any other sect. So, what is happening? Your Gods are dividing you, your beliefs in God are dividing you and yet you talk about the brotherhood of man, unity in God, and at the same time deny the very thing that you want to find out, because you cling to these beliefs as the most potent means of destroying limitation, whereas they but intensify it.

These things are so obvious. If you are a Protestant, you have a horror of the Roman Catholic; and if Roman Catholic, you have a horror of everybody else. That goes on everywhere, not only here. In India, among the Mohammedans, among all religious sects this goes on; because to all, belief—that cruel thing—is more vital, more important, than the discovery of truth, which is real humanity. Therefore, the people who believe so much in God are really not in love with life. They are in love with a belief, but not with life, and therefore their hearts and minds wither and become as nothing, empty, shallow.

Question: Do you believe in reincarnation?

KRISHNAMURTI: First of all, I do not know how many of you are conversant with the idea of reincarnation. I will very briefly explain to you what it means. It means that in order to reach perfection, you must go through a series of lives, gathering more and more experience, more and more knowledge, until you come to that reality, to that perfection. Briefly and crudely, without going into the subtleties of it, that is reincarnation: that you as the 'I', the entity, the ego, take on a series of forms, life after life, until you are perfect.

Now I am not going to answer whether I believe it or not, as I want to show that reincarnation is immaterial. Do not reject what I say immediately. What is the ego? What is this consciousness which we call the 'I'? I will tell you what it is, and please consider it; do not reject it. You are here to understand what I am saying, not to create a barrier between yourself and me by your belief. What is the 'I', that focal point which you call the 'I', that consciousness of which the mind is continually becoming aware? That is, when you are conscious of the 'I'? When you are conscious of yourself? Only when you are frustrated, when you are hindered, when there is a resistance; otherwise, you are supremely unconscious of your little self as 'I'. Is that not so? You are only conscious of yourself when there is a conflict. So, as we live in nothing else but conflict, we are conscious of that most of the time; and, therefore there is that consciousness, that conception, which is born of the 'I'. The 'I' in that conflict is nothing else but the consciousness of yourself as a form with a name, with certain prejudices, with certain idiosyncrasies, tendencies, faculties, longings, frustrations; and this, you think, must continue and grow and reach perfection. How can conflict reach perfection? How can that limited consciousness reach perfection? It can expand, it can grow, but it will not be perfection, however large, all-inclusive, because its foundations are conflict, misunderstandings, hindrances.

So as you say to yourself, "I must live as an entity beyond death, therefore I must come back to this life until I reach perfection."

Now then, you will say, "If you remove this conception of the 'I', what is the focal point in life?" I hope you are following this. You say, "Remove, free the mind from this consciousness of myself as an 'I', then what remains?" What remains when you are supremely happy, creative? There remains that happiness. When you are really happy, or when you are greatly in love, there is no 'you'. There is that tremendous feeling of love, or that ecstasy. I say that is the real. Everything else is false.

So let us discover what creates these conflicts, what creates these hindrances, this continual friction, let us find out whether it is artificial or real. If it is real, if this friction is intended to be the very process of life, then the consciousness of the 'I' must be real. Now, I say this friction is a false thing, that it cannot exist in a humanity where there is well-organized planning for the needs of human beings, where there is true affection. So let us find out if the 'I' is the false creation of a false environment, a false society, or if the 'I' is something permanent, eternal. To me, this limited consciousness is not eternal. It is the result of false environment and beliefs. If you were doing what you really wanted to do in life, not being forced to do some particular job which you loathe, if you were following your true vocation, fulfilling yourself in your true vocation, then work would no longer be friction. A painter, a poet, a writer, an engineer, who really loves his work, to him life is not a burden.

But your work is not your vocation. Environment and social conditions are forcing you to do a certain piece of work whether you like it or not, so you have already created a friction. Then certain moral standards, certain authorities have established various ideals as true, as false, as being virtuous, and so on, and you accept these. You have taken on this cloak without understanding, without discovering its right value, and therefore you have created friction. So gradually your whole mind is warped and perverted and in conflict until you have become conscious of that 'I' and nothing else. Therefore, you start with a wrong cause, produced by a wrong environment, and you have a wrong answer.

So whether reincarnation exists or does not exist is, to me, immaterial. What matters is to fulfill, which is perfection. You cannot fulfill in a future. Fulfillment is not of time. Fulfillment is in the present. So what is happening? Through friction, through continual conflict, memory is being created, memory as the 'I' and the 'mine', which becomes possessive. That memory has many layers, and constitutes that consciousness which we call the 'I'. And I say that this 'I' is the false result of a false environment, and hence its problems, its solutions, must be entirely false, illusory. Whereas, if you, as individuals, begin to awaken to the limitations of environment imposed on you by society, by religions, by economic conditions, and begin to question, and thereby create conflict, then you will dissipate that little consciousness which you call the 'I'; then you will know what is that fulfillment, that creative living in the present.

To put it differently, many scientists say that individuality, this limited consciousness, exists after death. They have discovered ectoplasm, and all the rest of it, and they say that life exists after death. You will have to follow this a little bit carefully, as I hope you have followed the other part; if not, you won't understand it. Individuality, this consciousness, this limited self-consciousness, is a fact in life. It is a fact in your life, isn't it? It is a fact, but it has no reality. You are constantly self-conscious, and that is a fact, but as I showed you, it has no reality. It is mere-

ly the habit of centuries of false environment which has made a fact of something which is not real. And though that fact may exist, and does exist, so long as that continues there cannot be fulfillment. And I say the fulfillment of perfection is not in the accumulation of virtues, not in postponement, but in complete harmony of living in the present. Sirs, suppose you are hungry now and I promise food to you next week, of what value is it? Or if you have lost someone whom you love greatly, even though you may be told or even though you may know for yourself as a fact that he lives on the other side, what of it? What matters, and in reality takes place, is that there is that emptiness, that loneliness in your heart and mind, that immense void; and you think you can get away from that, run away from it, by this knowledge that your brother, or your wife, or your husband, still lives. There is still in that consciousness death; there is still in that consciousness a limitation; there is still in that consciousness an emptiness, a continual gnawing of sorrow. Whereas, if you free the mind from that consciousness of the 'I' by discovering the right values of environment, which no one can tell you, then you will know for yourselves that fulfillment which is truth, which is God, or any name you like to give it. But through the developing of that limited self-consciousness which is the false result of a false cause, you will not find out what truth is, or what God is, what happiness is, what perfection is; for in that self-consciousness there must be continual conflict, continual striving, continual misery.

Question: Are you the Messiah?

KRISHNAMURTI: Does it matter greatly? You know, this is one of the questions I have been asked everywhere I go: by newspaper reporters for a story; by the audience because they want to know, as they think that authority shall convince them. Now, I have never denied or asserted that I am the Messiah, that I am the Christ returned; that does not matter. No one can tell you. Even if I did tell you it would be utterly valueless, and so I am not going to tell you, because, to me, it is so irrelevant, so unimportant, futile. After all, when you see a marvelous piece of sculpture, or a marvelous painting, there is a rejoicing; but I am afraid most of you are interested in who has done the picture, most of you are interested in who the sculptor is. You are not really interested in the purity of action, whether in a picture or a statue, or in thought; you are interested to know who is speaking. So it indicates that you have not the capacity to find out the intrinsic merit of an idea, but are rather concerned with who speaks. And I am afraid a snobbery is being cultivated more and more, a spiritual snobbery, just as there is a mundane snobbery, but all snobbery is the same.

So, friends, don't bother, but try to find out if what I am saying is true; and in trying to find out if what I am saying is true, you will be rid of all authority, a pernicious thing. For really creative, intelligent human beings, there cannot be authority. To discover if what I am saying is true, you cannot approach it by mere opposition, or by saying, "We have been told so," "It has been said," "Certain books have said this and that," "Our spirit-guides have said." You know that is the latest thing, "Our spirit-guides have said this." I do not know why you give more importance to those spirits who are dead than to the living. You know the living can always contradict you, therefore you do not pay much attention to them, whereas the spirits you know, they can always deceive.

We have trained our minds, not to appreciate a thing for itself, but rather for who has created it, who has painted, who has spoken. So our minds and hearts become more and more shallow, empty, and in that there is neither affection nor real, reasonable thought, but merely masses of prejudices.

Question: What is spirituality?

KRISHNAMURTI: I say it is harmonious living. Now wait a minute. I will explain to you what I mean. You cannot live harmoniously if you are a nationalist. How can you? If you are race-conscious, or class-conscious, how can you live intelligently, supremely, free from that consciousness of class? Or how can you live harmoniously when you are possessive, when there is that idea of mine and yours? Or how can you live intelligently, and therefore harmoniously, if you are bound by beliefs? After all, belief is merely an escape from the present conflict. A man that is in immense conflict with life, wanting to understand, has no belief, he is in the process of experimentation; he does not positively believe and then continue with the experiment. A scientist does not start with a belief in his experiments, he starts experimenting. And a man who is bound by authority, social or religious, surely he cannot live harmoniously, therefore spiritually, intelligently. Authority, then, is merely the process of imitation, falseness. A man who is full of thought is not free of authority, because authority merely makes him into an imitative machine, into a cog—whether in a social or religious machine. Therefore such a man can live harmoniously, and in that harmony his mind and heart are normal, sane, full, complete, not burdened with fear.

Question: Is the study of music, or art generally, of value to one who is desirous to attain the realization of which you speak?

KRISHNAMURTI: Do you mean to say you go and listen to music as though you were going to get something in return? Surely music is not merchandise, to be sold. You go there to enjoy yourself, not to get something in return. It is not a shop. Surely our whole idea of the realization of truth or of living ecstatically is not continual accumulation of things, accumulation of ideas, accumulation of sensations. You go and see a beautiful piece of painting, architecture—any of these things—because you enjoy them, not because you are going to get something in return. That is the real materialistic attitude, the attitude of exchange, trading. That is your approach to reality, that is your approach to God. You go to God with prayers, flowers, confessions, sacrifices, because in return you are going to get something. So your sacrifices, prayers, implorings, beggings, have no value, because you are looking for something in return. It is like a man that is kindly because you are going to give him something, and the whole process of civilization is based on that. Love is a merchandise to be bartered. Spirituality, or the realization of truth, is something you seek in return for doing some righteous action. Sir, it is not a righteous action when you seek something else in return for that kindly deed.

Question: If priests and churches, and similar organizations, are acting with men in a sense of first aid to relieve the symptoms until the Great Physician arrives to deal with the cause, is that wrong?

KRISHNAMURTI: So you make priests and religions as the first stepping stone. Is that it? You are waiting for somebody else to come and reveal to you the cause? You are saying, as far as I can make out, "As there are so many symptoms, as we are suffering superficially, that is, dealing with the symptoms, it is necessary to have the priests and churches." Now do you say that? Do you recognize that? Do you recognize and assert that

churches and priests are merely dealing with symptoms? If you really acknowledge that, then you will find out the cause. But you will not do that. You don't say that priests and churches deal superficially, symptomatically. If you really said that and felt that, then you would find out the cause for yourself immediately; whereas you do not say that. You say priests and churches will lead you to discover the cause, so the question is not truly put. To the vast majority of people, practically everybody, churches and priests will help you to go to the reality of truth: you do not say they deal with the symptoms. If you did, you would do away with them immediately, tomorrow. I wish you did! Then you would find out. Then no one need tell you what the cause is, because you are functioning intelligently, because you are beginning to question, not to accept. Then you are becoming real individuals, not machines driven by environment and fear. Then there will be more thoughtfulness, more affection, more humanity in the world, not these awful divisions.

Question: Seeing that human society has to be cooperative and collective, what value can the individual be to its success? Leadership suppresses the individual's freedom, and renders his uniqueness valueless.

KRISHNAMURTI: "Seeing that human society has to be cooperative and collective, what value can the individual be to its success?" Now let us find out if the individual, by becoming truly individual, will not cooperate. That is, instead of being driven to cooperation as you are now by circumstances—I should not say driven to cooperation, you are not cooperative— instead of being driven by conditions to act for yourselves, which is therefore not true, intelligent cooperation, is it possible to cooperate by becoming real individuals? I say it is possible, by becoming truly individual, that there will be true and natural cooperation, without being driven by circumstances; so let us inquire into it.

After all, are you individuals, functioning with your full volition? That, after all, is the true individual, is it not?—the man who functions with full freedom; otherwise you are not individuals, you are mere cogs in a machine that is being driven. So I say it is only when you are truly individuals that there will be real cooperation. Now what is an individual? Not a human being who is driven to action by environment, by circumstances. I say true individuality consists in freeing the mind from the environment of the false, and therefore becoming truly individual, and so there must be cooperation.

Please, it is already late, and I cannot go into details, but if you are interested you will think it over, and you will see that in this world, as it is constituted, each individual is fighting his neighbor, searching for his own self-security, protection, preservation. There cannot be cooperation. It is an impossibility. There can only be cooperation which is intelligent, human, creative, not selfish cooperation, when you as individuals, become full individuals. That is, when you see that to have true cooperation in the world, there must be no competitive search for self-security. That means altering the whole structure of our civilization, with its vested interest, with its class possessiveness, with its nationalities, race-consciousness, divisions of people by religions. When you, as individuals, are really free, when you see the significance of these things and their falseness, then you become truly individual, and then you will be able to cooperate intelligently; that is inevitable. What is keeping us apart is our prejudice, our lack of perception of right values, of all these hindrances which we, as individuals, have created; and it is only as individuals that we can break down this system. It means that you cannot have

any nationality, the sense of possessiveness, though you may have clothes, houses. That sense of possessiveness disappears when you have discovered your real needs, when your whole attitude is not that of possessive class consciousness. When every individual takes an interest in the welfare of the community, then there can be true cooperation. Now there is no cooperation because you are being merely driven like so many sheep, in one direction or another, by circumstances, and your leaders suppress you because you are but the means of exploitation, and you are exploited because your whole thought, your whole structure, is self-preservation at the expense of everybody else. And I say there is true self-preservation, true security, in the world plan as a whole, when you, as individuals, destroy those things that are keeping people apart, fighting each other in continual wars which are the result of nationalities and sovereign governments. And I assure you, you will not have peace, you will not have happiness, so long as these things exist. They but bring about more and more strife, more and more wars, more and more calamities, pains and sufferings. They have been created by individuals, and as individuals you have to begin to break them down and free yourselves from them, and then only will you realize that ecstasy of life.

April 1, 1934

Third Talk in Vasanta School Gardens

Friends,

This morning I will first try to answer some of the questions, and then I will try to make a résumé of what I have been saying, at the close of my answers.

Question: In order to discover lasting values, is meditation necessary, and, if so, what is the correct method of meditation?

KRISHNAMURTI: I wonder what people generally mean by meditation. As far as I can make out, the so-called meditation which is but concentration, is not meditation at all. We are used to this idea that by concentrating, by making tremendous effort to control the mind and fix it on a certain idea or concept, certain picture or image, by focusing the mind on a particular point, we are meditating.

Now, what is happening when you are trying to do that? You are trying to concentrate your mind on a particular idea and banish all other ideas, all other concepts; and trying to fix the mind on that idea, to force the mind to limit itself to that, whether it be a great thought, an image, or a concept which you have picked up in a book. What is happening when you are doing that? Other ideas come creeping in and you try to banish them away, and so this continual conflict is kept up. Ideas creep in which you do not want, in the attempt to fix your mind on a particular idea. You are but creating conflict; making the mind become smaller, contracting the mind, forcing the mind to fix itself on a particular idea; whereas, to me, the joy of meditation consists, not in forcing the mind, but trying to discover the full significance of each thought as it arises. How can you say which is a better idea and which is a worse idea, which is noble, which is ignoble? You can only say that when the mind has discovered their true values. So, to me, the joy of meditation consists in this process of discovering the right value of each thought. You discover by a natural process the significance of each thought, and therefore free the mind from this continual conflict.

Suppose you are trying to concentrate on an idea—you think of what you are going to wear, that idea comes into your mind, or whom you are going to see, or what you are going to have for lunch. Complete each thought, do not try to banish it away; then you will see that mind is no longer a battlefield of competing ideas. So your meditation is not limited to a few hours, or to a few moments during the day, but is a continual alertness of the mind and heart throughout the day; and that, to me, is true meditation. In that there is peace. In that there is a joy. But the so-called meditation you practice for discipline in order to get something in return is, to me, a pernicious thing, it is really destroying thought. Why are we forced to do that? Why do we force ourselves to think concentratedly for a few moments during the day of things which we think we like? Because we are doing the rest of the day something we do not like, which is not pleasant. Therefore, we say, "To find, to think about something which I like, I must meditate." So you are giving a false answer to a false cause. That is, environment— economic, social, religious—prevents you from doing, fulfilling what you want to do; and as it prevents you, you have to find moments, an hour or two, in which to live. So disciplining the mind, forcing it to a particular pattern then, is necessary, and hence the whole idea of discipline. Whereas, if you really understood the limitation of environment, and broke through it with action, then this process of disciplining the mind to act in a certain manner would become wholly unnecessary.

Please, you have to think it over rather carefully if you would see the significance of all this; because a disciplined mind—not a mind that is merely disciplined to carry out a technique—is a mind that has been trained along a certain particular pattern, and that pattern is the outcome of a false society, false ideas, false concepts. Whereas, if you are able to penetrate, and see what are the things that are false; then the mind is no longer a battlefield of contradictory ideas; and in that you will find there is true contemplation. The joy of thought then is awakened.

Question: What is the state of awareness which you speak of? Will you deal with it a little more fully?

KRISHNAMURTI: Sirs, we are used to continual effort to do anything; to think is to make tremendous effort. We are used to this ceaseless effort. Now, I want to put what, to me, is not an effort but a new way of living. When you know something is a hindrance, something is a poison, when your whole being becomes conscious of something which is poisonous, there is no effort to throw it out: you have already moved away from it. When you know something is dangerous, poisonous, and when you become fully conscious of it in your mind and heart, you have already become free of it. It is only when we do not know that it is poison, or when that poison gives pleasure and at the same time pain, then we play with it.

Now, we have created many hindrances, such as nationalism, patriotism, imitative following of authority, bowing down to tradition, the continual search for comfort. All these we have created through fear. But, if we know with our whole being that patriotism is really a false thing, a poisonous thing, then you have not to battle against it. You do not have to get rid of it. The moment you know it is a poisonous thing, it is gone. How are we going to discover it is a poisonous thing? By not identifying yourselves with either patriotism or antipatriotism. That is, you want to discover if patriotism is a poison; but if you identify yourself with either patriotism or the feeling of anti-patriotism, then you cannot discover what is true. Isn't it so? You want to discover if patriotism is a poison. Therefore the

first thing is to become aware, become conscious of the fact of nonidentification with either. So, when you are not trying to identify yourself with either patriotism, or the feeling against patriotism, then you begin to see the true significance of patriotism. Then you are becoming aware of its true value.

After all, what is patriotism? I am trying to help you to become aware of this poison now. It does not mean that you must accept or reject what I am saying. Let us consider it together, and see if it is not a poison; and the moment you see it is poison, you need not battle against it. It has gone. If you see a poisonous snake, you have moved away from it. You are not battling against it. Whereas, if you are uncertain that it is a poisonous snake, then you go and play with it. In the same way, let us try to find out without acceptance or opposition if patriotism is a poison or not.

First of all, when are you patriotic? You are not patriotic every day. You do not keep up that patriotic feeling. You are being trained carefully to patriotism at school, through history books saying that your country has beaten some other country, your country is better than some other country. Why has there been this training of the mind to patriotism, which, to me, is an unnatural thing? Not that you do not appreciate the beauty of one country perhaps more than other countries; but that appreciation has nothing to do with patriotism, it is appreciation of beauty. For instance, there are some parts of the world where there is not a single tree, where the sun is blazing hot; but that has its own beauty. Surely a man that likes shade, the dancing of leaves, surely he is not patriotic. Patriotism has been cultivated, trained, as a means of exploitation. It is not an instinctive thing in man. The instinctive thing in man is the appreciation of beauty, not to say "my country." But that has been cultivated by those who desire to seek foreign markets for their goods. That is, if I have the means of production in my hands, and have saturated this country with my products, and then I want to expand, I must go to other countries. I must conquer markets in other countries. Therefore I must have means of conquering. So, I say "our country," and I stimulate this whole thing through press, propaganda, education, history books, and so on, this sense of patriotism, so that at a moment of crisis we all jump to fight another country. And upon that feeling of patriotism the exploiters play until you are so bamboozled that you are ready to fight for the country, calling the others barbarians, and all the rest of it.

This is an obvious thing, not my invention. You can study it. It is obvious if you look at it with an unprejudiced mind, with a mind that does not want to identify itself with one or the other, but tries to find out. What happens when you find out that patriotism is really a hindrance to complete, full, real life? You do not have to battle against it. It has gone completely.

Comment: You would be up against the law of the land.

KRISHNAMURTI: The law of the land! Why not? Surely, if you are free of patriotism and the law of the land interferes with you, and takes you to war and you do not feel patriotic, then you may become a conscientious objector, or go to prison, then you have to fight the law. Law is made by human beings, and surely it can be broken by human beings. (Applause) Please don't bother to clap, it is a waste of time.

So what is happening? Patriotism, whether it is of the western kind, or of the eastern kind, is the same, a poison in human beings that is really distorting thought. So patriotism is a disease, and when you begin to realize, become aware that it is a disease, then you

will see how your mind is reacting to that disease. When, in time of war, the whole world talks of patriotism, you will know the falseness of it, and therefore you will act as a true human being.

In the same way, for instance, belief is a hindrance. That is, mind cannot think completely, fully, if it is tethered to a belief. It is like an animal that is tied to a post by a string. It does not matter if that string be long or short; it is tied, so that it cannot wander fully, freely, extensively, completely; it can only wander within the length of that string. Surely such wandering is not thinking: it is only moving within the limited circle of belief. Now, men's minds are tethered to a belief, and therefore they are incapable of thinking. Most minds have identified themselves with a belief, and therefore their thought is always circumscribed, limited by that belief or ideal; hence the incompleteness of thought. Beliefs separate people. So if you see that, if you really recognize with your whole being that belief is conditioning thought, then what happens? You become aware that your thought is conditioned, aware your thought is caught up, tethered to a belief. In the flame of awareness you will recognize the foolishness, and therefore you are beginning to free the mind from the conditioning, and hence you begin to think completely, fully.

Please experiment with this, and you will see that life is not a process of continual battle, battle against standards as opposed to what you want to do. There is then neither what you want to do, nor the standard, but right action, without personal identification.

Take another example. You are afraid of what your neighbor might say—a very simple fear. Now, it is no good developing the opposite, which is to say, "I don't care what the neighbor says," and do something in reaction to that opposition. But if you really become aware of why you are afraid of the neighbor, then fear ceases altogether. To discover that "why," the cause of it, you have to be fully aware in that moment of fear, and then you will see what it is: you are afraid of losing a job, you may not marry off your son or your daughter, you want to fit into society, and all the rest of it. So you begin to discover through this process of alertness of mind, this continual awareness; and in that flame the dross of the false standards is burned away. Then life is not a battle. Then there is nothing to be conquered.

You may not accept this. You may not accept what I am saying, but you can experiment. Experiment with these three instances I have given to you, fear, belief, patriotism, and you will see how your mind is tethered, conditioned, and therefore life becomes a conflict. Where the mind is enslaved, conditioned, there must be conflict, there must be suffering. Because, after all, thought is like the waters of a river. It must be in continual movement. Eternity is that movement. If you condition that free-flowing movement of thought, of mind and heart, then you must have conflict, and that conflict then must have a remedy, and then the process begins: the searching for remedies, substitutes, and never trying to find out the cause of this conflict. So through the process of full awareness, you liberate the mind and heart from the hindrances which have been set about them through environment; and as long as environment is conditioning the mind, as long as the mind has not discovered the true significance of the environment, there must be conflict, and hence the false answer which is self-discipline.

Question: When one has discovered for oneself that every method of escape from the present has resulted in futility, what more is there to be done?

KRISHNAMURTI: When you discover that you are escaping from conflict, that your mind is running away through superficial remedies, you want to know what remains. What does remain? Intelligence, understanding. Is that not so? Suppose you have some kind of sorrow, either the sorrow of death, or a momentary sorrow of some kind. You escape, when there is the sorrow of death, through this belief in reincarnation, or that life exists and continues on the other side. I went into that last night, so I will not go into it here. But when you recognize it is an escape, what happens? Then you are looking at the remedy to discover its significance, if it has any value; and in the process of discovering, there is born intelligence, understanding; and that supreme intelligence is life itself. You don't want any more.

Or suppose you have some kind of momentary sorrow, and you want to escape from it, run away and try to amuse yourself, try to forget it. In trying to forget, you never understand the cause of that sorrow. So you increase and multiply the means of forgetfulness; it may be a cinema, a church, or anything. So it is not a question of what remains after you have ceased to escape; but in trying to discover the value of the escapes which you have created for yourself, there is true intelligence, and that intelligence is creative happiness, is fulfillment.

Question: What is the fundamental cause of fear?

KRISHNAMURTI: Is not the fundamental cause of fear, self-preservation, with all its subtleties? For instance, you may have money, and therefore you are not bothering about the competition of getting a job; but you are afraid of something else, afraid that your life may come suddenly to an end and there might be extinction, or afraid of loss of money. So, if you look at it, you will see that fear will exist so long as this idea of self-preservation continues, so long as the mind clings to this idea of self-consciousness, which idea I explained last night. As long as that ego-consciousness remains, there must be fear; and that is the fundamental cause of fear. And I tried to explain last night also, how this limited consciousness which we call the 'I' is brought about, how it is created through false environment, and the fighting that is brought about by that environment. That is, as the system now exists, you have to fight for yourself to live at all, so that creates fear; and then we try to find remedies to get rid of this fear. Whereas, if you really altered the condition that creates this fear, then there is no need for remedies; then you are really tackling at the very source, the very creator of fear. Cannot we conceive of a state when you have not got to fight for your existence? Not that there are not other kinds of fear, which we will go into later; but it is this idea of nationality, this idea of race consciousness, class consciousness, the means of production in the hands of the few, and therefore the process of exploitation: it is these that prevent you from living naturally without this continual fight for self-preservation and security, which, I say, in an intelligent state is absurd. We are just like animals really, though we may call ourselves civilized, each one fighting for himself and his family; and that is one of the fundamental causes of fear. If you really understand environment and the battling against it, then you do not care, and fear loses its grip.

But there is a fear of another kind, the fear of inward poverty. There is the fear of external poverty, and then there is the fear of being shallow, of being empty, of being lonely. So, being afraid, we resort to the various remedies in the hope of enriching ourselves. Whereas, what is really happening? You are merely covering up that hollowness, that shallowness, by innumerable remedies. It may be the remedy of literature, by reading a great deal—not that I am against reading. It may be this exaggeration of sport, this continual rush, of keeping together at all costs, being on the run, belonging to certain groups, certain classes, certain societies, being in the clique, among the smart set. You know, we all go through it. All these but indicate the fear of that loneliness which you must inevitably face some day or another. And as long as that emptiness exists, that shallowness, that hollowness, that void, there must be fear.

To be really free of that fear, which is to be free of that emptiness, that shallowness, is not to cover it up by remedies; but rather to recognize that shallowness, become aware of it, which gives you then the alertness of mind to find out the values and the significance of each experience, of each standard, of each environment. Through that you will discover true intelligence; and intelligence is deep, profound, limitless, and therefore shallowness disappears. It is when you are trying to cover it up, trying to gain something to fill that emptiness, that the emptiness grows more and more. But, if you know that you are empty, not try to run away, in that awareness your mind becomes very acute, because you are suffering. The moment you are conscious that you are empty, hollow, there is tremendous conflict taking place. In that moment of conflict you are discovering, as you move along, the significance of experience—the standards, the values of society, of religion, of the conditions placed upon you. Instead of covering up emptiness, there is a depth of intelligence. Then you are never lonely even if you are by yourself or with a huge crowd, then there is no such thing as emptiness, shallowness.

Question: Will people act by instinct, or will someone have to point out the way always?

KRISHNAMURTI: Now, instinct is not a thing to be trusted. Is it? Because instinct has been so perverted, so bound by tradition, by authority, by environment, that you can no longer trust it. That is, the instinct of possessiveness is a false thing, an unnatural thing. I will explain to you why. It has been created by a society which is based on individual security; and therefore the instinct of possessiveness has been carefully cultivated throughout the generations. We say, "Instinctively I am possessive. It is human nature to be possessive"; but if you really look at it, you will see it has been cultivated by false conditions, and therefore the instinct of possessiveness is not true instinct. So we have many instincts which have been falsely fostered, and if you depend on another to lead you out of these false instinctive standards, then you will go into another cage; you will create another set of standards which will again pervert you. Whereas, if you really look into each instinct and not try to identify yourself with that instinct, but try to discover its significance, then out of that comes a natural spontaneous action, the true intuition.

You know, you have been here at my talks, fortunately or unfortunately, for the last four or five days, and merely listening to my talks is not going to do anything, is not going to give you wisdom. What gives wisdom is action. Wisdom is not a thing to be bought, or got from encyclopedias, or from reading philosophies. I have never read any philosophies. It is only in the process of action that you begin to discern what is false and what is true; and very few people are alert, eager for action. They would rather sit down and discuss, or attend churches, create mysteries out of nothing, because their minds are slothful, lazy, and behind that there is the fear of going against society, against the established order. So listening to my talks, or reading what I have said, is not going to awaken intelligence or lead you to truth, to that ecstasy of life which is in continual movement. What brings wisdom is to become aware of one of these hindrances, and to act. Take, as I said, the hindrance of patriotism or of belief, and begin to act, and you will see to what depth, to what profundity of thought it will lead you. You go far beyond any theoretical theologian, any philosopher; and in that action you will find out that there comes a time when you are not seeking for a result from your action, a fruit from your action, but the very action itself has meaning. As a scientist experiments, and in the process of experimenting there are results, but he continues experimenting; so, in the same way, in the process of experimenting, in the process of liberating the mind and heart from hindrances there will take place action, result. But the essential thing is that there is this continual movement of mind and heart. If all action is really the expression of that movement, then action becomes the new society, the new environment and therefore society is not being approximated to some ideal, but in that action, society is also moving, never static, never still, and morality is then a voluntary perception, not forced through fear, or imposed externally by society or by religion.

So, gradually, in this process of liberating the mind from the false, there is not the replacement of the false by the true, but only the true. Then you are no longer seeking a substitution, but in the process of discovering the false, you liberate the mind to move, to live eternally, and then action becomes a spontaneous, natural thing, and therefore life becomes, not a school in which to learn to compete, to fight, life becomes a thing to be lived intelligently, supremely, happily. And such a life is the life of a consummate human being.

April 2, 1934

Talk to Businessmen in Auckland

Friends,

I think that most of us think that it would be a marvelous world if there were no real exploitation, and that it would be a splendid world if every human being had the capacity to live naturally, fully, and humanly. But there are very few who want to do anything about it. As ideals, as a utopia, as a thing of a dream, everyone indulges in it, but very few desire action. You cannot bring about a utopia nor can there be the cessation of exploitation without action.

Now, there can be action, collective action, only if there is first of all individual thinking out of that problem. Every human being, in sane moments, feels the horror of real exploitation, whether by the priest, by the businessman, by the doctor, by the politician, or by anybody. We all feel really, in our hearts, the appalling cruelty of exploitation, if we have given a single moment's thought to it. And yet each one is caught up in this wheel, in this system of exploitation, and we are waiting and hoping that by some miracle a new system will come into being. And so, individually, we feel we have but to wait, let things take their natural course, and by some extraordinary means a new world will come into being. Surely, to create a new thing, a new world, a new conception of organization, individuals must begin. That is, the business people, or anyone in particular, must begin to find out if their action is really based on exploitation.

Now, as I said, there is the exploitation of the priest based on fear, there is the exploitation of the businessman based on his own aggrandizement, accumulation of wealth, greed, subtle forms of selfishness and security; and as you are all here supposed to be businessmen, surely you cannot leave every human problem aside and concern yourselves wholly with business. After all, businessmen are human beings, and human beings, so long as they are exploited, must have this rebellious spirit in them continually. It is only when you have reached a certain level where you are fairly secure that you forget all about this condition, about changing the world, or bringing about a certain attitude of spontaneous action towards life. Because we have reached a certain stage of security, we forget, and feel everything is all right; but behind it all one can feel that there cannot be happiness, human happiness, so long as there is real exploitation.

Now, to me, exploitation comes into being when individuals seek more than their essential needs; and to discover your essential needs requires a great deal of intelligence, and you cannot be intelligent so long as your needs are the result of the pursuit of security, or comfort. Naturally, one must have food, shelter, clothing, and all the rest of it; but to make this possible for everyone, individuals must begin to realize their own needs, the needs which are human, and organize the whole system of thought and action on that, and then only can there be real creative happiness in the world.

But now what is happening? We are fighting each other all the time, elbowing each other out, there is continual competitiveness, where each one feels insecure, and yet we go on drifting, without taking a definite action. That is, instead of waiting for a miracle to take place to alter this system, it needs a complete revolutionary change, which each one recognizes.

Although we may have a slight fear of world revolution, we all recognize the immense necessity of a change. And yet, individually, we are incapable of bringing about that change, because, individually, we have not given consideration, individually we have not tried to find out why there should be this continual process of exploitation. When individuals are really intelligent, then they will create an organization which will provide the essential needs for humanity, not based on exploitation. Individually we cannot live apart from society. Society is the individual and as long as individuals are merely continually seeking their own self-security, for themselves or their families, there must be a system of exploitation.

And there cannot be real happiness in the world if individuals, as yourselves, treat the world's affairs, human affairs, apart from business. That is, you cannot be, if I may say so, nationalistically inclined, and yet talk about the freedom of trade. You cannot consider New Zealand as the first important country, and then reject all other countries, because you feel, individually, the essential need for your own security. That is, sirs, if I may put it this way, there can be real freedom of trade, development of industries, and so on, only when there are no nationalities in the world. I think that is obvious. So long as there are tariff walls protecting each country there must be wars, confusion, and chaos; but if we were able to treat the whole world, not as divided into nationalities, into classes, but as a human entity; not divided by religious sects, by capitalist class and the worker class; then only is there a possibility of real freedom in trade, in cooperation. To bring this about you cannot merely preach or attend meetings. There cannot be mere intellectual enjoyment of these ideas, there must be action; and to bring about action, individually we must begin, even though we may suffer for it. We must begin to create intelligent opinion, and thereby we shall have a world where individuality is not crushed out, beaten to a particular pattern, but becomes a means of expression of

life; not the battered, conditioned shape which we call human beings. Most people want and realize there must be a complete change. I cannot see any way but by beginning as individuals, and then that individual opinion will become the realization of humanity.

Question: What intelligible meaning, may I ask, do you attach to the idea of a masculine God as postulated by practically the whole of the Christian clergy, and arbitrarily imposed upon the masses during the dark ages of the past and until the present moment? A God conceived of in terms of the masculine gender, must, by all the canons of sound and sane logic, be thought of, prayed to, importuned and worshipped in terms of personality. And a personal God—personal as we human beings necessarily are—must be limited in time, space, power and purpose, and a God so limited can be no God at all. In the very face of this colossal imposition, arbitrarily imposed upon the masses, is it any wonder that we find the world in its present catastrophic condition? God to be God must, in sober and sane reality, be the absolute and infinite totality of all existence, both negative and positive. Is that not so?

KRISHNAMURTI: Sir, why do you want to know whether God is masculine or feminine? Why do we question? Why do we try to find out if there is a God, if it is personal, if it is masculine? Is it not because we feel the insufficiency of living? We feel that if we can find out what this immense reality is, then we can mold our lives according to that reality; so we begin to preconceive what that reality must be or should be, and shape that reality according to our fancies and whims, according to our prejudices and temperaments. So we begin to build up by a series of contradictions and oppositions, an idea of what we think God should be; and, to me, such a God is no God at all. It is a human means of escape from the constant battles of life, from this thing which we call exploitation, from the inanities of life, the loneliness, the sorrows. Our God is merely a means of escape from these things; whereas, to me, there is something much more fundamental, real. I say there is something like God; let us not inquire into what it is. You will find out if you begin to really understand the very conflict which is crippling the mind and heart: this continual struggle for self-security, this horror of exploitation, wars, and nationalities, and the absurdities of organized religion. If we can face these and understand them, then we shall find out the real meaning instead of speculating; the real meaning of life, the real meaning of God.

Question: Do you follow Mohammed, or the Christ?

KRISHNAMURTI: May I ask why anyone should follow another? After all, truth or God is not to be found by imitating another: then we will only make ourselves into machines. Surely, need we, as human beings, belong to any sect, whether Mohammedanism, Christianity, Hinduism, or Buddhism? If you set up one person as your savior, or as your guide, then there must be exploitation; there must be the shaping of the world into a particular narrow sect. Whereas, if we really do not set anyone up in authority, but if we find out whatever they say, or any human being says, then we shall realize something which is lasting; but merely following another does not lead us anywhere. I take it that you are all Christians, and you say you are following Christ. Are you? Are human beings, whether they belong to Christianity or Mohammedanism or Buddhism, really following their leaders? It is impossible. They don't. So why call yourselves by different names and separate yourselves? Whereas, if we really altered the en-

vironment to which we have become such slaves, then we should be really gods in ourselves, not follow anybody. Personally, I do not belong to any sect, large or small. I have found truth, God, or whatever you like to call it, but I cannot transmit it to another. One can discover it only through consummate intelligence, and not through imitation of certain principles, beliefs, and personages.

Question: Is there an exterior force or influence known as organized evil?

KRISHNAMURTI: Is there? The modern businessman, the nationalist, the follower of religion—I call these people evils, organized evils; because, sirs, individually we have created these horrors in the world. How have religions come into being with their power to exploit people ruthlessly through fear? How have they grown into such formidable machines? We individually have created them through our fear of the hereafter. Not that there is no hereafter: that is quite a different thing altogether. We have created it, and in that machine we are caught; and it is only the very rare few who break away, and those people you call Christ, Buddha, Lenin, or X, Y, Z.

Then there is the evil of society as it is. It is an organized, oppressive machine to control human beings. You think if human beings are released they will become dangerous, they will do all kinds of horrors; so you say, "Let us socially control them, by tradition, by opinion, by the limitation of morality"; and it is the same thing economically. So gradually these evils become accepted as normal, healthy things. Surely it is obvious how through education we are made to fit into a system where individual vocation is never thought of. You are made to fit into some work; and so we create a dual life, throughout our lives, that of business from 10 to 5, or whatever it is, which has nothing to do with the other, our private, social, home-life. So we are living continually in contradiction, going occasionally, if you are interested, to church, to keep up the fashion, the show. We inquire into reality, into God, when there are moments of strife, moments of oppression, moments when there is a crash. We say, "There must be some reality. Why are we living?" So we gradually create in our lives a duality, and therefore we become such hypocrites.

So, to me, there is an evil. It is the evil of exploitation engendered by individuals through their longing for security, self-preservation at all costs, irrespective of the whole of human beings; and in that there is no affection, no real love, but merely this possessiveness which we term as love.

Question: Can you tell us how you have arrived at this degree of understanding?

KRISHNAMURTI: I am afraid it would take very long, and it may be very personal. First of all, sirs, I am not a philosopher, I am not a student of philosophy. I think one who is merely a student of philosophy is already dead. But I have lived with all kinds of people, and I have been brought up, as you perhaps know, to fulfill a certain function, a certain office. Again, that means, "exploiter." And I was also the head of a tremendous organization throughout the world, for spiritual purposes; and I saw the fallacy of it, because you cannot lead men to truth. You can only make them intelligent through education, which has nothing to do with priests and their means of exploitation—ceremonies. So I disbanded that organization; and, living with people, and not having a fixed idea about life, or a mind bound by a certain traditional background, I began to discover what, to me, is truth: truth to everybody—a life which one can live healthily, sanely, humanly; not based on exploitation, but on needs. I know what I need, and that is not very much, so whether I work

for it by digging in a garden, or talking, or writing, that is not of great importance.

First of all, to discover anything, there must be great discontent, great questioning, unhappiness; and very few people in the world, when they are discontented, desire to accentuate that discontent, desire to go through it to find out. They generally want the opposite. If they are discontented, they want happiness, whereas, for myself—if I may be personal—I did not want the opposite. I wanted to find out; and so gradually through various questionings and through continual friction, I came to realize that which one may call truth or God. I hope I have answered it.

Question: Tell us something of your idea of the hereafter.

KRISHNAMURTI: Isn't it extraordinary! This is supposed to be a meeting for business people, and we are talking about the hereafter, God, and all the rest. It indicates that we are not interested in our business at all; we are interested in this merely as a means of getting money to exist; and our human interests are divorced from our daily living.

Now, with regard to what lies hereafter. Perhaps you have read what some of the great scientists in Europe are saying: that there is a continuance after death. Some of them maintain that there is an individual continuance, others with equal emphasis deny it. It is pretty obvious that there is some kind of continuity, whether it is the thought-form of the entity that dies, or the expression of the world thought, and so on.

Now, let us find out, inquire into what we call individuality. When we ask the question, "Is there a hereafter?" why do we ask it? Because you want to know if you will continue as Mr. X when you die; or you want to know because you love someone tremendously, and that person has died. So let us find out what is this thing we call individuality—that is, my brother, my wife, my child, or myself: what is it? When you talk about Mr. X, what is that Mr. X? Is it not form, name, certain prejudices, a certain bank account, certain class distinctions? That is, Mr. X has become the focal point of this condition of society.

I hope I am explaining this. I will put it this way. An ordinary individual now, as he is, is nothing else but the focal point of the environment, of society, of religion, of moral edicts and economic conditions—as the ordinary individual, he is that. Isn't it so? That focal point, with its contradictions, prejudices, hopes, longings, fears, likes and dislikes, that constitutes that bundle which we call an individual, as Mr. X. Now, we want to know if that Mr. X shall live in the hereafter. There is the possibility that he may live, and he lives now. Wait a minute. That is not of importance, is it? Because what we call individuals are nothing else but the result of false environment. This focal point of the present state of individuality is really false, isn't it? An ordinary man has to fight in this world to live at all. He has to be competitive, ruthless, and he must belong to certain classes of society, bourgeois, proletariat, capitalist; or he belongs to certain religious sects called by various names, Christianity, Hinduism, Buddhism, and so on. Surely these environments are false when I have to fight my neighbor ruthlessly to live at all. Isn't there something rotten in such a state? Isn't there something abnormal in dividing ourselves into class distinctions? Isn't there something crude when we have to call ourselves Christians, Hindus, Mohammedans, or Buddhists?

So these false environments create friction in the mind, and mind identifies itself with that conflict, identifies itself as Mr. X. And then the question arises, "What happens? Shall I live, or not live?" As I say, there is a possibility that they may live; but in that living there is no happiness, creative intelligence, joy in life; it is a continual battle. Whereas, if we understand the true significance of all these environments placed on the mind—religious, social, and economic—therefore freeing the mind from conflict, we shall find out that there is a different focal unit, a different individuality altogether; and I say that individuality is continuous; it is not yours and mine. That individuality is the eternal expression of life itself, and in that there is no death, there is no beginning and end; in that there is a wider conception of life. Whereas, in this false individuality there must be death, there must be continual inquiry whether I shall live or shall not live. The fear is continual, haunting, pursuing.

Question: Do you think the social systems of the world will evolve to a state of international brotherhood, or will it be brought about through parliamentary institution, or by education?

KRISHNAMURTI: As society is organized, you cannot have international brotherhood. You cannot remain a New Zealander, and I a Hindu, and talk about brotherhood. How can there be brotherhood really, if you are restricted by economic conditions, by this patriotism which is such a false thing? That is, how can there be brotherhood if you remain as a New Zealander, holding on to your particular prejudices, your tariff walls, patriotism, and all the rest; and I a Hindu living in India, with my prejudices? We can talk about tolerance, leaving each other alone, or my sending you missionaries and your sending me missionaries, but there cannot be brotherhood. How can there be brotherhood when you are a Christian and I am a Hindu, when you are priest-ridden and I am also priest-ridden in a different way, when you have one form of worship and I have another?—which does not mean that you must come to my form of worship or that I must go into yours.

So, as things are, they will not result in brotherhood. On the contrary, there is nationalism, more sovereign governments, which are but the instruments of war. So, as social institutions exist, they cannot evolve into a magnificent thing, because their very basis, their foundation is wrong; and your parliaments, your education based on these ideas, will not bring about brotherhood. Look at all our nations. What are they? Nothing but instruments of war. Each country is better than the other, each country beating another, inflaming this false thing called patriotism. Please, you like certain countries, certain countries are more beautiful than others, and you appreciate it. You enjoy beauty as you enjoy a sunset, whether here, in Europe or America. There is nothing nationalistic, no patriotic feeling behind it—you enjoy it. Patriotism comes only when people begin to use your enjoyment to a purpose. And how can there be real brotherhood, through patriotism, when the whole form of government is based on class distinctions, when one class that has everything rules the other which has nothing, or sends representatives who have nothing to parliament? Surely this approach to human state, human unity is impossible. It is so obvious, it does not even need discussion.

So long as there are class distinctions developing into nationalities, based on exploitation by the possessive class, or the class which has the means of production in its hands, there must be wars; and through wars you are not going to get brotherhood. That is obvious. You can see that in Europe since the war: more national feeling, greater flag-waving, higher tariff walls. That, surely, is not going to produce brotherhood. It may produce brotherhood in the sense that there will be a great catastrophe and people will wake up and say, "For God's sake, let us wake up and be sensible." Eventually that may produce brotherhood; but nationalities are not going to produce brotherhood, any more than religious distinctions, which are really, if you come to think of it, based on refined selfishness. We all want to be secure in heaven—whatever that place is—safe, secure, certain, and so we create institutions, organizations, to bring about the certainty, and we call these religions, and thereby increase exploitation. Whereas, if we really see the falseness of all these things, not only perceive it intellectually but really feel it completely with our mind and heart, then there is a possibility of brotherhood. If we perceive it and act, then there is a voluntary, true, moral act. I call that a true moral act when we perceive a thing completely and act, and not when forced by circumstances, or there is brought about a brotherhood forced by the sheer brutal necessity of life. That is, when business people, the capitalist, the financiers, begin to see that this distinction does not pay, that they cannot make more money, they cannot be in the same position, then they will bring about environment forcing the individual to become brotherly; as now you are forced by environment to be unbrotherly, to exploit, so you will also be forced to cooperate. Surely that is not brotherhood: that is merely an action brought about by convenience, without human intelligence and understanding.

So, to really bring human intelligence into action, individuals must morally and voluntarily act and then they will create an organization in which they will be real fighters against exploitation. But that needs a great deal of perception, a great deal of intelligent action, and you can begin only with yourself; you can only tend your own garden, you cannot look after your neighbor's.

Question: Please be candid. Can we know truth as you do, cease to exploit, and still remain in business, or do you suggest we sell out? Could you go into trade and remain as you are?

KRISHNAMURTI: Sir, please, I am not dodging the issue. I will be perfectly candid. As the system is organized, unless you withdraw into a desert island where you cook and do everything for yourselves, there must be exploitation. Isn't that so? It is obvious. As long as the system is based on individual competition, security, possessiveness, as its foundation, there must be exploitation. But cannot you be free of that foundation because you are not afraid, because you have discovered what are your essential needs, because you are rich in yourself? Therefore, although you remain in trade, you find that your needs are very few; whereas, if there is poverty of mind and heart, your needs become colossal. But again, unless one is really honest, absolutely frank, and does not subtly deceive oneself, what I have said can be used to exploit further. I would not mind personally going into trade, but to me it would have no value, because I have no need to go into trade. Therefore, what is the use of my talking theoretically? Not that I have money; but I would do anything reasonable, sane, because my needs are very few, and I have no fear of being crushed out. It is when there is a fear of losing—the fear of the loss of security, preservation—that we fight. But if you are prepared to lose everything because you have nothing—well, there is no exploitation. This sounds ridiculous, absurd, savage, primitive, but if you really think about it sanely, if you give a few minutes of your real creative thought to it, you will see it is not so absurd as all that. It is the savage who is continually at the behest of his wants, not the man of intelligence. He does not cling to things, because inwardly he is supremely rich; therefore his external needs are very few. Surely we can organize a society which is based on needs, not on this exploitation through advertising. I hope I have answered your question, sir.

Question: Without wishing to exploit the speaker, I look upon him as one of the greatest of all exemplifiers of philosophic altruism, but I would much like him to tell his audience here this afternoon what belief he has in the ultimate millennium, that no doubt he and the whole of the human race seek.

KRISHNAMURTI: Sir, to have a perfect millennium means the savage must be as intelligent as anyone else, must have as perfect conditions as anyone else. That is, all human beings living in the world at the precise moment, at the same time, must all be happy. Surely that is the millennium, isn't it? That is what we mean when we talk about it. All right, sir. Wait a minute. Is such a thing possible? Surely it is not possible. We think a millennium is a moment when the ideal has come into being, when civilization has reached its highest pinnacle. It is like a human being who shapes his life to a certain ideal, and reaches the height. What happens to such a human being? He wants something else, there is a further ideal. Therefore, he never reaches the culmination. But when a human being lives, not trying to achieve, to succeed, to reach a height, but is living fully, humanly, all the time, then his action, which must be reflected in society, will not reach a pinnacle. It will be constantly on the move, therefore continually increasing, and not striving after a culmination.

April 6, 1934

Ojai, California, 1934

✳

First Talk in The Oak Grove

It is my purpose during these talks not so much to give a system of thought, as to awaken thought, and to do that I am going to make certain statements, naturally not dogmatic, which I hope you will consider, and as you consider them, there will arise many questions; if you will kindly put these to me, I will try to answer them, and thus we can discuss further what I have to say.

I wonder why most of you come here? Presumably you are seeking something. And what are you seeking? You cannot answer that question, naturally, because your search varies, the object of your search varies; the object of your search is constantly changing, so you do not definitely know what you seek, what you want. But you have established, unfortunately, a habit of going from one supposed spiritual teacher to another supposed spiritual teacher, of joining various organizations, societies, and of following systems; in other words, trying to find out what gives you greater and greater satisfaction, excitement.

This process of going from one school of thought to another, from one system of thought to another, from one teacher to another, you call the search for truth. In other words, you are going from one idea to another idea, from one system of thought to another, accumulating, hoping to understand life, trying to fathom its significance, its struggles, each time declaring that you have found something.

Now, I hope you won't say at the end of my talks that you have found something, because the moment you have found something you are already lost; it is an anchor to which mind clings, and therefore that eternal movement, this true search of which I am going to speak, ceases. And most minds are looking for a definite aim, with this definite desire to find, and when once there is established this desire, you will find something. But it won't be something living, it will be a dead thing that you will find, and therefore you will put that away to turn to another; and this process of continually choosing, continually discarding, you call acquiring wisdom, experience, or truth.

Probably most of you have come here with this attitude, consciously or unconsciously, so your thought is expended merely on the search for schemes and confirmations, on the desire to join a movement or form groups, without the clarity of the fundamental or trying to understand what these fundamental things of life mean. So as I said, I am not putting forward an ideal to be imitated, a goal to be found, but my purpose is rather to awaken that thought by which the mind can liberate itself from these things which we have established, which we have taken for granted as being true.

Now, each one tries to immortalize the product of environment; that thing which is the result of the environment we try to make eternal. That is, the various fears, hopes, longings, prejudices, likes, personal views which we glorify as our temperament—these are, after all, the result, the product of environment; and the bundle of these memories, which is the result of environment, the product of the reactions to environment, this bundle becomes that consciousness which we call the 'I'. Is that not so? The whole struggle is between the result of environment with which mind identifies itself and becomes the 'I', between that, and environment. After all, the 'I', the consciousness with which the mind identifies itself is the result of environment. The struggle takes place between that 'I' and the constantly changing environment.

You are continually seeking immortality for this 'I'. In other words, falsehood tries to become the real, the eternal. When you understand the significance of the environment, there is no reaction and therefore there is no conflict between the reaction, that is, between what we call the 'I' and the creator of the reaction, which is the environment. So this seeking for immortality, this craving to be certain, to be lasting, is called the process of evolution, the process of acquiring truth or God or the understanding of life. And anyone who helps you towards this, who helps you to immortalize reaction which we call the 'I', you make of him your redeemer, your savior, your Master, your teacher, and you follow his system. You follow him with thought, or without thought; with thought when you think that you are following him with intelligence because he is going to lead you to immortality, to the realization of that ecstasy. That is, you want another to immortalize for you that reaction which is the outcome of environment, which is in itself inherently false.

Out of the desire to immortalize that which is false you create religions, sociological systems and divisions, political methods, economic panaceas, and moral standards. So gradually in this process of developing systems to make the individual immortal, lasting, secure, the individual is completely lost, and he comes into conflict with the creations of his own search, with the creations which are born out of his longing to be secure and which he calls immortality.

After all, why should religions exist? Religions as divisions of thought have grown, have been glorified and nourished by sets of beliefs because there is this desire that you shall realize, that you shall attain, that there shall be immortality.

And again, moral standards are merely the creations of society, so that the individual may be held within its bondage. To me, morality cannot be standardized. There cannot be at the same time morality and standards. There can only be intelligence, which is not, which cannot be standardized. But we shall go into that in my later talks.

So this continual search in which each one of us is caught up, the search for happiness, for truth, for reality, for health—this continual desire is cultivated by each one of us in order that we may be secure, permanent. And out of that search for permanency, there must be conflict, conflict between the result of environment, that is the 'I', and the environment itself.

Now if you come to think of it, what is the 'I'? When you talk about 'I', 'mine', my house, my enjoyment, my wife, my child, my love, my temperament, what is that? It is nothing but the result of environment, and there is a conflict between that result, the 'I', and the environment itself. Conflict can only, and must inevitably, exist between the false and the false, not between truth and the false. Isn't that so? There cannot be conflict between what is true and what is false. But there can be conflict and there must be conflict between two false things, between the degrees of falseness, between the opposites.

So do not think this struggle between the self and the environment, which you call the true struggle, is true. Isn't there a struggle taking place in each one of you between yourself and your environment, your surroundings, your husband, your wife, your child, your neighbor, your society, your political organizations? Is there not a constant battle going on? You consider that battle necessary in order to help you to realize happiness, truth, immortality, or ecstasy. To put it differently: what you consider to be the truth is but self-consciousness, the 'I', which is all the time trying to become immortal, and the environment which I say is the continual movement of the false. This movement of the false becomes your ever-changing environment, which is called progress, evolution. So to me, happiness, or truth, or God, cannot be found as the outcome of the result of environment, the 'I', the continually changing conditions.

I will try to put it again, differently. There is conflict, of which each one of you is conscious, between yourself and the environment, the conditions. Now, you say to yourself, "If I can conquer environment, overcome it, dominate it, I shall find out, I shall understand"; so there is this continual battle going on between yourself and environment.

Now what is the 'yourself'? It is but the result, the product of environment. So what are you doing? You are fighting one false thing with another false thing, and environment will be false so long as you do not understand it. Therefore the environment is producing that consciousness which you call the 'I', which is continually trying to become immortal. And to make it immortal there must be many ways, there must be means, and therefore you have religions, systems, philosophies, all the nuisances and barriers

that you have created. Hence there must be conflict between the result of environment and environment itself; and, as I said, there can be conflict only between the false and the false; never between truth and the false. Whereas, in your minds there is this firmly established idea that in this struggle between the result of environment, which is the 'I', and the environment itself, lies power, wisdom, the path to eternity, to reality, truth, happiness.

Our vital concern should be with this environment, not with the conflict, not how to overcome it, not how to run away from it. By questioning the environment and trying to understand its significance, we shall find out its true worth. Isn't that so? Most of us are enmeshed, caught up in the process of trying to overcome, to run away from circumstances, environment; we are not trying to find out what it means, what is its cause, its significance, its value. When you see the significance of environment, it means drastic action, a tremendous upheaval in your life, a complete, revolutionary change of ideas, in which there is no authority, no imitation. But very few are willing to see the significance of environment, because it means change, a radical change, a revolutionary change, and very few people want that. So most people, vast numbers of people, are concerned with the evasion of environment; they cover it up, or try to find new substitutions by getting rid of Jesus Christ and setting up a new savior; by seeking new teachers in place of the old, but they do not ever inquire whether they need a guide at all. This alone would help, this alone would give the true significance of that particular demand.

So where there is a search for substitution, there must be authority, the following of leadership, and hence the individual becomes but a cog in the social and religious machinery of life. If you look closely you will see that your search is nothing but a search for comfort and security and escape; not a search for understanding, not a search for truth, but rather a search for an evasion and therefore a search for the conquering of all obstacles; after all, all conquering is but substitution, and in substitution there is no understanding.

There are escapes through religions, with their edicts, moral standards, fears, authorities; and escapes through self-expression— what you call self-expression, what the vast majority of people call self-expression, is but the reaction against environment, is but the effort to express oneself through reaction against that environment—self-expression through art, through science, through various forms of action. Here I am not including the true, spontaneous expressions of beauty, of art, of science; they in themselves are complete. I am talking of the man who is seeking these things as a means of self-expression. A real artist does not talk about his self-expression, he is expressing that which he intensely feels; but there are so many spurious artists, like the spurious spiritual people, who are all the time seeking self-expression as a means of getting something, some satisfaction which they cannot find in the environment in which they live.

Through this search for security and permanency, we have established religions with all their inanities, divisions, exploitations, as means of escape; and these means of escape become so vital, so important, because, to tackle environment, that is, the conditions about us, demands tremendous action, voluntary, dynamic action, and very few are willing to take that action. On the contrary, you are willing to be forced to an action by environment, by circumstances; that is, if a man becomes highly moral and virtuous through depression, you say what a nice man he is, how he has changed. For that change you depend upon environment; and so long as there is the dependence on environment for

righteous action, there must be means of escape, substitutions, call it religion or what you will. Whereas, for the true artist who is also truly spiritual there is spontaneous expression, which in itself is sufficient, complete, whole.

So what are you doing? What is happening to each one of you? What are you trying to do in your lives? You are seeking; and what are you seeking? There is a conflict between yourself and the constant movement of environment. You are seeking a means to overcome that environment, so as to perpetuate your own self which is but the result of that environment; or, because you have been thwarted so often by environment, which prevents you from self-expressing, as you call it, you seek a new means of self-expression through service to humanity, through economic adjustments, and all the rest of it.

Each one has to find out for what he is searching; if he is not searching, then there is satisfaction and decay. If there is conflict, there is the desire to overcome that conflict, to escape from that conflict, to dominate it. And as I have said, conflict can exist only between two false things, between that supposed reality which you call the 'I', which to me is nothing else but the result of environment, and the environment itself. And hence if your mind is merely concerned with the overcoming of that struggle, then you are perpetuating falseness, and hence there is more conflict, more sorrow. But if you understand the significance of environment, that is, wealth, poverty, exploitation, oppression, nationalities, religions, and all the inanities of social life in modern existence, not trying to overcome them but seeing their significance, then there must be individual action, and complete revolution of ideas and thought. Then there is no longer a struggle, but rather light dispelling darkness. There is no conflict between light and darkness.

There is no conflict between truth and that which is false. There is only conflict where there are opposites.

June 16, 1934

Second Talk in The Oak Grove

You may remember that yesterday I was talking about the birth of conflict, and how the mind seeks a solution for it. I want to deal this morning with the whole idea of conflict and disharmony, and show the utter futility of mind trying to seek a solution for conflict, because the mere search for the solution will not do away with the conflict itself. When you seek a solution, a means of dissolving the conflict, you merely try to superimpose, or substitute in its place, a new set of ideas, a new set of theories, or you try to run away from conflict altogether. When people desire a solution for their conflict, that is what they seek.

If you observe, you will see that when there is conflict, you are at once seeking a solution for it. You want to find a way out of that conflict, and you generally do find a way out; but you have not solved the conflict, you have merely shifted it by substituting a new environment, a new condition, which will in turn produce further conflict. So let us look into this whole idea of conflict, from where it arises, and what we can do with it.

Now, conflict is the result of environment, isn't it? To put it differently, what is environment? When are you conscious of environment? Only when there is conflict and a resistance to that environment. So, if you observe, if you look into your lives, you will see that conflict is continually twisting, perverting, shaping your lives; and intelligence, which is the perfect harmony of mind and heart, has no part in your lives at all. That is, environment is continually shaping, molding your lives to action, and naturally out of that continual twisting, molding, shaping, perversion, conflict is born. So where there is this constant process of conflict there cannot be intelligence. And yet we think that by continually going through conflict we shall arrive at that intelligence, that fullness, and that plenitude of ecstasy. But by the accumulation of conflict we cannot find out how to live intelligently; you can find out how to live intelligently only when you understand the environment which is creating conflict, and mere substitution, that is, the introduction of new conditions, is not going to solve the conflict. And yet if you observe, you will see that when there is conflict, mind is seeking a substitution. We either say, "It is heredity, economic conditions, past environment," or we assert our belief in karma, reincarnation, evolution; so we are trying to give excuses for the present conflict in which the mind is caught, and are not trying to find out what is the cause of conflict itself, which is to inquire into the significance of environment.

Conflict then can exist only between environment—environment being economic and social conditions, political domination, neighbors—between that environment, and the result of environment, which is the 'I'. Conflict can exist only so long as there is reaction to that environment which produces the 'I', the self. The majority of people are unconscious of this conflict—the conflict between one's self, which is but the result of the environment, and the environment itself; very few are conscious of this continuous battle. One becomes conscious of that conflict, that disharmony, that struggle between the false creation of the environment, which is the 'I', and the environment itself, only through suffering. Isn't that so? It is only through acuteness of suffering, acuteness of pain, acuteness of disharmony, that you become conscious of the conflict.

What happens when you become conscious of the conflict? What happens when in that intensity of suffering you become fully conscious of the battle, the struggle which is going on? Most people want an immediate relief, an immediate answer. They want to shelter themselves from that suffering, and therefore they find various means of escape, which I mentioned yesterday, such as religions, excitements, inanities, and the many mysterious avenues of escape which we have created through our desire to protect ourselves from this struggle. Suffering makes one conscious of this conflict, and yet suffering will not lead man to that fullness, to that richness, that plenitude, that ecstasy of life, because after all, suffering can only awaken the mind to great intensity. And when the mind is acute, then it begins to question the environment, the conditions, and in that questioning, intelligence is functioning; and it is only intelligence that will lead man to the fullness of life and to the discovery of the significance of sorrow. Intelligence begins to function in the moment of acuteness of suffering, when mind and heart are no longer escaping, escaping through the various avenues which you have so cleverly made, which are so apparently reasonable, factual, real. If you observe carefully, without prejudice, you will see that so long as there is an escape you are not solving, you are not coming face to face with conflict, and therefore your suffering is merely the accumulating of ignorance. That is, when one ceases to escape, through the well-known channels, then in that acuteness of suffering, intelligence begins to function.

Please, I do not want to give you examples and similes, because I want you to think it out, and if I give examples I do all the thinking and you merely listen. Whereas if you begin to think about what I am saying, you will see, you will observe for yourself how mind, being accustomed to so many substitutions, authorities, escapes, never comes to that point of acuteness of suffering which demands that intelligence must function. And it is only when intelligence is fully functioning that there can be the utter dissolution of the cause of conflict.

Whenever there is the lack of understanding of environment there must be conflict. Environment gives birth to conflict, and so long as we do not understand environment, conditions, surroundings, and are merely seeking substitutions for these conditions, we are evading one conflict and meeting another. But if in that acuteness of suffering which brings forth in its fullness a conflict, if in that state we begin to question environment, then we shall understand the true worth of environment, and intelligence then functions naturally. Hitherto mind has identified itself with conflict, with environment, with evasions, and therefore with suffering; that is, you say, "I suffer." Whereas, in that state of acuteness of suffering, in that intensity of suffering in which there is no longer escape, mind itself becomes intelligence.

To put it again differently, so long as we are seeking solutions, so long as we are seeking substitutions, authorities for the cause and the alleviation of conflict, there must be identification of the mind with the particular. Whereas if the mind is in that state of intense suffering in which all the avenues of escape are blocked, then intelligence will be awakened, will function naturally and spontaneously.

Please, if you experiment with this, you will see that I am not giving you theories, but something with which you can work, something which is practical. You have so many environments, which have been imposed on your by society, by religion, by economic conditions, by social distinctions, by exploitation and political oppressions. The 'I' has been created by that imposition, by that compulsion; there is the 'I' in you which is fighting the environment and hence there is conflict. It is no use creating a new environment, because the same thing will still exist. But if in that conflict there is conscious sorrow and suffering—and there is always suffering in all conflict, only man wants to run away from that struggle and he therefore seeks substitutes—if in that acuteness of suffering you stop searching for substitutes and really face the facts, you will see that mind, which is the summation of intelligence, begins to discover the true worth of environment, and then you will realize that mind is free of conflict. In the very acuteness of suffering lies its own dissolution. So therein is the understanding of the cause of conflict.

Also, one should bear in mind that what we call accumulation of sorrows does not lead to intensity, nor does the multiplication of suffering lead to its own dissolution; for acuteness of mind in suffering comes only when the mind has ceased to escape. And no conflict will awaken that suffering, that acuteness of suffering, when the mind is trying to escape, for in escape there is no intelligence.

To put it briefly again, before I answer the questions that have been given to me: First of all everyone is caught up in suffering and conflict, but most people are unconscious of that conflict; they are merely seeking substitutions, solutions and escapes. Whereas if they cease seeking escapes and begin to question the environment which causes that conflict, then mind becomes acute, alive, intelligent. In that intensity mind becomes intelligence and therefore sees the full worth and significance of the environment which creates conflict.

Please, I am sure half of you don't understand this, but it doesn't matter. What you can do, if you will, is to think this over, really think it over, and see if what I am saying is not true. But to think it over is not to intellectualize it, that is, to sit down and make it

vanish away through the intellect. To find out if what I am saying is true, you have to put it into action, and to put it into action you must question the environment. That is, if you are in conflict, naturally you must question the environment, but most minds have become so perverted that they are not aware that they are seeking solutions, escapes through their marvelous theories. They reason perfectly, but their reasoning is based on the search for escape, of which they are wholly unconscious.

So if there is conflict, and if you want to find out the cause of that conflict, naturally the mind must discover it through acuteness of thought and therefore the questioning of all that which environment places about you—your family, your neighbors, your religions, your political authorities; and by questioning there will be action against the environment. There is the family, the neighbor and the state, and by questioning their significance you will see that intelligence is spontaneous, not to be acquired, not to be cultivated. You have sown the seed of awareness and that produces the flower of intelligence.

Question: You say that the 'I' is the product of environment. Do you mean that a perfect environment could be created which would not develop the 'I' consciousness? If so, the perfect freedom of which you speak is a matter of creating the right environment. Is this correct?

Voices from audience: "No."

KRISHNAMURTI: Wait a minute. Can there ever be right environment, perfect environment? There cannot. Those people who answered "no" haven't thought it out fully, so let us reason together, go into it fully.

What is environment? Environment is created, this whole human structure has been created, by human fears, longings, hopes, desires, attainments. Now, you cannot make a perfect environment because each man is creating, according to his fancies and desires, new sets of conditions; but having an intelligent mind, you can pierce through all these false environments and therefore be free of that 'I' consciousness. Please, the 'I' consciousness, the sense of 'mine', is the result of environment; isn't it? I don't think we need discuss it because it is pretty obvious.

If the state gave you your house and everything you required, there would be no need of "my" house—there might be some other sense of 'mine', but we are discussing the particular. As that has not been the case with you, there is the sense of 'mine', possessiveness. That is the result of environment, that 'I' is but the false reaction to environment. Whereas if the mind begins to question the environment itself, there is no longer a reaction to environment. Therefore we are not concerned with the possibility of there ever being a perfect environment.

After all, what is perfect environment? Each man will tell you what to him is a perfect environment. The artist will say one thing, the financier another, the cinema actress another; each man asks for a perfect environment which satisfies him, in other words, which does not create conflict in him. Therefore there cannot be a perfect environment. But if there is intelligence, then environment has no value, no significance, because intelligence is then freed from circumstance, it is functioning fully.

The question is not whether we can create a perfect environment, but rather how to awaken that intelligence which shall be free of environment, imperfect or perfect. I say you can awaken that intelligence by questioning the full value of any environment in which your mind is caught up. Then you will see that you are free of any particular environment, because then you are functioning intelligently, not being twisted, perverted, shaped by environment.

Question: Surely you cannot mean what your words seem to convey. When I see vice rampant in the world, I feel an intense desire to fight against that vice and against all the suffering it creates in the lives of my fellow human beings. This means great conflict, for when I try to help I am often viciously opposed. How then can you say that there is no conflict between the false and the true?

KRISHNAMURTI: I said yesterday that there can be struggle only between two false things, conflict between the environment and the result of environment which is the 'I'. Now between these two lie innumerable avenues of escape which the 'I' has created, which we call vice, goodness, morality, moral standards, fears, and all the many opposites; and the struggle can exist only between the two, between the false creation of the environment which is the 'I', and the environment itself. But there cannot be struggle between truth and that which is false. Surely that is obvious, isn't it? You may be viciously opposed because the other man is ignorant. It doesn't mean you mustn't fight—but don't assume the righteousness of fighting. Please, you know there is a natural way of doing things, a spontaneous, sweet way of doing things, without this aggressive, vicious righteousness.

First of all, in order to fight, you must know what you are fighting, so there must be understanding of the fundamental, not of the divisions between the false things. Now we are so conscious, we are so fully conscious of the divisions between the false things, between the result and the environment, that we fight them, and therefore we want to reform, we want to change, we want to alter, without fundamentally changing the whole structure of human life. That is, we still want to preserve the 'I' consciousness which is the false reaction to environment; we want to preserve that and yet want to alter the world. In other words, you want to have your own bank account, your own possessions, you want to preserve the sense of 'mine', and yet you want to alter the world so that there shall not be this idea of 'mine' and 'yours'.

So what one has to do is to find out if one is dealing with the fundamental, or merely with the superficial. And to me the superficial will exist so long as you are merely concerned with the alteration of environment so as to alleviate conflict. That is, you still want to cling to the 'I' consciousness as 'mine', but yet desire to alter the circumstances so that they will not create conflict in that 'I'. I call that superficial thought, and from that there naturally is superficial action. Whereas if you think fundamentally, that is, question the very result of the environment which is the 'I', and therefore question the environment itself, then you are acting fundamentally, and therefore lastingly. And in that there is an ecstasy, in that there is a joy of which now you do not know because you are afraid to act fundamentally.

Question: In your talk yesterday you spoke of environment as the movement of the false. Do you include in environment all the creations of nature, including human forms?

KRISHNAMURTI: Doesn't environment continually change? Doesn't it? For most people it doesn't change because change implies continual adjustment, therefore continual awareness of mind, and most people are concerned with the static condition of the environment. Yet environment is moving because it is beyond your control, and it is false so long as you do not understand its significance.

"Does environment include human forms?" Why set them apart from nature? We are not concerned so much with nature, because we have almost brought nature under control, but we have not understood the environment created by human beings. Look at the relationship between peoples, between two human beings, and all the conditions which human beings have created that we have not understood, even though we have largely understood and conquered nature through science.

So we are not concerned with the stability, with the continuance of an environment which we understand, because the moment we understand it there is no conflict. That is, we are seeking security, emotional and mental, and we are happy so long as that security is assured and therefore we never question environment, and hence the constant movement of environment is a false thing which is creating disturbance in each one. As long as there is conflict, it indicates that we have not understood the conditions placed about us; and that movement of environment remains false so long as we do not inquire into its significance, and we can only discover it in that state of acute consciousness of suffering.

Question: It is perfectly clear to me that the 'I' consciousness is the result of environment, but do you not see that the 'I' did not originate for the first time in this life? From what you say it is obvious that the 'I' consciousness, being the result of environment, must have begun in the distant past and will continue in the future.

KRISHNAMURTI: I know this is a question to catch me about reincarnation. But that doesn't matter. Now let's look into it.

First of all you will admit, if you think about it, that the 'I' is the result of environment. Now to me it doesn't matter whether it is the past environment or present environment. After all, environment is of the past also. You have done something which you haven't understood, you did something yesterday, which you haven't understood, and that pursues you until you understand it. You cannot solve that past environment until you are fully conscious in the present. So it doesn't matter whether the mind is crippled by past or present conditions. What matters is that you shall understand the environment and this will liberate the mind from conflict.

Some people believe that the 'I' has had a birth in the distant past and will continue in the future. It is irrelevant to me, it has no significance at all. I will show you why. If the 'I' is the result of the environment, if the 'I' is but the essence of conflict, then the mind must be concerned, not with that continuance of conflict, but with freedom from that conflict. So it does not matter whether it is the past environment which is crippling the mind, or the present which is perverting it, or whether the 'I' has had a birth in the distant past. What matters is that in that state of suffering, in that consciousness, that conscious acuteness of suffering, there is the dissolution of the 'I'.

This brings in the idea of karma. You know what it means, that you have a burden in the present, the burden of the past in the present. That is, you bring with you the environment of the past into the present, and because of that burden, you control the future, you shape the future. If you come to think of it, it must be so, that if your mind is perverted by the past, naturally the future must also be twisted, because if you have not understood the environment of yesterday it must be continued today; and therefore, as you don't understand today, naturally you will not understand tomorrow either. That is, if you have not seen the full significance of an environment or of an action, this perverts your judgment of today's environment, of today's action born of environment, which

will again pervert you tomorrow. So one is caught up in this vicious circle, and hence the idea of continual rebirth, rebirth of memory, or rebirth of the mind continued by environment.

But I say mind can be free of the past, of past environment, past hindrances, and therefore you can be free of the future, because then you are living dynamically in the present, intensely, supremely. In the present is eternity, and to understand that, mind must be free of the burden of the past; and to free the mind of the past there must be an intense questioning of the present, not the considering of how the 'I' will continue in the future.

June 17, 1934

Third Talk in The Oak Grove

This morning I am only going to answer questions.

Question: What is the difference between self-discipline and suppression?

KRISHNAMURTI: I don't think there is much difference between the two because both deny intelligence. Suppression is the gross form of the subtler self-discipline, which is also repression; that is, both suppression as well as self-discipline are mere adjustments to environment. One is the gross form of adjustment, which is suppression, and the other, self-discipline, is the subtle form. Both are based on fear: suppression, on an obvious fear; the other, self-discipline, on fear born of loss, or on fear which expresses itself through gain.

Self-discipline—what you call self-discipline—is merely an adjustment to an environment which we have not completely understood; therefore in that adjustment there must be the denial of intelligence. Why has one ever to discipline one's self? Why does one discipline, force one's self to mold after a particular pattern? Why do so many people belong to the various schools of disciplines, supposed to lead to spirituality, to greater understanding, greater unfoldment of thought? You will see that the more you discipline the mind, train the mind, the greater its limitations. Please, one has to think this over carefully and with delicate perception and not get confused by introducing other issues. Here I am using the word self-discipline as in the question, that is, disciplining one's self after a certain pattern, preconceived or preestablished, and therefore with the desire to attain, to gain. Whereas to me the very process of discipline, this continual twisting of mind to a particular preestablished pattern, must eventually cripple the mind. The mind which is really intelligent is free of self-discipline, for intelligence is born out of the questioning of environment, and the discovery of the true significance of environment. In that discovery is true adjustment, not the adjustment to a particular pattern or condition, but the adjustment through understanding, which is therefore free of the particular condition.

Take a primitive; what does he do? In him there is no discipline, no control, no suppression. He does what he desires to do, this primitive. The intelligent man also does what he desires, but with intelligence. Intelligence is not born out of self-discipline or suppression. In the one instance it is wholly the pursuit of desire, the primitive man pursuing the object he desires. In the other instance, the intelligent man sees the significance of desire and sees the conflict; the primitive man does not, he pursues anything he desires and creates suffering and pain. So to me self-discipline and suppression are both alike—they deny intelligence.

Please experiment with what I have said about discipline, self-discipline. Don't reject it, don't say you must have self-discipline, because there will be chaos in the world—as if there were not already chaos; and again, don't merely accept what I say, agreeing that it is true. I am telling you something with which I have experimented and which I have found to be true. Psychologically I think it is true, because self-discipline implies a mind that is tethered to a particular thought or belief or ideal, a mind that is held by a condition; and as an animal that is tethered to a post can only wander within the distance of its rope, so does the mind which is tethered to a belief, which is perverted through self-discipline, wander only within the limitation of that condition. Therefore such a mind is not mind at all, it is incapable of thought. It may be capable of adjustment between the limitations of the post and the farthest point of its reach; but such a mind, such a heart cannot really think and feel. The mind and the heart are disciplined, crippled, perverted, through denying thought, denying affection. So you must observe, become aware how your own thought, how your own feelings are functioning, without wanting to guide them in any particular direction. First of all, before you guide them, find out how they are functioning. Before you try to change and alter thought and feeling, find out the manner of their working, and you will see that they are continually adjusting themselves within the limitations established by that point fixed by desire and the fulfillment of that desire. In awareness there is no discipline.

Let me take an example. Suppose that you are class-minded, class-conscious, snobbish. You don't know that you are snobbish, but you want to find out if you are; how will you find out? By becoming conscious of your thought and your emotions. Then what happens? Suppose that you discover that you are snobbish, then that very discovery creates a disturbance, a conflict, and that very conflict dissolves snobbishness. Whereas if you merely discipline the mind not to be snobbish, you are developing a different characteristic which is the opposite of being a snob, and being deliberate, therefore false, is equally pernicious.

So, because we have established various patterns, various goals, aids, which we are continually, consciously or unconsciously, pursuing, we discipline our minds and hearts towards them, and therefore there must be control, perversion. Whereas if you begin to inquire into the conditions that create conflict, and thereby awaken intelligence, then that intelligence itself is so supreme that it is continually in movement and therefore there is never a static point which can create conflict.

Question: Granted that the 'I' is made up of reactions from environment, by what method can one escape its limitations; or how does one go about the process of reorientation, in order to avoid conflict between the two false things?

KRISHNAMURTI: First of all, you want to know the method of escape from the limitations. Why? Why do you ask? Please, why do you always ask for a method, for a system? What does it indicate, this desire for a method? Every demand for a method indicates the desire to escape. You want me to lay down a system so that you may imitate that system. In other words, you want a system invented for you to superimpose on those conditions which are creating conflict, so that you can escape from all conflict. In other words you merely seek to adjust yourselves to a pattern, in order to escape from conflict or from your environment. That is the desire behind the demand for a method, for a system. You know life is not *Pelmanism*. The desire for a method indicates essentially the desire to escape.

"How does one go about the process of reorientation in order to avoid constant conflict between the two false things?" First of all, are you aware that you are in conflict, before you want to know how to get away from it? Or, being aware of conflict, are you merely seeking a refuge, a shelter which will not create further conflict? So let us decide whether you want a shelter, a safety zone, which will no longer yield conflict, whether you want to escape from the present conflict to enter a condition in which there shall be no conflict; or whether you are unaware, unconscious of this conflict in which you exist. If you are unconscious of the conflict, that is, the battle that is taking place between that self and the environment, if you are unconscious of that battle, then why do you seek further remedies? Remain unconscious. Let the conditions themselves produce the necessary conflict, without your rushing after, invoking artificially, falsely, a conflict which does not exist in your mind and heart. And you create artificially a conflict because you are afraid you are missing something. Life will not miss you. If you think it does, something is wrong with you. Perhaps you are neurotic, not normal.

If you are in conflict, you will not ask me for a method. Were I to give you a method you would merely be disciplining yourself according to that method, trying to imitate an ideal, a pattern which I have laid down, and therefore destroying your own intelligence. Whereas if you are really conscious of that conflict, in that consciousness suffering will become acute and in that acuteness, in that intensity, you will dissolve the cause of suffering, which is the lack of understanding of the environment.

You know we have lost all sense of living normally, simply, directly. To get back to that normality, that simplicity, that directness, you cannot follow methods, you cannot merely become automatic machines; and I am afraid most of us are seeking methods because we think that through them we shall realize fullness, stability, and permanency. To me methods lead to slow stagnation and decay and they have nothing to do with real spirituality, which is, after all, the summation of intelligence.

You speak of the necessity of drastic revolution in the life of the individual. If he does not want to revolutionize his outward personal environment because of the suffering it would cause to his family and friends, will inward revolution lead him to the freedom from all conflict?

KRISHNAMURTI: First of all, sirs, don't you also feel that a drastic revolution in the life of the individual is necessary? Or are you merely satisfied with things as they are, with your ideas of progress, evolution and your desire for attainment, with your longings and fluctuating pleasures? You know, the moment you begin to think, really begin to feel, you must have this burning desire for a drastic change, drastic revolution, complete reorientation of thinking. Now, if you feel that that is necessary, then neither family nor friends will stand in the way. Then there is neither an outward revolution nor an inward revolution; there is only revolution, change. But the moment you begin to limit it by saying, "I must not hurt my family, my friends, my priest, my capitalistic exploiter or state exploiter," then you really don't see the necessity for radical change, you merely seek a change of environment. In that there is merely lethargy which creates further false environment and continues the conflict.

I think we give the rather false excuse that we must not hurt our families and our friends. You know when you want to do something vital, you do it, irrespective of your family and friends, don't you? Then you don't consider that you are going to hurt

them. It is beyond your control; you feel so intensely, you think so completely that it carries you beyond the limitation of family circles, classified bondage. But you begin to consider family, friends, ideals, beliefs, traditions, the established order of things, only when you are still clinging to a particular safety, when there is not that inward richness, but merely the dependence on external stimulation for that inward richness. So if there is that full consciousness of suffering, brought about by conflict, then you are not held in the bondage of any particular orthodoxy, friends, or family. You want to find out the cause of that suffering, you want to find out the significance of the environment which creates that conflict; then in that there is no personality, no limited thought of the 'I'. But it is only when you cling to that limited thought of the 'I' that you have to consider how far you shall wander and how far you shall not wander.

Surely truth, or that Godhead of understanding, is not to be found by clinging either to family or tradition or habit. It is to be found only when you are completely naked, stripped of your longings, hopes, securities; and in that direct simplicity there is the richness of life.

Question: Can you explain why environment started being false instead of true? What is the origin of all this mess and trouble?

KRISHNAMURTI: Who do you think created environment? Some mysterious God? Please, just a minute; who created environment, the social structure, the economic, the religious structure? We. Each one has contributed individually, until it has become collective, and the individual who has helped to create the collective, now is lost in the collective, for it has become his mold, his environment. Through the desire for security—financial, moral, and spiritual—you have created a capitalistic environment in which there is nationality, class distinction, and exploitation. We have created it, you and I. This thing hasn't miraculously come into being. You will again create another capitalistic, acquisitive system of a different kind, with a different nuance, with a different color, so long as you are seeking security. You may abolish this present pattern, but so long as there is possessiveness, you will create another capitalistic state, with a new phraseology, a new jargon.

And the same thing applies to religions, with all their absurd ceremonies, exploitations, fear. Who has created them? You and I. Throughout the centuries we have created these things and yielded to them through fear. It is the individual who has created false environment everywhere. And he has become a slave, and that false condition has resulted in a false search for the security of that self-consciousness which you call the 'I', and hence the constant battle between the 'I' and the false environment.

You want to know who has created this environment and all this appalling mess and trouble, because you want a redeemer to lift you out of that trouble and set you in a new heaven. Clinging to all your particular prejudices, hopes, fears, and preferences, you have individually created this environment, so individually you must break it down and not wait for a system to come and sweep it away. A system will probably come and sweep it away and then you will merely become slaves to that system. The communistic system may come in, and then probably you will be using new words, but having the same reactions, only in a different manner, with a different tempo.

That is why I said the other day that if environment is driving you to a certain action, it is no longer righteous. It is only when there is action born out of the understanding of that environment that there is righteousness.

So individually we must become conscious. I assure you, you will then individually create something immense, not a society which is merely holding to an ideal and therefore decaying, but a society that is constantly in movement, not coming to a culmination and dying. Individuals establish a goal, strive after its attainment, and after attaining, collapse. They try all the time to reach some goal and stay at that stage which they have attained. As the individual, so the state—the state is trying all the time to reach an ideal, a goal. Whereas to me the individual must be in constant movement, must ever be becoming, not seeking a culmination, not pursuing a goal. Then self-expression, which is society, will be ever in constant movement.

Question: Do you consider that karma is the interaction between the false environment and the false 'I'?

KRISHNAMURTI: You know karma is a Sanskrit word which means to act, to do, to work, and also it implies cause and effect. Now karma is the bondage, the reaction born out of the environment which the mind has not understood. As I tried to explain yesterday, if we do not understand a particular condition, naturally the mind is burdened with that condition, with that lack of understanding; and with that lack of understanding we function and act, and therefore create further burdens, greater limitations.

So one has to find out what creates this lack of understanding, what prevents the individual from gathering the full significance of the environment, whether it be the past environment or the present. And to discover that significance, mind must really be free of prejudice. It is one of the most difficult things to be really free of a bias, of a temperament, of a twist; and to approach environment with a fresh openness, a directness, demands a great deal of perception.

Most minds are biased through vanity, through the desire to impress others by being somebody, or through the desire to attain truth, or to escape from their environment, or expand their own consciousness—only they call this by a special spiritual name—or through their national prejudices. All these desires prevent the mind from perceiving directly the full worth of the environment; and as most minds are prejudiced, the first thing that one has to become conscious of is one's own limitations. And when you begin to be conscious, there is conflict in that consciousness. When you know that you are really brutally proud or conceited, in the very consciousness of conceit it begins to dissipate, because you perceive the absurdity of it; but if you begin merely to cover it up, it creates further diseases, further false reactions.

So to live each moment now without the burden of the past or of the present, without that crippling memory created by the lack of understanding, mind must ever meet things anew. It is fatal to meet life with the burden of certainty, with the conceit of knowledge, because, after all, knowledge is merely a thing of the past. So when you come to that life with a freshness, then you will know what it is to live without conflict, without this continual straining effort. Then you wander far on the floods of life.

June 18, 1934

Fourth Talk in The Oak Grove

I shall first answer some of the questions that have been put to me, and then give a brief talk.

Question: Does intuition include past experience and something else, or only past experience?

KRISHNAMURTI: To me intuition is intelligence, and intelligence is not past experience, it is the understanding of past experience. I am going to talk presently about this whole idea of past experience, memory, intelligence, and mind, but I shall now answer this particular point, whether intuition is born of the past.

To me, the past is a burden, the past being but gaps in understanding; and if you really base your action on the past, on so-called intuition, it is bound to lead you astray. Whereas if there is spontaneous action in the ever-moving present, in that action is intelligence and that intelligence is intuition. Intelligence is not to be separated from intuition. Most people like to separate intuition from intelligence, because intuition gives them a certain security and hope. Many people say they act "on intuition," that is, they act without reason, without depth of thought. Many people accept a theory, an idea, because they say their "intuition" tells them that it is true. There is no reason behind it, they merely accept it because that theory or idea gives them some solution, some comfort. It is really not reason that is functioning, but it is merely their own hopes, their own longings which are directing their minds. Whereas intelligence is detached from environment and therefore there is reason, thought, behind it.

Question: How can I act freely and without self-repression when I know that my action must hurt those that I love? In such a case, what is the test of right action?

KRISHNAMURTI: I think I answered this question the other day, but probably the questioner wasn't here, so I will answer it again. The test of right action is in its spontaneity, but to act spontaneously is to be greatly intelligent. The majority of people have merely reactions which are perverted, twisted, and stifled because of the lack of intelligence. Where intelligence is functioning, there is spontaneous action.

Now the questioner wants to know how he can act freely and without self-repression when he knows his action must hurt those he loves. You know, to love is to be free—both parties are free. Where there is the possibility of pain, where there is the possibility of suffering in love, it is not love, it is merely a subtle form of possession, of acquisitiveness. If you love, really love someone, there is no possibility of giving him pain when you do something that you think is right. It is only when you want that person to do what you desire or he wants you to do what he desires, that there is pain. That is, you like to be possessed; you feel safe, secure, comfortable; though you know that comfort is but transient, you take shelter in that comfort, in that transience. So each struggle for comfort, for encouragement, really but betrays the lack of inward richness; and therefore an action separate, apart from the other individual naturally creates disturbance, pain, and suffering; and one individual has to suppress what he really feels in order to adjust himself to the other. In other words, this constant repression, brought about by so-called love, destroys the two individuals. In that love there is no freedom; it is merely a subtle bondage. When you feel very ardently that you must do something, you do it, sometimes cunningly and subtly, but you do it. There is always this urge to do, to act independently.

Question: Am I right in believing that all conditions and environment become right to a really intelligent mind? Is it not a question of seeing the art in the pattern?

KRISHNAMURTI: To an intelligent mind, environment yields its significance; therefore that intelligent mind is the master of environment, that mind is free of environment, is not conditioned by environment. What conditions the mind? The lack of understanding. Doesn't it? Not environment, environment does not limit the mind; what limits the mind is the lack of understanding of a particular condition.

Where there is intelligence, mind is not conditioned by any environment, because it is all the time conscious, aware, and functioning, and therefore discerning, perceiving the full worth of the environment. Mind can only become conditioned by the environment when it is lethargic and lazy, trying to escape from the condition itself. Though mind may think in that condition, it is not functioning truly, it is only thinking within that limited circle of condition, which to me is not thinking at all.

So what creates intelligence, what awakens intelligence is this perception of true values, and as the mind is crippled with so many values imposed on it by tradition, one has to be free of these past experiences, past burdens in order to understand the present environment. So the battle is between the past and the present. The struggle is between the background which we have cultivated through the centuries and the ever-changing circumstances in the present. Now, a mind that is clouded by the past cannot understand these swift changes of environment. In other words, to understand the present, mind must be supremely free of the past; that is, it must have a spontaneous appreciation of values in the present. I am going to talk about that later on.

"Is it not a question of seeing the art in the pattern?" Surely. That is, in the pattern of circumstances, in the pattern of environment, mind must see the subtle value, so hidden, so delicate; and to perceive that subtlety, that delicacy, the mind must be alive, pliable, acute, not burdened by values of yesterday.

Question: There seems to be the idea that liberation is a goal, a culmination. What is the difference in this case between striving for liberation and striving for any other culmination? Surely the idea of an end, a goal, a culmination is wrong. How then ought we to regard liberation if not in this way?

KRISHNAMURTI: I am afraid the questioner has not been hearing what I have been talking about; probably he has read some old books of mine and then has put the question.

Now, mind is seeking a culmination, a goal, an end, because mind wants to be certain, assured. Take away all the assurances and certainties from the mind, which are subtle forms of self-glorification or of the craving for self-continuance. Take all that away from the mind, strip it naked, and then you will see that the mind is battling again for security, for shelter, because from that security it can judge, it can function, it can act safely like an animal tethered to a post.

As I said, liberation is not an end, it is not a goal: it is the understanding of right values, eternal values. Intelligence is ever becoming, it has no end, no finality. In the desire to attain there is subtle craving for self-continuance, glorified self-continuance; and every struggle, every effort to attain liberation indicates an escape from the present. This summation of intelligence, which is liberation, is not to be understood through effort. After all, you make an effort when you want, when you desire to acquire something. But liberation is not to be acquired, truth is not to be acquired. So where there is a craving for liberation, for a cul-

mination, for attainment, there must be an effort to sustain, to preserve, to perpetuate that consciousness which we call the 'I'. The very essence of that 'I' is an effort to reach a culmination, because it lives in a series of movements of memory, moving towards an end.

"But then, how ought we to regard liberation if not in this way?" Why regard it at all? Why do you want liberation? Is it because I have been talking about it for the last ten years? Or is it because you want to escape from conditions, or because it will give you greater excitement, greater stimulation, greater intellectual domination? Why do you want liberation? You say, "I am not happy, and if I can find liberation there will be happiness; because I am in misery, if I find this other, then misery will disappear." If you say so, then you are merely seeking substitution.

Liberation is not to be "regarded" in any way. It is born. It comes into being only when the mind is not trying to escape from the condition in which it is caught, but rather to understand the significance of that condition which creates conflict. You see, as you don't understand the condition, the environment which creates conflict, you seek an idea, a culmination, an end, a goal, saying to yourself, "If I understand that, this will disappear," or, "If I have that, I can impose that on this condition." So it is but a subtle form of continual escape from the present. All ideals, beliefs, goals and culminations are but ways out of the present. Whereas if you really come to think of it, the more you are pursuing an end, a goal, an aim, a belief, an ideal, the more you are burdening the future, because you are escaping from the present and therefore creating more and more limitation, conflict, sorrow.

Question: Some people say your idea is that we should become liberated now, while we have the opportunity, and that we can be-

come Masters later on, at some other time. But if we are to become Masters at all, why is it not good for us to begin to set our feet on that way now?

KRISHNAMURTI: Is there opportunity now for you to be liberated? What do you mean by opportunity? How could you be liberated now? By some miraculous process? And later on become a Master? Sir, what is a Master, and what is liberation? What is Masterhood? Surely if it is not liberation it cannot be Masterhood. If liberation is not the summation of intelligence in the present, surely that intelligence is not going to be acquired in some far distant future. So you want liberation now and Masterhood afterwards? I wonder why you want liberation now. I am afraid liberation has no meaning when you want it. And this idea of becoming a Master—the questioner must think that life is like passing an examination, becoming something—I am afraid this becoming a Master, becoming liberated has no meaning to you. Don't you see when you really don't want to become anything, but live completely in one day, in the richness of a single day, you will know what Masterhood or liberation is. This wanting is continually creating a future which can never be fulfilled, therefore you are living incompletely in the present.

During the last three days I have been talking about mind and intelligence. Now to me there is no division between mind and intelligence. Mind stripped of all its memories and hindrances, functioning spontaneously, fully, being aware, creates understanding, and that is intelligence, that is ecstasy; that to me is immortality, timelessness. Intelligence is timelessness, and intelligence is mind itself. This intelligence is the real, is mind itself, it is not to be divided from mind; this intelligence is ecstasy, it is ever-becoming, ever in movement.

Now memory is but the impediment to that intelligence; memory is independent of that intelligence; memory is the perpetuation of that 'I' consciousness which is the result of environment, of that environment the full significance of which the mind has not seen. So memory stupefies, thwarts the ever-becoming intelligence, the ever-moving, timeless intelligence. Mind is intelligence, but memory has imposed itself on mind. That is, memory being that 'I' consciousness, identifies itself with the mind, and the 'I' consciousness comes as it were between intelligence and the mind, thus dividing, stupefying, thwarting, perverting it. So memory, identifying itself with mind, tries to become intelligence, which to me is wrong— if I may use the word "wrong" here—because mind itself is intelligence, and it is memory that perverts the mind and so clouds intelligence. And hence mind seems ever to seek that timeless intelligence, which is the mind itself.

So what is memory? Isn't memory incident, experience, fear, hope, longing, belief, idea, prejudice and tradition, action, deed, with their subtle and complex reactions? The moment there is hope, longing, fear, prejudice, temperament, it conditions the mind, and that conditioning creates memory, which obscures the clarity of mind which is intelligence. This memory rolls through time, coagulating and hardening itself into the self-consciousness of the 'I'. When you talk about the 'I', it is that. It is the crystallizing, the hardening of the memory of your reactions, the reactions of experience, incidents, beliefs, ideals, and after becoming a solidified mass, that memory becomes identified and confused with the mind. If you think it over you will see this. Self-consciousness, or that consciousness of the particular, the 'I', is nothing else but the bundle of memory, and time is nothing else but the field in which it can function and play. So this hardened mass of reactions cannot be resolved, cannot resolve itself backwards in time through analysis, the analysis of the past, because this very looking back, this analysis of the past is one of the tricks of memory itself. You know, taking an unhealthy pleasure in reasserting and reconditioning the past in the present is the constant activity, the métier of memory, isn't it? Please, this is not cleverness, this is not a philosophical concept. Just think it out for a minute, and you will see that this is true. There is this mass of reactions born out of condition, environment, prejudice, various longings, and all these, therefore there is the thing which you call the 'I'.

Then there is born this idea that you must dissolve the 'I', because of what I have been saying. Or you yourself feel the stupidity of it, so you begin to unwind; memory begins to unwind itself backward into the past, which is the process of self-analysis. And if you really come to think of it, memory itself is taking an unhealthy pleasure in reconditioning the past in the present. And likewise, the future of memory is a greater hardening through further craving, further accumulation of experiences and reactions. In other words, time is memory or self-consciousness. You cannot resolve or dissolve self-consciousness by going into the past. The past is but the accumulation of memory, and delving into the past is not going to resolve that consciousness in the present; nor going into the future—which is but further accumulation, further craving, further reaction and hardening, which we call beliefs, ideals, hopes—the future which is still involved in time. As long as this process of memory as past and future continues, intelligence can never act with completeness or fullness in the present.

Intuition as commonly understood is based on the past, the past accumulation of memory, past accumulation of experiences, which is but a warning to act carefully—or freely—in the present. As I said, this timelessness is not a philosophical concept to me,

it is a reality, and you will see that it is a reality if you experiment with what I am saying. That is, you will see that it is a reality if your mind is not clogged by the past accumulation which you call memory, which functions and directs you in the present, preventing you from being fully intelligent and therefore living completely in the present.

So liberation or truth or God is the release of the mind, which is itself intelligence, from the burden of memory. I have explained to you what I mean by memory, not the memory of facts or falsehoods, but the burden placed on the mind through self-consciousness which is memory, and that memory is the reaction to the environment which has not been understood. Immortality is not the perpetuation of that 'I' consciousness, which is but the result of a false environment, but immortality is the freedom, the release of the mind from the burden of memory.

June 19, 1934

Fifth Talk in The Oak Grove

This morning I want to talk about fear, which creates, which necessitates compulsion, influence.

Now, we have divided mind into thought, reason, intellect; but, as I explained in my last talk, to me mind is intelligence, self-creative but clouded over by memory; mind, which is intelligence, is clouded over by memory and is confused with that 'I' consciousness, the result of environment. So mind becomes enslaved by the environment which it itself has created through craving, and therefore there is fear continually. Mind has created environment, and as long as we do not understand that environment there must be fear. We do not give our complete thought to environment and we are not fully conscious of it, so mind becomes enslaved to that environment and thereby there is fear; and compulsion is the instrument of fear. So naturally the lack of understanding of environment is brought about by that lack of intelligence, and because we do not understand environment, fear is thereby created, and fear necessitates influence, either outer or inner.

And how is this continual compulsion created, which has become the instrument, this penetrating instrument of fear? Memory clouds the mind, and this, I have said over and over again, is the result of the lack of understanding of the environment which creates conflict, and memory becomes self-consciousness. This mind, clouded over, limited and confined by memory, seeks perpetuation of the result of environment which is the 'I'; so in perpetuating the 'I', mind seeks the adjustment, alteration, or modification of environment, its growth and expansion. You know, mind is continually seeking adjustment to the environment; but adjustment to environment does not bring about understanding, nor can we see the significance of that environment by merely modifying the state of mind or trying to change or expand that environment. Because mind is continually seeking its own protection, it gets clouded over by memory which has become confused, identified with self-consciousness—that self-consciousness which desires to perpetuate itself; therefore it tries to alter, adjust, modify the environment, or in other words, mind seeks to make the 'I', as it thinks, immortal, universal, and cosmic. Isn't it so?

So mind, which seeks immortality, really desires the continuance of this 'I' consciousness, the perpetuation of environment; that is, so long as mind clings to the idea of 'I' consciousness, which is but the lack of understanding of environment and therefore the cause of conflict, so long will it seek, in that limitation, its own perpetuation, and this per-

petuation we call immortality, or that cosmic consciousness in which the particular still remains. So long as mind, which is intelligence, is held in the bondage of memory, which is the 'I' consciousness, there is the search of the false for the false. This 'I', as I explained, is the false reaction to environment; there is a false cause and it is ever seeking a false solution, a false effect, a false result. So when the mind clouded by memory is seeking to perpetuate itself as self-consciousness, it is seeking false immortality, a false cosmic expansion, or whatever you like to call it.

In this process of the perpetuation of the 'I', that self-preserving memory, in the perpetuation of that 'I' is born fear—not superficial fear, but the fundamental fear with which I shall deal presently. Remove that fear, which has as its outward expression nationality, growth, achievement, success—remove that fundamental fear, the anxiety for the perpetuation of that 'I', and all fears cease. So fear exists as long as there is this desire for the perpetuation of that thing which is false; this 'I' is false, therefore you must have a false reaction, which is fear itself. And where there is fear there must be discipline, compulsion, influence, domination, the search for power which the mind glorifies as virtue and as divine. If you really think of it you will see that where there is intelligence there cannot be the hunt for power.

Now all life is molded by fear and conflict, and hence by compulsion, by the enforcing of decrees and fetters which some consider virtuous and worthy, and others baneful and evil. Isn't that so? These are the restraints you have established in your search for perpetuation, free from fear; in that search you have created disciplines, codes, and authorities, and your life is molded, controlled, and shaped by compulsion of various forms and degrees. Some call that compulsion virtuous, others evil.

We have first of all, outward compulsion which is the restraint of environment upon the individual. The ordinary person whom you call unevolved, unspiritual, is controlled by environment, outward environment, that is, by religion, codes of conduct, moral standards, political and social authority; he is a slave to all these because all these are rooted in the economic needs of the individual. Aren't they? Remove entirely the economic needs upon which the individual depends, then codes of conduct, moral standards, political, economic, and social values disappear. So in these restraints of the outer environment which create conflict between the individual and the outer environment, in which the individual is crushed, warped, twisted, he becomes increasingly unintelligent. The individual who is merely conditioned all the time by outward environment, shaped by certain rules, laws, reactions, edicts, moral standards—the more and more you crush him, the less and less intelligent he becomes. But intelligence is the understanding of environment, seeing its subtle significance freed from compulsion.

These restraints imposed on the individual, which he calls outer environment, have as their exponents the quacks and the exploiters in religion, in popular morality, and in the political and economic life of man. The exploiter is the individual who uses you consciously or unconsciously, and you yield to him consciously or unconsciously, because you do not understand; you become the exploited economically, socially, politically, religiously, and he becomes your exploiter. So in that way life becomes a school, a frame, a steel frame, in which the individual is beaten into shape, in which he becomes merely a machine—the individual becomes merely a cog in a machine, thoughtless and rigidly limited. Life becomes a continual

struggle, a battle, and therefore he has established this false idea that life is a series of lessons to be learned, to be acquired, so that he may be forewarned, so that he may meet life anew tomorrow, but with his preconceived ideas. Life becomes merely a school, not a thing to be lived, to be enjoyed, to be lived ecstatically, fully, without fear.

The outer environment forces the individual, crushes him into this steel frame of standards, of morality, of religious ideas, of moral edicts, and as the individual is crushed from the outside, he seeks and escapes into a world which he calls the inner. Naturally, when the mind is being twisted, shaped, perverted by outer environment, and there is constant conflict outside, constant battle, constant false adjustments, the mind hopes for tranquillity, for happiness, for a different world; so the individual builds up a romantic haven of escape in which he seeks compensation for the loss and suffering in the outer world.

Please, as I said, you are here to find out, to criticize, not to oppose. You can oppose after you have thought over very carefully what I have been saying. You can put up barriers if you wish to, but first find out fully what it is that I want to convey; and to do that you must be super critical, aware, intelligent.

As I have said, being crushed by outward circumstances which create suffering, and in an effort to escape from those outward circumstances, the individual creates an inner world, begins to develop an inner law and creates his own individual restraints, which he calls self-discipline, or cooperation with that which he has learned to call his high self.

Most people—the so-called spiritual people—have rejected the outer force of environment and its influence, but have developed an inner law, an inner standard, an inner discipline, which they call bringing the high self down to the low; that is, in other words, merely substitution. So there is self-discipline. Then there is that which is called the inner voice, whose power and control is far greater even than the outward environment. But what is, after all, the difference between the one and the other, the outer and the inner? They are both controlling, perverting the mind, which is intelligence, through this desire for self-perpetuation. And also you have what you call intuition, which is merely the unfettered fulfillment of your own secret hopes and desires. So you have filled the inner world, what you call the inner world, with all these—self-discipline, the inner voice, intuition. All, if you come to think of it, are subtle forms of that same conflict, carried into a different world in which there is no understanding, but merely a molding, an adjusting to a more subtle, what you call a more spiritual, environment.

You know, in the outer world some have sought and found social distinctions, and likewise the so-called spiritual people merely seek in this inner world, and generally find, their spiritual peers and superiors; and again as there is conflict in the outer between individuals, so there is created in this inner world a spiritual conflict between ideals, attainment, and their own cravings. You see then what has been created.

In the outer world there is no expression for the mind clouded by memory, for that 'I' consciousness there is no expression, because the environment is too strong, too powerful, too crushing; there you fit into the mold, or if you don't, you are broken. So you develop an inner or more subtle form of environment, in which exactly the same process takes place. That environment which you have created is an escape from the outer, and there again you have standards, moral laws, intuitions, the high self, inner voice, and to them you are constantly adjusting. This is a fact.

In essence these restraints which we call the outer and inner, are born of craving, and so there is fear; and from fear there comes restraint, compulsion, influence, and the desire for power, which are but the outward expressions of fear. Where there is fear there cannot be intelligence, and as long as we have not understood that, there must be this division in life as the outer and the inner, and therefore our actions must always be influenced, either compelled by the outer, and therefore false, or compelled by the inner, which is equally false, because in the inner also you are trying merely to adjust to certain other standards.

Fear is created when the false seeks a perpetuation of itself in the false environment. And so what happens to our action, which is our daily conduct, to our thought and emotion, what is happening to these?

Mind and heart are shaping themselves to environment, external environment, but when they find that they cannot, for the compulsion becomes too strong, they then turn to an inner condition in which the mind and heart seek perfect ease and satisfaction. Or they have thoroughly satisfied themselves through economic, social, religious, or political achievements, and then they turn to the inner, there also to succeed, to be successful, to attain; and to attain, they must have always a culmination, a goal, which but becomes the condition to which the mind and heart are continually adjusting themselves.

So in the meantime, what happens to our feelings, to our emotions, to our thoughts, to our love, to our reason? What happens when you are merely adjusting, when you are merely modifying, altering? What happens to anything—what happens to a house whose walls you are merely decorating though its foundations are rotten? So, likewise, our thoughts and our emotions are merely taking shape, altering themselves, modifying themselves after a pattern, either the external or the inward pattern; or according to an external compulsion or an inward direction. So greatly are our actions being limited through influence, that all reason merely becomes the imitation of a pattern, an adjustment to a condition, and love becomes but another form of fear. Our whole life—after all our life is our thoughts and our emotions, our joys and our pains—our whole life remains incomplete, our whole process of thought or the expression of that life is merely an adjustment, a modification, never a fullness, a completeness. And hence there arises problem after problem, the adjustment to environment which must be constantly changing, and conformity to patterns, which also must vary. So you go on with this battle, and this battle you call evolution, the growth of self, the expansion of that consciousness which is but memory. You have invented words to pacify your mind, but continue with this struggle.

Now, if you really ponder over this—and I think you have an opportunity during these days, those of you who stay quietly here—if you recognize this and without the desire to alter, without the desire to modify, become aware of this outward environment, of these circumstances, conditions, and the inner world in which there are the same conditions, the same environments, which you have called merely by more subtle, more lovely names; if you really become aware of this; then you will begin to understand the true significance of the outer and the inner; there is an immediate perception, the release of life, then mind becomes intelligence and it can function naturally, creatively, without this constant battle. Then mind—intelligence— recognizes the obstacles, and because of its understanding of these obstacles, it penetrates; there is no adjustment, there is no modification, there is only understanding. Hence intelligence does not depend on the outer or the inner, and in that awareness there is no desire, no craving, but the perception of what is true. To perceive what is true, there cannot be craving.

You know, when there is a craving, your mind is already clouded, is already perverted, because mind identifies itself with one and rejects the other—where there is craving there is no understanding; but when mind does not identify itself with the 'I' but becomes aware of both the outer and the inner, of the subtle divisions, of the various emotions, of the delicate nuances of mind dividing itself as memory and intelligence— then in that awareness you will see the full significance of the environment which we have created throughout the centuries, that environment which we call the outer, and that which we call the inner, both of which are continually changing, adjusting themselves to each other.

All that you are now concerned with is modification, alteration, adjustment, and therefore there must be fear. Fear has its instruments in compulsion, and compulsion exists only when there is no understanding, when intelligence is not functioning normally.

June 22, 1934

Sixth Talk in The Oak Grove

I will give a brief talk first and then answer some of the questions that have been put to me.

I dealt yesterday with the whole idea of fear and how it necessitates compulsion; this morning I am going to deal again, briefly, with the way incompleteness creates compulsion. Where there is incompleteness there is the desire for guidance, for authority, for that molding influence which has become tradition, tradition which is no longer thought but which acts merely as a guide. Whereas, to me, tradition should be a means of awakening thought, not dampening, killing thought. Where there is insufficiency, there must be compulsion; and out of this compulsion is born a particular mode of life or a method of action, and therefore further conflict, further struggle, further pain. That is, where one, consciously or unconsciously, feels the poignancy of insufficiency, there must be conflict, there must be misery and a sense of shallowness and emptiness and of the utter futility of life. One may not be conscious of this insufficiency, or one may be conscious of it.

So where there is insufficiency, what is the process of the mind? What happens when one becomes conscious of this emptiness, this shallowness within one's self? What do we do when we feel, when we become conscious of this emptiness, of this void in ourselves? We desire to fill that emptiness, and we look for a pattern, for a mold created by another; we imitate, follow that pattern, we discipline ourselves in that mold which another has established, hoping that we may thereby fill this emptiness, this shallowness of which we have become more or less conscious.

That pattern, that mold begins to influence our lives, compelling us to adjust ourselves, our minds, our hearts and actions to that particular pattern. So we begin to live, not within our own experience, within our own understanding, but within the expression, the ideas, the limitations of another's experience. That is what is happening. If you really think about it for a while, you will see that we begin to reject our own particular experiences and the understanding of these experiences, because we feel that insufficiency, and we turn to imitate, to copy and to live through another's experience. And when we look to another's experience and do not live by our own understanding, there naturally comes more and more insufficiency, more and more conflict; but also if we say to ourselves that we must live by our own experience, our own understanding, we again

turn that into an ideal, into another pattern, and after that pattern we shape our lives.

Suppose that you say to yourself, "I am not going to depend on another's experience, but will live by my own," then surely you have already created a mold for your adjustment. When you say, "I shall live by my own experience," you are already placing a limitation on your thought, for this idea that you must live by your own understanding creates complacency, which is only an ineffectual adjustment leading to stagnation. You know, most people say that they will reject the outward pattern which they are constantly imitating, and will try to live within their own understanding. They say, "We will do only what we understand"; and thereby they create another pattern which they weave into their lives. And then what happens? They become more and more satisfied; hence they slowly decay.

We look, for the dissipation of this insufficiency, to mere action, because where there is insufficiency and emptiness our one desire is to fill that emptiness, and so we look at action merely to fill that. Again, what do we do when we look to an action to complete that insufficiency? We are merely trying through accumulation to fill that void, and so we are not trying to find out what the cause of insufficiency is.

Please, when you feel that you are insufficient, what happens? You try to fill that insufficiency, you try to become rich, and you say that to become rich, to become complete, you must look to another, so you begin to adjust your own thoughts and feelings to the ideas and experiences of another. But this does not give you richness, this does not bring about completeness or fulfillment. And then you say to yourself, "I will try to live by my own understanding," which has its dangers, as I pointed out, leading to complacency; and if you merely look to action, saying, "I shall go out into the world and act so as to become rich, complete," you are again, by substitution, trying to fill that void. Whereas if you become aware through action, then you will find out the cause of insufficiency. That is, instead of seeking completeness, you create action, through intelligence.

Now what is action? It is, after all, what we think and feel. And as long as you are not aware of your own thinking, of your own feeling, there must be insufficiency, and no amount of outward activity is going to replenish you. That is, only intelligence can dispel this emptiness, and not accumulation; and intelligence is, as I have pointed out, perfect harmony of mind and heart. So if you understand the functioning of your own thought and your own emotion, and thereby in that action become aware, then there is intelligence, which dispels insufficiency and which does not try to replace it by sufficiency, completeness, because intelligence itself is completeness.

So when there is completeness there cannot be compulsion. But disharmony, incompleteness, creates separation between mind and heart. Isn't that so? What is disharmony? It is the consciousness of the division between what you think and what you feel, and thereby in that distinction there is conflict. Whereas to me, to think and to feel is the same. So having conflict and disharmony, and having divided the mind from feelings, we then further separate and divide mind and heart from intelligence— intelligence which to me is truth, beauty, and love. That is, conflict, which as I have explained is the struggle between the result of environment, which is the 'I' consciousness, and the environment itself—that conflict between the result of environment and environment itself, brings about struggle which produces disharmony. We divide mind from emotion, and having divided mind from emotion, we proceed still further to divide intelligence from mind and

heart; whereas to me they are one. Intelligence is thought and emotion in perfect harmony, and therefore intelligence is beauty itself, inherently, not a thing to be sought after.

When there is great conflict, great disharmony, when there is the full consciousness of emptiness, then there arises the search for beauty, truth, and love to influence and to direct our lives. That is, being aware of that emptiness, you externalize beauty in nature, in art, in music, and begin to surround yourself artificially with these expressions in order that they may become, in your life, influences for refinement, culture, and harmony. Isn't that the process the mind goes through? As I said, through conflict we have divided intelligence from mind and emotion, and then there comes the consciousness of that insufficiency, that void. Then we begin to seek happiness, completeness, in art, in music, in nature, in religious ideals, and these begin to influence our lives, to control, to dominate and to guide us, and we think that in this way we shall arrive at that completeness; we hope through the accumulation of positive influences and experiences that we can overcome disharmony and conflict. This is merely going further and further away from that which is intelligence, and therefore from truth, beauty, and love, which is completeness itself.

That is, in our feeling of insufficiency, incompleteness, we begin to accumulate, hoping to become complete through this gathering of experiences and the enjoyment of other people's ideas and patterns. Whereas to me, incompleteness disappears when there is intelligence, and intelligence itself is beauty and truth. We cannot see this so long as mind and heart are divided, and they divide themselves through conflict. We separate intelligence itself from mind and heart, and this process goes on continually, this process of separation and the search for fulfillment. But fulfillment lies in intelligence itself, and to awaken that intelligence is to find out what creates disharmony and therefore division.

What creates disharmony in our lives? The lack of understanding of environment, of our surroundings. When you begin to question and understand environment, its full worth and significance, not try to imitate or follow it or adjust yourselves to it or escape from it, then there is born intelligence, which is beauty, truth, and love.

Question: In your opinion, would it be better for me to become a deaconess of the Protestant Episcopal church, or could I be of greater service to the world by remaining as I am?

KRISHNAMURTI: I suppose the questioner wants to know how to help the world, not whether she should join some church or other, which is of little importance.

How is one to help the world? Surely by not creating more sectarian divisions, by not creating more nationalism. Nationalism is, after all, the growth, the fulfillment of economic exploitation, and religions are the crystallized outcome of certain sets of beliefs and creeds. If one wants really to help the world, it cannot be, from my point of view, through any organized religion, whether it be Christianity with its innumerable sects, or Hinduism with its innumerable sects, or any other religion. These are, in reality, pernicious divisions of mind, of humanity. And yet we think that if all the world became Christian, then there would be the brotherhood of religions, and the unity of life. To me religion is the false result of a false cause, the cause being conflict, and religion merely a means of escape from that conflict. So the more you develop and strengthen the sectarian divisions of religion, the less true brotherhood there will be; and the more you

strengthen nationalism, the less will be the unity of man.

Question: Is greed the product of environment or of human nature?

KRISHNAMURTI: What is human nature? Isn't it itself the product of environment? Why divide them? Is there such a thing as human nature apart from environment? Some believe that the distinction between human nature and environment is artificial, for by altering the environment they say that human nature can be changed and molded. After all, greed is merely the result of false environment, therefore of human nature itself.

When the individual tries to understand his environment, the conditions in which he lives, then because there is intelligence there can be no greed. Then greed would not be a vice or a sin to be overcome. You do not understand and alter the environment which produces greed, but you fear the result and call it sin. But the mere search for perfect environment, therefore perfect human nature, cannot produce intelligence; but where there is intelligence there is the understanding of the environment, therefore freedom from its reactions. Now environment or society forces you, urges you to be self-protective. But if you begin to understand the environment which produces greed, then in seeing the significance of environment, greed vanishes altogether, and you do not then replace it by its opposite.

Question: I understand you to say that conflict ceases when it is faced without the desire to escape. I love someone who doesn't love me, and I am lonely and miserable. I honestly think I am facing my conflict, and I am not seeking an escape; but I am still lonely and miserable. So what you say has not worked. Can you tell me why?

KRISHNAMURTI: Perhaps you are merely trying to use my words as a means of escape; perhaps you are using my words, my ideas to fill your own emptiness.

Now you say you have faced the conflict. I wonder if you really have. You say you love someone; but you really want to possess that person, therefore there is conflict. And why do you want to possess? Because you have the idea that through possession you will find happiness, completeness.

So the questioner has not really faced the problem, he desires to possess the other and hence is limiting his own affection. Because after all, when you really love someone, in that love there is freedom from possession. We have occasionally, rarely, that sense of intense affection in which there is no possessiveness, acquisitiveness. And this leads us back to what I just now said in my talk, that possessiveness exists so long as there is insufficiency, the lack of inward richness; and that inward richness exists not in accumulations but in intelligence, in the awareness of action in conflict, caused by the lack of understanding of environment.

Question: Does not the very fact that people come to hear you make of you a teacher? And yet you say we should not have teachers. Should we then stay away?

KRISHNAMURTI: You should stay away if you make of me a teacher, if you make of me your guide. If I am creating in your lives an influence, if by my words and actions I am compelling you towards a certain action, then you should stay away; then what I say is to you worthless, it has no meaning, then you will make of me a teacher who exploits you. And in that there can be no understanding, no richness, no ecstasy, nothing but sorrow and emptiness. But if you come to listen so that you can find out how to awaken intelligence, then I am not your exploiter, then I am merely an incident, an experience which enables you to penetrate the environment that is holding you in bondage.

But most people want teachers, most people want guides, Masters, either here on the physical plane or on some other plane; they want to be guided, to be compelled, to be influenced to do right, to act rightly, because in themselves they have no understanding. They do not understand environment, they do not understand the various subtleties of their own thoughts and emotions; therefore they feel that if they follow another they will come to fulfillment; which, as I explained yesterday, is another form of compulsion. As there is compulsion here, forcing you into a certain groove because there is no intelligence, so you seek teachers in order to be influenced, to be guided, to be molded, and again in that there is no intelligence. Intelligence is truth, completeness, beauty, and love itself. And no teacher, no discipline can lead you to it; because they are all forms of compulsion, modifications of environment. It is only when you fully understand the significance of environment and see its value, only then is there intelligence.

Question: How can one determine what shall fill the vacuum created in the process of eliminating self-consciousness?

KRISHNAMURTI: Sir, why do you want to eliminate self-consciousness? Why do you think it is important to dissolve self-consciousness, or that 'I', that egotistic limitation? Why do you think it is necessary? If you say it is necessary because you seek happiness, then that self-consciousness, that limited particularity of the ego will still continue. But if you say, "I see conflict, my mind and heart are caught up in disharmony, but I see the cause of this disharmony, which is the lack of understanding of environment which has created that self-consciousness,'' then there is no void to be filled. I am afraid the questioner has not understood this at all.

Please let me explain this once again. What we call self-consciousness, or that 'I' consciousness, is nothing else but the result of environment; that is, when the mind and heart do not understand environment, the surroundings, the conditions in which an individual finds himself, then through the lack of that understanding, conflict is created. Mind is clouded by this conflict, and this continual conflict creates memory and becomes identified with mind and thus this idea of 'I', of ego-consciousness, becomes hardened. Hence, there is further conflict, suffering, and pain. But the understanding of the circumstances, the surroundings, the conditions which create this conflict does not come through substitution but through intelligence, which is mind and love; that intelligence which is ever self-creating, ever in movement. And that to me is eternity, a timeless reality.

Whereas, you are seeking the perpetuation of that consciousness which is the result of environment, which you call the 'I', and that 'I' can disappear only when there is the understanding of environment. Intelligence then functions normally, without restraint or compulsion. Then there is not this frightful struggle, this search for beauty, search for truth, and the constant battle of possessive love, because intelligence itself is complete.

June 23, 1934

Seventh Talk in The Oak Grove

Let us for a moment, imaginatively at least, look over the world from a point of view which will reveal the inner workings and the outer workings of man, his creations and his battles; and if you can do that imaginatively for a moment, what do you see spread before you? You see man imprisoned by innumerable walls, walls of religion, of social, political, and national limitations, walls created by his own ambitions, aspirations, fears, hopes, security, prejudices, hate, and love. Within these barriers and prisons he is held, limited by the colored maps of national boundaries, racial antagonisms, class struggles, and cultural group distinctions. You see man throughout the world imprisoned, enclosed by the limitations, the walls of his own creation. Through these walls and through these enclosures he is trying to express what he feels and what he thinks, and within these he functions with joy and with sorrow.

So you see man throughout the world as a prisoner, imprisoned within the walls of his own creation, within the walls of his own making; and through these enclosures, through these walls of environment, through the limitation of his ideas, ambitions, and aspirations—through these he is trying to function, sometimes successfully, and sometimes with hideous struggle. And the man who succeeds in making himself comfortable in the prison, we call successful, whereas the man who succumbs in the prison, we call a failure. But both success and failure are within the wall of the prison.

Now when you look at the world in that way you see man in that limitation, in that enclosure. And what is that man, what is that individuality? What is his environment, and what are his actions? That is what I want to talk about this morning.

First of all, what is individuality? When you say, ''I am an individual,'' what do you mean by it? I think you mean by that—without giving subtle philosophical or metaphysical explanations—you mean by individuality, the consciousness of separation, and the expression of that separate consciousness which you call self-expression. That is, individuality is that full recognition, full consciousness of separate thought, separate emotion, limited and held in the bondage of environment; and the expression of that limited thought and of that limited feeling, which are the same essentially, he calls his self-expression. This self-expression of the individual, which is but the consciousness of separation, is either forced and compelled by circumstances to take some particular channel of action; or, in spite of circumstances, expresses intelligence, which is creative living. That is, as an individual he has become conscious of his separative action, is compelled, forced, circumscribed, urged to function along some particular channel which he does not choose at all. Most people are forced into work, activities, vocations for which they are not at all suited. They spend the rest of their existence in battling against these circumstances and so waste all their energies in struggle, pain, suffering, and occasionally in pleasure. Or a man pierces through the limitations of environment because he understands its full significance, and lives intelligently, creatively, whether in the world of art, music, science, or of professions, without the sense of separation through expression.

This expression of creative intelligence is very rare, and though it has the appearance of individuality or separativeness, to me it is not individuality but intelligence. Where there is true intelligence functioning, there is not the consciousness of individuality; but where there is frustration, effort, and struggle against circumstances, there is the consciousness of individuality which is not intelligence.

The man who is functioning intelligently and who is therefore free of circumstances we call creative, divine. To a man who is in prison, the liberated man, the intelligent man is as a god. So we need not discuss that man who is free, because we are not concerned with him; the majority of people are not concerned with him, and I am not going to deal

with that freedom because liberation, divinity, can be understood, realized, only when you have left the prison. You cannot understand divinity in prison. So it is utterly futile, merely metaphysical or philosophical, to discuss what is liberation, what is divinity, what is God; because what you can now discern as God must be limited, since your mind is circumscribed, held in bondage; therefore I will not describe that.

As long as this spontaneous, intelligent expression which we call life, which is that exquisite reality, is thwarted, there is merely the accentuation of the consciousness of the individual. The more you battle against environment without understanding, the more you struggle against circumstances, the more you become conscious, in that effort, of your limitation.

Please, do not suppose the opposite of that limited consciousness to be complete annihilation, or mechanical functioning, or group activity. I am showing you the cause of individuality, how individuality arises; but with the dissipation, the disappearance of that limited consciousness, it does not follow that you become mechanical, or that there will be a collective functioning through the focus of a single dominating individual. Because intelligence is free of the particular which is the individual, as well as of the collective (for after all, the collective is but the multiplicity of individuals), and there is the disappearance of this limited consciousness which we call individuality, it does not follow that you become mechanical, collective; but rather that there is intelligence, and that intelligence is cooperative, not destructive, not individualistic or collective.

Every man then is thwarted, and conscious of his own separateness he functions and acts in and through environment, battling against it and making colossal efforts to adjust, modify, and alter circumstances. Isn't this what you are all doing? You are thwarted in your love, in your vocation, in your actions; and in the struggle against your limitations you become acute in your consciousness, and you begin to modify and alter circumstances, environment. Then what happens? You merely increase the walls of resistance, for modification or alteration is but the result of the lack of understanding; when you understand you don't seek to modify, to alter, to reform.

So in modification, adjustment, alteration, in your efforts to break through the limitations, the walls, there is what you call activity. For the vast majority of people action is nothing but the modification of environment, and this action leads to the enlarging of the walls of prison, or the limitation of environment. If you don't understand something and merely try to modify it, your action must increase the barriers, must build up new sets of barriers; your efforts merely enlarge the prison. And these barriers, these walls man calls environment; and the functioning within them he calls action.

I wonder if I have explained this. Without understanding the significance of environment, man struggles to alter, modify that environment, and thereby but heightens the walls of his prison, though he thinks he has removed them. These walls are environment, ever changing, and action to him is but the modification of this environment.

So there is never a release, never a completeness, a richness in this action; there is but increasing fear, and never fulfillment. The multiplication of problems is the whole process of the existence of the individual, of yourself. You think you have solved one problem, and in its place there grows another, and so you continue to the very end of life, and when there is no problem at all, then you call that death. When there is no possibility of a further problem, naturally that to you is annihilation and death.

And again, is not your affection, love, born of fear and hedged about by jealousy,

suspicion, and oppressed by possessiveness and sorrow? For this love is born out of the desire to possess, born of insufficiency, born of incompleteness. And thought is merely the reaction to limitation, to environment. Isn't it? When you say, "I think," "I feel," you are reacting to environment and not trying to pierce through that environment. But intelligence is the process of piercing through environment, not the reaction to environment. That is, when you say, "I think," you mean you have certain sets of ideas, beliefs, dogmas, and creeds. And as an animal that is tethered to a post wanders within the length of its rope, so you wander within the limitation of these beliefs, dogmas, and creeds. Surely that is not thinking. That is merely having reactions to bondage, to beliefs, dogmas, and creeds; these reactions produce an effort, a conflict, and that conflict you call thinking, but it is merely like walking round and round within the walls of a prison. Your action is but reaction to this prison, producing further fear, further limitation; isn't that so?

When we talk about action what do we mean? Movement within the limitation of environment, that movement confined to a fixed idea, a fixed prejudice, a fixed belief, dogma, or creed; such movement within that limitation you call action. So the more you act, the less intelligent and free you become, because you have always this fixed point of safety, of security, this dogma or creed; and as you begin to act from that, naturally you are only creating further limitations, further walls of restriction. Then your action is not creative, your action is not born of intelligence, which is completeness itself. Therefore there is no joy, no ecstasy, no fullness of life, no love.

So, not having that creative intelligence which is the comprehension of environment, man begins to play within the walls of his prison, he begins to embellish and decorate the prison and he makes himself comfortable within its walls; and he thinks and hopes to bring beauty into that ugly prison. Therefore he begins to reform, he searches out societies which talk about brotherhood, but which are also within the prison; he tries to become free while remaining possessive. So this beautifying, reforming, playing, seeking comfort within the walls of that prison, he calls living, functioning, acting. And as there is no intelligence, no creative ecstasy of living, he must ever be crushed down by the false structure which he has raised. Thus he begins to resign himself to the prison because he sees he cannot alter, he cannot break down these limitations; because he has not the desire or the intensity of suffering which demands the breaking down of that prison, he resigns himself to it and takes flight into romanticism or escapes through the glorification of his own self. Now this glorification of his own self he calls religion, spiritualism, occultism, either scientific or spurious.

Isn't that what each one does? Please, is this not applicable to you? Don't say this applies to the individual whom we are observing from the top of the world. This individual is yourself, your neighbor, every one of you. So as I talk of these things, don't look at your neighbor or think of some distant friend, which is but an immediate escape. Rather, as I am talking, let the mirror of intelligence be created in front of you, so that you can see the picture of yourself, without a twist, without bias, and with clarity. Out of that clarity will be born action, not lethargic thought or the mere modification of environment.

Again, if you are not imaginative or romantic, if you do not seek what is called God or religion, you create about you a whirlpool of bustle, you become inventors of schemes, you begin to reform your environment, to alter your prison walls, and you increase further the activities in that prison.

You begin, if you are not imaginative or romantic or mystic, to create greater and greater activity within that prison, calling yourself reformers, and so create greater and greater limitation, restriction, and chaos in the prison. Hence you have unnatural divisions called religions and nationalities, caused or created by exploiters and perpetuated for their own profession and benefit.

Now what is religion? What is the function of religion as it is? Don't imagine some marvelous, true, and perfect religion; we are discussing what exists, not what should exist. What is this religion to which man has become a slave, to which he has succumbed unintelligently, hopelessly, to be slaughtered on the altar by the exploiter? How has it been created? It is the individual who has created it through the desire for his own security, which naturally creates fear. When you begin the search for your own security through what you call spirituality, which is spurious, you must have fear. When mind seeks security, what does it expect? To be assured of a condition in which it can be at ease, a point of certainty from which it can think and act, and to live perpetually in that condition. But a mind that seeks certainty is never assured. It is the mind that does not seek certainty that can become assured. It is the mind which has no fear, which sees the futility of an aim, of a culmination, of an achievement, that lives intelligently, therefore with surety, and so is immortal.

Thus the search for security must create fear, and from fear is born the desire for creeds and beliefs in order to ward off that fear. With your beliefs, your creeds, dogmas, and authorities, you push fear into the background. To ward off fear you seek guides, Masters, systems, because you hope that by following them, by obeying them, by imitating them you will have peace, you will have comfort. They are the tricksters who become priests, exploiters, preachers, mediators, swamis, and yogis.

Don't nod your head in approval, because you are all in this chaos. You are all caught up in it. You can only nod your head in approval when you are free of it. In listening to me and nodding your head you show mere intellectual approval of an idea which I am expressing. And what value has that?

Where there is the craving for security there must be fear, so mind and heart seek out spiritual trainers to learn from them ways of escape. As in a circus the animals are trained to function for the amusement of spectators, so the individual through fear seeks out these spiritual trainers whom he calls priests and swamis, who are the defenders of spurious spirituality and the inanities of religion. Naturally the function of spiritual trainers is to create amusements for you, and so they invent ceremonies, disciplines, and worship; all these pretend to be beautiful in expression, but degenerate into superstition. This is but knavery under the cloak of service.

Discipline is merely a form of adjustment to an environment of a different kind, and yet the battle continues constantly within you even though through discipline you are stifling that creative intelligence. And worship, which in reality is most lovely, which is affection, love itself, becomes objectified, exploited, worthless, without any significance or value.

Naturally out of all this fear is born the search for security, the search for God or truth. Can you ever find God? Can you ever find truth? But truth exists; God is. You cannot find truth, you cannot find God, because your search is but an escape from fear, your search is but a desire for a culmination. Therefore, when you seek out God, you are merely seeking a comfortable resting place. Surely that is not God, that is not truth; that is merely a place, an abode of stagnation from which all intelligence is banished, in which all creative life is extinct. To me the very search for God or truth is the very denial of it. The mind that is not seeking a culmination, a goal, an end, shall discover truth. Then divinity is not an externalized, unfulfilled desire, but that intelligence which is itself God, which is beauty, truth, completeness.

As I said, we have created unnatural divisions which we call religions and social organizations for human life. After all, these social organizations are essentially based on our needs, our needs of shelter, food, and sex. The whole structure of our civilization is based on that. But this structure has become so monstrous, and we have glorified our needs so fearfully that our needs for shelter, food, and sex, which are simple, natural, and clean, have become complicated and made hideous, cruel, appalling, by this colossal and ever-crumbling structure which we call society, and which man has created.

After all, to discover our needs in their simplicity, in their naturalness, in their cleanliness, in their spontaneity, demands tremendous intelligence. The man who has discovered his needs is no longer caught by environment.

But because there is so much exploitation, so much unintelligence, so much ruthlessness in glorifying these needs, this structure which we call nationalism, economic independence, political and social organizations, class divisions, prestige of peoples and their racial cultures—this structure exists for the exploitation of man by man and leads him to conflict, disharmony, war, and destruction. After all, this is the purpose of all class distinctions, this is the function of all nationalities, sovereign governments, racial prejudices, this utter spoliation and exploitation of man by man, leading to war.

Now this is how things are, this whole structure, the creation of our human mind which we have individually built up. These monstrous, cruel, appalling social and religious distinctions, dividing, separating, disuniting human beings, have created havoc in the world. You as individuals have created them; they haven't come into being naturally, mysteriously, spontaneously. Some miraculous god has not created them. It is the individual who has created them, and you alone as individuals can destroy them. If we wait for some other monstrous system to come into being to create a new condition for you to live in, then you will become only a slave again to that new condition. In that there can be no intelligence, no spontaneous, creative living.

As an individual you must begin to perceive the true significance of environment, whether it is of the past or of the present, that is, perceive the true significance of continually changing circumstances; and in the perception of that which is true in environment, there must be great conflict. But you do not desire conflict, you want reforms, you want someone to reform the environment. As most people are in conflict and try to escape from that conflict by seeking a solution, which can be but a modification of environment, as most people are caught up in conflict, I say: Become intensely conscious of that conflict, don't try to escape it, don't try to seek out solutions for it. Then in that acuteness of suffering you will discern the true significance of environment. In that clarity of thought there is no deception, no security, no withholding, and no limitation.

This is intelligence, and this intelligence is pure action. When action is born of that intelligence, when action is itself intelligence, then you do not seek that intelligence or buy it through action. There is then completeness, sufficiency, richness, the realization of that eternity which is God. And that completeness, that intel-

ligence prevents forever the creation of barriers and prisons.

June 24, 1934

Eighth Talk in The Oak Grove

This morning I am going to answer questions.

Question: Do I understand you to mean that the ego, made from the effects of environment, is the visible shell, surrounding a unique and immortal nut? Does that nut grow or shrivel or change?

KRISHNAMURTI: You know, some of you bring the spirit of speculation, the spirit of gambling into your inquiry as to what is truth. Just as you speculate in the stock market to get rich quickly, and thus exploit others, cheat others, through this pernicious habit of gambling, so does a philosophical mind indulge in its habit of speculation. With that attitude of mind you begin to inquire if there is an immortal and enduring soul, entity, or being which is complete in itself, or an ever-increasing, growing, expanding individuality.

Now why do you want to know? What lies behind this inquiry, this spirit of speculation? Wouldn't it be better not to inquire, not to speculate, but rather to ascertain if the environment creates that conflict resulting in that individual consciousness, of which I spoke yesterday? Would that not be better than merely to speculate, because all speculation about these matters must be utterly false, since one cannot possibly conceive, in that state of limitation, in that state of conflict between the result of environment and environment itself, one cannot conceive that reality, that eternal life which is truth. If you say that it is consciousness ever increasing, ever expanding, or that it is complete in itself, eternal, I think it is incorrect, because it is neither of these two things from the point of view of that which is intelligence. If you are merely speculating to discover whether that being grows, or eternally is, then the result will be a pattern, a metaphysical or philosophical concept according to which you will, consciously or unconsciously, mold your lives. Therefore such a pattern will be merely an escape, an escape from that conflict which alone can free man from his speculation, from his gambling.

So if you become conscious of the conflict, then you will see in its intensity the meaning of eternity; that is, when you begin to free the mind and heart from all conflict there is intelligence, and then timelessness has a different significance altogether. It is a fulfillment, not a growth. It is ever becoming, not towards an end, but inherently. You can understand this intellectually, superficially, but you cannot understand it fundamentally in all its depth, richness, if the mind and heart are merely seeking a metaphysical refuge, or taking delight in philosophical speculations.

Question: If the eternal is intelligence and therefore truth, then it is not bothered by the false which is the 'I' and the environment. Similarly, there is no inducement to the false, the 'I', the environment, to be troubled about the eternal, truth, intelligence; for, as you have said repeatedly, the one cannot be reached by the other, no matter how great is the effort. And it also appears that throughout the thousands of years of human life, the eternal has not made much headway in dissipating the false and creating truth. As they seem to be unrelated, according to you, why not let the eternal be the eternal, and let the false get worse if it pleases? In a word, why bother about anything at all?

KRISHNAMURTI: Why bother about it? Why do you bother about anything in life? Because there is conflict, because man is caught in sorrow, in pain, transient joys, innumerable struggles, vain gropings, subtle fancies, and romanticisms which are always collapsing; because there is continual strife in the mind, you begin to inquire why this struggle exists. If there is not a struggle, why bother about it? I quite agree with the questioner, why bother about anything if there is not this struggle, the struggle of earning money and keeping that money, the struggle of adjusting yourself to your neighbors, environment and conditions and demands, the struggle to be yourself, to express what you feel. If you don't feel that there is a struggle, then don't bother, let it alone. But I do not think there is a single human being in the world—except perhaps the savages in remote places away from civilization—who is not in the struggle, in the ceaseless search for security, for comfort, driven by fear. In that struggle man begins to create ideas concerning truth as ways of escape.

I say there is a mode of life in which conflict ceases altogether, a way to live spontaneously, naturally, ecstatically. This to me is a fact, not a theory. And I would like to help those who are in sorrow, who are not seeking an end, who are trying to discover the cause of this conflict; those who are not seeking a solution—because there is no solution—to awaken in themselves that intelligence which dissipates, through understanding, the cause of conflict. But if you are not in conflict then there is nothing more to be said. Then you have ceased to think, then you have ceased to live, because you have merely found a security, a shelter away from this constant movement of life, which without understanding becomes a conflict, but when understood becomes a delight, an ecstasy, a continual movement, timeless; and that is eternity.

So what is this conflict? Conflict, as I said, can only exist between two false things, conflict cannot exist between understanding and ignorance, conflict cannot exist between truth and that which is false. So man's whole conflict, his pain and his suffering, lies between two false things, between what he considers the essential and the inessential. Let us consider what these two false things are; not what was created first, not the old question: which came first—the chicken or the egg? That is again a metaphysical laziness of the speculative mind which is not really thinking.

So long as we do not understand the true worth of the environment which creates the individual who battles against it, there must be struggle, there must be conflict, there must be ever-increasing restraint and limitation. Therefore action, as I said yesterday, creates further barriers. And mind and heart—which to me are the same, I divide them for convenience of speech—are impaired and clouded over by memory, and memory is the result born of the search for security, it is the outcome of adjustment to environment, and that memory is continually clouding the mind that is intelligence itself, and therefore dividing it from intelligence; that memory creates the lack of understanding, that memory creates the conflict between the mind and environment. But if you can approach environment anew and not be burdened by this memory of the past which is but a careful adjustment and therefore merely a warning; if you are that intelligence, that mind which is continually renewing itself, not adjusting, modifying itself to a condition, but meeting everything anew, like the sun on a fresh morning, like the evening stars, then in that freshness, in that alertness, there comes the comprehension of all things. Therefore conflict ceases altogether, because intelligence and conflict cannot exist together. Disharmony ceases when intelligence is functioning in its plenitude.

Question: When a person I love, without attachment or longing, comes into my thoughts and I dwell on them pleasantly for a moment, is this what you decry as not living fully in the present?

KRISHNAMURTI: What is living fully in the present? I will try again to explain what I mean. A mind that is in conflict, in struggle, is continually seeking an escape; either the memory of the past unconsciously precipitates itself in the mind, or the mind deliberately turns back into the past and lives in the delight of that past, which is one form of escape. Or else the mind in conflict, in struggle, which is without understanding, seeks a future, a future that you call a belief, a goal, a culmination, an achievement, a success, and escapes to that. It is the function of memory to be cunning and to escape from the present. This process of looking back is but one of the tricks of memory which you call self-analysis, which but perpetuates memory, and therefore limits and confines the mind, banishing intelligence.

So there are these various forms of escape, and when mind has ceased to escape through memory, when memory no longer clouds the mind and heart, there is then that ecstasy of living in the present. This can only be when mind is no longer taking delight in the past or the future, when mind does not create division; in other words, when that supreme intelligence which is truth, which is beauty, which is love itself, is functioning normally, without effort—then in that state intelligence is timeless, and then there is not this fear of not living in the present.

Question: When love is freed of all possessiveness, does this not necessarily result in asceticism and hence abnormality?

KRISHNAMURTI: If you were free of possessiveness, you would not ask this question. Before you have come to that immense thing, you are already afraid, and are therefore building a protective wall which you call asceticism. So let us consider first, not whether it will be asceticism and therefore abnormality, when you are free of possessiveness, but whether that possessiveness itself creates the struggle and produces the abnormal.

Why is there this idea of possession? Is it not born out of insufficiency, out of incompleteness? And because of that insufficiency, sex and other problems assume great importance, and hence possessiveness plays a tremendous part in the lives of people. In completeness, which is intelligence itself, there is no abnormality. But being insufficient, incomplete, knowing poverty, emptiness, utter loneliness and shallowness of thought and emotion, we depend on other people, on books, on literature, on ideas, on philosophy to enrich our lives, and thus we begin to acquire, store up. This process of storing up for guidance in the present is but the functioning of memory which depends on knowledge, which is of the past and therefore dead.

As a man of many possessions looks for comfort in his things, so the man of poverty, of shallowness, of incompleteness, looks to the possession of his friend, of his wife, or of his love; and out of this possessiveness comes the battle and the constant gnawings of mind and heart. And when there is freedom from these conflicts, which can come only through awareness, through the understanding of environment, and not through effort—when there is this freedom, this understanding, then there is no possessiveness and hence there is no abnormality.

After all, the ascetic is one who eschews life because he does not understand it. He runs away from life, from life with all its expressions; whereas intelligence does not seek to escape from anything, because there is nothing to be put away; intelligence is complete, and in that completeness there is no division.

Question: If priests are exploiters, why did Christ found the apostolic succession and Buddha his sangha?

KRISHNAMURTI: First of all, how do you know? You have been told, you have read of it in books. How do you know they are not the fabrications of priests for their own profession, for their own benefit? An authority seasoned through the mists of time becomes invulnerable, and then man accepts that authority as being final. Why accept the Christ or the Buddha, or anyone, including myself? Let us rather ascertain whether priests are exploiters, not merely accept that they are not, simply because Christ is supposed to have established the apostolic succession. That is only the habit of a lazy mind that wants to settle everything by authority, by precedent, saying that because someone has said it, therefore it must be true, it does not matter whether that someone is great or small.

So let us find out. As I tried to explain yesterday, religions are the outcome of man's search for security. And therefore when a mind is seeking shelter, certainty, a place where it can rest, an assurance of immortality, when a mind seeks these, then there must be those to comfort and satisfy that mind. You may call them priests, exploiters, mediators, swamis; all these are of the same type. Now when you are seeking shelter, there is always the fear of losing it; when you are seeking gain, naturally with it comes the fear of loss. So the fear of loss drives you continually to this search for security, which to me is utterly false. And therefore a false cause creates a false product; and this product is the priest, the swami, the exploiter.

Why do you want a priest at all? As a convenient person for marrying you or burying you, or to give you a blessing which will wash away all your so-called sins? There is no such thing as sin—there is only the lack of understanding, and that lack of understanding cannot be washed away by any priest, whether he claims apostolic succession or not. Intelligence alone can free you from that lack of understanding, not the benedictions of a priest, or going to an altar or to the grave.

Do you go to a priest because he will awaken your intelligence, give you stimulation? Then treat this as you treat drink. If you are addicted to drink, it is a pity, because all dependence reveals a lack of intelligence, and then there must be suffering. And man is caught up in this suffering continually, although he does not and will not see the cause; he therefore multiplies means and ways of escape. But the cause is the very search for security, for this certainty which does not exist.

The mind which is intelligent seeks no security, because there is no place, no abode where it can rest. Intelligence itself is tranquillity, creativeness, and as long as there is not that intelligence there must be suffering. Running away from the cause of suffering is not going to give you that intelligence; on the contrary, it makes you more blind, more ignorant; and more and more you will suffer. What gives you perception immediately, directly, is that full intensity of awareness in the present. To understand the environment, whatever it be, is intelligence. Then you are really beyond all priests, then you are beyond all limitations, beyond the gods themselves.

Question: You refer to two forms of action: reaction to environment, which creates conflict, and penetration of environment, which brings freedom from conflict. I understand the first, but not the second. What do you mean by the penetration of environment?

KRISHNAMURTI: There is the reaction to environment when the mind does not understand the environment, and acts without understanding, thereby further increasing the limitation of environment. That is one form of action in which most people are caught up. You react to one environment which creates a conflict, and to escape from that conflict you create another environment which you hope will bring you peace, which is but acting in environment without understanding that the environment may change. That is one form of action.

Then there is the other which is to understand environment and to act, which does not mean that you understand first and then act, but the very understanding itself is action; that is, it is without the calculation, modification, adjustment, which are the functions of memory. You see environment as it is, with all its significance, in the mirror of intelligence, and in that spontaneity of action there is freedom. After all, what is freedom? To move so that there are no barriers, to leave no barriers behind, or create them as you go along. Now the creation of barriers, the creation of environment is the function of memory, which is self-consciousness, which divides mind from intelligence. To put it again differently: action between two false things, the environment and the result of environment, action between these must ever create, must ever increase barriers and therefore diminish, banish intelligence. Whereas, if you recognize this—recognition is not a matter of intellect, recognition must be born of your complete being—then in that full awareness there takes place a different action, which is not burdened by memory—and I have explained what I mean by memory. Therefore every movement of thought and emotion takes a different nuance, a different significance. Then intelligence is not a division between the object which is environment and the creator which you call the self. Then intelligence does not divide, and therefore is itself the spontaneity of action.

June 25, 1934

Ninth Talk in The Oak Grove

This morning I want to deal with the idea of values. Our whole life is merely a movement from value to value, but I think there is a way, if I may use that word with consideration and delicacy, whereby the mind can be freed from the sense of valuation. We are accustomed to values and their continual change. What we call the essential soon becomes the unessential, and in the process of this continual change of values lies conflict. As long as we do not understand the fundamental in the change of values, and the cause of that change, we shall ever be caught up in the wheel of conflicting values.

I want to deal with the root idea of values, whether it is fundamental, whether mind which is intelligence, can always act spontaneously, naturally, without imparting values to environment. Now wherever there is dissatisfaction with environment, with circumstances, that discontent must lead to the desire for change, for reform. What you call reform is merely the creation of new sets of values and the destruction of the old. In other words, when you talk of reform, you really mean mere substitution. Instead of living in the old tradition with established values, you want, with the change of circumstances, to create new sets of values; that is, where there is this sense of valuation, there must be the

idea of time and therefore continual change of values.

In times of stagnation, in times of settled comfort, that which is but the gradual transformation of values we call the struggle between the old generation and the new. That is, in times of peace and quietness, there takes place a gradual change of values, mostly unconscious, and this change, this gradual change, we term the struggle between the old and the young. In times of upheaval, in times of great conflict, violent and ruthless changes in values take place, which we call revolution. The swift change of values, which we call revolution, is violent, ruthless. The slow, gradual change of values is the continual battle that takes place between the settled, comfortable, stagnating mind and the circumstances that are forcing that stagnating mind into new conditions so that it has to create a new set of values.

So then, these circumstances change slowly or rapidly, and the creation of new values is merely the result of adjustments to ever changing environment. Therefore values are merely the pattern of conformity. Why should you have values at all? Please don't say, "What will happen to us if we do not have values?" I haven't come to that, I haven't said that yet. So please follow this. Why should you have values? What is this whole idea of searching for values but a conflict between the new and the old, the ancient and the modern? Aren't values merely a mold, established by yourself or by society, to which mind, in its laziness, in its lack of perception, desires to conform? Mind seeks a certainty, a conclusion, and in that search it acts; or it has trained itself to develop a background, and from that background it functions; or it has a belief, and from that belief it begins to color its activities. Mind demands values so that it will not be at a loss, so that it will always have a guide to follow, to imitate. Hence values become merely the molds in which the mind stagnates, and even the purpose of education seems to be to compel mind and heart to accept new conformities.

So all reforms in religion, in moral standards, in social life, and political organizations are merely the dictates of desire for adjustment to ever-changing environment. That is what you call reform. Environments are constantly changing; circumstances are continually in movement, and reforms are made only because of the need for adjustment between the mind and the environment, not because the mind pierces through the environment and therefore understands it. These new values are glorified as being fundamental, original, and true. To me they are nothing else but subtle forms of coercion and conformity, subtle forms of modification; and these new values help, futilely, to bring about a scrappy reformation, a deceitful transformation of cloaks which we call change.

So through this ever-increasing conflict, divisions and sects are created. Each mind creates a new set of values according to its own reactions to the environment, and then begins the division of peoples; there come into being class distinctions and fierce antagonisms between creeds, between doctrines. And out of the immensity of this conflict, experts come into activity and call themselves reformers in religion and healers of social and economic ills. Being experts, so blinded are they by their own expertise, that they merely increase division and struggle. These are the religious reformers, social reformers, and economic and political reformers, all experts in their own limitations, and all dividing our life and human functioning into compartments and conflict.

Now, to me, life cannot be divided that way at all. You can't think you are going to change your soul and yet be a nationalist; you can't be class conscious and yet talk about brotherhood, or create tariff walls around your own particular country and talk about the unity of life. If you observe, this is what you are doing all the time. You may have plenty of money, well-established conditions about you and be possessive, nationalistic, and class conscious, and yet divide that separative consciousness from your spiritual consciousness in which you try to be brotherly, follow ethics, morality, and try to realize God. In other words, you have divided life into various compartments and each compartment has its own special values, and you thereby only create further conflict.

This division, this reliance on experts, is nothing else but the laziness of the mind, so that it need not think, but merely conform. Conformity, which is but the creation and destruction of values, is environment to which mind is constantly adjusting itself, and so mind becomes increasingly bound and enslaved. But conformity must exist so long as mind is bound by environment. So long as mind has not understood the significance of environment, circumstances, conditions, there must be conformity. Tradition is but the mold for the mind, and a mind that imagines itself free from tradition merely creates its own mold. A man who says, "I am free of tradition," has probably another mold of his own to which he is a slave.

So freedom is not in going from an old mold into a new one, from an old stupidity into a new stupidity, or from restraint of tradition to the license of mindlessness, of lack of mind. And yet you will observe that those people who talk a great deal about freedom, liberation, are doing that; that is, they have put away their old tradition and have now a pattern of their own to which they conform, and naturally this conformity is but mindlessness, the absence of intelligence. What you call tradition is merely outer environment with its values, and what you call freedom from tradition is but enslavement to some inner environment and its values. One is imposed, and the other self-created; aren't they? That is, circumstances, environment, conditions, are imposing certain values and making you conform to those values, or you develop your own values to which you are again conforming. In both cases there is merely adjustment, not comprehension of environment. From this there arises, naturally, the question whether mind can ever discover lasting values, so that there will not be this constant change, this constant conflict created by values which one has established for oneself, or which have been imposed on one externally.

What is it that we call changing values? To me these changing values are but cultivated fears. There must be the change of values so long as there are essentials and unessentials, so long as there are opposites, and the whole idea and the great worship of success, in which we include gain and loss and achievement—as long as these exist and the mind is pursuing these as its aim, its goal, there must be the changing of values, and therefore conflict.

Now what is it that creates the changing of values? Mind, which is also heart, is befogged and clouded by memory, and is ever undergoing a change, modifying or altering itself, is depending ever on the movement of circumstances, the lack of understanding of which creates memory. That is, as long as mind is clouded by memory, which is the outcome of adjustment to environment, and not the understanding of environment, that memory must come between intelligence and environment, and therefore there cannot be the full comprehension of environment.

This memory, which you call mind, is giving and imparting values, isn't it? That is the whole function of memory, which you call mind. That is, mind, instead of being itself intelligence which is direct perception,

mind clouded by memory is giving values as true and false, essential and unessential, according to its cunning, according to its calculating fears and its search for security. Isn't that so? That is the whole function of memory, which you call the mind, but which is not mind at all. To the majority of people, except perhaps here and there to one rare, happy person, mind is merely a machine, a storehouse of memory which is continually giving values to the things it meets, to experiences. And the imparting of values depends on its subtle calculations, cunning, and deceitfulness, based on fear and the search for security.

Though there is no such thing as fundamental security—it is obvious, the moment you begin to think, observe awhile, that there is no such thing as security—memory seeks security after security, certainty after certainty, essential after essential, achievement after achievement. As the mind is constantly seeking security, the moment it has that security, it regards as unessential what it has left behind. Again, it is only imparting values, and thus in this process of movement from goal to goal, from essential to essential, in the process of this constant movement, its values are changing, always colored by its own security and anxiety for its perpetuation.

So mind-heart, or memory, is caught up in the struggle of changing values, and this battle is called progress, the evolutionary path of choice leading to truth. That is, mind, seeking security and reaching its goal, is not satisfied with it, therefore again moves on and again begins to give new values to all things in its path. This process of movement you call growth, the evolutionary path of choice between the essential and the unessential.

This growth is to me nothing else but memory conforming and adjusting itself to its own creation which is the environment; and fundamentally there is no difference between that memory and the environment. Naturally, action is always the result of calculation when it is born of this conformity and adjustment. Isn't it? When mind is clouded over by memory, which is but the result of the lack of understanding of environment, such a mind, befogged by memory, must in its action seek an escape, a culmination, a motive, and therefore that action is never free, it is always limited and is always creating further bondages, further conflict. So this vicious circle of memory, burdened by its conflict, becomes the creator of values. Values are environment, and mind and heart become its slaves.

I wonder if you have understood all this. No, I see someone shaking his head. Let me put the same idea differently and perhaps make it clear, if I can.

As long as mind does not understand environment, that environment must create memory, and the movement of memory is the changing of values. Memory must exist so long as the mind is seeking a culmination, a goal; and its action must ever be calculated, can never be spontaneous—by action I mean thought and emotion—and therefore that action must ever lead to greater and greater burdens, greater and greater limitation. The growth of this limitation, the extension of this prison, is called evolution, the path of choice towards truth. That is how mind functions for most people, and so the more it functions, the greater becomes the suffering, the greater the intensity of struggle. The mind creates ever new and greater barriers and then seeks further escapes from that conflict.

So how is one to free the mind from giving values at all? When the mind imparts values, it can only impart them through the fog of memory and therefore cannot understand the full significance of environment. If I examine or try to understand circumstances through the various deeprooted prejudices—

national, racial, social, or religious prejudices—how can I understand environment? Yet that is what mind attempts, the mind which is befogged by memory.

Now intelligence imparts no values, which are but the measures, standards, or calculations, born out of self-protectiveness. So how is there to be this intelligence, this mirror of truth, in which there are only absolute reflections and no perversions? After all, the intelligent man is the summation of intelligence; his is an absolute, direct perception without twists and perversions which result when memory functions.

What I am saying can only apply to those who are really in conflict, not to those who want to reform, who want to do patchwork. I have explained what I mean by reform, by patchwork—it is an adjustment to an environment, born out of the lack of understanding.

How is one to have this intelligence which destroys struggle and conflict and the ceaseless effort which wears out mind itself? You know, when you make an effort, you are as a piece of wood that is being whittled away continually until there is no wood left at all. So if there is this continual effort, this constant wear, mind ceases to be itself; and effort only exists so long as there is conformity or adjustment to environment. Whereas if there is immediate perception, immediate, spontaneous understanding of environment, there is no effort to adjust oneself. There is an immediate action.

So how is one to awaken this intelligence? Now, what happens in moments of great crisis? In that rich moment when memory is not escaping, in that acute, intense awareness of the circumstance, of the environment, there is the perception of what is true. You do this in moments of crisis. You are fully conscious of all circumstances, of the condition about you, and also you are aware that mind cannot escape. In that intensity which is not relative, in that intensity of acute crisis, intelligence is functioning and there is spontaneous understanding.

After all, what is it that we call a crisis, a sorrow? When the mind is lethargic, when it has gone to sleep, when it has conditioned itself in contentment, in stagnation, there comes an experience to awaken you, and that awakening, that shock, you call crisis, sorrow. Now if that crisis or conflict is really intense, then you will see in that state of acuteness of mind and heart, that there is an immediate perception. That intensity becomes relative only when memory comes in with its calculations, modifications, and clouds.

Please, I hope you will experiment with what I am saying. Each one has moments of crisis. They occur very often; if one is aware, they occur every minute. Now in that crisis, in that conflict, observe, without the desire for a solution, without the desire for escape, without the desire to overcome it. Then you will see that mind has understood instantaneously the cause of conflict, and in understanding the cause, there is the dissolution of the cause. But we have so trained the mind to escape, to let memory cloud the mind, that it is very difficult to become intensely aware. Hence we seek means and ways of escape or of awakening that intelligence, which to me is again false. Intelligence functions spontaneously if the mind ceases to escape, ceases to seek solutions.

So when the mind is not imparting values, which is mere conformity, when there is spontaneous understanding of the prison, which is environment, then there is the action of intelligence, which is freedom.

As long as the mind, clouded by memory, imparts values, action must create further walls of prison; but in the spontaneous understanding of the walls of the prison, which is environment, in that understanding there is the action of intelligence, which is freedom; because that action, that intelligence, is not

creating or imparting values. Values must exist—values which are circumstances and therefore bondage, conformity to environment—these values of conformity, of circumstances, must exist so long as there is fear, which is born of the search for security. And when the mind, which is intelligence, sees the full significance of environment and therefore understands environment, there is spontaneous action which is intelligence itself, and therefore that intelligence is not imparting values, but is completely understanding the circumstances in which it exists.

June 28, 1934

Tenth Talk in The Oak Grove

From the questions that have been put to me, my talks seem to have created some confusion, I think because we are caught up in the words themselves and do not go deeply into their meaning or use them as a means of comprehension.

To me there is a reality, an immense living truth; and to comprehend that, there must be utter simplicity of thought. What is simple is infinitely subtle, what is simple is greatly delicate. There is a great subtlety, an infinite subtlety and delicacy, and if you use words merely as a means of getting to that delicacy, to that simplicity of thought, then I am afraid you will not comprehend what I want to convey. But if you would use the significance of words as a bridge to cross, then words would not become an illusion in which the mind is lost.

I say there is this living reality, call it God, truth, or what you like, and it cannot be found or realized through search. Where there is the implication of search, there must be contrast and duality; whenever mind is seeking, it must inevitably imply a division, a distinction, a contrast, which does not mean that mind must be contented, mind must be stagnant. There is that delicate poise, which is neither contentment, nor this ceaseless effort born of search, of this desire to attain, to achieve; and in that delicacy of poise lies simplicity, not the simplicity of having but few clothes or few possessions. I am not talking of such simplicity, which is merely a crude form, but of simplicity born of this delicacy of thought, in which there is neither search nor contentment.

As I said, search implies duality, contrast. Now where there is contrast, duality, there must be identification with one of the opposites, and from this there arises compulsion. When we say we search, our mind is rejecting something and seeking a substitute that will satisfy it, and thereby it creates duality, and from this there arises compulsion. That is, the choice of the one is the overcoming of the other, isn't it?

When we say we seek out or cultivate a new value, it is but the overcoming of that in which the mind is already caught up, which is its opposite. This choice is based on attraction to one or fear of the other, and this clinging through attraction, or rejection through fear, creates influence over the mind. Influence then is the negation of understanding and can exist only where there is division, the psychological division from which there arise distinctions such as class, national, religious, sex. That is, when the mind is trying to overcome, it must create duality, and that very duality negates understanding and creates the distinctions which we call class, religion, sex. That duality influences the mind, and hence a mind influenced by duality cannot understand the significance of environment or the significance of the cause of conflict. These psychological influences are merely reactions to environments from that center of 'I' consciousness, of like and dislike, or antitheses, and naturally where there are antitheses, opposites, there can be no comprehension.

From this distinction there arises the classification of influences as beneficial and evil. So as long as mind is influenced—and influence is born of attraction, opposites, antitheses—there must be the domination or compulsion of love, of intellect, of society, and this influence must be a hindrance to that understanding which is beauty, truth, and love itself.

Now, if you can become aware of this influence, then you can discern its cause. Most people seem to be aware superficially, not at the greatest depth. It is only when there is awareness at the greatest depth of consciousness, of thought and emotion, that you can discern the division that is created through influence, which negates understanding.

Question: After listening to your talk about memory, I have completely lost mine, and I find I cannot remember my huge debts. I feel blissful. Is this liberation?

KRISHNAMURTI: Ask the person to whom you owe the money. I am afraid that there is some confusion with regard to what I have been trying to say concerning memory. If you rely on memory as a guide to conduct, as a means of activity in life, then that memory must impede your action, your conduct, because then that action or conduct is merely the result of calculation, and therefore it has no spontaneity, no richness, no fullness of life. It does not mean that you must forget your debts. You cannot forget the past. You cannot blot it out of your mind. That is an impossibility. Subconsciously it will exist, but if that subconscious, dormant memory is influencing you unconsciously, is molding your action, your conduct, your whole outlook on life, then that influence must ever be creating further limitations, imposing further burdens on the functioning of intelligence.

For example, I have recently come from India; I have been to Australia and New

Zealand where I met various people, had many ideas and saw many sights. I can't forget these, though the memory of them may fade. But the reaction to the past may impede my full comprehension in the present, it may hinder the intelligent functioning of my mind. That is, if my experiences and remembrances of the past are becoming hindrances in the present through their reaction, then I cannot comprehend or live fully, intensely, in the present.

You react to the past because the present has lost its significance, or because you want to avoid the present; so you go back to the past and live in that emotional thrill, in that reaction of surging memory, because the present has little value. So when you say, "I have completely lost my memory," I am afraid you are fit for only one place. You cannot lose memory, but by living completely in the present, in the fullness of the moment, you become conscious of all the subconscious entanglements of memory, the dormant hopes and longings which surge forward and prevent you from functioning intelligently in the present. If you are aware of that, if you are aware of that hindrance, aware of it at its depth, not superficially, then the dormant subconscious memory, which is but the lack of understanding and incompleteness of living, disappears, and therefore you meet each movement of environment, each swiftness of thought anew.

Question: You say that the complete understanding of the outer and inner environment of the individual releases him from bondage and sorrow. Now, even in that state, how can one free himself from the indescribable sorrow which in the nature of things is caused by the death of someone he really loves?

KRISHNAMURTI: What is the cause of suffering in this case? And what is it that we call suffering? Isn't suffering merely a shock to the mind to awaken it to its own insufficiency? The recognition of that insufficiency creates what we call sorrow. Suppose that you have been relying on your son or your husband or your wife to satisfy that insufficiency, that incompleteness; by the loss of that person whom you love, there is created the full consciousness of that emptiness, of that void, and out of that consciousness comes sorrow, and you say, "I have lost somebody."

So through death there is, first of all, the full consciousness of emptiness, which you have been carefully evading. Hence where there is dependence there must be emptiness, shallowness, insufficiency, and therefore sorrow and pain. We don't want to recognize that; we don't see that that is the fundamental cause. So we begin to say, "I miss my friend, my husband, my wife, my child. How am I to overcome this loss? How am I to overcome this sorrow?"

Now all overcoming is but substitution. In that there is no understanding and therefore there can only be further sorrow, though momentarily you may find a substitution that will completely put the mind to sleep. If you don't seek an overcoming, then you turn to seances, mediums, or take shelter in the scientific proof that life continues after death. So you begin to discover various means of escape and substitution, which momentarily relieve you from suffering. Whereas, if there were the cessation of this desire to overcome and if there were really the desire to understand, to find out, fundamentally, what causes pain and sorrow, then you would discover that so long as there is loneliness, shallowness, emptiness, insufficiency, which in its outer expression is dependence, there must be pain. And you cannot fill that insufficiency by overcoming obstacles, by substitutions, by escaping or by accumulating, which is merely the cunning of the mind lost in the pursuit of gain.

Suffering is merely that high, intense clarity of thought and emotion which forces you to recognize things as they are. But this does not mean acceptance, resignation. When you see things as they are in the mirror of truth, which is intelligence, then there is a joy, an ecstasy; in that there is no duality, no sense of loss, no division. I assure you this is not theoretical. If you consider what I am now saying, with my answer to the first question about memory, you will see how memory creates greater and greater dependence, the continual looking back to an event emotionally, to get a reaction from it, which prevents the full expression of intelligence in the present.

Question: What suggestion or advice could you give to one who is hindered by strong sexual desire?

KRISHNAMURTI: After all, where there is no creative expression of life, we give undue importance to sex, which becomes an acute problem. So the question is not what advice or suggestion I would give, or how one can overcome passion, sexual desire, but how to release that creative living, and not merely tackle one part of it, which is sex; that is, how to understand the wholeness, the completeness of life.

Now, through modern education, through circumstances and environment, you are driven to do something which you hate. You are repelled, but you are forced to do it because of your lack of proper equipment, proper training. In your work you are being prevented by circumstances, by conditions, from expressing yourself fundamentally, creatively, and so there must be an outlet; and this outlet becomes the sex problem or the drink problem or some idiotic, inane problem. All these outlets become problems.

Or you are artistically inclined. There are very few artists, but you may be inclined, and that inclination is continually being perverted, twisted, thwarted, so that you have no means of real self-expression, and thus undue importance comes to be given either to sex or to some religious mania. Or your ambitions are thwarted, curtailed, hindered, and so again undue importance is given to those things that should be normal. So, until you understand comprehensively your religious, political, economic, and social desires, and their hindrances, the natural functions of life will take an immense importance, and the first place in your life. Hence all the innumerable problems of greed, of possessiveness, of sex, of social and racial distinctions have their false measure and false value. But if you were to deal with life, not in parts but as a whole, comprehensively, creatively, with intelligence, then you would see that these problems, which are enervating the mind and destroying creative living, disappear, and then intelligence functions normally, and in that there is an ecstasy.

Question: I have been under the impression that I have been putting your ideas into action; but I have no joy in life, no enthusiasm for any pursuit. My attempts at awareness have not cleared my confusion, nor have they brought any change or vitality into my life. My living has no more meaning for me now than it had when I started to listen to you seven years ago. What is wrong with me?

KRISHNAMURTI: I wonder if the questioner has, first of all, understood what I have been saying before trying to put my ideas into action. And why should he put my ideas into action? And what are my ideas? And why are they my ideas? I am not giving you a mold or a code by which you can live, or a system which you can follow. All that I am saying is, that to live creatively, enthusiastically, intelligently, vitally, intelligence must function. That intelligence is perverted, hindered, by what one calls memory, and I have explained what I mean by that, so I won't go into it again. So long as there is this constant battle to achieve, so long as mind is influenced, there must be duality, and hence pain, struggle; and our search for truth or for reality is but an escape from that pain.

And so I say, become aware that your effort, your struggle, your impinging memories are destroying your intelligence. To become aware is not to be superficially conscious, but to go into the full depth of consciousness so as not to leave undiscovered one unconscious reaction. All this demands thought; all this demands an alertness of mind and heart, not a mind that is cluttered up with beliefs, creeds, and ideals. Most minds are burdened with these and with the desire to follow. As you become conscious of your burden, don't say you mustn't have ideals, you mustn't have creeds, and repeat all the rest of the jargon. The very "must" creates another doctrine, another creed; merely become conscious and in the intensity of that consciousness, in the intensity of awareness, in that flame you will create such crisis, such conflict, that that very conflict itself will dissolve the hindrance.

I know some people come here year after year, and I try to explain these ideas in different ways each year, but I am afraid there is very little thought among the people who say, "We have been listening to you for seven years." I mean by thought, not mere intellectual reasoning, which is but ashes, but that poise between emotion and reason, between affection and thought; and that poise is not influenced, is not affected by the conflict of the opposites. But if there is neither the capacity to think clearly, nor the intensity of feeling, how can you awaken, how can there

be poise, how can there be this alertness, awareness? So life becomes futile, inane, worthless.

Hence the very first thing to do, if I may suggest it, is to find out why you are thinking in a certain way, and why you are feeling in a certain manner. Don't try to alter it, don't try to analyze your thoughts and your emotions; but become conscious of why you are thinking in a particular groove and from what motive you act. Although you can discover the motive through analysis, although you may find out something through analysis, it will not be real; it will be real only when you are intensely aware at the moment of the functioning of your thought and emotion; then you will see their extraordinary subtlety, their fine delicacy. So long as you have a "must" and a "must not," in this compulsion you will never discover that swift wandering of thought and emotion. And I am sure you have been brought up in the school of "must" and "must not" and hence you have destroyed thought and feeling. You have been bound and crippled by systems, methods, by your teachers. So leave all those "musts" and "must nots." This does not mean that there shall be licentiousness, but become aware of a mind that is ever saying, "I must," and "I must not." Then as a flower blossoms forth of a morning, so intelligence happens, is there, functioning, creating comprehension.

Question: The artist is sometimes mentioned as one who has this understanding of which you speak, at least while working creatively. But if someone disturbs or crosses him, he may react violently, excusing his reaction as a manifestation of temperament. Obviously he is not living completely at the moment. Does he really understand if he so easily slips back into self-consciousness?

KRISHNAMURTI: Who is that person that you call an artist? A man who is momentarily creative? To me he is not an artist. The man who merely at rare moments has this creative impulse and expresses that creativeness through perfection of technique, surely you would not call him an artist. To me, the true artist is one who lives completely, harmoniously, who does not divide his art from living, whose very life is that expression, whether it be a picture, music, or his behavior; who has not divorced his expression on a canvas or in music or in stone from his daily conduct, daily living. That demands the highest intelligence, highest harmony. To me the true artist is the man who has that harmony. He may express it on canvas, or he may talk, or he may paint; or he may not express it at all, he may feel it. But all this demands that exquisite poise, that intensity of awareness, and therefore his expression is not divorced from the daily continuity of living.

June 29, 1934

Eleventh Talk in The Oak Grove

What we call happiness or ecstasy is, to me, creative thinking. And creative thinking is the infinite movement of thought, emotion, and action. That is, when thought, which is emotion, which is action itself, is unimpeded in its movement, is not compelled or influenced or bound by an idea and does not proceed from the background of tradition or habit, then that movement is creative. So long as thought—and I won't repeat each time emotion and action—so long as thought is circumscribed, held by a fixed idea, or merely adjusts itself to a background or condition and therefore becomes limited, such thought is not creative.

So the question which every thoughtful person puts to himself is how can he awaken this creative thinking; because when there is this creative thinking, which is infinite movement, then there can be no idea of a limitation, a conflict.

Now, this movement of creative thinking does not seek in its expression a result, an achievement; its results and expressions are not its culmination. It has no culmination or goal, for it is eternally in movement. Most minds are seeking a culmination, a goal, an achievement, and are molding themselves upon the idea of success, and such thought, such thinking is continually limiting itself. Whereas if there is no idea of achievement but only the continual movement of thought as understanding, as intelligence, then that movement of thought is creative. That is, creative thinking ceases when mind is crippled by adjustment through influence, or when it functions with the background of a tradition which it has not understood, or from a fixed point, like an animal tied to a post. So long as this limitation, adjustment exists, there cannot be creative thinking, intelligence, which alone is freedom.

This creative movement of thought never seeks a result or comes to a culmination, because result or culmination is always the outcome of alternate cessation and movement, whereas if there is no search for a result, but only continual movement of thought, then that is creative thinking. Again, creative thinking is free of division which creates conflict between thought, emotion, and action. And division exists only when there is the search for a goal, when there is adjustment and the complacency of certainty.

Action is this movement which is itself thought and emotion, as I explained. This action is the relationship between the individual and society. It is conduct, work, cooperation, which we call fulfillment. That is, when mind is functioning without seeking a culmination, a goal, and therefore thinking creatively, that thinking is action, which is the relationship between the individual and society. Now if this movement of thought is clear, simple, direct, spontaneous, profound, then there is no conflict in the individual against society, for action then is the very expression of this living, creative movement.

So to me there is no art of thinking, there is only creative thinking. There is no technique of thinking, but only spontaneous creative functioning of intelligence, which is the harmony of reason, emotion, and action, not divided or divorced from each other.

Now, this thinking and feeling without a search for a reward, a result, is true experiment, isn't it? In real experiencing, real experimenting, there cannot be the search for result, because this experimenting is the movement of creative thought. To experiment, mind must be continually freeing itself from the environment with which it conflicts in its movement, the environment which we call the past. There can be no creative thinking if mind is hindered by the search for a reward, by the pursuit of a goal.

When the mind and heart are seeking a result or a gain, thereby complacency and stagnation, there must be practice, an overcoming, a discipline, out of which comes conflict. Most people think that by practicing a certain idea, they will release creative thinking. Now, practice, if you come to observe it, ponder over it, is nothing but the result of duality. And an action born of this duality must perpetuate that distinction between mind and heart, and such action becomes merely the expression of a calculated, logical, self-protective conclusion. If there is this practice of self-discipline, or this continual domination or influence by circumstances, then practice is merely an alteration, a change towards an end; it is merely action within the confines of the limited thought which you call self-consciousness. So practice does not bring about creative thinking.

To think creatively is to bring about harmony between mind, emotion, and action.

That is, if you are convinced of an action, without the search of a reward at the end, then that action, being the result of intelligence, releases all hindrances that have been placed on the mind through the lack of understanding.

I am afraid you are not getting this. When I put forward a new idea for the first time, and you are not accustomed to it, naturally you find it very difficult to understand; but if you will think over it, you will see its significance.

Where the mind and heart are held by fear, by lack of understanding, by compulsion, such a mind, though it can think within the confines, within the limitations of that fear, is not really thinking, and its action must ever throw up new barriers. Therefore its capacity to think is ever being limited. But if the mind frees itself through the understanding of circumstances, and therefore acts, then that very action is creative thinking.

Question: Will you please give an example of the practical exercise of constant awareness and choice in everyday life?

KRISHNAMURTI: Would you ask that question if there were a poisonous snake in your room? Then you wouldn't ask, "How am I to keep awake? How am I to be intensely aware?" You ask that question only when you are not sure that there is a poisonous snake in your room. Either you are wholly unconscious of it, or you want to play with that snake, you want to enjoy its pain and its delights.

Please follow this. There cannot be awareness, that alertness of mind and emotion, so long as mind is still caught up in both pain and pleasure. That is, when an experience gives you pain and at the same time gives you pleasure, you do nothing about it. You act only when the pain is greater than the pleasure, but if the pleasure is greater, you do nothing at all about it, because there is no acute conflict. It is only when pain over-balances pleasure, is more acute than pleasure, that you demand an action.

Most people wait for the increase of pain before they act, and during this waiting period, they want to know how to be aware. No one can tell them. They are waiting for the increase of pain before they act, that is, they await for pain through its compulsion to force them to act, and in that compulsion there is no intelligence. It is merely environment which forces them to act in a particular way, not intelligence. Therefore when a mind is caught up in this stagnation, in this lack of tenseness, there will naturally be more pain, more conflict.

By the looks of things political, war may break out again. It may break out in two years, in five years, in ten years. An intelligent man can see this and intelligently act. But the man who is stagnating, who is waiting for pain to force him to action, looks to greater chaos, greater suffering to give him impetus to act, and hence his intelligence is not functioning. There is awareness only when the mind and heart are taut, are in great tenseness.

For example, when you see that possessiveness must lead to incompleteness, when you see that insufficiency, lack of richness, shallowness must ever produce dependence, when you recognize that, what happens to your mind and heart? The immediate craving is to fill that shallowness; but apart from that, when you see the futility of continual accumulation, you begin to be aware of how your mind is functioning. You see that in mere accumulation there cannot be creative thinking; and yet mind is pursuing accumulation. Therefore in becoming aware of that, you create a conflict, and that very conflict will dissolve the cause of accumulation.

Question: In what way could a statesman who understood what you are saying, give it expression in public affairs? Or is it not more likely that he would retire from politics when he understood their false bases and objectives?

KRISHNAMURTI: If he understood what I am saying, he would not separate politics from life in its completeness; and I don't see why he should retire. After all, politics now are merely instruments of exploitation; but if he considered life as a whole, not politics only—and by politics he means only his country, his people, and the exploitation of others—and regarded human problems not as national but as world problems, not as American, Hindu or German problems, then, if he understood what I am talking about, he would be a true human being, not a politician. And to me, that is the most important thing, to be a human being, not an exploiter, or merely an expert in one particular line. I tried to explain that yesterday in my talk. I think that is where the mischief lies. The politician deals with politics only; the moralist with morals, the so-called spiritual teacher with the spirit, each thinking that he is the expert, and excluding all others. Our whole structure of society is based on that, and so these leaders of the various departments create greater havoc and greater misery. Whereas if we as human beings saw the intimate connection between all these, between politics, religion, the economic and social life, if we saw the connection, then we would not think and act separatively, individualistically.

In India, for example, there are millions starving. The Hindu who is a nationalist says, "Let us first become intensely national; then we shall be able to solve this problem of starvation." Whereas to me, the way to solve the problem of starvation is not to become nationalistic, but the contrary; starvation is a world problem, and this process of isolation but further increases starvation. So if the politician deals with the problems of human life merely as a politician, then such a man creates greater havoc, greater mischief, greater misery; but if he considers the whole of life without differentiation between races, nationalities, and classes, then he is truly a human being, though he may be a politician.

Question: You have said that with two or three others who understand, you could change the world. Many believe that they themselves understand, and that there are others likewise, such as artists and men of science, and yet the world is not changed. Please speak of the way in which you would change the world. Are you not now changing the world, perhaps slowly and subtly, but nevertheless definitely, through your speaking, your living, and the influence you will undoubtedly have on human thought in the years to come? Is this the change that you had in mind, or was it something immediately affecting the political, economic and racial structure?

KRISHNAMURTI: I am afraid I have never thought of the immediacy of action and its effect. To have a lasting, true result, there must be behind action, great observation, thought, and intelligence, and very few people are willing to think creatively, or be free from influence and bias. If you begin to think individually, you will then be able to cooperate intelligently; and as long as there is no intelligence there cannot be cooperation, but only compulsion and hence chaos.

Question: To what extent can a person control his own actions? If we are, at any one time, the sum of our previous experience, and there is no spiritual self, is it possible for a person to act in any other way than

that which is determined by his original inheritance, the sum of his past training, and the stimuli which play upon him at the time? If so, what causes the changes in the physical processes, and how?

KRISHNAMURTI: "To what extent can a person control his own actions?" A person does not control his own actions if he has not understood environment. Then he is only acting under the compulsion, the influence of environment; such an action is not action at all, but is merely reaction or self-protectiveness. But when a person begins to understand environment, sees its full significance and worth, then he is master of his own actions, then he is intelligent; and therefore no matter what the condition he will function intelligently.

"If we are, at any one time, the sum of our previous experience, and there is no spiritual self, is it possible for a person to act in any other way than that which is determined by his original inheritance, the sum of his past training, and the stimuli which play upon him at the time?"

Again, what I have said applies to this. That is, if he is merely acting from the burden of the past, whether it be his individual or racial inheritance, such action is merely the reaction of fear; but if he understands the subconscious, that is, his past accumulations, then he is free of the past, and therefore he is free of the compulsion of the environment.

After all, environment is of the present as well as of the past. One does not understand the present because of the clouding of the mind by the past; and to free the mind from the subconscious, the unconscious hindrances of the past, is not to roll memory back into the past, but to be fully conscious in the present. In that consciousness, in that full consciousness of the present, all the past hindrances come into activity, surge forward, and in that surging forward, if you are aware, you will see the full significance of the past, and therefore understand the present.

"If so, what causes the changes in the physical processes, and how?" As far as I understand the questioner, he wants to know what produces this action, this action which is forced upon him by environment. He acts in a particular manner, compelled by environment, but if he understood environment intelligently, there would be no compulsion whatever; there would be understanding, which is action itself.

Question: I live in a world of chaos, politically, economically and socially, bound by laws and conventions which restrict my freedom. When my desires conflict with these impositions, I must break the law and take the consequences, or repress my desires. Where then, in such a world, is there any escape from self-discipline?

KRISHNAMURTI: I have spoken about this often, but I will try again to explain it. Self-discipline is merely an adjustment to environment, brought about through conflict. That is what I call self-discipline. You have established a pattern, an ideal, which acts as a compulsion, and you are forcing the mind to adjust itself to that environment, forcing it, modifying it, controlling it. What happens when you do that? You are really destroying creativeness; you are perverting, suppressing creative affection. But if you begin to understand environment, then there is no longer repression or mere adjustment to environment, which you call self-discipline.

How then can you understand environment? How can you understand its full worth, significance? What prevents you from seeing its significance? First of all, fear. Fear is the cause of the search for protection or security, security which is either physical, spiritual, religious or emotional. So long as

there is that search there must be fear, which then creates a barrier between your mind and your environment, and thereby creates conflict; and that conflict you cannot dissolve as long as you are only concerned with adjustment, modification, and never with the discovery of the fundamental cause of fear.

So where there is this search for security, for a certainty, for a goal, preventing creative thinking, there must be adjustment, called self-discipline, which is but compulsion, the imitation of a pattern. Whereas when the mind sees that there is no such thing as security in the piling up of things or of knowledge, then mind is released from fear, and therefore mind is intelligence, and that which is intelligence does not discipline itself. There is self-discipline only where there is no intelligence. Where there is intelligence, there is understanding, free from influence, from control and domination.

Question: How is it possible to awaken thought in an organism wherein the mechanism requisite for the apprehension of abstract ideas is absent?

KRISHNAMURTI: By the simple process of suffering; by the process of continual experience. But you see, we have taken such shelter behind false values that we have ceased to think at all, and then we ask, "What are we to do? How are we to awaken thought?" We have cultivated fears which have become glorified as virtues and ideals, behind which mind takes shelter, and all action proceeds from that shelter, from that mold. Therefore there is no thinking. You have conventions, and the adjusting of oneself to these conventions is called thought and action, which is not at all thought or action, because it is born of fear, and therefore cripples the mind.

How can you awaken thought? Circumstances, or the death of someone you love, or a catastrophe, or depression, force you into conflict. Circumstances, outer circumstances, force you to act, and in that compulsion there cannot be the awakening of thought, because you are acting through fear. And if you begin to see that you cannot wait for circumstances to force you to act, then you begin to observe the very circumstances themselves; then you begin to penetrate and understand the circumstances, the environment. You don't wait for depression to make you into a virtuous person, but you free your mind from possessiveness, from compulsion.

The acquisitive system is based on the idea that you can possess, and that it is legal to possess. Possession glorifies you. The more you have, the better, the nobler you are considered. You have created that system, and you have become a slave to that system. You can create another society, not based on acquisitiveness, and that society can compel you as individuals to conform to its conventions, just as this society compels you to conform to its acquisitiveness. What is the difference? None whatever. You as individuals are merely being forced by circumstances or law to act in a particular direction, and therefore there is no creative thinking at all; whereas if intelligence is beginning to function, then you are not a slave to either society, the acquisitive or the nonacquisitive. But to free the mind, there must be great intensity; there must be this continual alertness, observation, which itself creates conflict. This alertness itself produces a disturbance, and when there is that crisis, that intensity of conflict, then 'mind, if it is not escaping, begins to think anew, to think creatively, and that very thinking is eternity.

June 30, 1934

Twelfth Talk in The Oak Grove

I think most people have lost the art of listening. They come with their particular problems, and think that by listening to my talk their problems will be solved. I am afraid this will not happen; but if you know how to listen, then you will begin to understand the whole, and your mind will not be entangled by the particular.

So, if I may suggest it, don't try to seek from this talk a solution for your particular problem, or an alleviation of your suffering. I can help you, or rather you will help yourself only if you think anew, creatively. Regard life, not as several isolated problems, but comprehensively, as a whole, with a mind that is not suffocated by the search for solutions. If you will listen without the burden of problems, and take a comprehensive outlook, then you will see that your particular problem has a different significance; and although it may not be solved at once, you will begin to see the true cause of it. In thinking anew, in relearning how to think, there will come the dissolution of the problems and conflicts with which one's mind and heart are burdened, and from which arise all disharmony, pain, and suffering.

Now, each one, more or less, is consumed by desires whose objects vary according to environment, temperament, and inheritance. According to your particular condition, to your particular education and upbringing, religious, social, and economic, you have established certain objectives whose attainment you are ceaselessly pursuing, and this pursuit has become paramount in your lives.

Once you have established these objectives, there naturally arise the specialists who act as your guides towards the attainment of your desires. Hence the perfection of technique, specialization, becomes merely the means to gain your end; and in order to gain this end, which you have established through your religious, economic, and social conditioning, you must have specialists. So your action loses its significance, its value, because you are concerned with the attainment of an objective, not with the fulfillment of intelligence which is action; you are concerned with the arrival, not with that which is fulfillment itself. Living becomes merely the means to an end, and life a school in which you learn to attain an end. Action therefore becomes but a medium through which you can come to that objective which you have established through your various environments and conditions. So life becomes a school of great conflict and struggle, never a thing of fulfillment, of richness, of completeness.

Then you begin to ask, what is the end, the purpose of living. This is what most people ask; this is what is in the minds of most people here. Why are we living? What is the end? What is the goal? What is the purpose? You are concerned with the purpose, with the end, rather than with living in the present; whereas a man who fulfills never inquires into the end because fulfillment itself is sufficient. But as you do not know how to fulfill, how to live completely, richly, sufficiently, you begin to inquire into the purpose, the goal, the end, because you think you can then meet life, knowing the end—at least you think you can know the end—then, knowing the end, you hope to use experience as a means towards that end; hence life becomes a medium, a measure, a value to come to that attainment.

Consciously or unconsciously, surreptitiously or openly, one begins to inquire into the purpose of life, and each one receives an answer from the so-called specialists. The artist, if you ask him what is the purpose of life, will tell you that it is self-expression through painting, sculpture, music, or poetry; the economist, if you ask him, will tell you that it is work, production, cooperation,

living together, functioning as a group, as society; and if you ask the religionist he will tell you the purpose of life is to seek and to realize God, to live according to the laws laid down by teachers, prophets, saviors, and that by living according to their laws and edicts you may realize the truth which is God. Each specialist gives you his answer about the purpose of life, and according to your temperament, fancies, and imagination you begin to establish these purposes, these ends, as your ideals.

Such ideals and ends have become merely a haven of refuge because you use them to guide and protect yourself in this turmoil. So you begin to use these ideals to measure your experiences, to inquire into the conditions of your environment. You begin, without the desire to understand or to fulfill, merely to inquire into the purpose of environment; and in discovering that purpose, according to your conditioning, your preconceptions, you merely avoid the conflict of living without understanding.

So mind has divided life into ideals, purposes, culminations, attainments, ends; and turmoil, conflict, disturbance, disharmony; and you, yourself, the self-consciousness. That is, mind has separated life into these three divisions. You are caught up in turmoil and so through this turmoil, this conflict, this disturbance which is but sorrow, you work towards an end, a purpose. You wade through, plow through this turmoil to the goal, to the end, to the haven of refuge, to the attainment of the ideal; and these ideals, ends, refuges have been designed by economic, religious, and spiritual experts.

Thus you are, at one end, wading through conditions and environment, and creating conflict while trying to realize ideals, purposes, and attainments which have become refuges and shelters at the other. The very inquiry into the purpose of life indicates the lack of intelligence in the present; and the man who is fully active—not lost in activities, as most Americans are, but fully active, intelligently, emotionally, fully alive—has fulfilled himself. Therefore the inquiry into an end is futile, because there is no such thing as an end and a beginning; there is but the continual movement of creative thinking, and what you call problems are the results of your plowing through this turmoil towards a culmination. That is, you are concerned with how to overcome this turmoil, how to adjust yourselves to environment in order to arrive at an end. With that your whole life is concerned, not with yourself and the goal. You are not concerned with that, you are concerned with the turmoil, how to go through it, how to dominate it, how to overcome it, and therefore how to evade it. You want to arrive at that perfect evasion which you call ideals, at that perfect refuge which you call the purpose of life, which is but an escape from the present turmoil.

Naturally, when you seek to overcome, to dominate, to evade, and to arrive at that ultimate goal, there arises the search for systems and their leaders, guides, teachers, and experts; to me all these are exploiters. The systems, the methods, and their teachers, and all the complications of their rivalries, enticements, promises and deceits, create divisions in life known as sects and cults.

That is what is happening. When you are seeking an attainment, a result, an overcoming of the turmoil, and not considering the 'you', the 'I' consciousness, and the end which you are ceaselessly and consciously, or unconsciously, pursuing, naturally you must create exploiters, either of the past or the present; and you are caught up in their pettiness, their jealousies, their disciplines, their disharmonies and their divisions. So the mere desire to go through this turmoil ever creates further problems, for there is no consideration of the actor or the manner of his

action, but merely the consideration of the scene of turmoil as a means to get to an end.

Now to me, the turmoil, the end, and the 'you' are the same; there is no division. This division is artificial, and it is created by the desire to gain, by the pursuit of acquisitive accumulation, which is born of insufficiency.

In becoming conscious of emptiness, of shallowness, one begins to realize the utter insufficiency of one's own thinking and feeling, and so in one's thoughts there arises the idea of accumulation, and from that is born this division between 'you', the self-consciousness, and the end. To me, as I said, there can be no such distinction, because the moment you fulfill there can no longer be the actor and the act, but only that creative movement of thought which does not seek a result, and so there is a continual living, which is immortality.

But you have divided life. Let us consider what this 'I', this actor, this observer, this center of conflict is. It is but a long, continuous scroll of memory. I have discussed memory very carefully in my previous talks, and I cannot go into details now. If you are interested, you will read what I have said. This 'I' is a scroll of memory in which there are accentuations. These accentuations or depressions we call complexes, and from these we act. That is, mind, being conscious of insufficiency, pursues a gain and therefore creates a distinction, a division. Such a mind cannot understand environment, and as it cannot understand it, it must rely on the accumulation of memory for guidance; for memory is but a series of accumulations which act as a guide towards an end. That is the purpose of memory. Memory is the lack of comprehension; that lack of comprehension is your background, and from that proceeds your action.

This memory is acting as a guide towards an end, and that end, being preestablished, is merely a self-protective refuge which you call ideals, attainment, truth, God or perfection. The beginning and the end, the 'you' and the goal, are the results of this self-protective mind.

I have explained how a self-protective mind comes into being; it comes into being as the result of the consciousness or awareness of emptiness, of void. Therefore it begins to think in terms of achievement, acquisition, and from that it begins to function, dividing life and restricting its actions. So the end and the 'you' are the result of this self-protective mind; and turmoil, conflict and disharmony are but the process of self-protection, and are born out of this self-protection, spiritual and economic.

Spiritually and economically you are seeking security, because you rely on accumulation for your richness, for your comprehension, for your fullness, for your fulfillment. And so the cunning, in the spiritual as well as in the economic world, exploit you, for both seek power by glorifying self-protection. So each mind is making a tremendous effort to protect itself, and the end, the means, and the 'you' are nothing else but the process of self-protection. What happens when there is this process of self-protection? There must be conflict with circumstances, which we call society; there is the 'you' trying to protect itself against the collective, the group, the society.

Now, the reverse of that isn't true. That is, don't think that if you cease to protect yourself you will be lost. On the contrary, you will be lost if you are protecting yourself due to the insufficiency, due to the shallowness of thought and affection. But if you merely cease to protect yourself because you think through that you are going to find truth, again it will be but another form of protection.

So, as we have built up through centuries, generation after generation, this wheel of self-protection, spiritual and economic, let us find out if spiritual or economic self-protection is real. Perhaps economically you may assert self-protection for a while. The man who has money and many possessions, and who has secured comforts and pleasures for his body, is generally, if you will observe, most insufficient and unintelligent, and is groping after so-called spiritual protection.

Let us inquire however if there really is spiritual self-protection, because economically we see there is no security. The illusion of economic security is shown throughout the world by these depressions, crises, wars, calamities, and chaos. We recognize this, and so turn to spiritual security. But to me there is no security, there is no self-protection, and there never can be any. I say there is only wisdom, which is understanding, not protection. That is, security, self-protection, is the outcome of insufficiency, in which there is no intelligence, in which there is no creative thinking, in which there is constant battle between the 'you' and society, and in which the cunning exploit you ruthlessly. As long as there is the pursuit of self-protection there must be conflict, and so there can be no understanding, no wisdom. And as long as this attitude exists, your search for spirituality, for truth, or for God is vain, useless, because it is merely the search for greater power, greater security.

It is only when the mind, which has taken shelter behind the walls of self-protection, frees itself from its own creations that there can be that exquisite reality. After all, these walls of self-protection are the creations of the mind which, conscious of its insufficiency, builds these walls of protection, and behind them takes shelter. One has built up these barriers unconsciously or consciously, and one's mind is so crippled, bound, held, that action brings greater conflict, further disturbances.

So the mere search for the solution of your problems is not going to free the mind from creating further problems. As long as this center of self-protectiveness, born of insufficiency, exists, there must be disturbances, tremendous sorrow and pain; and you cannot free the mind of sorrow by disciplining it not to be insufficient. That is, you cannot discipline yourself, or be influenced by conditions and environment, in order not to be shallow. You say to yourself, "I am shallow; I recognize the fact, and how am I going to get rid of it?" I say, do not seek to get rid of it, which is merely a process of substitution, but become conscious, become aware of what is causing this insufficiency. You cannot compel it; you cannot force it; it cannot be influenced by an ideal, by a fear, by the pursuit of enjoyment and powers. You can find out the cause of insufficiency only through awareness. That is, by looking into environment and piercing into its significance there will be revealed the cunning subtleties of self-protection.

After all, self-protection is the result of insufficiency, and as the mind has been trained, caught up in its bondage for centuries, you cannot discipline it, you cannot overcome it. If you do, you lose the significance of the deceits and subtleties of thought and emotion behind which mind has taken shelter; and to discover these subtleties you must become conscious, aware.

Now to be aware is not to alter. Our mind is accustomed to alteration which is merely modification, adjustment, becoming disciplined to a condition; whereas if you are aware, you will discover the full significance of the environment. Therefore there is no modification, but entire freedom from that environment.

Only when all these walls of protection are destroyed in the flame of awareness, in which there is no modification or alteration or adjustment, but complete understanding of the significance of environment with all its delicacies and subtleties—only through that understanding is there the eternal; because in that there is no 'you' functioning as a self-protective focus. But as long as that self-protecting focus which you call the 'I' exists, there must be confusion, there must be disturbance, disharmony, and conflict. You cannot destroy these hindrances by disciplining yourself or by following a system or by imitating a pattern; you can understand them with all their complications only through the full awareness of mind and heart. Then there is an ecstasy, there is that living movement of truth, which is not an end, not a culmination, but an ever-creative living, an ecstasy which cannot be described, because all description must destroy it. So long as you are not vulnerable to truth, there is no ecstasy, there is no immortality.

July 1, 1934

New York City, New York, 1935

⁕

First Talk in The Town Hall*

Friends,

Most of us are trying to solve our many difficulties and problems within the artificial distinction which we have created between the group and the individual. Now, to me, such a distinction as the individual, opposed to the group, perverts and destroys clarity of thought, and such perversion will lead, naturally, to many repressions and exaggerations between the individual and the group.

As we search for ways and means out of this chaos, clever and complicated methods and solutions are offered, and each individual chooses the solution according to his particular idiosyncrasy, depending on his social upbringing and religious fancies.

I do not want to add, to those already existing, any new theories or explanations. To me, the real solution of our problems is through intelligence, which must be direct, simple; when there is such intelligence we can then understand life as a whole.

Now, this intelligence is not to be awakened by following any group or any system or by obeying one's own particular idiosyncracies and fancies. To awaken true intelligence we must first inquire into the

*This report also contains the substance of the talk given by Krishnamurti in Hollywood on March 3, and in Chicago on March 7, 1935.

many stupidities which cripple the mind and heart, and not seek a definition of intelligence; because, when we find out what the stupidities are and free the mind from them through constant awareness, we shall then be able to know for ourselves what true intelligence is.

In finding out for ourselves the limitations environment has placed about us and in discerning its true significance and thus sloughing off the stupidities, we shall begin to realize what is true intelligence. The expression of that intelligence in action is immortality; it is the blessedness of living in the present.

You have many ideas concerning completeness of life and immortality. But, to me, this immortality, this richness, this completeness of life can only be understood and lived when the mind is wholly free from the limitations, the stupidities, that environment, past and present, inherited or acquired, is continually placing about us.

So please do not, if I may suggest, look to me for new explanations during this talk, or for a set of formulas, or definitions. Such explanations and formulas offer only means of escape from conflict. Most minds desire to copy, imitate, follow, because they cannot think for themselves, or else the conflict is so intense that they would rather escape through systems, through definitions, through explanations. It is only by continually being aware of the environment and the imposition of its ever-increasing stupidities, it is only by constantly questioning these, that we stop the escapes, and come face to face with conflict, which gives us the capacity to understand environment intelligently.

What I want to explain during this talk is how we create stupidities; without understanding this continual, unconscious creation, the mere inquiry into what is intelligence gives us but another escape. So, our whole inquiry should be directed towards what is stupidity and its cause, rather than towards what is intelligence.

As I said, until we try to free the mind from those stupidities which environment, past and present, has created about us, and by which it is crippling our action, until we perceive them and understand their true significance, until then our inquiry into intelligence is but futile.

The purpose of my talk is to help you to find out what are the stupidities and how you can be free of them.

Now, each expert, each authority, each sect, each party, offers a way out of this increasing conflict which we know exists. Each puts forward an idea, a theory, a method for the solution of this terrifying tangle. We can divide, I think, these theorists, or the people who give explanations, into two kinds: those who are turned outward, and those turned inward.

The man who is turned outward says that all human problems can be solved by controlling environment. That is, he says human thought can be changed, altered, controlled, through organization, whether of work or of the means of production and distribution, and so forth. He regards man as clay, to be conditioned by environment, and so by the controlling of that environment and in the perfecting of the group, the individual will have an opportunity to express himself. That is, he will no longer be antisocial because, being

mere clay to be conditioned, his environment can be controlled and so his ambitions, his outlook, his desires will never be opposed to the group and be antisocial. Man then will be conditioned according to a new set of ideas and theories so that he can never come, as an individual, into conflict with the group or with society.

If you think that man is nothing else than matter to be conditioned, to be shaped, to be controlled, then there is nothing more to be said. Then life is very simple. Let us all, then, work for the mere perfection of environment, following a certain set of theories and ideas, and be conditioned by them.

Now, I am not against or for this point of view. I want to go into it more fully. If man is merely a social entity, and if altering circumstances and environment and creating in him the habit of seeking the well-being of the group alone, so that he shall not be antisocial—if that is all, then, it seems to me, life becomes very shallow, a series of unfulfilled, superficial actions.

Also, you have the man turned inward, who says that life is nothing but spirit. Leave it, he says, to the highest in man and let him follow that highest, as shown by the teachers, by the various philosophical systems; let him become more religious, let him follow the great leaders, let him have discipline, enter spiritual organizations and obey spiritual authority, and be guided through fear, so that he will eventually conquer circumstances, environment.

Thus you have the exaggerations of the man who is turned outward and the exaggerations of the man who is turned inward: the person who says that man is nothing more than clay and therefore to be ever conditioned; and the other, the man turned inward, the so-called spiritual man who insists first on the change of heart.

So you have these two types. Emphasis or exaggeration of the one or the other destroys its own end. The man who says environment first and the man who says spirit first, each through his exaggerations and his false emphasis, will destroy his own ends. Whereas to me the solution, or rather the manner of thought, the true awakening of intelligence which alone can resolve the innumerable conflicts and problems, social and individual, lies in the perfect equilibrium between the two, beyond and above the two, and that equilibrium is the simple and the direct way.

To study the various systems, philosophic as well as economic, to study them all thoroughly so as to be able to compare, requires great effort, and few have the time, the capacity, or the inclination, to penetrate through their complicated reasoning and theories. And what happens when you haven't time to inquire into the explanations of innumerable competing experts? You choose one who you like, whom you think is reasonable; and as you haven't the time to go into his system thoroughly, you merely accept his authority. The greater the expert, the greater the authority, the greater the following.

So, gradually the followers become blind and merely accept dogmas, and the leaders destroy the followers, and the followers in turn destroy the leaders. Gradually we create another set of stupidities based on a new set of dogmas which were originally theories and we become slaves to them.

Now, to me, theories are of very little value; because a man who is constantly in conflict with environment, both the past and the present, is continually discerning, penetrating, trying to understand, and therefore he is living completely in the present. To such a man there is no need for theories or explanations. But that requires great persistency of thought, great awareness, great penetration into the true significance of ever-changing environment. As the majority of people cannot do that, they accept theories which become their masters, facts, realities.

Naturally, this also applies to religious experts whom we regard as our spiritual guides. Now take religion, that is, religion as an organized belief, and you will see that the authority of the expert is supreme. The pattern is set out and you are forced through the pressure of public opinion, through fear, and so forth, to follow. This worship of authority, this worship of the expert without knowing his limitations is, to me, the very root of exploitation.

So, the whole process of living, which should be a continual fulfillment and therefore a continual penetration into reality, into what is true, is completely destroyed through this worship of authority, of specialists, of creeds, of theories. The whole process is to make the individual subservient, to make him obey and follow. Thus he gradually becomes unconscious of everything but the pattern, and he exists as much as he can within the edicts of that pattern, and he calls that living. Environment becomes only the mold to shape him. So, then, the individual, as he is now, is nothing else than the exaggerated expression of environment, environment being the past and the present, the inherited and the acquired.

To me, this is not true individuality. Through the understanding of the significance of environment, past and present, and therefore being free from it, intelligence is awakened, and the expression of that intelligence is true individuality.

Now, you are conditioned by environment. You are the result of your past and present environment, and what you express, calling it individuality or self-expression, is nothing but the expression of that conditioning environment. To me, the true expression of individuality is that intelligence which is awakened through freeing the mind from the conditioning environment of the past and the present.

The next thing we have to find out is whether any system can help to awaken this intelligence. Or does it merely impose another set of stupidities, further limitations? Because, if we can find a perfect system, then we can give ourselves over to it and become intelligent.

To me, systems are but the crystallization of thought, and the group is but the expression of that thought. Can they, these crystallized thoughts, by your following them, awaken intelligence? Or have you to begin, not considering yourself as an individual, or as a group, to discern for yourself the stupidities created through the false division of the group and of the individual? That is, not considering yourself as an individual or as a group, to think anew, to think from the very beginning so as to be able to grasp the true significance of each environment, each limitation. Because, if we cannot be so active emotionally and mentally, apart from a system, the mere following of a system and being active in it does not awaken intelligence.

Now, such intelligence, when it is awakened, can truly cooperate, not with stupidities but with other intelligences. Take, for instance, what is happening with regard to war. To understand the whole question of war we must think from the very beginning, not from the nationalistic, racial, class point of view. Inherently, war is wrong. There is no excuse for war so long as there is intelligence functioning. But, as we are mostly ruled by politicians, exploiters, and by such kind, we are forced into one war after another, and many reasons are given for the unavoidability and the necessity of wars.

As long as you do not think clearly, fundamentally, from the very beginning, with regard to this question, one day you will be for peace and the next day you will be for war, because you have not discovered for yourself fundamentally the appalling cruel-ties, the racial hatreds, the exploitations which create war. Only when there is an awakened intelligence, not only on your part but on the part of politicians, the rulers, will there be peace.

To discover what is true, one requires great intelligence. Intelligence, to me, is not book knowledge. You may be very learned and yet be stupid. You may read many philosophies and yet not know the bliss of creative thinking, which can exist only when the mind and heart begin to free themselves through conflict, through constant awareness, from the stupidities of the past and from those that are being built up. Then only is there the ecstasy of that which is true.

Can anyone else tell you what is true? Can anyone tell you what is God? No one can: you have to discover it for yourself. So, to find out what is true, what is the significance of life, what is immortality, without which life becomes a chaotic triviality, a senseless, blind suffering, you must have intelligence; and to awaken that intelligence you must strip the mind and heart of stupidities.

The first cause of stupidity is that consciousness which clings to the particular and therefore creates the distinction between the group and itself, that consciousness whose very essence is the thought of acquisitiveness, of 'mine'. This limited consciousness is the very root and cause of stupidity, suffering.

One of its manifestations is the constant craving for security, security in the realm of one's entire being, physically, emotionally, and mentally. In search of that security there is bound to be conflict between what we call the individual and the group, the exaggerations of the individual as against the group, leading to constant friction, struggle, and suffering.

You can see that this search for physical security expresses itself in possessions, with all its cruelties, exploitations, and the rather terrifying stupidities such as nationalism, class wars, racial hatred.

Also, emotionally, love has become but possessiveness. It has lost its creative ecstasy. It is a series of possessive conflicts. Its tenderness, its great depths, its eternal quality, its profound ecstasy are destroyed through this desire to hold.

Then there is the mental craving for certainty. That is why there is the worship of authority, the worship of teachers. That is why the incessant demand for the ultimate, so that your mind can cling to it. That is why your constant inquiry into truth, into God; and the man who assures you of the certainty of God, of truth, of immortality, you worship, as it gives you comfort, security.

Gradually this demand for security destroys intelligence. Mind, through experience, accumulates carefully guarded and self-defensive securities, memories, which prevent constant adjustment to the eternal movement of life.

Experience is most of the time creating securities, self-defensive memories, and with this barrier you meet life, which must inevitably bring conflict and suffering. This does not mean that you must forget the past. What I want to explain is that, as physically we seek security, so mentally we seek to move from uncertainty to certainty, which in turn becomes uncertain, in which there is never a moment of complete, inescapable aloneness.

I assure you, when there is complete nakedness, utter hopelessness, then in that moment of vital insecurity there is born the flame of supreme intelligence, the bliss of truth. In the search for security there arises fear, which begets many illusions, false disciplines, repressions, perversions, the fear of death and the inquiry into the hereafter.

Why are so many interested in the hereafter? Because life here is so superficial, so conditioned by environment, so conflicting, chaotic, unreasonable, without joy, without ecstasy; hence they look to the future, and from this arises the inquiry into the hereafter.

Immortality is a continual becoming, not of that consciousness which we call the 'I', but of that intelligence which is freed from the particular as well as from the group, from that consciousness which creates distinctions. That is, when the mind is stripped of all illusion or ignorance it is able to discern the infinite present. It is a thing which you cannot explain, you cannot reason about. It is beyond all argument. It has to be experienced. It has to be lived. It demands great persistency and constant purposefulness.

Now this seems to me to be the state of the world. The chaos caused by the conflict of many theories leads to stupid practices and divisions; and, as time passes, we are merely accumulating knowledge of theories, increasing bitter divisions, creating mass movements for conflicting experiments, and in this conflict in which we are immersed, intelligence, which is the true expression and mode of life, is wholly forgotten.

This is the state of the world about us. What should be our action? What should be our attitude, our thought? Are you going to wait for the perfection of environment through revolution, through economic changes, through political upheaval? This waiting is but an escape, this looking to the future is but another escape through hope, it is but a postponement. Or, will you, not considering yourselves as individuals or as groups, begin to think anew, from the very beginning, thus shaking off the many stupidities that have become virtues, the many things you have taken for granted, accepted, so that in the true simplicity and directness of thought, which is supreme intelligence, there may come the fruition of action? Which are you going to do: wait for the future, hoping that environment will be perfected through some miracle, through someone else's action; or become so intensely aware, through your own conflict with environment in which there is no possibility of escape, that there is completeness of action?

For most people this is the problem: merely to wait, marking time; or to be able to discern the true significance of life with its conflicts and sorrows, and not create a new set of stupidities, a new set of illusions, and therefore to live directly and simply. The one leads to utter disorder, superficiality, boredom, to such superficial lives as most people lead, whether in the intensity of work or in the lack of work; the other, to the ecstasy of immortality.

Everywhere there is a despair, waiting for some action, waiting for governments to change conditions. And, in the meantime, your own lives are becoming more and more superficial, shallow, with all the inanities of modern society and the inanities of the so-called spiritual people.

As I said in the very beginning of my talk, intelligence is the only solution that will bring about harmony in this world of conflict, harmony between mind and heart in action. No system, the mere alteration of environment, is ever going to free man from ignorance and illusion, which are the causes of suffering. You yourself, through your own awareness, in your own completeness, can discern the true significance of these many limiting barriers. This alone will bring about lasting intelligence, which shall reveal immortality.

March 11, 1935

Second Talk in the Town Hall

Friends,

Before answering some of the questions that have been sent to me, I should like to say that what I have been saying and what I am going to say is not a new intellectual toy, not a new set of theories over which we can wrangle for mere mental stimulation; nor is it meant to give a new sensation to an already jaded emotion. The true significance and depth of its meaning is to be discovered only when you experiment with it; otherwise it will have no value in a world where there is constant conflict.

To make an experiment, one has to begin with oneself. After all, you cannot begin experimenting with somebody else. You won't know either the result or the significance of that experiment if you do not test it out for yourself.

So instead of considering your neighbor, you should begin to find out how to experiment truly with yourself. To help the world one must begin with oneself. If one can truly experiment with oneself so that there is a continual adjustment, not the adjustment to a stereotyped self-discipline, not the blind following of a pattern, not the ceaseless practice of an idea, then such an experiment in living will bring about a significant change in action, in conduct, in one's whole being.

I would suggest that instead of considering superficially the ideas that I put forward, you experiment with them to see whether they have any practical value in your daily life.

Most of us are nurtured in certain prejudices, traditions, and fears, forced by environment to follow and to obey, and through that background we think and act. This background has become an unconscious part of us, and from this unconscious center we start thinking, feeling and acting. All our actions, springing from that limitation of the mind and heart, naturally become more and more limited, more and more narrow, more and more conditioned. Thus the unconscious being, those habitual thoughts and feelings which we haven't questioned or understood, is continually perverting, interfering with and darkening the conscious actions. If we do not understand and so become free from that background with which we have grown up, naturally those prejudices, those fears will be continually interfering with and conditioning the conscious. Consciousness is action, is discernment. So our action is continually being limited, being conditioned through fear, through tradition. Instead of liberating us, freeing us, action but increases our conflict, our problems, and so living becomes but a series of conflicts, a series of struggles.

To escape from these struggles, we have created certain illusions as releases, which have become realities to us. That is, we have innumerable problems and conflicts, and in order to escape from them we have established certain regular, acknowledged releases. These releases are organized religion, acquisitiveness, establishing and following a tradition, and the many escapes through sensation.

If you are aware of your actions, you will notice that this is what is happening to most of you, that you are functioning through an established background of tradition, or of fear, and therefore increasing your conflict, your struggles. Instead of freeing yourselves through action, you establish various releases or escapes, and these become so real, so demanding, that the mind finds it immensely difficult to free itself from them.

To free yourselves from the cause of increasingly limited action, that is, from the unconscious, is not to dig into the past, but to become aware in action in the present. Instead of looking to see if you are slaves to tradition, to fear, to prejudice, become fully aware in your action, and in that flame of awareness the cause of limitation, such as

fear, will reveal itself. That is, if you are fully awakened, fully aware in an action which demands your complete being, then you will perceive that all these hidden, unconscious perversions spring forth and prevent your acting fully, completely. Then is the time to deal with them, and if the flame of awareness is intense, that flame consumes these limiting causes.

Instead of following a pattern, a well-laid line of action, which, again, is bound to cripple thought and emotion, if one can be fully aware in the moment of action—and this can only be when thought and feeling are intense—then the hidden and unexplored depths of one's consciousness reveal themselves. Whereas if you merely examine the unconscious through self-analysis, you will find that your actions become more and more restricted, more and more superficial, therefore losing their significance, their depth, and so life becomes shallow and empty. If you begin to be aware, to deal with a question integrally, as a whole, completely, then you will see how into your mind will creep all the various conditioning, defensive thoughts, inherited or acquired. Then you will discover—if you really experiment with it—that the mind and heart are not in conflict, do not contradict each other, but are the very fountain, the source of that which you are seeking, that creative ecstasy, truth.

Instead of seeking peace, happiness, or trying to find out what truth or immortality is, or if there is a God; if, in the flame of awareness, the mind and heart can free themselves from fear, prejudice, perversions, conditioning causes, then that consciousness is the real ecstasy of life, of truth.

Question: What should one do to get rid of loneliness and fear?

KRISHNAMURTI: First let us discover what we now do, and then we can inquire what we should do. If we are lonely, what do we do? We try to escape from loneliness through companionship, through work, amusement, worship, prayer, all the well-known and cunningly well-established escapes. Why do we do that? We think that we can cover up loneliness by these escapes, through these releases. Can we ever cover up a thing that is inherently diseased? We may momentarily cover up loneliness, but it continues all the time.

So, where there is escape, there must be the continuance of loneliness. For loneliness there is no substitution. If we can understand this with all our being, completely, if we can understand that there is no possibility of escape from loneliness, from fear, then what happens? Most of you will not be able to answer, because you have never completely faced the problem. You don't know what would happen if all the avenues of escape had been completely blocked up and there were not the least possibility of escape.

I suggest that you experiment with it. When you are lonely, be fully aware and you will see that your mind wants to run away, wants to escape. When the mind is aware that it is escaping and at the same time perceives the absurdity of escape, in that understanding loneliness truly disappears.

Please, when you are confronted with a problem and there is no possibility of a way out, then the problem ceases, which does not mean an acceptance of it. Now, you are seeking a remedy for loneliness, a substitution, and therefore the problem is not the significance of loneliness, but what is the remedy for loneliness, what is the best way to escape from it or to cover it up. But when the mind is no longer seeking an escape, then loneliness or fear has a very different significance.

Now, you cannot accept my word for it: all you can say is that you do not know. You do not know whether loneliness and fear will

disappear, but by experimenting you will understand the whole significance of loneliness. If we merely seek a remedy for loneliness or fear, we become very superficial, don't we? To the man who has everything he wants, or the man who wants everything, life becomes very shallow. In merely seeking remedies, life becomes meaningless, empty; whereas, if you are really confronted with a burning problem and there is no possible way of escape, then you will see that that problem does a miraculous thing to you. It is no longer merely a problem; it is intensely vital, it is to be examined, to be lived with, to be understood.

Question: Do you think one should compromise in everyday life?

KRISHNAMURTI: Do you think there is a possibility of a compromise between war and peace? That is, if you really think that war, killing for any patriotic reason or for any other reason, is fundamentally wrong, do you think you could compromise with regard to creating or taking part in a war? In the same way, between acquisitiveness and nonacquisitiveness, do you think there can be any compromise?

There is compromise if at one moment you are acquisitive and the next moment you are nonacquisitive. If one is not acquisitive, if one is not really pursuing acquisitiveness, if one is not driven by it, then there is no compromise. But, when you are possessive and are being driven by circumstances, by ideas and ideals, to be nonacquisitive, then you begin to compromise, then you begin to search out the best and least harmful way to compromise.

If you are truly free from acquisitiveness, though you may live in this world of possessions, there is no compromise. You have to find out whether you are acquisitive. This is very simple. To do this, do not begin to analyze your actions, which only leads to the limitation of action, but be fully aware in the moment of action itself.

Time will not give you freedom from acquisitiveness. That is, you cannot learn non-acquisitiveness through postponement into a future; you can become free from acquisitiveness only in the present, and not eventually. You can only discern its significance now, instantly. But, as we do not want to discern this immediately, we say, deceiving ourselves, that we shall learn nonacquisitiveness later on, through the years to come. In the present only can we understand the stupidity of acquisitiveness, and not in the future. The freedom from acquisitiveness is not the result of slow evolutionary growth of the mind and heart.

A friend of mine became a priest some ten years ago. He said to me the other day that it had taken him ten years to see the foolishness of his act. I wondered whether it had; or was it that he was so carried away by his desires, by his emotions, by his fears, by traditions, that he was not able to think clearly then, and he began to think clearly only when he was disillusioned? What happened was that he was emotionally carried away and influenced by fear, by authority, by tradition. Had he been fully aware at the moment of his decision, he would not have taken ten years to discover the foolishness of that act.

The question is: should there be compromise? Naturally there is compromise when you are acquisitive and at the same time do not want to be acquisitive. In that conflict of the opposites there must be compromise. There is no solution to that, and when life becomes a continual conflict between the opposites, then it is a meaningless and a stupid struggle. But if you truly discern the whole significance of acquisitiveness, then in that freedom there is richness, the enduring beauty of life.

Question: You say that memory is a barrier. Why?

KRISHNAMURTI: Anything that we perceive directly, understand completely, leaves no scar on the mind. If you live in an experience wholly, although you may recall the incident, it will not produce those reactions which you use for your self-defense. If I have an experience whose significance I do not completely understand, then mind but becomes a center of conflict and this conflict continues until I understand that experience wholly. As long as the mind is burdened with these conflicts, it is but a storehouse of defensive reactions, called memories, and with such protective memories we approach life, thus creating a barrier between life and ourselves, from which ensues all conflict, fear and suffering. This is what we are doing most of the time. Instead of being in that state of creative emptiness, mind becomes merely a storehouse of defensive memories. This bundle of defensive reactions we call the 'I', that limited consciousness.

With that limited consciousness, which is but a series of self-protective, invulnerable layers of memories, you approach life and all its experiences. Experiences, instead of dissipating these many layers and so releasing the creative force of life, merely create and add further defensive memories, and so life becomes a continued conflict, confusion and suffering. Instead of being completely vulnerable to life, being completely empty—not in the negative sense of the word—being wholly without self-defense, mind has become a machine of warning, of guiding, to protect and defend itself. To me, such self-protective, defensive memories are fundamental barriers, for they prevent the complete fruition of life, which alone is truth.

Consider for yourself how your mind is not vulnerable. Complete vulnerability is wisdom. When you have an experience, observe what happens. All your prejudices, your memories, your defensive responses come forward and tell you how to act, how to conduct yourself. So already you have made up your mind how to deal with the new, the fresh.

After all, to understand truth, God, the unknown, or whatever name you care to give to it, mind and heart must come unprepared, insecure. In the vitality of insecurity, there is the eternal.

In protecting yourselves, you have built up cunning securities, certainties, subtle memories, and it requires great intelligence to free yourselves from them. You cannot brush them aside or try to forget them. You can discover these barriers only in the full awareness of action itself.

Your listening to me must also be an experience. If you are at all interested and alive to what I am saying, you will see that you are meeting it with all kinds of objections. You do not approach openly, with a desire to find out, to experiment. It is only when the mind and heart are pliable, alert, and are not slaves to theories, certainties, assurances, that you begin to discover the barriers of memories as self-protective, defensive reaction. These scars which we call memories continually come between the movement of life, which is eternal, and ourselves, causing conflict, suffering.

Question: How can I awaken intelligence?

KRISHNAMURTI: Why do you want to awaken intelligence? Can you really awaken intelligence, or does the mind strip itself of the many stupidities and thus find itself to be intelligence? Please see the significance of the question. The questioner wants to know what he should do to awaken intelligence. He wants to know the method, the manner, the technique. When the mind desires to know how, it is really seeking a definite system, and then it becomes a slave to that system. Whereas, if you begin to discover for yourself what are stupidities, then the mind becomes exquisitely, delicately alert. It is in discovering and understanding what are the stupidities and in eschewing them that there is the awakening of true intelligence.

When you ask, how is one to awaken intelligence, you are really demanding rules and regulations, so that you can force your mind along a particular groove. This you would call a positive way of dealing with life, to tell you exactly what to do. It is really a negation of thought, making you a slave to a certain system. Whereas, if you truly were beginning to be aware of your environment, past and present, of your own thought, your own actions, then in discovering what is stupid, you would awaken true intelligence. Definitions of intelligence tend to enslave the mind and heart.

We can find out for ourselves what are stupidities. One need not give a whole list of them. We must discover for ourselves the true cause of stupidity. If we can do that, then we need not take an inventory of stupidities.

What is the cause of stupidity? All thought, emotion and action springing from the limited consciousness, the 'I', gives rise to stupidity. So long as mind is merely a self-defensive, acquisitive entity, any action springing from that must lead to confusion and suffering.

Question: What exactly do you mean by environment?

KRISHNAMURTI: There is an outer environment, as the country, the place, the class and so on; then there is the inward environment of tradition, of ideas inherited and acquired. So we can divide environment as external and inward, but there is not really such a definite division, as the two are closely inter-woven.

Take for example a person born in India. He is brought up in a certain religious system, with many beliefs, with caste prejudices, with social and economic advantages and disabilities, and so on. With this inherited background, he develops further conditioning of mind and heart. He not only has inherited from his parents, from his religion, from his country and from his race, a certain conditioning, but also he is adding to that his own reactions, his own memories, prejudices, based on his inherited background.

There is with him all the time the background of prejudices, inherited and acquired, thoughts, inherited and acquired, fears, desires, cravings, hopes, memories. All that constitutes environment. With that background, with that conditioned mind, he approaches life; he tries to understand this constant movement of life. That is, from a fixed point he attempts to meet life that is eternally beckoning. Naturally then there must be conflict between that fixed point and that thing which is ever living, moving. Where there is conflict, there is the desire for release, escape; and religion becomes but one of the defensive reactions against intelligence. Religions, class consciousness, acquisitiveness, all these but become the avenues of escape, the shelters from the conflict which ensues between that fixed point or prejudice, memories, fears, the limited consciousness, the 'I', and the movement of life.

There can be true understanding, real joy of living, only when there is complete unity, or when there is no longer the fixed point, that is, when mind and heart can follow freely and swiftly the wanderings of life, of truth. In that there is ecstasy. That is immortality.

As long as one has not discerned the true significance of environment, mind and heart are held to that fixed point of limited con-sciousness. From this there arises conflict and sorrow, the constant battle between that fixed point and the eternal movement of life. From this there is born a defensive reaction against life, against intelligence.

Life becomes a series of conflicts and releases. You have so completely surrounded yourself with these illusions, with these escapes, that to you they have become realities from which you hope to have happiness and peace, but they can never give this. Through continual awareness, through penetration, through constant alertness of mind, questioning, doubting, the walls of that fixed point of consciousness, that center with its illusions, must be worn down. Then only is there immortality.

To understand immortality, life, requires great intelligence, not some stupid mysticism. It requires ceaseless discernment, which can exist only when there is constant penetration, wearing away the walls of tradition, acquisitiveness, self-protective reactions. You may escape into some illusion which you call peace, immortality, God, but it will have no reality, for there will still be doubt, suffering. But what will free the mind and heart from sorrow, from illusions, is the full awareness of that eternal movement of life. This is to be discerned only when the mind is free from that center, from that fixed center of limited consciousness.

March 13, 1935

Third Talk in the Town Hall

Friends,

I want to give a brief talk before answering the questions, to explain something which perhaps may be difficult to understand. I will try to make it as simple and clear as possible.

I think most of us are trying to find out what is true happiness, for without being intelligently happy, life becomes very superficial, futile, and rather dreary. And so, in search of what we call happiness, we go from one experience to another, from one belief to another, from one theory to another, until we find such beliefs, such ideas, as give us satisfaction. Now these satisfactions are but escapes. The very search for happiness must result in a series of escapes; it may be, as I said, through authority, through sensation, through the mere multiplication of experiences, and the increase of power, these escapes become standards or values by which we cover up conflict.

After all, when you are conscious of conflict, there is disturbance which creates unhappiness; and to escape from that unhappiness you seek various experiences and develop certain values, standards, measures, which become your escape. So gradually you become unconscious of all except those standards, those patterns, and your life is nothing else than a living imitation of these values which you have established in your search for happiness.

If you examine, you will see that your mind and heart are held in a series of standards or values. Being so bound, mind is always giving further values, establishing further standards, and is ever sitting in judgment. Until the mind frees itself from this continual process of attributing values, it is never fresh, new; never creatively empty, if I may use that word without being misunderstood. For in creative emptiness alone is there the birth of truth.

Conflict, suffering, is the process of breaking up this habit of attributing values. You have a set of values established through experience, through tradition, and these values have become your guides; with these past standards and values you approach a fresh experience, which must naturally create a conflict. This suffering is nothing else than

the breaking up of old values to which the mind clings.

Now, it is the very essence of stupidity to escape from conflict through a series of established values, or through forming a new set of values. The very essence of intelligence is to understand life or experience with an unburdened mind and heart, anew, afresh.

Instead of meeting life without any preconceived demands, you come to it with a mind and heart already prejudiced, almost incapable of swift adjustment, quick pliability. The lack of this instantaneous discernment of the movement of life creates sorrow. Conflict is the indication of bondage, which cannot be conquered, but whose significance must be understood. All conquering of obstacles through a new set of values is but another form of escape.

You might say that a mind which does not give values is really the mind of a primitive. It is true in one sense; the primitive meets life unconsciously, incompletely, without understanding its significance fully. But to meet life completely and to understand its significance fully, requires a mind that is unconditioned by the past, and this can come about only through intense awareness, through discernment. This demands, unlike the mind of the primitive, integrated action in the present without the urge of fear or the search for a reward. It is the intelligence of complete aloneness.

It is only when the unburdened and vulnerable mind and heart meet life, the unknown, the immeasurable, that there is the ecstasy of truth. When the mind is not burdened with values, with memories, with preconceived beliefs, and is able to meet the unknown, in that meeting there is born wisdom, the bliss of the present.

So conflict is the very process of awakening man to full consciousness; and if we are not continually aware, we create a series of escapes which we call values, though they may be changing, and through those values we try to find happiness.

Values become the medium of escape. A mind that is in conflict and meets it without trying to interpret that conflict according to certain values becomes fully, completely aware. Then that mind and that heart shall awaken to the reality of life, the bliss of the present.

Question: Do you advocate renunciation and self-abnegation as a means of finding personal happiness?

KRISHNAMURTI: Personal happiness does not exist. So there are no means to it. There is only the creative ecstasy of life, whose expressions are many. This idea of sacrifice, renunciation, self-abnegation, is false. You think that happiness is to be found through giving up certain things, following certain actions. So you are really trading in, exchanging your sacrifice, your abnegation, for happiness. There is no abnegation or renunciation, but only understanding; and in that there is creative happiness which is not personal, individualistic.

Let me put it differently. I begin to accumulate because I think happiness lies through accumulation, but I find at the end of a certain time that possession does not bring me happiness. Therefore I begin to renounce possessions and try to possess and pursue abnegation; which is only another form of acquisitiveness. But if I discern the inherent significance of possessiveness, then in that there is creative happiness.

Question: Isn't it true that the essential can be found in all the phases of life, in everything?

KRISHNAMURTI: I do not think that there is the essential or the unessential. What is the essential? What is the unessential? One day I want a thing and that becomes the most essential, the most important, and in the very possession of it, it has become the unessential. Then I want some other thing; and so I go on, moving from one essential which becomes the unessential, to another essential which in its turn becomes the unessential.

In other words, where there is a craving there can never be lasting discernment. As most people are slaves to craving, they are in constant conflict of the essential and the unessential. From possessiveness merely of things, which no longer gives satisfaction, you move to mental and emotional possession of virtues, of truth, of God. From things, which were once essential, you have moved "forward" to abstraction. This abstraction becomes the essential.

Can't we look at life, not from this point of view of the essential and the unessential, but from that which is intelligent, comprehensive? Why have we this division of the essential and the unessential, the important and the unimportant? Because we are always thinking in terms of acquisition, gain; but if we look at it from the point of view of understanding, then this division ceases, then we are meeting life continually as a whole. This is one of the most difficult things to do, because we have been and are being trained in religious and economic systems which impose certain sets of values. To a mind that is really not attributing values but is trying to live completely, without the desire of gain; to such a mind there are no degrees of changing values, and therefore there is no conflict between the impermanent and the permanent, between the stationary, and the constant movement of life.

Question: It is all right for you to talk about fundamental things of life, but what about the ordinary man?

KRISHNAMURTI: What are we discussing? We are discussing, as far as I am concerned, how to live intelligently, and therefore divinely, humanly; not with this competitive, ruthless brutality of acquisitiveness, of exploitation, whether by a class or by a teacher, economic or religious. All this applies, naturally, to us all, that is, to the ordinary man. I do not segregate myself from the average, from the ordinary man. People who are concerned about the ordinary man have separated themselves from him. They are concerned about the average man. Why? They say, "I can give up tradition, but what about the man in the street? If he gives it up, there will be chaos." So he must have a tradition, while the people who are concerned about him need not.

Now if you are not thinking in terms of distinctions, either of class or of needs, if you discern the significance of a thing in itself, then you will help that man in the street to free himself without imposition from, let us say, tradition. That is, if you are convinced of the futility of tradition, if you see the significance of it, then you will naturally help the other without imposition, without exploitation. In understanding the fundamental things of life intelligently, you will help the other to extricate himself from this cruel chaos.

If we, all of us here, really felt deeply about these things, really understood, we should act with intelligence. First, surely, one must begin with oneself. One must deal with the fundamental things because they are the simplest; and in a civilization that is becoming more and more complex, if we don't understand for ourselves these simple and fundamental things, we shall but add to the confusion, exploitation and ignorance.

So what we are discussing applies to everyone, and as you have the opportunity, which, unfortunately, not everyone has, if you become conscious, aware, and begin to understand and therefore act, such action will help to dispel ignorance, the cause of suffering.

Question: How can one cope with memory and the obsession of its pictures?

KRISHNAMURTI: First of all, by understanding how memory is formed, how it is created. Now, as I tried to explain the other day, memory is nothing else than incompleted action. I am not including in that the capacity to recall incidents. But memory is the residue, the scar of action which has not been completely lived or completely understood. Until that action is wholly understood, the memory of it or scar on the mind continues. The mind is mostly the residue or the scars of many incompleted, unfulfilled actions. If one is class-conscious or if one is religiously prejudiced, naturally one cannot meet experience wholly, completely; one approaches it with this bias, which creates inevitably a conflict. As long as one does not understand the cause and the significance of that conflict, completely, wholly, there must be further scars or barriers as memories. In that conflict, if one merely escapes or seeks substitutions, then memory as a barrier must be continually perverting the completeness of understanding, which alone is the fulfillment of action. I hope I am not explaining it in very complicated language.

For instance, suppose a man born in India has certain religious prejudices. With these perversions of thought, he approaches life. Naturally he does not discern its full significance, because he is always looking at life through these perversions, and therefore there must be conflict. From this he develops a series of self-defensive memories, barriers, which he calls values. Such defensive reactions must further pervert the comprehension of experience or of life.

When one fully realizes that prejudice or any other perversion is continually corrupting, twisting, the fullness of understanding, then one begins to be aware; in that awareness one discovers the hindrances. It is only through the flame of awareness, through full consciousness, not through self-analysis, that one can discern the prejudices, the escapes, the self-defensive values which are continually twisting experience. In the very fullness of experience itself are the barriers against discernment to be discovered and understood, and not through intellectual self-analysis or self-dissection. If you are intensely aware in the fullness of experience, then you will see how the perversions, impediments, limitations, spring forth.

If the mind and heart can free themselves from these values, which are but memories stored up for self-defensive purposes, that you have inherited or acquired, then life is an eternal becoming. But that requires, as I said, great purposefulness, an incessant inquiry into the cause and significance of suffering, conflict. If you are sitting at ease with life, or merely seeking satisfaction, the bliss of the eternal present is not for you. It is only in moments of great crisis, great conflict, that the mind frees itself from all these self-protective accumulations and accretions. Then only is there the ecstasy of life, truth.

Question: If everyone gave up all possessions, as you suggest, what would happen to all business and the ordinary pursuits of life? Are not business and possessions necessary if we are to live in the world?

KRISHNAMURTI: I have never said give up. I have said that acquisitiveness is the cause of competition, of exploitation, of class distinctions, of wars and so on. Now if one discerns the real significance of possessiveness, whether of things or of people or of ideas, which is ultimately the craving for power in different forms, if the mind can free itself from that, then there can be intelligent happiness and well-being in the world. We have through many centuries built up a system of acquisitiveness, of possessiveness, seeking personal power and authority. Now as long as that exists in our hearts and minds, we may change the system momentarily through revolution, through crisis, through wars, but as long as that craving exists, it will inevitably lead, in another form, to the old system. And, as I said, the freedom from acquisitiveness is not to be learned eventually, through postponement; it must be discerned immediately, and that is where the difficulty lies. If we cannot see the falseness of possessiveness immediately, we shall then not be able individually, and therefore collectively, to have a different civilization, a different way of living.

So my whole attack, if I may use that word, is not on any system, but on that desire for possessiveness, acquisitiveness, leading finally to power.

You think now possessiveness gives happiness. But if you think about it deeply, you will see that this craving for power has no end. It is a continual struggle in which there is no cessation of conflict, suffering. But it is one of the most difficult things, to free the mind and heart from acquisitiveness.

You know, in India we have certain people called sannyasis, who leave the world in search of truth. They have generally two loincloths, the one they put on, and one for the next day. A sannyasi, in search of truth, sought various teachers. In his wanderings he was told that a certain king was enlightened, that he was teaching wisdom. So this sannyasi went to the king. You can see the contrast between the king and the sannyasi: the king who had everything, palaces, jewels, courtiers, power; and the sannyasi who had only two loincloths. The king instructed him concerning truth. One day, while the king was teaching him, the palace caught fire. Serenely the king continued with his teaching, while the sannyasi, that holy man, was greatly disturbed because his other loincloth was burning.

You know, you are all in that position. You may not be possessive with regard to clothes, houses, friends, but there is some hidden pursuit of gain to which you are attached, to which you cling, which is eating your hearts and minds away. As long as these unexplored, hidden poisons exist, there must be continual conflict, suffering.

Question: You say that you are affiliated with no organization, yet obviously you are trying to make people think along certain lines. Can the world thought be changed without an organization whose purpose it is to bring your ideas constantly before the public?

KRISHNAMURTI: I wonder if I am making you think along a certain definite line. I hope not. I am trying to show that thinking is necessary, being in love is necessary; and to think deeply and to be greatly in love, you cannot have a storehouse of self-defensive reactions or memories. Surely when you are in love, you are vulnerable. If I am only making you think along certain lines, then please beware of me, because then I will force you and thus exploit you, and you will exploit me for your own various ends.

What I am saying is that to live greatly, to think creatively, one must be completely open to life, without any self-protective reaction, as you are when you are in love. So you must be in love with life. This requires great intelligence, not information or knowledge, but that great intelligence which is awakened when you meet life openly, completely, when

the mind and heart are utterly vulnerable to life.

You ask, "Can the world thought be changed without an organization whose purpose it is to bring your ideas constantly before the public?" Naturally not, you must have an organization; that is obvious. So we need not discuss it. But when you talk about organization, I think you mean quite a different thing. To convert people to certain beliefs, to force them, to urge them through opinion, through pressure, to adopt a certain method, certain ideas—for that purpose most organizations are formed, not merely for printing books and distributing them. That is how all religions are formed. That is how the followers destroy the teachers, by making their teachings into absolute dogmas which become the authority for exploitation. For that purpose, organization of the wrong kind is necessary. Whereas, if you are interested in these ideas which I am explaining, you will naturally help to print and to distribute books, but without the desire to convert, to exploit.

Question: Even after they have passed beyond the need of organized authority, most people are troubled with the inner conflict of choice between desire and fear. Can you explain how to distinguish, or what you consider true desire?

KRISHNAMURTI: Is there such a thing as true desire? The essential desire and the unessential desire? One day you want a hat, another day a car, and so on, satisfying your cravings. Yet another day you want to attain the highest truth or God. You pass through a whole series of desires. What is the essential in all this? Things are essential; love is essential; the understanding of truth is essential. So why separate desire into false and true, important and unimportant? Can't you look at it differently, meet desire intelligently?

Your minds are so crippled with contradictory values that you cannot discern truly.

I wonder if I am explaining this. Suppose you are possessive. Don't say to yourself, "Well, I have heard this afternoon that I mustn't be possessive, so I will get rid of that desire." Don't develop a contradictory resistance. If you are possessive, be completely and wholly aware of it; then you will see what happens. The mind must free itself from this contradictory desire, the comparative desire which is really a self-protective reaction against suffering; then you will discern the whole significance of acquisitiveness. You can only understand acquisitiveness, or any other problem, in its isolation, not by bringing it into comparison, into opposition. When there is no contradictory or opposite desire, then only is there the discernment of the true significance of desire. The continual contradiction in desire creates fear, and where there is fear, there must be escape. And so there ensues a ceaseless battle between desire, reason, the urge for fulfillment, and their opposites.

In this battle, intelligence, true fulfillment, is wholly lost. As long as mind is caught up in the conflict of opposites, there can be only an escape, a substitution as the essential and the unessential, the false and the true. In this there is no creative happiness.

Question: Are there not times when one needs to separate oneself from outward confusion to aid in the realization of true self?

KRISHNAMURTI: If you put needs first, then they become your masters and intelligence is destroyed. To find out your needs requires intelligence, for needs are constantly changing, constantly renewing themselves. But if you set out to find exactly what your needs are, and having discovered them you limit yourself to those needs, then your life will become very superficial, narrow, small.

So in the same way, if you are seeking solitude merely in order to find out what truth is, then solitude becomes only a means of escape. But in your search during your active life there come naturally periods of solitude. These moments of solitude then are not false; they are natural, spontaneous.

Question: You said on Monday that to have true intelligence, one must have passed through a state of great aloneness. Is this the only way of arriving at true intelligence?

KRISHNAMURTI: Let us consider what we do now. We are seeking security, constantly hedging ourselves in with certainties. Whenever there comes a state of utter uncertainty, doubt, we take immediate flight from it. So we have established comforting securities, certainties. Please think it over and you will see that this is so. And it is only when you are stripped of all hope, in the sense of security, certainty, only when you are completely naked, stripped of all protective measures and reactions, that there is the ecstasy of truth. In those moments of complete aloneness, which only come when all escapes and their significance have been truly discerned, is there the blessedness of the present.

March 15, 1935

Rio de Janeiro, Brazil, 1935

✳

First Talk in Rio de Janeiro*

Friends,

As there have been so many misconceptions and misunderstandings in the newspapers and magazines concerning me, I think it would be best if I made a statement to clarify the position. People generally desire to be saved by another, or by some miracle, or by philosophical ideas; and I am afraid that many come here with this desire, hoping that by merely listening to me they will find an immediate solution to their many problems. Neither the solution to their problems nor their so-called salvation can come through any person or any system of philosophy. The understanding of truth or of life lies through one's own discernment, through one's own perseverance and clarity of thought. Because most of us are too lazy to think for ourselves, we blindly accept and follow persons or cling to ideas which become our means of escape in times of conflict and suffering.

First of all, I want to explain that I do not belong to any society. I am not a Theosophist nor a Theosophical missionary, nor have I come here to convert you to any

*This talk contains also the substance of the first talk in São Paulo, April 21, 1935.

particular form of belief. I do not think it is possible to follow anyone, or to adhere to a certain belief, and at the same time have the capacity for clear thought. That is why most parties, societies, sects, religious bodies, become means of exploitation.

Nor do I bring an oriental philosophy, urging you to accept it. When I speak in India I am told there that what I say is a western philosophy, and when I come to the western countries, they tell me that I bring an oriental mysticism which is impractical and useless in the world of action. But if you really come to think of it, thought has no nationality, nor is it limited by any country, climate, or people. So please do not consider that what I am going to say is the result of some peculiar racial prejudice, idiosyncrasy, or personal peculiarity. What I have to say is actual, actual in the sense that it can be applied to the present life of man; it is not a theory based on some beliefs and hopes, but it is practicable and applicable to man.

Now, the full significance of what I am going to say can be understood only through experimenting and so through action. Most of us like to discuss philosophical questions in which our daily actions have no part; whereas, that of which I speak is not a philosophy or a system of thought, and its deep significance can be understood only through experiment, through action.

What I say is not a theory, an intellectual belief to be merely discussed, to be argued over; it demands a great deal of thought; and only in action, not by intellectual disputation, can you find out whether it be true and practical. It is not a system to be memorized, nor is it a set of conclusions which can be learned and automatically carried out. It must be understood critically. Now criticism is different from opposition. If you are really critical, you will not merely oppose, but you will try to find out whether what I say has any intrinsic merit in itself. This demands clarity of thinking on your part, so that you can pierce through the illusion of words, not allowing your prejudices, either religious or economic, to prevent you from thinking fundamentally. That is, you have to think from the very beginning, simply and directly. All of us have been brought up with many prejudices and preconceptions; we have been nurtured in festering traditions and limited by environment, and so our thought is continually perverted and twisted, thus preventing the simplicity of action.

Take, for example, the question of war. You know, so many discuss the rightness and the wrongness of war. Surely there cannot be two ways of looking at that question. War, defensive or offensive, is fundamentally wrong. Now to think from the very beginning with regard to that question, mind must be entirely free of the disease of nationalism. We are prevented from thinking fundamentally, directly, simply, because of the prejudices which have been exploited through ages under the guise of patriotism, with its absurdities.

So we have created through the centuries many habits, traditions, prejudices, which prevent the individual from thinking completely, fundamentally, about vital human questions.

Now to understand the many problems of life, with its varieties of suffering, we must discover for ourselves the fundamental motives and causes, with their results and effects. Unless we are fully conscious of our actions, their cause and effect, we shall exploit and be exploited, we shall become slaves to systems and our actions will be merely mechanical and automatic. Until we can consciously free our actions from their limiting effect, through the understanding of the significance of their cause, unless we consciously free ourselves from the old forms of thought which we have built about us, we shall not be able to penetrate the innumerable illusions which we have created around us and in which we are entrammelled.

Each one has to ask himself what he is seeking, or whether he is merely being driven by circumstances and conditions, and is therefore irresponsible, thoughtless. Those of you who are really discontented, critical, must have asked yourselves what it is that each individual is seeking. Are you seeking comfort, security, or the understanding of life? Many will say that they are seeking truth; but if they were to analyze their longing, their search, it would be seen that they are really looking for comfort, security, an escape from conflict and suffering.

Now if you are seeking comfort, security, it must be based on acquisition and so on exploitation and cruelty. If you say you are seeking truth, you will become a prisoner to illusion, for truth cannot be run after, searched out; it must happen. That is, its ecstasy is to be known only when the mind is utterly stripped of all the illusions which it has created in the search for its own security and comfort. Then only is there the dawning of that which is truth.

To put it differently, we have to ask ourselves on what are our life, thought, and action based. If we can answer this completely, truthfully, then we can find out for ourselves who is the creator of illusions, of these supposed realities to which we have become prisoners.

If you really think about it, you will see that your whole life is based on the pursuit of individual security, safety, and comfort. In this search for security, naturally there is born fear. When you are seeking comfort, when the mind is trying to evade struggle, conflict, sorrow, it must create various avenues of escape, and these avenues of escape become our illusions. So fear, which is the outcome of individual search for security, is the breeder of illusions. This drives you from one religious sect to another, from one philosophy to another, from one teacher to another, to seek that security, that comfort. This you call the search for truth, for happiness.

Now, there is no security, no comfort, but only clarity of thought which brings about the understanding of the fundamental cause of suffering, which alone will liberate man. In this liberation lies the blessedness of the present. I say that there is an eternal reality which can be discovered only when the mind is free from all illusion. So beware of the person who offers you comfort, for in this there must be exploitation; he creates a snare in which you are caught like a fish in a net.

In the search for comfort, security, life has come to be divided into the religious or the spiritual, and the economic or the material. Material security is sought through possessions which give power, and through that power you hope to realize happiness. To attain this material security, power, there must be exploitation, the exploitation of your neighbor through a system deliberately set up and which has become hideous in its many cruelties. This search for individual security, in which is included one's own family as well, has created class distinctions, racial hatreds, nationalism, ending eventually in wars. And curiously, if you consider it, religion which should denounce war, helps its furtherance. The priests, who are supposed to be the educators of the people, encourage all the inanities that nationalism creates and which blind people in moments of national hatred. And you create the system, based on individual security and comfort, which you call religion. You have created the religious organizations which are merely crystallized forms of thought and which assure personal immortality. I will go into this question of immortality in one of my later talks.

So through the search for individual security, through the demand for individual continuance, you have created a religion that exploits you through priestcraft, through ceremonies, through so-called ideals. The system which you call religion and which has been created through your own demand for security has become so powerful, so realistic, that very few free themselves from its weight of crushing tradition and authority. The very beginning of true criticism lies in questioning the values that religion has set about us.

Now in this frame each one is held; and as long as one is a slave to unexplored, unquestioned environment and values, both past and present, they must pervert the completeness of action. This perversion is the cause of conflict between the individual who is seeking security, and the many; between the individual and the continual movement of experience. As individually we have created this system of exploitation and crushing limitation, we have individually and consciously to break it down by understanding the foundation of this structure and not by merely creating new sets of values, which will only be another series of escapes. Thus we shall begin to penetrate into the true significance of living.

I maintain that there is a reality, give it what name you will, which can be understood and lived only when the mind and heart have penetrated into the illusions and are free from their false values. Then only is there the eternal.

April 13, 1935

Second Talk in Rio de Janeiro

Friends,

In this brief introductory talk, before answering some of the questions that have been put to me, I want to express some ideas which should be thought over with critical intelligence. I do not want to go into details, but when you think over what I say and carry it out in action, you will see its practical importance in this world of cruel and terrifying chaos.

The first thing we have to understand is that as long as there is a distinction between the individual and the group there must be conflict, there must be exploitation, there must be suffering. The conflict in the world is really between the individual who is seeking fulfillment, and the group. In the expression of his unique force as an individual, he must inevitably come into conflict with the many, and this conflict only increases the division between the two. The mere superficial imposition of the one upon the other or the extermination of the one by the other, cannot rid the world of exploitation and repressive cruelties.

So long as we do not understand the true relationship between the individual and the group, and his true function among the many, there will be a continual warfare. To me, this distinction between the individual and the group is artificial and untrue, though it has assumed a reality. So long as we do not truly understand how the consciousness of the group has come into being and what is the individual and his function, there must be a continual friction.

Before answering the questions this evening, I want to try to explain what I mean by the individual. The group consciousness is but the expansion of that of the individual, so let us concern ourselves with the thought and action of the individual. Though what I say may appear new to you, please examine it without prejudice.

The individual is the result of the past, expressing himself through the present environment; the past being the inherited, the incomplete, and the present, that which is created by incompleteness. The past is nothing but uncompleted thought, emotion, and action; that is, thought, emotion, or action conditioned and limited by ignorance.

To put it differently, if a person has developed a certain background through traditions, through economic environment, through heredity, through religious training, and is trying to express himself through the limitation of that background, naturally then his actions, thoughts, and feelings must be limited, conditioned. That is, his mind is perverted, twisted by his past, and with that limitation he is trying to meet life and understand its experiences. So ignorance is the accumulation of the results of action through the many hindrances whose significance the individual has not wholly understood. These hindrances have been built up by the mind for its self-protection.

Each one is constantly seeking and creating security for himself, and therefore his whole reaction to life is one of continual self-defense. As long as the mind and heart are seeking measures to protect themselves through defensive ideals and values, there must be ignorance, which prevents the mind from acting fully, completely, and so it develops its own particularity which we call individuality, and which must inevitably come into conflict with the many other individualities. This is the fundamental cause of suffering.

Now, to me, the true significance of individuality consists in freeing the mind from this past, from this ignorance with its limiting environment. In this process of liberation, there is born true intelligence, which alone will free man from suffering, from cruelties and exploitation.

So when the mind is free from the habit and the tradition of seeking and creating values for its self-protection, through accumulation, which is ignorance, and meets life completely, utterly naked, free, then only is there the lasting discernment of that which is true.

Question: Is it possible to live without exploitation, individual and commercial?

KRISHNAMURTI: Most of us are carried away by the mere sensation of possession. We desire to acquire, and therefore we begin to accumulate more and more, thinking that through accumulation we shall find happiness, security. As long as there is accumulative and acquisitive desire, there must be exploitation; and we can be free from that exploitation only when we begin to awaken intelligence through the destruction of self-protective values. But if we try merely to discover what our needs are and limit ourselves to those needs, then our life will become small, shallow, and petty. Whereas, if we lived intelligently, without self-protective accumulations, then there would be no exploitation, with its many cruelties. To try to solve this problem by merely controlling man's economic conditions or by mere renunciation, seems to me a wrong approach to this complicated problem. It is only through the voluntary and intelligent understanding of the futility and ignorance of self-protectiveness, that there can come the freedom from exploitation.

To awaken intelligence is to discover, through doubt and questioning, the true significance of the values which we have acquired, of the traditions, whether religious, social, or economic, which we have inherited or have consciously built up. In such questioning, if it is real and vital, there is the intelligent discovery of needs. This intelligence is the assurance of happiness.

Question: Should we break our swords and turn them into plowshares, even though our country is attacked by an enemy? Is it not our moral duty to defend our country?

KRISHNAMURTI: To me war is fundamentally wrong, either defensive or aggressive. The system of acquisitiveness on which this whole civilization is based must naturally create class, racial, and national distinctions, leading inevitably to war, which you may call offensive or defensive according to the dictates of commercial leaders and politicians. As long as this exploiting economic system exists, there must be war; and the individual who is faced with the problem of whether he shall fight or not, will decide according to his acquisitiveness, which he sometimes calls patriotism, ideals, and so on. Or, understanding that this whole system must inevitably lead to war, he, as an individual, will begin to free himself intelligently from this system. And this alone is to me the true solution.

By our acquisitiveness we have built up through the many centuries this crushing system of exploitation which is destroying all our sensibilities, our love for one another. And when we ask, "Should we not fight for our country, is it not our moral duty?" there is something inherently wrong, something fundamentally cruel in the very question itself. To be free from this extreme stupidity— war—man has to relearn to think from the very beginning. As long as humanity is divided by religion, by sects, by creeds, by classes, by nationalities, there must be war, there must be exploitation, there must be suffering. It is only when the mind begins to free itself from these limitations, only when the mind pours itself into the heart, that there is true intelligence, which alone is the lasting solution to the barbaric cruelties of this civilization.

Question: How can we best help humanity to understand and live your teachings?

KRISHNAMURTI: It is very simple: by living them yourself. What is it that I am teaching? I am not giving you a new system, or a new set of beliefs; but I say, look to the cause that has created this exploitation, lack of love, fear, continual wars, hatred, class distinctions, division of man against man. The cause is, fundamentally, the desire on the part of each one to protect himself through acquisitiveness, through power. We all desire to help the world, but we never begin with ourselves. We want to reform the world, but the fundamental change must first take place within ourselves. So, begin to free the mind and heart from this sense of possessiveness. This demands, not mere renunciation, but discernment, intelligence.

Question: What is your attitude towards the problem of sex, which plays such a dominant part in our daily life?

KRISHNAMURTI: It has become a problem because there is no love. Isn't that so? When we really love, there is no problem, there is an adjustment, there is an understanding. It is only when we have lost the sense of true affection, that profound love in which there is no sense of possessiveness, that there arises the problem of sex. It is only when we have completely yielded ourselves to mere sensation, that there are many problems concerning sex. As the majority of people have lost the joy of creative thinking, naturally they turn to the mere sensation of sex, which becomes a problem, eating their minds and hearts away. As long as you do not begin to question and understand the significance of environment, of the many values which you have built up about you in self-protection and which are crushing out fundamental, creative thinking, naturally you must resort to many forms of stimulation. From this arise innumerable problems for which there is no solution except the fundamental and intelligent understanding of life itself.

Please experiment with what I am saying. Begin to find out the true significance of religion, of habit, of tradition, of this whole system of morality that is continually forcing, urging you in a particular direction; begin to question its whole significance without prejudice. Then you will awaken that creative thought which dissolves the many problems, born of ignorance.

Question: Do you believe in reincarnation? Is it a fact? Can you give us proofs from your personal experience?

KRISHNAMURTI: The idea of reincarnation is as old as the hills; the idea that man, through many rebirths, going through innumerable experiences, will come at last to perfection, to truth, to God. Now what is it that is reborn, what is it that continues? To me, that thing which is supposed to continue is nothing but a series of layers of memory, of certain qualities, certain incompleted actions which have been conditioned, hindered by fear born of self-protection. Now that incomplete consciousness is what we call the ego, the 'I'. As I explained at the beginning in my brief introductory talk, individuality is the accumulation of the results of various actions which have been impeded, hindered by certain inherited and acquired values, limitations. I hope I am not making it very complicated and philosophical, I will try to make it simple.

When you talk of the 'I', you mean by that a name, a form, certain ideas, certain prejudices, certain class distinctions, qualities, religious prejudices, and so on, which have been developed through the desire for self-protection, security, comfort. So, to me, the 'I', based on an illusion, has no reality. Therefore the question is not whether there is reincarnation, whether there is a possibility of future growth, but whether the mind and heart can free themselves from this limitation of the 'I', the 'mine'.

You ask me whether I believe in reincarnation or not because you hope that through my assurance you can postpone understanding and action in the present, and that you will eventually come to realize the ecstasy of life or immortality. You want to know whether, being forced to live in a conditioned environment with limited opportunities, you will through this misery and conflict ever come to realize that ecstasy of life, immortality. As it is getting late I have to put it briefly, and I hope you will think it over.

Now, I say there is immortality, to me it is a personal experience; but it can be realized only when the mind is not looking to a future in which it shall live more perfectly, more completely, more richly. Immortality is the infinite present. To understand the present with its full, rich significance, mind must free itself from the habit of self-protective acquisition; when it is utterly naked, then only is there immortality.

Question: In order that we may grasp truth, shall we work alone or collectively?

KRISHNAMURTI: If I may suggest, leave the question of truth aside; rather let us consider whether it is intelligent to work for individual gain or for the collective. For centuries each one has sought his own security, and so he has been ruthless, aggressive, exploiting, thus creating confusion and chaos. Considering all this, you, the individual, will voluntarily begin to work for the welfare of the whole. In this voluntary act, the individual will never become mechanical, automatic, a mere instrument in the hands of the group; therefore, there can never be a con-

flict between the group and the individual. The question of individual creative expression as opposed to and in conflict with the group will disappear only when each one acts integrally in the fullness of understanding. This alone will bring about intelligent cooperation in which compulsion, either through fear or greed, has no place. Do not wait to be driven to act collectively, but begin to awaken that intelligence, stripping away all acquisitive stupidities, and then there will be the joy of collective work.

April 17, 1935

Second Talk in São Paulo*

Friends,

Many questions have been put to me concerning the personal future of individuals and their hopes, whether they will succeed in certain business, whether they should leave this country and establish themselves in North America, who is the right person to marry, and so on. I cannot answer such questions as I am not a fortuneteller. I know these are questions which are real and disturbing, but they have to be solved by each one for himself.

I have chosen from among the innumerable questions that have been put to me, those that are representative; but I feel it would be futile and a waste of time for you and for me if what I am going to say, and have said, were accepted by you as some philosophical theory with which the mind can amuse itself. I have something vital to say which is applicable to life, something which, when understood, will help you to solve the many problems in your daily life.

I am not answering these questions from any particular point of view, for I feel that

*See footnote on page 127.

all problems should be dealt with, not separately, but as a whole. If we can do this, our thoughts and actions will become sane and balanced.

Please do not dismiss some of these questions as being bourgeois or as asked by the leisured class. They are human questions and should be considered as such, not as belonging to any particular class.

Question: How do you regard mediumship and communication with the spirits of the dead?

KRISHNAMURTI: You can laugh it off or take it seriously. In the first place, do not let us discuss whether the spirits exist or not, but let us consider the desire which prompts us to communicate with them, for that is the most important part in the question.

With the majority of people who go in for that kind of thing, in their communication with the dead there is the desire to be guided, to be told what to do, as they are in constant uncertainty with regard to their actions, and they hope that by communicating with those who are dead they shall find guidance, thus sparing themselves the trouble of thinking. So the desire is for guidance, for direction, in order that they may not make mistakes and suffer. It is the same attitude that some have with regard to the Masters, those beings who are considered more advanced, and so able to direct man through their messengers and so forth and so on.

The worship of authority is the denial of understanding. The desire not to suffer breeds exploitation. So this search for authority destroys fullness of action, and guidance brings about irresponsibility, for there is a strong desire to sail through life without conflict, without suffering. For this reason one has beliefs, ideals, systems, in the hope that struggle and suffering can be avoided. But these beliefs, ideals, which have become escapes, are the very cause of conflict, creating greater illusions, greater suffering. So long as the mind seeks comfort through guidance, through authority, the cause of suffering, ignorance, can never be dissolved.

Question: In order to attain truth, must one abstain from marriage and procreation?

KRISHNAMURTI: Now, truth is not an end, a finality that can be attained through certain actions. It is that understanding born of continual adjustment to life, which demands great intelligence; and because most people are not capable of this self-defenseless adjustment to the movement of life, they create certain theories and ideals which they hope will guide them. So man is held in the frame of traditions, prejudices, and binding moralities, dictated by fear and the desire for self-preservation. This has come about because he is unable to discern continuously the significance of life in constant movement, and so he has developed certain "musts" and "must nots." A complete and a rich living, by which I mean a most intelligent life, not a self-protective, defensive existence, demands that the mind shall be free of all taboos, fears, and superstitions, without "must" and "must not," and this can only be when the mind wholly understands the significance and the cause of fear.

For most people there is conflict, suffering, and a ceaseless adjustment in marriage; and for many the desire to attain truth is but an escape from this struggle.

Question: You deny religion, God, and immortality. How can humanity become more perfect, and so happier, without believing in these fundamental things?

KRISHNAMURTI: It is because with you it is only a belief in God, in immortality, it is because you merely believe in these things, that there is so much misery, suffering, and exploitation. You can discover whether there is truth, immortality, only in the completeness of action itself, not through any belief whatsoever, not through the authoritative assertion of another. Only in the fullness of action itself is reality revealed.

Now to most people, religion, God, and immortality are simply means of escape. Religion has merely helped man to escape from the conflict, the suffering of life, and therefore from understanding it. When you are in conflict with life, with its problems of sex, exploitation, jealousy, cruelty, and so on, as you do not fundamentally desire to understand them—for to understand them demands action, intelligent action—and as you are unwilling to make the effort, you unconsciously try to escape to those ideals, values, beliefs which have been handed down. So immortality, God, and religion have merely become shelters for a mind that is in conflict.

To me, both the believer and the non-believer in God and immortality are wrong, because the mind cannot comprehend reality until it is completely free of all illusions. Then only can you affirm, not believe or deny, the reality of God and immortality. When the mind is utterly free from the many hindrances and limitations created through self-protectiveness, when it is open, wholly naked, vulnerable in the understanding of the cause of self-created illusion, only then all beliefs disappear, yielding place to reality.

Question: Are you against the institution of the family?

KRISHNAMURTI: I am, if the family is the center of exploitation, if it is based on exploitation. (Applause) Please, what is the good of merely agreeing with me? You must act to alter this. The desire for perpetuation creates a family which becomes the center of exploitation. So the question is really: can one ever live without exploiting? Not whether family life is right or wrong, not whether having children is right or wrong, but whether family, possessions, power, are not the result of the desire for security, self-perpetuation. As long as there is this desire, family becomes the center of exploitation.

Can we ever live without exploitation? I say we can. There must be exploitation as long as there is the struggle for self-protection; as long as the mind is seeking security, comfort, through family, religion, authority or tradition, there must be exploitation. And exploitation ceases only when the mind discerns the falseness of security and is no longer ensnared by its own power of creating illusions. If you will experiment with what I say, you will then understand that I am not destroying desire, but that you can live in this world, richly, sanely, a life without limitations, without suffering. You can discover this only by experimenting, not by denying, not through resignation nor by merely imitating. Where intelligence is functioning—and intelligence ceases to function when there is fear and the desire for security—there can be no exploitation.

Most people are waiting for a change to take place that will miraculously alter this system of exploitation. They are waiting for revolutions to realize their hopes, their unfulfilled longings; but in so waiting they are slowly dying. For I think that mere revolutions do not change the fundamental desires of man. But if the individual begins to act with intelligence, without compulsion, irrespective of present conditions or of what revolutions promise in the future, then there is a richness, a completeness whose ecstasy cannot be destroyed.

April 24, 1935

Third Talk in Rio de Janeiro

Friends,

Throughout the ages and in the present civilization also, one sees how the clever individual exploits the group, and the group in its turn exploits the individual. There is this constant interaction between the individual and the group as society, religions, the ideas of leaders and of dictators. There is also the exploitation of women by men in certain countries, and in others, women exploit men. There is a subtle or a gross form of exploitation taking place where there is vested interest, whether in private property or in religion or in politics.

It is always difficult to penetrate through to the real significance beyond the words, and not be misled by them. By fully understanding the present significance of morality, we shall discover for ourselves the new morality and its details in action. Most people, after hearing me, say that I have only given them vague ideas which are not at all practical. But I am not here to give you a new set of rules or a new mode of action, which would be but another form of exploitation, another cage to imprison you. You would merely be leaving an old prison for a new one, which would be utterly futile. Whereas, if you begin to examine and discover the basis of the present code of conduct, of the whole structure of morality, then in the very process of discovery of the true cause of what we call morality, you will begin to discern the manner of true individual action, which will then be moral. This action of intelligence, freed from enticement or compulsion, is true morality.

Our present-day morality is based on the protection of the individual; it is a closed system which acts as a covering to hold the individual within the group. The individual is treated like some vicious animal that must be kept in the cage of morality. We have become slaves to a group-morality which each of us has helped to build up out of his own individual desire for security and comfort. Each one of us has contributed to this system of morality, which is based on acquisition and cunning self-protection. In the closed system of this so-called morality, we have created static religions with their static gods, dead images, petrified thoughts. This closed prison of morality has become so powerful, so compulsive, that most individuals live in fear of breaking away from it, and merely imitate the rules and conduct of the prison.

Now, through this closed morality we cannot find truth, nor through mere escape from it. If we merely escape from this morality by the destruction of the old code without understanding, we shall but create another form of self-protection, another prison. As long as the mind is seeking safety, searching out ways and means of assuring its own security, it must inevitably create laws and systems for its own protection. This search for self-protection denies the understanding of reality. Reality can be discerned only when the mind is utterly naked, wholly denuded of this idea of self-protection.

So you have to become intensely aware of the cause of this prison, of this continual building up of securities, comforts, and escapes, in which the mind is engaged. When you are fully aware of the cause, then the mind itself begins to discern the true manner of acting in the very moment of experience, and so morality becomes purely individual. It cannot be made a means of exploitation. Knowing the cause and being continually aware of it, the mind itself begins to break through the covering of this self-protective morality, which has become so crushing, so destructive of intelligence. In that awareness, which is the awakening of intelligence, the mind breaks through to the flow of reality, which cannot become a static religion, a means of exploitation, nor can it be petrified in a prayer book of the priests.

Question: Would mere economic and social revolution solve all human problems, or must this be preceded by an inner, spiritual revolution?

KRISHNAMURTI: Revolution may come, and instead of a capitalistic system, suppose you establish a communistic form of government; but do you think that mere external revolution will solve the many human problems? Under the present system you are forced to adjust yourself to a certain method of thought, of morality, of earning money. If a different system is established through revolution, there will be another form of compulsion, perhaps for the better; but how can mere compulsion ever bring about understanding? Are you satisfied to continue living unintelligently in the present system, hoping and waiting for some miraculous external change to take place which will also alter your mind and heart? Surely there is only one way, which is to see that this present system is based on selfish exploitation in which each individual is ruthlessly seeking his own security, and so fighting to preserve his own distinctions and acquisitions. Understanding this, the intelligent man will not wait for a revolution to come but will begin to alter fundamentally his action, his morality, and will begin to free his mind and heart of all acquisitiveness. Such a man is free of the burden of any system, and so can live intelligently in the present. If you really desire to find out the true way of action, try to live in the present, with the comprehension of the inevitable.

Question: I belong to no religion, but I am a member of two societies which give me knowledge and spiritual wisdom. If I give these up, how can I ever reach perfection?

KRISHNAMURTI: If you understand the futility of all organized religious bodies, with their vested interests, with their exploitation, the utter stupidity of their beliefs based on authority, superstition, and fear, if you truly grasp the significance of this, then you will not belong to any religious sect or society. Do you think that any society or any book can give you wisdom? Books and societies can give you information; but if you say that a society can give you wisdom, then you merely rely on it, and it becomes your exploiter. If wisdom could be acquired through a religious society or sect, we should all be wise, for we have had religions with us for thousands of years. But wisdom is not to be acquired in that manner. Wisdom is the understanding of the continual flow of life or reality, which is to be discerned only when the mind is open and vulnerable, that is, when the mind is no longer hindered through its own self-protective desires, reactions, and illusions. No society, no religion, no priest, no leader is ever going to give you wisdom. It is only through our own suffering, from which we try to escape by joining religious bodies and by immersing ourselves in philosophical theories, it is only through being aware of the cause of suffering and in freedom from it that wisdom is born naturally and sweetly.

Question: I desire many things from life which I do not have. Can you tell me how to get them?

KRISHNAMURTI: Why do you want many things? We all must have clothes, food, shelter. But what is behind the desire for many things? We want things because we think that through possessions we shall be happy, that through acquisition we shall obtain power. Behind this question lies the desire for power. In the pursuit of power there is suffering, and through suffering, there is the awakening of intelligence which reveals the utter futility of power. Then there is the understanding of needs. You may not want many physical things; perhaps you may see the absurdity of many possessions, but you may want spiritual power. Between this and the desire for many things there is no difference. They are alike; the one you call materialistic, and to the other you give a more refined name, spiritual. But in essence they are only ways of seeking your own security, and in that there can never be happiness or intelligence.

Question: You seem to deny the value of discipline and moral standards. Will not life be a chaos without discipline and morality?

KRISHNAMURTI: As I said at the beginning of my talk this evening, we have turned morality and discipline into a shelter for our own protection, without any deep significance, without any reality. Are there not wars, ruthless exploitation, utter chaos in the world, in spite of your disciplines, your religions, your rigid frames of morality? So let us look into this structure of morality and discipline that we have built up and which has exploited us, which is destroying human intelligence. In the very examination of this closed structure of morality and discipline, with great care and without prejudice, you will begin to understand and develop that true morality which cannot be systematized, petrified.

The morality, the discipline that you have now is based on the individual's search for his own safety, security, through religion and economic exploitation. You may talk about love and brotherhood on Sundays, but on Mondays you exploit others in your various occupations. Religion, morality, discipline,

merely act as a cover for hypocrisy. Such a morality, from my point of view, is immoral. As you ruthlessly seek economic security, out of which is born a morality suited for that purpose, so you have created religions all over the world which promise you immortality through their closed and peculiar disciplines and moralities. As long as this closed morality exists, there must be wars and exploitation, there cannot be the real love of man. This morality, this discipline, is really based on egotism and the ruthless search for individual security. When the mind frees itself from this center of limited consciousness which is based on self-aggrandizement, then there comes the exquisite and delicate adjustment to life which does not demand rules and regulations, but which is consummately intelligent, expressing itself in the integrated action of true discernment.

Question: I do not care what happens after death, but I am afraid of dying. Must I fight this fear, and how can I overcome it?

KRISHNAMURTI: By living in the present. Eternity is not in the future, it is ever in the present. There is no remedy or substitution for fear, except the understanding of the cause of fear itself. The mind is being continually limited by the memories of the past, and these memories are hindering the fulfillment of action in the present. So there is no completeness of action in the present, which creates fear of death.

This is not an intellectual feat, living in the present. It demands understanding of action and freeing the mind from illusion. The mind has the power to create illusion, and with that we are mostly occupied— creating illusions, escapes, covering over things we do not want to understand. The mind is creating illusions as a means of escape, and these illusions, with their power, prevent the completeness of action and the full comprehension of the present. Thus the old illusions are creating new and further hindrances, limitations. That is why we begin to think in terms of time as a means of understanding, growing. Understanding is ever in the present, not in the future. And the mind refuses to discern immediately because this involves an intelligent revolt against all that it has built up in its search for its own security.

Question: I allow my imagination to wander fearlessly. Is this right?

KRISHNAMURTI: Actually you may be afraid of many things. This imaginative flight is another escape from the problems of life. If it is an escape, it is utterly wasteful of mental energy. That energy can become creative and effective only when it has liberated itself from fears and illusions which traditions and self-protective desires have imposed upon it.

Question: Are you preaching individualism?

KRISHNAMURTI: I am afraid the questioner has not quite understood what I have said. I am not advocating individualism at all. Unfortunately, the vast majority have hardly an opportunity for individual expression. They may think they are acting voluntarily, freely; but sadly they are merely machines, functioning in a particular groove under the compulsion of circumstances and environment. So how can there be individual fulfillment, which is the highest form of intelligence? What we call individual expression, in the case of the vast majority of people, is nothing but a reaction in which there is very little intelligence.

But there is a different kind of individuality, that of uniqueness, which is the result of voluntary and comprehending ac-

tion. That is, if one understands environment and acts with discerning intelligence, then there is true individuality. This uniqueness is not separative, for it is intelligence itself.

Intelligence is alone, unique. But if you merely act through the compulsion of circumstances, then, though you may think you are an individual, your actions are but reaction in which there is no true intelligence. Because the present individual is merely a reaction in which there can be no intelligence, there is chaos in the world, each individual seeking his own security and thoughtless fulfillment.

Intelligence is unique; it cannot be divided as yours and mine. It is only the absence of intelligence that can be separated into units as yours and mine, and this is the ugliness of distinction out of which is born exploitation, cruelty, and sorrow.

May 4, 1935

Fourth Talk in Rio de Janeiro

Friends,

Each one is trying to find happiness, truth, or God, giving to the object of his search a different name according to his intellectual capacities, religious upbringing, and environment. You have come here hoping to discover a certainty around which you can build your whole life and action.

Now why are you seeking the ultimate certainty, that reality which you hope will give you happiness, explain the cruelty and the suffering of man? What is the cause of your search? Fundamentally, the reason for this search—the human reason, not some intellectual reason—is that, as there is so much suffering in you and about you, you want to escape from the present to some idealistic utopia of the future, to an intellectual system of thought, or to an authority of faith and assurance. A man who is profoundly in love is not in search of love or happiness; but the man who is not in love, who is not happy, who is suffering, seeks the opposite of that in which he is caught. Finding yourself in misery, in great emptiness, despair, you begin to seek a way out, an escape. This escape is called the search for reality, truth, or by whatever name you like to give to it.

Most people who say they are seeking happiness, are really trying to escape, trying to run away from the conflict, the misery, the nothingness in which they are caught. Being uncertain of love, of thought, one's whole search is directed towards certainties and satisfactions; for love and thought are constantly seeking certainties to which they can anchor themselves. These are called realities, happiness and inquiries after immortality. You want to be assured that there is something enduring, something more than this confusion and misery.

If you really consider—and please don't merely listen intellectually to what I am saying—if you really consider your own search and examine it, then you will see that you are trying to escape from this confusion and misery to what you imagine to be a reality, a happiness. You want a drug, a dope which will satisfy you, which will put you peacefully to sleep. The only actuality, the only reality that we can fully comprehend, is this confusion, this misery, this conflict; and to escape from this is but to create illusion. If you escape from actuality, you can only go to illusions, to hopes, to longings, which have no reality. So the way out of actuality must inevitably lead to illusion, though this illusion may have assumed a reality through time and tradition.

Now please don't say, "Is there nothing beyond confusion, nothing beyond misery?" I want to explain how our minds act, what our reactions are; and in properly and thoroughly understanding this, we can then proceed with care to something which can be understood only through actuality, not through illusions. Please let me repeat that the search for happiness, truth, or reality is born out of the desire to escape from the prison of suffering, and is therefore fundamentally false; and unless you discern this clearly, understand it fully, what I say further on in my talk will not be completely understood. So I will go into it thoroughly.

When we suffer through the loss of someone we love, or there is in our lives the emptiness of unfulfillment or the despair of utter uncertainty, we begin to create the opposite and pursue that image, hoping that it will lead us to peace, fulfillment, completeness. So we are drawn, consciously or unconsciously, subtly or grossly, further and further away from actuality, from the suffering of the present.

Suppose that you have lost someone by death. You suffer and you begin to ask about the hereafter, whether it is a fact or not. Then you begin to investigate the theory of reincarnation. What is it that you are really doing? You are trying to get away from suffering. So explanations and so-called facts merely act as drugs to dull the acuteness of suffering. Where there is the desire to escape there must be the creation of illusion. As we do suffer constantly, we have created innumerable illusions, and our present search for reality is nothing but the search for a greater and more magnificent illusion.

If you understand this completely, then you will perceive the utter futility of the search for happiness, for certainty, for truth, or whatever you may call it. You will no longer be concerned with the measuring of the immeasurable. Once and for all, the mind must rid itself of this desire to escape, and only then is it prepared to discover the fundamental cause of suffering; for suffering is the main reality with which each one of us is acquainted.

Now to understand fundamentally the cause of suffering, the mind must be free from ideals, because ideals are nothing but forms of escape from actuality. When the mind becomes aware of itself, it will perceive that it is merely imitating patterns, following objectives, beliefs, ideals, which it has established for itself as a means of running away from confusion. Mind thus superimposes those beliefs and ideals on confusion and suffering. In other words, ideals are merely illusions which give you hope and encouragement to avoid the present. In case you don't completely understand this, I will take an example.

There is the ideal of brotherhood and of brotherly love. Now what is happening in actuality? There are wars, nationalities, divisions of classes, of man against man, exploitations, the grouping of men into religions which separate them by dogmas. In actuality, that is what is happening. So what is the good of your ideal? You will say, "We are going to work up to that ideal eventually." But of what value is that in the present? Why do you want ideals when you know definitely that there cannot be brotherhood so long as there are the distinctions created by religion, acquisitiveness, and exploitation in which you are living? Your ideals are only sentimental soporifics for people who do not want to act in the present. Whereas, if you had no ideals at all, but saw the actuality of confusion and cruelty, without being blinded by hopes that have become ideals, then in solving these problems there would naturally be brotherhood, there would be true unity between all men. So ideals really give you the opportunity not to face the present corruption and exploitation, in which you are taking part.

Most minds are pursuing the authority of beliefs and ideals, because they do not want to comprehend the present; and that is one of the main reasons why they never find out

and therefore dissipate for themselves the cause of suffering.

Now we have built up through many centuries an environment of such illusions as authority, imitativeness, beliefs, ideals, which give us the opportunity of subtle escape. People suffer within that prison of limitation and they try to find solutions for their suffering within it, within the illusions they have built around themselves. But there are others who truly discern the illusory nature of this structure, and because they suffer much more intensely and intelligently and are not willing to escape into the future, in that very acuteness of suffering they discover the true freedom from suffering itself.

So you have to ask yourself whether you are seeking a solution for your suffering within the circle of illusion, within the environment of centuries, and thus creating further illusions and entrenching yourself more within that prison; or whether you are seeking to break through the many illusions that you have built about yourself through the centuries. For in the process of discernment, the cause of suffering is known and dissolved. It is only then, and not until then, that the mind is able to discern truth. The very search for reality is an illusion, because it is but an escape. When all escapes and illusions have been cleared away by understanding, then only can the mind perceive that which is enduring, the immeasurable.

Question: What do you think of charity and social philanthropy?

KRISHNAMURTI: Social philanthropy is giving back to the victim a little of what the philanthropist has ruthlessly got out of him. You first exploit him, make him work innumerable hours and all the rest of it, and amass a great deal of wealth by cunning, cheating, and then turn around magnanimously and give a little to the poor victim.

(Laughter) I don't know why you are laughing, because you are doing the same thing, only differently. You may not be cunning, clever, ruthless enough to amass wealth and become a philanthropist; but you are spiritually, idealistically amassing what you call knowledge, in order to protect yourself.

Charity is unconscious of itself; there is no accumulation first and then distribution. It is like the flower, natural, open, spontaneous.

Question: Should the Ten Commandments be destroyed?

KRISHNAMURTI: Aren't they already destroyed? Do they exist now? Perhaps in the prayer book, petrified, to be worshipped as ideals, but in actuality they do not exist. For many centuries man has been guided through fear, forced, compelled to act according to certain standards; but the highest form of morality is to do a thing for its own sake, not for a motive or for a reward. Now, instead of being coerced to follow a pattern, we have to find out individually what is true morality. This is one of the most difficult things to do, to find out for oneself how to act truly; it demands intelligence, a continual adjustment, not the following of a law or a system, but an intense awareness, discernment in the moment of action itself. And this can be only when the mind is liberating itself, with understanding, from fear and compulsions.

Question: Is there God?

KRISHNAMURTI: I wonder what value it would have if I said yes or no. To deny or assert would not reveal the reality. One has to discover for oneself. Therefore you cannot accept or deny. If I said yes, what would happen? It would be another belief to be added to your museum of beliefs. If I said no, that also would belong to a museum, of another type. One way or the other, it is of no importance to you. If I said yes, I would become an authority, and you might perhaps mold your life on that pattern; if I said no, that would also lay down a pattern. You cannot approach this problem, whether there is God or not, with any prejudice either for or against. What you can do is, prepare the soil of the mind and see what happens. That is, let the mind free itself from all illusions, from all fears, prejudices, and longings, and be without any expectation whatsoever; then such a mind can discern whether there be God or not. One has a speculative mind, and for intellectual amusement one tries to solve this question; but such a mind cannot find a true answer. All that you can do is to break through the falseness, the illusions that you have created about yourselves. And this demands, not an inquiry into the existence of God, but the action of completeness, of your whole being, in the present.

Question: Are not priests necessary to lead the ignorant to righteousness?

KRISHNAMURTI: Certainly not. But who are the ignorant? This question can be put only to each one of you and not to a vague mass called the ignorant. The mass is you. Do you need priests? Who is to say who are the ignorant? No one. So being ignorant, do you need a priest, and can a priest ever lead you out of that ignorance to righteousness? If you merely consider that an ignorant man, vaguely existing somewhere whom you don't know, needs a priest, then you perpetuate exploitation and all the tricks of religion. No one can lead you to righteousness except you yourself, through your own understanding, through your own suffering.

Question: Is it possible to reach perfection among the imperfect?

KRISHNAMURTI: Where else can you realize perfection, where else can you understand perfection, except among the imperfect? But this whole idea of gaining perfection is so fundamentally wrong. Please, you have to think about this carefully. When you talk of perfection, you mean gaining an end, a certainty, a power which can give you security, from which there can never arise conflict, sorrow. Perfection is not an end, an absolute, fixed point, but a continual becoming. When the mind is free from the opposites, then there is a continual movement, a continual flow of reality. Perfection is the action, the continual flow of reality, not an absolute objective to which you are progressing through innumerable experiences, memories, lessons, suffering. To understand this flow of life, mind must be free entirely from finalities, from certainties, which are but the outcome of the desire for self-protection.

If you consider what I have been saying this evening, you will discern the enclosure which we have created through the many centuries, in which we have become prisoners, thus destroying our creative intelligence. If the mind can begin to break down the walls of that prison, through comprehension, then there is action without sorrow, normal and true.

Question: Is not egotism the root of religious and economic exploitation?

KRISHNAMURTI: Sir, that is obvious. It is egotism that has created the cages of religion; it is egotism that creates the exploitation of people. The questioner knows this, but what does he do about it? We know that there is ruthless exploitation by the clever and the cunning, that there is poverty amidst plenty. But has the questioner asked himself whether he is not also taking part in this cruel and stupid acquisitive battle? If he really felt the appalling cruelty of all this and

acted intelligently, he would be as a flame, consuming the stupidities around him.

May 10, 1935

Fifth Talk in Rio de Janeiro

Friends,

I have been told that what I say is too complicated, too impracticable, and impossible for daily life in which each one has to fight for his own living. Some reject without thought what I say, and others, equally thoughtlessly, accept it without further examination, hoping that it will fit into their already existing system. So the renewing power of action is denied.

Now we are concerned with living, and living implies, not only bread, shelter, clothes, and work, but also love and thought. We cannot understand the full significance of living if we deal separately and singly with the problem of work, of love, or of thought. As they are interrelated and inseparable, they must be understood comprehensively, as a whole. It is only the people who are comfortably settled in life, who are following the traditional pattern or system, that try to separate work from living, and they hope to overcome the conflict which arises from this division by considering each problem exclusively.

There are many so-called spiritual people who consider work, occupation, as something materialistic and merely to be tolerated. They are concerned only with truth and God. And there are others who concern themselves solely with reorganizing society for the welfare of the whole. If we want to understand action, which is living, we have to take it as a whole, not divide it into watertight compartments, as most people do. Living is the harmonious action of thought, emotion, and work; and when these are in contradiction with each other, then there is suffering, conflict, disharmony. We are seeking—aren't we?—to live harmoniously, to live completely in our actions, to fulfill. To do so there must be the highest intelligence, which is to be without fear, exploitation, without seeking reward. From this there arises the renewing freedom of action. Each one is fundamentally seeking, trying to live in this action; but in seeking to discover that harmonious movement of living, he is very often led astray by some unimportant question, such as what system he should follow, whether there are Masters, whether there is truth, God.

Why don't we live this intelligent, harmonious action? If we accomplish this, then life becomes simple, supremely purposeful and creative. So why don't we who are seeking this harmonious living—at least there are many who constantly assert that they are seeking—realize it? One of the main reasons is that we consider the many problems of life separately and exclusively, as I have tried to explain. From this division there arises false thinking, which creates exploitation in work and the complications and confusion which inhibit love. These can be understood and solved only by right thinking.

To find out what right thinking is, let us discover first what is false in our thought. If we can know for ourselves that which is false in our thinking, then we shall know naturally, without imposition, what is the true. Through the mass of false ideas, through the screen of many illusions, there cannot be the perception of the true. So we have to concern ourselves with trying to discover what is false.

Now, our thought is based on habit, the habit of centuries to which it has become accustomed. It is following a pattern, a system; it is shaping itself after an ideal which it has established as a means of escape from the present conflict. As long as thought is following a system, a habit, or merely conforming to an established tradition, an ideal, there

must be false thinking. You follow a system or mold yourself after a pattern because there is fear, the fear of right and wrong which has been established according to the tradition of a system. If thought is merely functioning in the groove of a pattern without understanding the significance of environment, there must be conscious or unconscious fear, and such thought must inevitably lead to confusion, to illusion and false action.

The traditional habit of thought with regard to work is the pursuit of individual economic security, safety, and comfort. So we have developed a system throughout the world in which exploitation has become righteous and acquisitiveness is honored. Out of this there naturally arises the conflict of classes, nationalism and wars.

The very foundation of our love is possessiveness, out of which arise jealousy and the complexities and problems of sex. Now, to try to solve any one of these problems exclusively, not as a part of the whole, is to create and perpetuate conflict and suffering, from which arise further illusions and false thinking.

So long as thought is seeking and following a pattern, conforming to an environment which it has not understood and merely acting from habit, there must be conflict and disharmony. So the first thing, if you really want to understand the beauty of living and its richness, is to become aware of the environment, both of the past and of the present, to which the mind has become attached; and in understanding the illusions which it has created for its own protection, there comes naturally, without the mind having to search after it, that spontaneous, intelligent action which is the highest consummation of life.

All this applies to those who desire to understand and to live supremely, but not to those who merely seek comfort, nor to those who are satisfied with explanations, for explanations are so much dust in the eyes. So if you would find such a life, there must be the purification of the mind through doubt, and that means the deep understanding of traditions and ideals, the dissipation of the many illusions which the mind has created in the search for its own protection. Thus when there is true discernment there is the ecstasy of the immeasurable, which cannot be imagined or preconceived, but only experienced.

Question: Can we not be guided in our daily life by the wise advice given to us by the voices and spirits of the dead?

KRISHNAMURTI: Some of you, I see, are impatient with this question; you may think that it is stupid to seek advice from the spirits. To make this question applicable to others as well, let us simplify it. Some of you may not go to séances, may not indulge in automatic writing, but you do not mind seeking Masters, who perhaps may live in a far-off country, and accepting their messages through their messengers. Fundamentally, what is the difference? None whatever. Both are seeking guidance from others. Some try to get into touch with those who are dead, through mediums, automatic writing, and other childish means; and there are others who seek guidance from those whom they call Masters, through their representatives, which is equally childish. So please do not condemn those who go to mediums and attend séances, when you yourselves diligently seek messages and systems given by those whom you call the representatives of Masters. There are others who depend upon priests and ceremonies, traditions and conventionalities for their guidance. They are all in the same category.

Now behind this question, whether one should seek advice and guidance from spirits, from Masters through their representatives, from saviors through their priests, is the desire to take shelter under the cover of authority. We are not concerned, for the moment, with the question of whether the Masters and the so-called spirits exist or not. Why do you search out guidance and advice, why do you desire direction? That is the problem. You give far greater value to the dead, to the hidden, to the past, than to the living and the present, because out of the dead, the hidden, and the past, your mind can carve its own pleasant images, and live with these illusions completely satisfied; but the present and the living will not let you sleep with contentment. So to escape from this conflict, which is but to evade the present, you seek guidance, advice. A man who seeks guidance, a man who is creating idols to worship, will live in fear; he will be exploited and his intelligence slowly destroyed, as is being done all over the world. The desire to seek guidance from spirits and Masters through their representatives arises from the fear of sorrow.

Can anyone, no matter who, save you from sorrow? If you can be saved by another, then the problem of authority ceases. You have merely to search out the most convenient and suitable authority and worship it. But I say no one can save you from sorrow except you yourself, through your own understanding. It is only your own discernment of the cause of suffering, not the explanations of another, that can open the doors to the greatest bliss, to the ecstasy of understanding. So long as you are seeking advice and guidance, which are but a means of escape from conflict, so long as you do not discern for yourself the cause of suffering but merely get confused by explanations, none can save you from sorrow—no priest, no book, no theory, no system, no spirit, no Master. Because that reality, that freedom from sorrow is in yourself, and through yourself alone can you go to it.

Question: Have the teachings attributed to the great teachers—Christ, Buddha, Hermes, and others—any value for the attainment of the direct path to truth?

KRISHNAMURTI: If you will not misunderstand, I would say that their teachings become valueless because the human mind, being so subtle, so cunning in its desire for self-protection, twists the teachings to suit its own purposes and creates systems and ideals as a means of escape, out of which grow petrified churches and exploiting priests. Religions throughout the world, through their systems and the trickery of their organized exploitation, seek to teach man to love, to think, to live sanely, intelligently; but how can a system create love or teach you to think selflessly? As you do not want to do this, as you are unwilling to live completely, integrally, with vulnerable mind and heart, you have created a system which has become your master, a system that is contrary to and destructive of thought and love. So it is utterly useless to multiply systems. If the mind frees itself from the illusion of its own self-protective demands and cravings, then there will be love, intelligence; then there will not be this division created by religions and beliefs; man will not be against man.

Question: If it is a fact that your future as a World Teacher was foretold, then is not predestination a fact in nature, and are we not therefore merely slaves of our appointed destiny?

KRISHNAMURTI: If your action is conditioned by the past, by fear or by environment, and is thus made incomplete, there must be tomorrow to complete that action. That is, if your thought is limited, hindered by tradition, by class consciousness or by fear, or by religious prejudice, then it cannot complete itself in action; therefore it creates its own destiny, its own limitation. That is, your own incomplete action brings forth its own limited future. Where there is incomplete action there is suffering, which creates its own bondage. True action is choiceless, but if action is hindered by the prejudice of choice, then all further actions must inevitably create greater and narrower limitations. So, instead of merely inquiring whether there is predestination or not, begin to act completely. In perceiving the necessity for complete action, you will discern in action itself the prejudices of centuries which begin to impede that action, curtailing its fulfillment. When there is the flow of action which is intelligence, then life is a continual becoming without the conflict of choice.

Question: What is human will power?

KRISHNAMURTI: It is nothing but a reaction against resistance. The mind has created, through its desire for self-protection and comfort, many hindrances and barriers, thus bringing about its own incompleteness, its own sorrow. To free itself from this sorrow, the mind begins to battle against these self-created resistances and limitations. In this conflict there is born and developed will, with which the mind identifies itself, thus giving birth to the 'I' consciousness. If these barriers did not exist, there would be continual fulfillment in action, not an overcoming of a conflict. You are trying to kill out, to conquer these self-imposed limitations, which only give birth to resistance which we call will. But if we understood why these barriers were created, then there would not be an overcoming, a conquering, which but creates further resistance. These barriers, these hindrances have come into being through the desire for self-protection, and hence there is a conflict between the movement of eternal life and that desire. From this conflict arise sorrow and the many carefully cultivated escapes. Where there is escape there must be illusion, there must be the erection of barriers.

Will is but another of the illusions which have been created in search of self-protection; and it is only when the mind liberates itself from its own center of illusions and is creatively empty that there is discernment of that which is true. Discernment is not the result of will, as will springs from resistance. Will is the outcome of the conflict of choice, but discernment is choiceless.

Question: What is action?

KRISHNAMURTI: Action is that unimpeded movement of intelligence, unhindered by fear, by compulsion, by the conflict of self-protective choice. Such pure action is the very expression of life itself. Now, this is not a philosophical answer to be treated merely as a theory, impracticable in daily life. We are concerned with action every moment of the day, and we shall know the ecstasy of this unimpeded action when the mind is renewing itself through fulfillment. We shall understand the full significance of action when thought is free and unhindered. That is, when you have pierced through the false illusions, false values, which you have created, which have become your environment, your burden, then there is the flow of reality, of life, which is action itself. You have individually to begin to discern the significance of acquisitiveness upon which our whole structure of thought and action is based. In disentangling yourself from it, there arises suffering only when there is no comprehension, only when there is compulsion. But to realize the ecstasy of this unimpeded action, thought must free itself from the molds of ideals, awakening that unique uncertainty, the uncertainty of nonaccumulation. When the mind is capable of discernment without the

conflict of choice, then there is the ecstasy of action.

May 18, 1935

Talk in Niteroi

Friends,

Most people throughout the world, it does not matter where they are, are discontented, disturbed by the existing conditions, and they are trying to find a lasting way out of this misery and chaos. Each expert offers his own particular form of solution, and, as it generally happens, he contradicts the other experts. So each specialist forms a group around his theory, and soon the purpose of helping humanity is forgotten, while discussions and wrangles take place between various parties and experts.

Not being an expert, I am not putting forward a new system or a new theory for the solution of the many problems; but what I should like to do is to awaken individual intelligence, so that each one, instead of becoming a slave to a system or to an expert, begins to act intelligently, for out of that alone can come a cooperative and constructive action. If each one of us is able under all circumstances to discern for himself what is true action, then there will not be exploitation, then each one will fulfill truly and live a harmonious and complete life.

Naturally, what I say will apply to those people who are discontented, who are in revolt, who are trying to find an intelligent way of action. This applies to those who are in sorrow and desire to free themselves from all exploitation.

Everyone is concerned with that awakening, through conflict and struggle between himself and the group, between himself and another individual. There is established authority, whether ancient or modern, which is continually urging, twisting the individual to function in one particular way. We have a whole system of thought, cultivated through the ages, to which each one of us has contributed, in whose ruthless movement each one, consciously or unconsciously, is caught up. So there is a collective and an individual consciousness, sometimes running parallel, often diametrically opposed. This opposition is the awakening of sorrow.

Our conflict, dissatisfaction, and struggle is between that which is the established authority, and the individual; between that which is centuries old tradition, and the eager desire on the part of the individual not to be suffocated by tradition, by authority, but to fulfill; for in fulfillment alone is there creative happiness.

In the world of action, which we call the material world, the economic world, the world of sociology, there is a system which prevents the true fulfillment of the individual. Even though each one thinks that he is acting individually in this present system, if you really examine it, you will see that he is but acting as a slave, as an automaton of the established order. That system has within it class distinction, based on acquisitive exploitation, leading to nationalism and wars; it has placed the means of accumulating wealth in the hands of the few. If the individual is at all able to express, to fulfill, he will be in constant revolt against this system; because, if you examine it, you will see that it is fundamentally unintelligent, cruel.

If the individual wants to understand this external system, he must first become aware of the prison in which he is held, the prison which he has created through his own aggressive acquisitiveness, and begin to break it down through his own individual suffering and intelligence.

Then there is an inner system, equally cruel and exploiting, which we call religion. I mean by religion the organized system of thought which holds the individual in the groove of a particular pattern. After all, Christianity, Hinduism, Buddhism, are so many sets of beliefs, ideas, precepts, which have become seasoned in fear and tradition, which force the individual through faith and illusory hope to think and to act along one particular line, blindly and unintelligently, with the help of exploiting priests. Each religion throughout the world, with its vested interests, with its beliefs, dogmas, and traditions, is separating man from man, as nationalism and classes are doing. It is utterly futile to hope that there will be one religion throughout the world, either Hinduism, or Buddhism, or Christianity, although it is the dream of the missionaries. But we can approach this whole idea of religion from a totally different point of view.

Please listen patiently and without prejudice to what I have to say, because religion, like politics, is a very touchy subject. If a person is religious, he usually becomes so dogmatic, so violent when one begins to question the whole structure of religion, that he is incapable of thinking clearly and straightly. So I would beg those of you who are listening to me, perhaps for the first time, to listen without any antagonism and with a desire to find out the significance of what I am saying.

If we can understand life and live here in this world with love, supremely and intelligently in the present, then religion becomes vain and useless. Because we have been constantly told by exploiters that we cannot do this ourselves, we have come to believe that we must have a system to follow. So without being helped to free himself, man is encouraged to follow a system and is held, through fear, a prisoner to authority which he hopes will guide him through the various conflicts and perplexities of life.

To get rid of the idea of religion merely, without deep understanding, will naturally lead to superficial activities, reaction and thought. If we are really able to live with profound intelligence, then we shall not create an escape from our miseries and struggles; which is what religion has become. That is, because we find life so difficult, with so many problems and apparently unending miseries, we want an escape; and religions offer a very convenient method of escape. Every Sunday people go to church to pray and to practice brotherly love, but the rest of the week they are engaged in ruthless exploitation and cruelty, each one seeking his own security. So people are living a hypocritical life: Sunday for God, and the rest of the week for self-security. Thus we use religion as a convenient escape to which we resort in moments of difficulty and misery.

So, through this system which is called religion, with its beliefs and ideals, you have found an authorized escape from the incessant battle of the present. After all, ideals, which religions and religious bodies offer, are nothing but escapes from the present.

Now why do we want ideals? It is because, as we cannot understand the present, the everyday existence with its cruelties, sorrows and ugliness, we want to steer ourselves across this life by some ideal. Hence ideals themselves become, fundamentally, an escape from the present. Our mind is caught up in creating many escapes from the present which alone is the eternal. Being imprisoned in those, mind must naturally be in constant battle with the present. So, instead of seeking new methods, new prisons, we ought to understand for ourselves how the mind is creating for itself these avenues of escape. Hence the question is: Are you satisfied to live in this prison of illusion, in this prison of make-believe with its stupidities and suffering? Or are you as individuals dissatisfied, in revolt? Are you willing to disentangle yourselves from this system, thus discovering

for yourselves what is true? If you are merely satisfied to remain in the prison, then the only thing that will awaken you is sorrow; but when that sorrow comes, you seek an escape from it, and so you create yet another prison. So you go on from one suffering to another, only to enter into greater bondage. But if you realize the utter futility of escape of any kind, either of ideals or beliefs, then you will, with intense awareness, perceive the true significance of beliefs, traditions and ideals. In understanding their deep significance, the mind, free from all illusion, is able to discern truth, the everlasting.

So instead of merely seeking new systems, new methods to replace the present mode of thought, of exploitation, of subtle escapes, take the actuality as it is, with all its exploitations, cruelties, bestialities, and understand the whole significance of this system; and this can be done only when there is great suffering. Out of this intense questioning and inquiry you will realize for yourself that consummation of all human existence, which is intelligence. Without that realization life becomes shallow, empty, and suffering merely a constant recurrence without an end.

So if those who are suffering try to understand the full depth of the present, without any fear or any desire for escape, then without the need of priests and saviors, there is the realization of that which is the lasting, of that which cannot be measured by words.

Question: If the intelligence of most people is so limited that they cannot find truth for themselves, are not Masters and teachers necessary to show them the way?

KRISHNAMURTI: If we merely consider that the unintelligent need the intelligent, we shall keep the unintelligent ever as unintelligent. If you think that a stupid man needs a guide, a Master, then you will create circumstances to hold him in stupidity. If the intelligent perceive the necessity to help the stupid, not towards any particular system or belief or dogma, but to be intelligent, then the unintelligent will not be exploited. But the question is not whether the stupid man needs Masters, saviors, but whether you need them. In truly questioning this need, you will discover that no one can save you, that no one can give you understanding; for understanding lies through your own discernment. Intelligence is not the gift of Masters and teachers, but it is of your own creative perception and action.

Question: Cannot man be liberated through science?

KRISHNAMURTI: It may save man from many sorrows, but there is a great deal of suffering, misery, and exploitation, even though science is far advanced. Each one knows the bestiality and ugliness of war, the result of vested interest and nationalism. In what way has science prevented this suffering, this disease? It is the heart of man that must be changed, but why wait for some future day when it is now in your power to bring about a sane and intelligent alteration?

Question: I should like to know if we need to pray, and how to pray.

KRISHNAMURTI: Sir, isn't it the fundamental idea of prayer to seek aid and understanding beyond ourselves? If that is so, we are depending on something, which makes us weaker in our own intelligence.

Question: Is the soul a reality?

KRISHNAMURTI: Again I would ask the audience to listen without prejudice, without bigotry, to this point. When you talk about the "soul," you mean a something between the material and the spiritual, between body and God. So you have divided life into matter, spirit, and God. Isn't that so? If I may say this, you who talk about "soul" know nothing about it, you are accepting it merely on authority, or it is based on some hope, on some unfulfilled longing. You have accepted on authority many fundamental ideas, as you have accepted "soul" to be a reality.

Please consider what I am going to say, without any prejudice either in favor of or against the idea of soul, and without any preconceived ideas, in order to discover what is true. The only actuality of which we are fully cognizant, with which we have to concern ourselves, is suffering; we are conscious of that constant unfulfillment, limitation, incompleteness which causes conflict and suffering. This consciousness of sorrow is the only actuality from which you can start, and it is only in understanding the cause of suffering and being intelligently free from it, that there comes the ecstasy of reality. When the mind has disentangled itself from all illusions and hopes, then there is the bliss of reality.

Through all this conflict and misery, one feels that there must be a reality, a God, an infinite intelligence, or whatever one may call it. That feeling may be merely a reaction from this agony, and therefore unreal, and so its pursuit must lead to ever-increasing illusions; or it may be the intrinsic desire to discover truth which cannot be measured or systematized. If we can discover what creates conflict and who is the creator of sorrow, then in uprooting the cause of this there can be the true felicity of man. This almost ceaseless battle, this seemingly unending sorrow, is created by that limited consciousness which we call the 'I'. We have created about ourselves many false values, false ideals, to which the mind has become a slave. There is a constant struggle taking place between these illusions and the present, and there must ever be conflict as long as these self-protective illusions exist. This conflict creates in our minds the idea of the particular, the 'I'. So from this limited consciousness arises division as the 'I', the impermanent, and the 'I', the permanent, the eternal. When the mind is wholly free from the self-protective illusions and false values which are the cause of limited consciousness and of its many stupidities, then each one shall realize for himself whether there is truth or not.

If I merely said there is a soul, I should but add another belief to your many beliefs. So of what value would it be? Whereas, the only actuality of which we are conscious is this struggle, this suffering, this exploitation to which we have become slaves; and in intelligently freeing ourselves, not escaping from it, we shall discern the lasting in the transient, the real in the illusion.

May 28, 1935

Montevideo, Uruguay, 1935

✳

First Talk in Montevideo

Friends,

There is a distinct art of listening, especially to those ideas to which, perhaps, you are not quite accustomed. So I would beg of you to listen without prejudice to what I am going to say, which does not mean that you must have a negative mind. Some of you here may think that you possess already a definite mode of life and therefore it is not very important to listen carefully; and to those who have come out of curiosity, there is very little to be said.

To listen properly, there must be neither opposition nor antagonism. Most people have a certain background of tradition, prejudice, hope, and fear, which they put forward as a defense; and this, which is but opposition, they call criticism. If, for instance, you are Christian or you belong to some other religion or to some political party, you will try, with your particular prejudices, to oppose what I am going to say. This is not true criticism. But there is an active form of criticism which demands a clear and an open mind—being conscious of one's prejudices, one's limitations, and at the same time trying to find out the intrinsic value of what the speaker has to say. So, putting aside the background of tradition and habit of thought in which mind constantly dwells, pursue critically, without accepting what I am going to say.

What I have to say is fundamentally simple, and not very philosophical, metaphysical or complicated. As I happen to come from India, people are apt to think that what I say is metaphysical and impractical, and so often brush aside the ideas which I try to put forward.

Now to understand the present chaos with all its miseries, conflicts and difficulties, real criticism is required; not acceptance, but an active form of critical examination. If you merely accept a new set of ideas or a new system of thought, you are only substituting the new in place of the old, and so do not fundamentally understand the cause of suffering and the many problems that confront each one of you.

My intention is not to put forward a new theory or a new system of thought, or a new practice or discipline, but to awaken that understanding of the present; for in understanding the existing chaos and suffering in which man is caught, he will know for himself how to live completely, intelligently, and divinely.

In your suffering, you are apt to turn to the established authority or create a new one, which will not in any way help you to understand and free yourself from the cause of suffering. But if you truly understood the significance of the present, then you would not turn to any authority whatsoever, but being intelligent, actively conscious, you would be able to adjust yourself constantly to the movement of life.

So, if each one can understand the present, then he will discover for himself how to live intelligently and supremely. That is, by discovering and eradicating the cause of existing chaos, of human suffering, of spiritual and economic exploitation, each one will truly fulfill.

In his search for security and comfort, man has consciously or unconsciously separated life into two divisions: we might call these divisions, for the moment, the material and the spiritual. The material—the economic or the social world—is based entirely on acquisitiveness, which has developed, naturally, class distinctions. That is, each one in his individual search for his own security, his own comfort, has created an economic and social system of ruthless exploitation. Out of this is born the disease of nationalism, with all its absurdities and cruelties, which must engender wars and the divisions of people. The means of acquiring wealth, the machine, in the hands of the few, has led to immense suffering; and to maintain this vested interest, separate political parties have been formed which disregard man entirely, using him only to further their own power and importance. In fact, this system is based wholly on individual and family security, which must inevitably create ruthless exploitation, the distinction of classes, nationalism, and wars. In this complicated tradition of false values which he has so sedulously built up through the centuries, the individual is caught. Briefly, without going into many details which you can think out for yourself, this system of thought and habit is influencing, dominating, coercing the individual to conform to this civilization of acquisition.

Then, in the world of the spiritual there is also acquisitiveness, only in a different form. Perhaps to some of you this may appear strange, while you may be familiar with the ordinary material form of acquisitiveness. As this may be new to you, please listen advisedly and carefully.

In the world of the spiritual, the search for security is expressed through the desire for immortality. In each one there is the desire to remain permanent, eternal. This is what all religions promise, an immortality in the hereafter, which is but a subtle form of egotistic security. Now, anyone that promises this selfish continuance, which you call immortality, consciously or unconsciously becomes your authority. Look at the various religions in the world and you will see that out of your own desire for security, for salvation, for continuance, you have created a subtle and cruel authority to which you have become utterly enslaved, which is constantly crippling your thought, your love.

Now, to interpret this authority, you must have mediators whom you call priests, who become in fact your exploiters. (Applause) Perhaps you applaud rather too quickly—because you are the creators of these exploiters. (Laughter, applause) Some of you may not consciously create these spiritual authorities, but subtly, unknowingly, you are creating other kinds of exploiters. You may not go to a priest, but this does not mean that you are not exploiting or exploited.

Where there is the desire for security, certainty, there must be authority, and you give yourself over entirely to those people who promise to guide you, to help you to realize that security. So religions have become throughout the world the receptacle of vested interest, and of organized, closed belief. (Applause) Sirs, may I suggest something?

Please don't bother to applaud, as it is a waste of time.

As religions promise immortality, so they have created ideals, which have become merely a means of escape from the present. After all, what are all your ideals? They but offer a subtle means of flight from actuality. Let me take an example which perhaps will make this clear.

You profess the ideal of brotherly love, and that is the ideal with which the majority of you have been brought up. But what is taking place in actuality? There is the distinction of classes, of religions with their beliefs, dogmas and divisions, and of nationalism with its exploitation and wars. So what is the good of your ideals? Ideals but become drugs which prevent you from thinking clearly and understanding fully the present.

Religions, with their beliefs, dogmas and creeds, have become tremendous barriers between human beings, dividing man against man, limiting him and destroying his intelligence. Please understand what I mean by religion. I mean, by religion, organized thought and belief which have become receptacles of vested interest and in which authority is firmly rooted.

So, having created these two divisions in life, the material and the spiritual, we turn in moments of great crisis, great suffering and misery, to experts along these two lines. In moments of intense suffering, we seek comfort from these authorities and experts. And what happens when you look up to another? Gradually and unconsciously you create authority, you give yourself over to it entirely and become merely a part of that system of thought; and, as there are innumerable experts along these two lines, you become tools in their hands to fight other experts and their groups.

What is your answer to all this? On the one hand you can say that man is nothing but clay, matter to be molded, and that he is but the result of environment, to be controlled and shaped. If this is so, then the whole question of his creative expression and fulfillment, his intelligent happiness and moral action, is of no great importance and of no special consequence. If you think fundamentally that man is nothing but clay to be fashioned by circumstances, then you must create circumstances, laws, authorities that will ruthlessly control, dominate individual expression and action. Or, if man is not mere clay to be conditioned, to be molded into a particular shape, then there must be a complete revolution in your ideas and actions.

That is, sirs, there are only two possibilities: one of complete domination and control; and the other, the voluntary creation of right environment for the fulfillment of man. You must belong to one or the other of these; you cannot play with both. Either you consider man as merely a social entity, and therefore you ruthlessly shape and control his whole social and creative action; or, if he is not merely that, but something much more, then there must be a fundamental revolution in your thought and action.

If you voluntarily discern this, then your acquisitive action, your thought based on security, must undergo a complete change. If you consider that man has within himself the greatest capacity for intelligence, then you must remove the innumerable fears, punishments and rewards with which you guide and dominate him. But if you think that man is merely clay to be shaped, then you will increase all the fears and punishments which will dominate and coerce him.

So you, as individuals, will have to discover for yourselves upon what your action is based, whether upon compulsion or upon voluntary understanding. We see so much exploitation, so much misery and suffering, and we don't seem to find a comprehensive answer. We are satisfied by one day's remedy. But if we can really, fundamentally understand this problem of compulsion, domination, then we shall find a true and lasting answer to the many aches and agonies of life. This means that as each one has been so twisted, perverted, limited by past and present environment, he must now begin to question the true significance of the innumerable values to which he has become a slave. To do this there must be a continual awakened interest and alertness to free the mind from all pressure and influence, to make it clear, simple, so that there is direct discernment of what is true.

We have three kinds, if I may so divide it, of individual, egotistic expression. One is the search for immortality, the desire for selfish continuance, which prevents the complete understanding of the present, the only eternity. As long as the mind is pursuing its own egotistic continuance, thinking that this is immortality, there cannot be the flow of reality, that unique intelligence which is not yours or mine. To understand and realize this, mind must be free from that consciousness which has been created through many hindrances, through authority, through values based on acquisitive and self-protective fears. When the mind is free from its own egotistic limitations and impediments, when it is creatively empty, there is born that reality which is immeasurable, not to be discussed but to be experienced, lived.

Then there is that selfish acquisitiveness of things, that possessiveness, with all its subtle cruelties and exploitations, by which the mind seeks to establish its own security and comfort.

Finally, there is the pursuit of sensation.

Now if you desire to understand truth, mind must be free from these impediments and limitations. As individuals you must become conscious, fully conscious of your actions. You cannot give yourself over to authority, to experts, but you must be con-

tinually aware of your action, and its cause; then the mind will discern the bondage, the hindrance in which thought is caught. So gradually the mind, which is now crippled, unconscious, becomes conscious and thereby discovers the limitations which it has created for itself in search of its own security. And when the mind is utterly naked, then there is that creative intelligence, that continual becoming.

Question: What is your truth?

KRISHNAMURTI: There cannot be your truth and my truth. There is only truth, and you can understand its unique quality only when the mind is free of "yours" and "mine." The 'you' and the 'me' are only memories, based on self-protective and accumulative reaction against intelligence. When the mind is free from that sense of "mine," then there is life, there is truth.

There is only love, but when you imprison it within the walls of possessiveness, then it becomes "yours," and its beauty fast withers away.

Question: If you live in an eternal now, having annihilated the idea of time and broken the ties that bind you to the past, how can you speak about your past and about your previous experiences? Are not these memories, ties?

KRISHNAMURTI: If action is born out of a prejudice, a hindrance, then it creates further limitation and brings sorrow. But if it is the outcome of discernment, then action is ever renewing itself and is never limiting. This liberation of action does not mean that you cannot remember incidents, but those past incidents will no longer control action.

If one acts through the background of many prejudices, surely that action, being impeded, must inevitably create a further limitation of the mind. If one has a background of religious prejudices, action must create conflict in the present. But if one begins to question and thus understand the significance of values, traditions, ideals, past accumulations which make up the background, then the mind shall know the beauty of action without sorrow. Experiment with what I am saying and you will know. We have many prejudices, fears, accumulative values, which are continually thwarting fulfillment in action, and so there is an ever-increasing incompleteness and the burden of tomorrow.

June 21, 1935

Second Talk in Montevideo

Friends,

Many questions have been put to me, and before I answer some of them I will say a few words by way of introduction.

I think it would be rather vain and absurd if you merely dismissed what I say as being communistic or anarchistic, or by saying that it is nothing new. To find out whether it is of any significant value, and to test whether it has any essential quality of truth, one must experiment with it and not merely dismiss it. To find out the quality of any idea that I put forward, you must carry it into action, with deliberate and conscious thought. Only then can you know the renewing quality of action in daily life—for we are concerned most with that intelligent action which shall reveal the richness, the fullness of life. To discover for ourselves the manner of this action, there must not be mere rejection or blind acceptance of the ideas which I have been trying to explain, but there must be true and conscious experiment. Then you will know the ever-renewing quality of action.

To live supremely, intelligently, we must find out for ourselves what are the hindrances or the prejudices that impede the free flow of reality. In understanding the significance of their cause and their existence, we shall voluntarily, without any compulsion, abandon them. Then only can there be the movement of reality.

There is, amongst other hindrances, one that does incalculable damage to the mind. Before I explain what that impediment is, please do not jump to conclusions or think in terms of opposites. To understand its deep significance, mind must be very pliable and not merely conclusive, as this prevents the continuous penetration of reality.

One of the greatest hindrances to the flow of reality, is authority. It is one of the most destructive barriers which we have created in our desire for self-protection and security. For convenience, let us divide authority into the inner and the outer. The outer authority is environment, tradition, habit, the closed morality of religion, the authority of experts, and the authority of vested interests. There is this outward environment which is continually impressing and forcing itself upon the individual, conditioning and perverting him. As long as we do not understand this limiting pressure of environment with its corroding influence, compelling us to act according to a particular pattern which is often considered as voluntary action, as long as we do not discern its true significance, there must be a continual conflict and suffering, thus ever increasing the limitation of action.

By reacting to this outward compulsion, we begin to develop an inner authority, an inner law based on fear, on the self-protective memory of security and comfort, according to which we are continually adjusting and paralleling our conduct, and which in its own subtle way controls and limits thought and action and thus creates its own conflict and suffering.

So we have the compulsion from without, and from within, which has been developed through our own desire for security, certainty, and which is continually perverting and twisting discernment.

If the mind would understand reality, it must become wholly unburdened, fresh and uninfluenced. That is, you must become fully conscious, fully aware of the subtle influence of vested interests on the one hand, which I have explained as environmental, and on the other of that inward compulsion based on acquisitive and self-protective fear and memory. When you begin to be aware, when you begin to perceive that influence or authority in any form, gross or subtle, must pervert thought, then the mind, in freeing itself from its limitations, is capable of true discernment. For the action of authority, based fundamentally on self-protective desire, must ever increase stupidity and its illusions, destroying creative action, until gradually the individual is nothing but automatic reactions. When the individual consciously understands the deep significance of authority, when the mind is completely naked, creatively empty, then there is bliss.

Many questions have been put to me, and I have chosen some which I think are representative. If your particular question is not chosen, please listen to the questions which I shall answer, and I think you will see that I am answering your question also.

Question: You gave us the impression in your first talk that you were destroying the old values and clearing the way. In the following talks, are you going to build anew, giving us the essence of your teaching?

KRISHNAMURTI: Now, I cannot destroy values which have been created by each individual, and which have become the means of exploitation either by society or by religion. You, by your own effort, by your own understanding of the true significance of existing values, can begin to destroy those

that are essentially false. If I merely destroy the old and establish a new set of values, you are none the freer, you will only become prisoners to the new. There is no fundamental difference, only a change of prisons. So please understand the purpose of these talks. Truth cannot be handed to you. You, through your own creative understanding, have to discover for yourself the true in the false. If I merely built a new system or structure of thought, it would become another kind of authority and prison, whereas if you, through your own discernment, begin to discover what is true, you are then releasing that creative energy of intelligence which is truth. Truth is unique; it is not many-sided; it is complete. Each one must come to it without any compulsion, without following anyone, without any adjustment to a system or pattern. You have to battle against the false values that man has created through centuries, which are now being imposed on him ruthlessly, those values which you as individuals have established for yourselves in the desire for self-protection and security.

It does not much matter what name you give to me; and it cannot matter very much to you what I am. What matters is whether you in your suffering are truly destroying the false values that enclose you, or creating further barriers that shall imprison man.

The questioner asks, "In the following talks, are you going to build anew, giving us the essence of your teaching?" Most of us are seeking explanations. Explanations are merely so much dust in the eyes. If you take even one of the ideas which I have put forward, and become aware of its full significance, you are then beginning to release creative intelligence. You will find fulfillment through your own action, and not through any particular system of thought.

Question: Do you believe that a man of low culture, oppressed, earning a miserable wage, with a wife and children to support, can save himself spiritually and economically without help and guidance?

KRISHNAMURTI: Economically, man certainly cannot be individualistic, which he has been through these many centuries, causing chaos, exploitation and misery. But spiritually, if I may use that much abused word, he must be a complete individual. That is, when he begins to discover for himself and discard the false values which he has established through his search for protection and security, he awakens in himself true intelligence. At present he is being driven ruthlessly, in this false, individualistic system.

When you begin voluntarily to question, to investigate and discard the false values which religions and society have established, you awaken that unique intelligence which is creative cooperation, and not compulsory, slavish adjustment. Without this intelligence you act merely like so many machines.

For the fundamental change which shall bring about collective cooperation there must be complete, true, and individual freedom of thought; but it is one of the most difficult things to realize, for we have been trained through centuries to obey and to adjust ourselves to a standard. The desire to create authority and to follow it is subtly ingrained in us. When there is a problem, we seek help, which we too easily find. Thus gradually and almost unconsciously we establish authority, to which we give ourselves over completely, until there is no thought apart from the system, apart from the established tradition and ideas.

Now the questioner wants to know whether a man of low state, low education, can realize that spiritual and true intelligence, that uniqueness. He can if he begins vigorously to question and to discover the significance of established values, and thus release creative thought. Unfortunately, such

people have very little time to themselves, they are overworked, they are exhausted at the end of the day. But you who are supposed to be educated, who have leisure, can see to it that these others have also the right environment in which to live and think, and are not ceaselessly imposed upon and exploited.

The deep quality of intelligence is not found through mere education; it is not the result of slavish obedience to authority, or of the imposition of social morality, but it happens through the diligent discovery of right values. When there is such unique intelligence, then there will not be exploitation, domination, and the cruel pursuit of selfish success.

Question: How can we be certain that happiness will result from the destruction of scientific, religious, moral, and psychological prejudices?

KRISHNAMURTI: You want a guarantee from me that by giving up something you will get something else in return. (Laughter) We approach life with the mentality of a merchant, and do not see that prejudice is inherently false. We want, before we renounce what we possess, to be assured that we shall receive something in return. And this is true of the whole pursuit of virtue. But the mentality that renounces in order to attain something else can never find happiness; such a mentality can never understand the pure quality of truth, which is to be understood only for its own beauty, not as a recompense.

Now if you think seriously about it, you will see that our whole system of thought is based on this idea of recompense. After all, the cultured man acts without seeking a reward. This requires, not only the recognition of the falseness of reward, but the understanding, the discernment of intrinsic values. If you are a true artist or a man who really loves his work, then you are not seeking a reward. It is only the person who is not in love with life that is constantly seeking, in a gross or subtle manner, a recompense or reward, for his actions are born out of fear; and how can such a person understand the swiftness, the subtle quality of truth?

Question: Are you trying to free the individual, or awaken in him the desire for freedom?

KRISHNAMURTI: If you are not suffering, if you are not in conflict, if there is no problem, no crisis in your life, then there is very little to be said. That is, if you are asleep, then the action of life must first awaken you. But what happens generally when you begin to suffer? You immediately seek a remedy that will ease your suffering. So gradually in your search for comfort, you again put yourself to sleep through your own effort; and what another can do is merely to point out how you are doing this. You put yourself to sleep by seeking comfort, which you call the search for God, for truth. When the mind is awakened through a shock, which you call suffering, that is the true moment to inquire into the cause of suffering, without seeking comfort. If you observe, you will see that when there is acute suffering, your thought is searching out a remedy, a comfort. And you do find a remedy, which but dulls the mind and turns it away from the cause of suffering, thus creating an illusion.

To put it differently, when the mind dwells in an accustomed groove of thought, then there is no conflict, then there is no suffering, no awakened interest in life. But when you have an experience of some kind that gives you a shock, which is called suffering and which awakens you from habit, then your immediate reaction is to seek another comfort to which thought can again become accustomed. The mind is searching constantly for certainties so that it shall be secure and not be disturbed, and hence life becomes full of fears and defensive reactions. But experience is continually destroying our certainties, and yet subtly we seek to create others. So life becomes a continual process of struggle and suffering, creation and destruction. But if the mind did not seek finalities, conclusions and securities, then it would find that there is constant adjustment, an understanding of the significance of the movement of life; and in that alone is there lasting reality, in that alone is there happiness.

Question: What do you mean by "religion"? I feel myself reunited to God through Christ. And through whom are you reunited to God?

KRISHNAMURTI: I mean by religion: organized belief, creed, dogma, and authority. That is one form of religion. Then there is the religion of ceremonies, which is but sensation and pageantry. Then there is the religion of personal experience. The first forces the individual to conform to a certain pattern for his own good through fear, through faith, dogma, and creed. The second impresses divinity on the worshipper through show and pageantry. With the third, personal experience, we shall deal presently.

Now, organized religion must inevitably create divisions and conflict between men. You see this throughout the world. Hinduism, like Christianity, Buddhism and other organized religions, has its own peculiar beliefs and dogmas, which are almost impenetrable barriers between men, destroying their love. And what value, what significance have these religions, when they are fundamentally based on fear? If you discern the falseness of organized belief, that through any particular belief you cannot understand reality, nor through any authority whatsoever can intelligence be awakened, then you as individuals, not as an organized group, will free yourselves from this destructive imposition. This means that you must question from the very beginning the whole idea of belief; but this involves great suffering, for it is not a mere intellectual process. A man who only inquires intellectually into the question of belief shall find nothing but dust. If a man who is deeply suffering, questions this whole structure based on fear and authority, then he shall find those waters of life which shall quench his thirst.

Then there is that personal experience which is also called religious experience. It requires greater frankness, greater effort on our part to unravel the illusions that are connected with this. When there is so much confusion, misery, and uncertainty, we want to find stability, peace, and happiness. That is, instead of discerning the cause of this suffering, we want to run away from conflict to something that will give us contentment and constant hope. So with this craving we create and develop illusions that give us intense satisfaction, encouragement, and happiness, whose sensation and thrill we generally call religious experience. If you really examine impersonally, without any prejudice, these so-called religious experiences, you will see that they are nothing but self-evolved compensations for suffering. So what people call religious experience is merely an escape into an illusion which they call a reality, in which they live, thinking that it is God, truth, and so on. If you are suffering, instead of seeking happiness, the opposite, discern the fundamental cause of suffering, and begin to free yourself from that cause; then there is that reality which cannot be measured by words.

A mind that desires to understand truth must be free from these three illusions: from organized belief, with its authority and dogmas; from ceremonies, with their pageantry

and sensation; and from those self-created illusions with their satisfactions and destructive happiness. When the mind is really without any prejudice, is not seeking a reward or cultivating a deity or hoping for immortality, then in that clear discernment there is the birth of reality.

Question: I am a priest, and I think I am fairly representative of the priesthood in general. I have had no revelation or mystic experience whatever; but what I preach from the pulpit I sincerely believe, because I have read it in sacred books. My words give consolation to those who listen to me. Should I give up helping them and leave my ministry because I have no such direct experience?

KRISHNAMURTI: Sir, what is it that you call helping people? If you want to pacify them, drug them to sleep, then you must have revelation and authority. Because there is so much suffering, we think that by giving comfort to people we are helping them. This giving of comfort is nothing but putting them to sleep; thus the comforter becomes the exploiter.

Don't merely laugh at the question and pass it by, saying that it does not apply to you. What is it that you are seeking? If you are seeking comfort, then you will find comforters and be drugged into contentment. But what can anyone truly teach you? What another can help you to do is to discern for yourself whether you are escaping from actuality into an illusion. This means that the person who talks, who preaches, must himself be free from illusions. Then he will be able to help people even without reading sacred books. He will help the individual to keep awake, alive to the actualities of life, freed from all illusion. In discerning an illusion the mind frees itself from it, through deep understanding, and destroys the creator of illusion, which is that center of limited consciousness, the 'I', the ego.

If you want really to help man because you yourself perceive the utter chaos and suffering that exists, you will not give him any drug that will put him to sleep, but will help him to discover for himself those causes which impede the birth of intelligence. It is difficult to teach truly without dominating, asserting; and both the teacher and the pupil must be free from the subtle influence of authority, for authority perverts and destroys all understanding.

Question: Do you believe in God?

KRISHNAMURTI: What is important is to find out why you seek God; for when you are happy or when you are in love, you do not seek love, happiness. Then you don't believe in love, you are love. It is only when there is no joy, no happiness, that you try to seek it. You are seeking God because you say to yourself, "I cannot understand this life, with its misery, injustice, with its exploitations and cruelties, with its changing love and its constant uncertainties. If I can understand the reality which is God, then all these things will pass away."

To a man in a prison, freedom can be only in imaginative flight. Your search for reality, for God, is but an escape from actuality. If you begin to free yourself from the cause of suffering, free the mind from the brutalities of personal ambition and success, from the craving for individual security, then there is truth, reality. Then you will not ask another if there is God. The search for God to the vast majority of people is but an escape from conflict, suffering. They call this escape religion, the search for eternity; but what they are really seeking is merely a drug to put them to sleep.

The fundamental cause of man's suffering is his egotism, expressing itself in many ways, essentially in his search for security through immortality, possessiveness, and authority. When the mind is free from these causes which create conflict, then you will understand, without beliefs, that which is immeasurable, that which is reality. A mind weighed down with belief, with prejudice, a mind that is prepared, cannot discover the unknown. The mind must be wholly naked, without any support, without any longing or hope. Then there is reality, which cannot be measured by words.

So do not seek vainly for that which is, but discover the impediments, the hindrances that prevent the mind from perceiving truth. When the mind is creatively empty there is the immeasurable.

Question: What is immortality?

KRISHNAMURTI: To understand immortality and its real significance, your mind must be free of all religious prejudice. That is, you have already an idea of what immortality must be, which is the outcome of intense desire to continue as a limited consciousness. All the religions throughout the world promise this egotistic immortality. If you would understand immortality, mind must be free of this craving for individual continuance.

Now, when you say that 'I' must continue, what is this 'I'? The 'I' is nothing but the form, the name, certain qualities and memories, certain fears and prejudices, certain limited desires and unfulfilled actions. All these compose the 'I' which becomes that limited consciousness, the ego. You desire that this limited consciousness shall continue. That is, when you ask if there is immortality, you are inquiring whether the 'I' will continue, that 'I' which is inherently a frustrated consciousness.

To put it differently, in truly creative moments of thought or of expression, there is no consciousness as the 'I'. It is only in moments of conflict, suffering, that the mind becomes conscious of its own limitation, which is called the 'I'; and we have become so accustomed to limitation that we crave for its continuance, thinking that this is immortality. Thus anyone who guarantees to you this immortality, becomes your authority. Grossly or subtly, that authority begins to exploit you through fear. So you who are seeking this selfish, illusory immortality, are creating exploiters with all their cruelties. But if you are really free of that limited consciousness with its illusions, hopes, and fears, then there is the eternal movement, the continual becoming, not of the 'I', but of life itself.

Question: Don't you think that any movement or social upheaval that succeeds in educating the younger generation without any religious ideas or thought of the hereafter, is a positive step in human progress?

KRISHNAMURTI: Religious ideas do not merely limit themselves to the hereafter. It is much more profound. The desire to be secure gives birth to the thought about the hereafter and to many other subtleties which create fear, and to be free from it needs great discernment. Only a mind that is insecure will understand truth; a mind that is not prepared, that is not conditioned by fear, shall be open to the unknown. So let us concern ourselves with limitations and their cause.

The question is this: Can we train children not to seek security? Now, to educate another, you must begin with yourself. Are you fundamentally free of this idea of security? Are you entirely vulnerable to life, without any self-protective wall? To discover this, begin to be aware, begin to question all the values that now enclose the mind. Then you will discover, through your own intel-

ligent awakening, the true significance of security.

June 26, 1935

Third Talk in Montevideo

Friends,

Many questions have been sent to me regarding the present social conditions: alcoholism, prostitution, civilization, and so on. I have been asked, also, why I do not join certain societies and political parties in order to help the world.

In reply to all these many questions, I feel that if we can really grasp the fundamental principle underlying our human struggle, then we shall understand these problems and truly solve them. We must understand the fundamental causes of struggle and suffering and then our action will inevitably bring a complete change. Our whole interest should be turned, not towards solving any one particular problem, not towards any particular end or definite objective, but towards understanding life as an integrated whole. To do this, limitations that have been placed on the mind, crippling thought and action, must be discerned and dissolved. If thought is really free from the innumerable impediments we have imposed upon it in our search for security, then we will meet life as a whole, and in this lies great bliss.

Now, the mind creates and becomes a slave to authority, and hence action is being constantly impeded, crippled, which is the cause of suffering. If you observe your own thought, you will see how it is caught between the past and the present. Thought is continually paralleling, guiding itself by the past, and adjusting itself to the future; thus action becomes incomplete in the present, which creates in our minds the idea of non-fulfillment, out of which comes the fear of death, the consideration of the hereafter, and the many limitations born of incompleteness. If the mind can completely understand the significance of the present, then action becomes fulfillment without creating further conflict and suffering, which is but the result of limited action, of impediments placed on thought through fear.

To release thought in order that action may flow without creating for itself limitations and barriers, mind must be free from this continual imposition of the past, and also free from the future pattern which is but an escape from the present. Please, this is not as complicated as it sounds. Watch your own mind functioning and you will see that it guides itself by the past, or it is adjusting itself to a future ideal or pattern, so the significance of the present is completely covered over. In this way, action is creating its own limitation, instead of liberating thought and emotion; action is being constantly influenced by the past and the future.

The past is tradition, those values which we have accepted and the significance of which we have not deeply understood. Then there are moral values against which you are constantly measuring your action. If you deeply examine these values, you will discern that they are based on self-protection and security, and merely adjusting action to such values is not fulfillment, nor is it moral. Again, observe yourself and you will see how memory is ever placing a limitation on your thought and so on action. This memory is really a self-protective adjustment to life, which is often called self-discipline. Such discipline is nothing but a defensive system against sorrow, a cunning protection and guard against experience, life itself. So the past, which is tradition, values, habits, memories, is conditioning thought, and thus action is incomplete.

The future is nothing but an escape from actuality, through an ideal to which we try to adjust the present, the immediate action.

These ideals are merely safeguards, hopes, illusions born of incompleteness and frustration. So the future is placing a hindrance in the way of action and fulfillment. Thought, which should be in constant movement, is attaching itself either to the past or the future, and out of this comes that limited consciousness, the 'I', which is but incompleteness.

Now to understand reality, the deep significance of the movement of life, which is the eternal, thought must be free from this attachment to and influence of the past and the future; mind must be completely naked, without any escape or support, without the power of creating illusion. In that clarity, in that simplicity, there is born, as the flower, truth, the ecstasy of life.

Question: Intellectually I understand what you say, but how am I to put it into action?

KRISHNAMURTI: I doubt, if I may say so, that you really understand what I am saying, even intellectually; for when you talk of understanding intellectually, you mean that you theoretically grasp an idea, but not its deep significance, which can be caught only in action. Most of us want to avoid action, because that necessarily creates circumstances and conditions which bring about conflict; and thought, being cunning, avoids disturbance, suffering. So it says to itself, "I understand intellectually, but how am I to put it into action?" You never ask how to put an idea into action if that idea is of real significance to you. The man who says, "Tell me how to act," does not wish to think deeply about the matter but merely desires to be told what to do, which creates the pernicious system of authority, following, and sectarianism.

I am afraid the majority of you, after hearing these talks, will say, "You have given us nothing practical." Your mind is accustomed to systematized thought and unconscious action, and you are willing to follow any new system which will give you further security. If you take one idea which I put forward and really go into it deeply through action, then you will discover the ever-renewing quality of complete action, and from this alone comes the true ecstasy of life.

Question: Do you believe in the existence of the soul? Does this continue to live infinitely after the death of the body?

KRISHNAMURTI: Most people believe in the existence of the soul in some form or other. Now you will not understand what I am going to say if, in defense, you merely oppose it, or quote some authority for your belief which is cultivated through tradition and fear; nor can this belief be called intuition when it is only a vague hope.

Illusion divides itself infinitely. The soul is a division, born of illusion. There is first the body, then there is the soul that occupies it, and finally there is God or reality: this is how you have divided life.

Now the limited consciousness of the 'I', is the result of incomplete actions, and this limited consciousness is creating its own illusions and is caught in its own ignorance; and when the mind is free from its own ignorance and illusion, then there is reality, not 'you' becoming that reality.

Please do not accept what I say, but begin to question and understand how your own belief has come into being. Then you will see how subtly the mind has divided life. You will begin to understand the significance of this division, which is a subtle form of egotistic desire for continuance. As long as this illusion, with all its subtleties, exists, there cannot be reality.

As this is one of the most controversial subjects and there exists so much prejudice with regard to it, one has to be very careful not to be swayed by opinion for or against the idea of the soul. In understanding reality,

this question as to whether there is a soul or not, will be answered. To understand reality, mind must be utterly free from the limitation of fear, with its craving for egotistic continuance.

Question: What have you to say about the sexual problem?

KRISHNAMURTI: Why has sex become a problem? It is a problem because we have lost that creative force which we call love. Because there is no love, sex becomes a problem. Love has become merely possession, and not that supremely intelligent adjustment to life. When we have lost that love and merely depend on sensation, then love and sex become a cruel problem. To understand this question deeply and to live greatly with love, mind must be free from the desire to possess. This requires great intelligence and discernment.

There are no immediate remedies for these vital problems. If you really want to solve them intelligently, you must alter the fundamental causes which create these problems. But if you merely deal with them superficially, then action springing from them will create greater and more complicated problems. If you deeply understand the significance of possessiveness—in which there is cruelty, oppression, indifference— and the mind frees itself from that limitation, then life is not a problem, nor a school in which to learn; it is a life to be lived completely, in the fullness of love.

Question: Do you believe in free will, in determinism, or in inexorable karma?

KRISHNAMURTI: We have the capacity to choose, and as long as this exists, however conditioned and however unjust, there must be limited freedom. Now our thought is conditioned by past experiences, memories; therefore it cannot be truly free. If you want to understand the eternal present, if you want to complete your action in the present, you must understand the cause of limitation, from which arises this division between consciousness and impeded consciousness. It is this limited consciousness, with its impeded action, that creates incompleteness, causing suffering. If action is not creating further limitations, then there is the continual movement of life.

Karma, or the limitation of action in the present, is created through impeded consciousness of values, ideals, hopes which each one has not wholly understood. Only through deep discernment of these hindrances, can the mind liberate itself from the limitation of action.

Question: I am enthusiastic about the united Christian front in a Christ-centric religion. I accept only the value which organizations have in themselves, and lay emphasis on the individual effort to find personal salvation. Do you believe that the united Christian front is feasible?

KRISHNAMURTI: Each religion maintains that there is only one true religion, itself, and tries to bring within its fold, within its limitation, people who are suffering. Religions thus create divisions between man and man. The point is: Why do you want a religion of any kind, religion being an organized system of beliefs, dogmas and creeds? You cling to it because you hope that it will act as a guide, giving you comfort and solace in times of trouble. So organized religion becomes a shelter, an escape from the continual impact of experience and of life. Through your own desire for protection you create an artificial structure which you call religion, which is in essence a comforting dope against actuality.

If the mind discerns its own process of building up shelters and so avoiding life, then it will begin to disentangle itself from all unquestioned values which now limit it. When man truly realizes this, there will not be the spectacle of one religion competing with others for him, but he will be free from his own self-created illusions, and so awaken in himself that true intelligence which alone can destroy all the artificial distinctions and the many cruelties of intolerance.

Question: Your observations upon authority were greeted in some quarters as an attack upon the churches. Don't you think you should make it clear to your listeners that this word attack *is misapplied? Should not your efforts be better understood and be regarded as a means of enlightenment? For do not attacks lead to conflict, and is not harmony your objective?*

KRISHNAMURTI: Should not traditions, beliefs, dogmas be questioned? Should not the social, moral values which we have built up for centuries be doubted and their significance discovered? By questioning deeply there will be individual conflict, which will awaken intelligence and not mere stupid revolt. This intelligence is true harmony. Harmony is not the blind acceptance of authority nor the easy satisfaction in unquestioned value.

Sir, what I am saying is very simple. We have now about us many values, traditions, ideals, which we accept unquestioningly; for when we begin to question, there must be action, and being afraid of the result of such action, we go on meekly accepting, subjugating, adjusting ourselves to these false values, which will remain false as long as we merely accept them and do not voluntarily discern their significance. But when we begin to question and try to understand their deep significance, conflict must inevitably arise.

Now, you cannot understand the true significance of values intellectually. You begin to discern it only when there is conflict, when there is suffering. But unless you are greatly aware, suffering will merely lead to the search for comfort. And the man who gives you comfort becomes your authority, and so you acquire other values which you again accept unquestioningly, thoughtlessly. In this vicious circle thought is held, and our suffering goes on day after day until we die, and so we come to hope that in the hereafter there will be happiness. Such an existence, with fear and bondage to authority, is a wasted life without fulfillment.

If you begin to discern for yourself the deep significance of values that have been established, then you will discover for yourself how to live intelligently, supremely. This action of intelligence is true harmony. So do not seek mere harmony, but awaken intelligence. Do not try to cover up the existing disharmony and chaos, but fully understand its cause, which is our egoistic desires, pursuits, and ambitions.

Question: How can you talk about human suffering when you yourself have never experienced it?

KRISHNAMURTI: We want to judge others. Instead of basing your understanding of what I say on whether I have suffered or not, become aware of your own suffering, and then see if what I say has any value. If it has not, then whether I have suffered or not has no significance whatsoever. When the mind discerns and frees itself from the cause of its own suffering, then a life without exploitation, a life of deep love, is possible.

Question: Do you believe that there is some truth in spiritualistic phenomena, or are they only autosuggestions?

KRISHNAMURTI: Even after you have examined spiritualistic phenomena under very strict conditions—for there is so much charlatanism and deception about all this—of what value is it?

What lies behind this question? Most of us want to know because we desire to be guided, or because we want to get into touch with those whom we have lost, hoping thus to free ourselves from loneliness, or cover up our agony with explanations. So, with most of us, the desire behind this question is, "How can I escape from suffering?" You want to be guided through life in order to avoid suffering, in order not to come into conflict with actuality. Hence you abandon the authority of a church, a sect, or an idea, and rely on this new spiritualistic authority. But authority still guides and dominates you as before. Your life, through control, through escape, becomes more and more shallow, more and more incomplete. Why give more authority, more understanding to the dead than to the living?

Where there is a desire to be guided, to seek security in authority, life must inevitably become a great sorrow and a great emptiness. The richness of life, the depth of understanding, the bliss of love can come only through the discernment of the false, of that which is illusory.

Question: Should we destroy desire?

KRISHNAMURTI: We want to destroy desire because desire creates conflict and suffering. You cannot destroy desire; if you could, you would become but an empty shell. But let us discover what causes suffering, what prompts us to destroy our desire.

Desire is continually trying to fulfill, and in its fulfillment there is pain, suffering, and joy. Thus mind becomes merely the storehouse of memories, to guide, to warn. In order that desire, in its fulfillment, may not create suffering, mind begins to limit and protect itself with values and impositions based on fear. Thus gradually desire becomes more and more limited, narrow, and out of this limitation comes suffering which urges us to conquer and destroy desire, or forces us to find a new objective for desire.

If we destroy desire, there is death; and if we merely change the objective of desire, find new ideals for desire, then it is only an escape from conflict, and so there can be no richness, no completeness. If there is no pursuit of limited, egotistic objectives or ideals, then desire is itself the continual movement of life.

Question: If, as you say, immortality exists, we assume that, without desiring it, we shall inevitably realize it in the natural course of experience, thus not creating exploiters. But if we desire it, then we shall make of those who offer us immortality our conscious or unconscious exploiters. Is this what you wish to convey?

KRISHNAMURTI: I tried to explain how we create authority which necessitates exploitation. You create authorities in your desire for egotistic continuance, which you call immortality. If you crave for that limited consciousness, the 'I', to continue, then he who gives you the promise of its endurance becomes your authority, which brings about the formation of a sect, and so on.

Now immortality is not egotistic continuance at all. The realization of that which is immeasurable can only be when the mind is no longer bound to its own limited consciousness, when it is no longer pursuing its own security. As long as the mind is seeking its own protection, comfort, creating its own particular limitation, there cannot be eternal becoming.

Question: Is man in any sense superior to woman?

KRISHNAMURTI: The question is surely put by a woman! Intelligence is neither superior nor inferior; it is unique. So don't let us discuss who is superior or who is inferior, but rather discover how to awaken that divinity. You can do it only by constant awareness. Where there is fear there is the submission to the many stupidities and compulsions of religion, of society, or to your wife, your husband or your neighbor. But when the mind, in its own awareness and suffering, deeply penetrates into the illusion of security with its many false values, then there is intelligence, an eternal becoming.

June 28, 1935

Talk at the University, Montevideo

Friends,

To bring about a mass action there must be individual awakening; otherwise, the mass merely becomes an instrument in the hands of the few for the purpose of exploitation. So either you lend yourself to be exploited, or you begin to awaken true intelligence, which is to live completely, fully, without exploitation.

Now, what is it that will awaken the individual from his self-satisfied, egotistic accumulations? The continual process of awakening the mind from its own limitation is true experience. When there is this action of experience on a limited mind, the awakening is called suffering. For most of us, the desire to cling to certainties, securities, to habits of thought, to traditions, is so great that anything which comes to shake us out of that groove of safety, out of those established values, thus creating insecurity, we call suffering. When there is suffering, there is an intense craving to escape from it, and so the mind creates further illusory values that are satisfying and consoling. These values are established through defensive reaction against intelligence. What we call values, moralities, are really based on this self-defensive reaction against the movement of life. To these values mind has become an unconscious slave.

We have ideals, values, traditions, in which we are constantly taking shelter when there is conflict or suffering. Intelligence, which is perception of the false and which is awakened through suffering, is again put to sleep by establishing other sets of values which will give us an illusory comfort. So we move from one illusion to another. There must be constant conflict and suffering until the mind is free from all illusions, until there is creative intelligence.

Question: Is it one of the duties of teachers to show children that war in any of its forms is inherently wrong?

KRISHNAMURTI: What would happen to a teacher who really taught the whole significance and stupidity of war? He would soon be without a job. So, knowing that, he begins to compromise. (Laughter) You all laugh, you say it is perfectly true, but you are the very people who are maintaining this whole system of thought. If you really, humanly felt the ugliness and cruelty of war, you as individuals would not contribute to all the steps leading up to nationalism and eventually to war. After all, war is merely the result of a system based on exploitation, on acquisitiveness. We hope by some miracle that this whole system will change. We do not want to act individually, voluntarily, freely, but we are waiting for a system to be created by others in which individually we will have no responsibility. If that happens, we shall merely become slaves to another system.

If a teacher really feels that he must not teach war, because he understands the full significance of it, then he will act. A man who deeply and intelligently feels the cruelty of a thing in itself will act and not consider what will happen to him. (Applause)

Question: What should be the real purpose of education?

KRISHNAMURTI: If you think that man is nothing but a machine, clay to be molded, to be shaped according to a particular pattern, then you must have ruthless compulsion, rigorous discipline; for then you do not want to awaken individual intelligence, creative thinking, but you merely want the individual to be conditioned for a particular system. That is what is happening throughout the world, in some cases subtly, in others in a gross form. You see compulsion in various forms exercised over human beings, thus gradually destroying their intelligence, their fulfillment.

Most of you who are religiously inclined, and who talk about God and immortality, do not fundamentally believe in individual fulfillment, for in the very structure of religious thought, through fear, you allow compulsion and imposition. Either there must be individual fulfillment, or the complete mechanization of man. There cannot be compromise between the two. You cannot say that man must fit into a pattern, must comply, follow, obey, have authority, and at the same time think that he is a spiritual entity.

Once you begin to understand the deep significance of human life, then there will be true education. But to understand this, mind must free itself from authority and tradition by discerning their true significance. The superficial questions concerning this will be answered when you delve profoundly into all the subtleties of authority. There must inevitably be the subtle and gross form of compulsion when the mind is seeking security, safety. So a mind that would liberate itself from compulsion must not seek the limitation of security, certainty. To understand the deep significance of authority and compulsion, you need very delicate and careful thought.

Question: You deny authority, but are you not creating authority too, by all you have to say or teach to the world, even if you insist that people must not recognize any authority? How can you prevent people from following you as their authority? Can you help it?

KRISHNAMURTI: If a man desires to obey and to follow someone, no one can prevent him; but it is most unintelligent, leading to great unhappiness and frustration. If those of you who are listening to me really begin to think deeply about authority, you will not follow anyone, including myself. But as I said, it is much easier to follow and to imitate than to really free thought from the limitation of fear and so from compulsion and authority. The one is an easy giving over of oneself to another, in which there is always the idea of getting something in return, whereas in the other there is absolute insecurity; and as people prefer the illusion of comfort, security, they follow authority with its frustration. But if the mind discerns the illusory nature of comfort or security, there is born intelligence, the new, the vital life.

Question: A person who is religiously minded but who has the power to think deeply may lose his religious faith after listening to you. But if his fear remains, what advantage will that be for him?

KRISHNAMURTI: What creates faith in man? Fundamentally, fear. You say, "If I get rid of faith, then I shall be left with fear, and

so have gained nothing." So you prefer to live in an illusion, clinging to its fantasies. In order to escape from fear, you create faith. Now when through deep thinking you dissolve faith, then you are face to face with fear. Then only can you resolve the cause of fear. When all the avenues of escape have been thoroughly understood and destroyed, then you are face to face with the root of fear: only then can the mind liberate itself from the clutch of fear.

When there is fear, then religions and authorities, which you have created in your search for security, offer you the opiate which you call faith, or the love of God. Thus you merely cover up fear, which expresses itself in hidden and subtle ways. So you continue rejecting old faiths and accepting new ones; but the real poison, the root of fear, is never dissolved. As long as there is that limited consciousness, the 'I', there must be fear. Until the mind liberates itself from this limited consciousness, fear must remain in one form or another.

Question: Do you think it is possible to solve social problems by transforming the state into an all-powerful machine in every field of human endeavor, having one man rule supreme over the state and the nation? In other words, has fascism any useful feature in it? Or is it rather to be fought against, as war must be, as an enemy of man's highest welfare?

KRISHNAMURTI: If in any organization there exist class or hierarchical distinctions based on acquisitiveness, then such an organization will be an impediment to man. How can there be the well-being of man if your attitude towards life is nationalistic, class-conscious or acquisitive? Because of this, people are divided into nations ruled by sovereign governments which create wars. As possessiveness and nationalism divide, so religions with their beliefs and dogmas separate people. So long as these exist, there must be divisions, wars, disputes, and conflicts.

To understand any of these problems, we must think anew, which demands great suffering; and as very few are willing to go through that, we accept political parties, with their jargon, and think that thereby we are dissolving the fundamental problems.

July 6, 1935

Buenos Aires, Argentina, 1935

＊

First Talk in Buenos Aires

Friends,

Most of us are aware of the many forms of conflict, of sorrow and of exploitation that exist about us. We see men exploiting their fellow men, men exploiting women and women exploiting men; we see the division of classes, nationalities, wars, and other great cruelties. Each one must have asked himself what shall be his individual action in all this chaotic and stupid condition. One is either entirely unconscious of all this or, being conscious, must often have had the thought not to add or submit to the impositions and cruelties in the world.

In the hope of finding a way out of this suffering, most of you come to listen to these talks. You will be disappointed if you are merely seeking a new system of action or a new method to overcome suffering. I am not going to give a new system or a pattern after which to mold yourselves, for that would in no way solve the many difficulties and sorrows. The mere adjustment to a plan, without deep thought and understanding, will only lead to greater confusion and emptiness. But if you are able to discern for yourselves how to act truly, then your own intelligence will always guide you under all circumstances. If you look to an expert, you become merely one of the many cogs in the machinery of his system of thought. Besides, among the experts and specialists themselves there is much contradiction and dissension. Each expert or specialist forms a party around his system of thought, and then these parties become the cause of further confusion and exploitation.

Now, as I said, I am not offering a new mold into which you can fit yourself; but if you are able to discover and understand profoundly the cause of suffering, then you will find for yourself the true method of action which cannot be systematized. For life is in continual movement, and a mind that is incapable of adjustment must inevitably suffer.

To understand and to discern the deep significance of life, you must come to it with a pliable and an eager mind. The mind must be critical and aware. The opposition of cultivated prejudices and of the traditional background of defensive reactions becomes a great impediment to clear understanding. That is, if you are Christians, you have been brought up in a certain tradition, with prejudices, hopes and ideals, and through that background, through those prejudices, you look at life with its ever-changing expressions. Often this is thought to be the critical understanding of life, but it is only the creation of further defensive opposition.

If I may suggest it, during this evening try to put away your prejudices, try to forget that you are a Christian, a communist, a socialist, an anarchist, or a capitalist; and examine what I am going to say. Do not merely dismiss what I say as being communistic, anarchistic, or as nothing new. To understand life with which, after all, we are concerned, we must not confuse theory with actuality; theories and ideals are merely expressions of hopes, longings, which offer an escape from actuality. If we can face actuality and discern its true value, then we shall find out what is of lasting significance and what is utterly vain and destructive.

So I am not going to discuss any theory. Theories are utterly useless. If we can discern the significance of actuality, through questioning, we shall begin to awaken that intelligence which shall be a constant, active, and directing principle in life.

Now we have certain established values, religious and economic, according to which we are guiding our life. We have to inquire whether these values are crippling, perverting our thought and action. In deeply understanding what we have created about us, which has become our prison, we shall not fall into another set of false values and illusions. This does not mean that you must accept my values, or accept my interpretation, or belong to any particular group that you may think I represent. I do not belong to any society, to any religion, or to any organization or party.

Man is almost suffocated in the prison of false values, of which he is unconscious. Through deep questioning and suffering he becomes aware of that which he has built about himself, and not through mere acceptance of what another says; if he merely accepted, he would fall into another prison, into another cage. If you individually and intelligently inquired into the system to which each one has contributed, then, through the understanding born of suffering, you would know for yourself the true manner of action.

What are these values, seasoned in tradition and illusion, based on? If you discern deeply, you will see that these values and ideals are based on fear, which is the outcome of individual search for security. In search of this security, we have divided life as material and spiritual, economic and religious. Now such an artificial division is entirely false, for life is an integrated whole. We have created this artificial distinction; and in understanding the cause of this separation between the spiritual and material, we shall know the integrated action of life as a whole. So let us first understand this structure which we call religion.

There is in each one of you, in one form or another, a desire for continuance, a search for spiritual security which you call immortality. He who offers or promises this security, this egotistic continuance, this selfish immortality, becomes your authority, to be worshipped, to be prayed to, to be followed. Thus you slowly give yourself over to that authority, and so fear is cunningly and subtly cultivated. To lead you to that promised immortality, a system, called religion, becomes a vital necessity. To maintain this artificial structure, beliefs, ideals, dogmas and creeds are required. And to interpret, to administer and to uphold this self-created prison of man, you must have priests. Thus priests throughout the world become exploiters.

In search of your individual security, which you call immortality, you begin to create many illusions and ideals, which become the means of gross or subtle exploitation. To assure you and to interpret the craving for your own security in the hereafter and in the present, there must be mediators, messengers, who, through your fear, become your exploiters. So it is you yourselves who are fundamentally the creators of exploiters, whether economic or spiritual. To understand this religious structure which has become a means of exploiting man throughout the world, you must understand your own desire and the ways of its subtle and cunning action.

Religion, which is an organized form of stupidity, has become your destroyer. It has become an instrument of power, of vested interest, of exploitation. You as individuals must awaken to this structure of opposition to intelligence, which is the result of your own fears, desires, cravings, and secret pursuits.

Religion, for most people, is nothing but a reaction against intelligence. You may not be religious, you may not believe in immortality, but you have secret desires prompting you to exploit, to be cruel, to dominate, which must inevitably create conditions forcing and stimulating man to seek comfort, security, in an illusion. Whether you are inclined to be religious or not, fear permeates human beings and their actions, and must create illusion of some kind: the religious illusion, or the illusion of power, or the intellectual conceit of ideals.

Throughout the world man is in search of this immortal security. Fear makes him seek comfort in an organized belief, which is called religion, with its creeds and dogmas, with its pageantry and superstition. These organized beliefs, religions, fundamentally separate man. And if you examine their ideals, their moralities, you will see that they are based on fear and egotism. From organized belief there follows vested interest, which subtly becomes the cruel authority for exploiting man through his fear.

So you see how man through his own fear, through self-created authority, through closed and egotistic morality, has allowed himself to be slavishly bound; he has lost the capacity to think and so to live creatively, happily. His action, born out of this suffocation and limitation, must ever be incomplete, ever destructive of intelligence.

The individual, through search for his own security, has created through many centuries a system based on acquisitiveness, fear, and exploitation. To this system of his own making he has become an utter slave. The selfish conditioning of family, and its own security, has created an environment which forces the individual to become ruthless. Into the hands of the most cunning and the ruthless, the few, has come the machine, which affords the means of exploitation. Out of all this there is born the absurd division of classes, nationalities, and wars. Every sovereign government, with its particular nationality, must inevitably create war, for its acts are based on vested interest.

Thus you have on the one side religion, and on the other material conditions, which are continually twisting, perverting man's thought and action.

Almost all people are unconscious both of the intelligence and of the stupidity about them. But how can each one realize what is stupidity and what is intelligence, if his thought and action are based on fear and authority? So individually we have to become aware, conscious of these limiting conditions.

Most of us are waiting for some miracle to take place which will bring order out of this chaos and suffering. Every one of us will have to become individually conscious, aware, in order to discover what is limiting and stupid. Out of this deep discernment there is born intelligence; but it is impossible to understand what this intelligence is if the mind is limited and stupid. To try intellectually to grasp the meaning of intelligence is utterly vain and arid. In discovering for ourselves and being free from the many stupidities and limitations, each one will realize a life of love and understanding.

Through fear, we have created certain hindrances which are continually impeding the full movement of life. Take the stupidity of nationalism, with all its absurdities, cruelties, and exploitations. What, as individuals, is your attitude, your action towards it? Do not say that it is not important, that you are not concerned with it, that you don't touch politics; if you examine it fundamentally, you will see that you are part of this machine of exploitation. You as an individual will have to become conscious of this stupidity and limitation.

Equally you have to become aware of the stupidity and limitation of authority in religion. When you once become conscious of it, then you will see the deep significance of the hold it has on you. How can you think clearly, feel fully, completely, when unquestioned authoritative values cripple the mind and the heart?

So we have many stupidities and limitations which are slowly destroying intelligence, such as ideals, beliefs, dogmas, nationalism and the possessive idea of family; and of these we are almost unconscious. And yet each one is trying to live fully, happily, trying to find out intelligently what is God, what is truth. But how can a limited mind, how can a mind that is enclosed by innumerable barriers, understand what is supremely intelligent, beautiful? To understand the supreme, mind must be free of the impediments and illusions created through fear and acquisitiveness.

How are you to become conscious, aware of these shelters and illusions? Only through conflict, through suffering; not by discussing intellectually, for that is dealing with this question but partially.

Let me explain what I mean by conflict. Suppose you begin to realize that organized belief, religion, is fundamentally separating man from man, preventing him from living fully, deeply, and by not yielding to its demands and stupidities, you begin to create vital conflict. Then you will find that your family, your friends and public opinion are against you, which will create great suffering in you. It is only when you suffer and do not try to escape from suffering, when you see that explanations are futile, when all escapes have been stopped, it is only then that you will begin to discern truly, fundamentally, deeply in your mind and heart, what are the limitations that prevent the free flow of reality, of life. If you merely accept what I say and repeat after me that nationalism, beliefs, authorities are hindrances, then you will create only another authority and take transient and illusory shelter under it. If you as individuals truly understand this whole structure of fear and exploitation, then only can there be fulfillment, an ever-becoming of life, immortality. But this demands intelligence, not knowledge; a deep understanding born of action, not of acceptance, not of following a particular person or pattern, nor of trying to adjust yourself to a system or to an authority.

If you would understand the beauty of life, with its deep movement and its happiness, then the mind and heart must become aware of those values and impediments that are preventing fulfillment in action. It is limitation, egotism, that prevent discernment, that cause suffering, and so there is no fulfillment.

July 12, 1935

Second Talk in Buenos Aires

Friends,

Many questions have been handed in, and before I answer some of them I should like to give a brief introductory talk.

I do not think that any human problem can be solved isolatedly, by itself. Each one of us has many problems, many difficulties, and we try to deal with them exclusively, not as a part of an integral whole. If we have a political problem, we try to solve it apart, let us say, from religion. Or if there is an individual religious problem, we try to solve it apart from the social problem, and so on. That is, there are individual and at the same time collective problems, which we try to deal with separately. Because we do this, we only create further confusion and further misery. By merely solving one problem isolatedly, we create others, and so the mind becomes entangled in a net of unsolved problems.

Now let us understand the problem which must be in the minds of most people: that of individual fulfillment and collective work. If collective work becomes compulsory, as it is becoming, and each individual is forcibly pulled into it, then individual fulfillment disappears and each one becomes merely a slave to a collective idea or a collective system of authority. So the point is: How can we bring about collective work and at the same time realize individual fulfillment? Otherwise, as I said, we become mere machines, cogs that automatically function.

If we can understand the deep significance of individual fulfillment, then collective work will not be a destructive force or an impediment to intelligence.

Each one must discover intelligence for himself, whose expression will then be true fulfillment. If he does not, if he merely follows a plan laid down, then it will not be a fulfillment, but only a conformity through fear. If I laid down a plan or gave you a system whereby you could, by imitating, arrive at fulfillment, it would not be a fulfillment at all; it would be merely an adjustment to a particular pattern. Please see this point very clearly, for otherwise you will think I am but destroying. If you merely imitate, there cannot be fulfillment. The constant conformity to a particular mold is the basis of our religious thought and moral action; and living is no longer a complete and deep fulfillment, an integrated understanding of life,

but merely conformity to a certain system, through fear and compulsion. This is the very beginning of authority.

To fulfill, there must be the greatest intelligence. This intelligence is different from knowledge. You may read many books, but it will not give you intelligence. Intelligence can be awakened only through action, through the understanding of action as an integrated whole.

To discuss and intellectually discover what is intelligence would be, I feel, a waste of time and energy, for that would not lift the burden of ignorance and illusion. Instead of inquiring what is intelligence, let us discover for ourselves what are the hindrances placed upon the mind which prevent the full awakening of intelligence. If I were to give an explanation of what is intelligence, and you agreed with my explanation, your mind would make of it a well-defined system, and through fear would twist itself to fit into that system. But if each one can discover for himself the many impediments placed on the mind, then, through awareness, not through self-analysis, the mind will begin to liberate itself, thus awakening true intelligence which is life itself.

Now one of the greatest impediments placed on the mind is authority. Please understand the whole significance of that word, and don't jump to the opposite conclusion. Please don't say, "Must we be free of law; can we do what we like; how can we be free of morality, authority?" Authority is very subtle; its ways are many; its permeating influence is so delicate, so cunning, that it needs great discernment, not hasty and thoughtless conclusions, to realize its significance.

When there is deep understanding there is no division of authority as the outer and the inner, as applicable to the mass or to the few, as the externally imposed or the inwardly cultivated. But unfortunately there exists this division of external and inward authority. The external is the imposition of standards, traditions, ideals, which merely act as an enclosure to restrain the individual, treating him as an animal to be trained according to certain demands and conditions. You see this happening all the time in the closed morality of religions, in the standards of systems and parties. As a reaction against this imposition of authority we develop an inner guide, a system, a discipline according to which we try to act, and thus force experience to fit itself into this groove of protected desires and hopes.

Where there is authority and a mere adjustment to it, there cannot be fulfillment. Each individual has created this authority, through fear and the desire for security. You have to understand your own desire, which is creating authority and to which you are a slave; you cannot merely disregard it. When the mind discerns the deep significance of authority, and frees itself from fear with its subtle influences, then there is the dawning of intelligence, which is true fulfillment. Where there is intelligence there is true cooperation, and not compulsion; but where there is no intelligence, collective work becomes mere slavery. True collective work is the natural outcome of fulfillment, which is intelligence. In awakening intelligence, each one helps to create the opportunity, the environment for others also to fulfill.

Question: It is being said in some newspapers and elsewhere that you have led a gay and useless life; that you have no real message, but are merely repeating the gibberish of the Theosophists who educated you; that you are attacking all religions except your own; that you are destroying without building anything new; that your purpose is to create doubt, disturbance, and confusion in the minds of the people. What have you to say to all this?

KRISHNAMURTI: I think I had better answer this question point by point. (Shouts from the audience: "It is an infamy! The question is libelous!") Sirs, just a minute. Please don't feel that I am insulted, and that you have to defend me. (Applause)

Someone has said that I have led a gay and useless life. I am afraid he cannot judge. To judge another is entirely false, for to judge means that your mind is a slave to a particular standard. As a matter of fact, I have not led a so-called gay life, fortunately or unfortunately; but that doesn't make me an object of worship. I say that the tendency in people to worship another, no matter who it is, is destructive of intelligence; but to understand and love another cannot be included in worship which is born of subtle fear. Only a limited mind will judge another, and such a mind cannot understand the living quality of life.

It is said that I have no real message, but am "merely repeating the gibberish of the Theosophists who educated me." As a matter of fact, I do not belong to the Theosophical Society, or to any other society. To belong to any religious organization is detrimental to intelligence. (Objections from the audience) Sirs, that is my opinion. You need not agree with it. But you have to find out whether or not what I say is true, and not merely object. It happens that when I talk in India, they tell me that I am teaching Hinduism, and when I talk in the Buddhist countries, they tell me that what I say is Buddhism, and the Theosophists and others say that I am explaining anew their own special doctrines. What matters is that you who are listening understand the significance of what I am saying, and not whether someone thinks that I am repeating the gibberish of a particular society. Out of your own suffering, through your own understanding of action, comes true intelligence, which is true fulfillment. So what is of great importance is not whether I belong to any society or am merely rehashing old ideas, but that you deeply understand the significance of the ideas which I have put forward, thus completing them in action. Then you will discover for yourself whether what I am saying is true or false, whether it has any essential value in life. Unfortunately, we are very apt to believe anything that appears in print. If you can really think through one idea completely, then you will find the real beauty of action, of life.

It is said that I am attacking all religions except my own. I do not belong to any religion. For me, all religions are but defensive reactions against life, against intelligence.

The questioner suggests that my purpose is to create doubt, disturbance, and confusion in the minds of the people. Now, you must have the purifying balm of doubt in order to understand; otherwise you merely become slaves of vested interest, whether it be of organized religion or of money and social tradition. If you begin to question truly the values which now enclose and hold you, though it may cause confusion and disturbance, if you persist in deeply understanding them in action, there will be clarity and happiness. But clarity or comprehension does not come about superficially, artificially; there must be deep questioning.

Doubt is the awakener of intelligence, born of suffering. But the man whose mind is held in the vice of vested interest, of power and exploitation, declares doubt to be pernicious, a fetter which causes confusion and brings about destruction. If you would truly awaken intelligence, you must begin to understand the significance of values through doubt and suffering. If you would realize the movement of life, of reality, mind must be denuded of all self-defensive values.

Question: It is clear to me that you are determined to destroy all our cherished ideals. If these are destroyed, will not civilization collapse and man return to savagery?

KRISHNAMURTI: First of all, I cannot destroy your ideals which you have created. If I could destroy them, you would create others in their place and so be prisoners to these. What we have to find out is, not whether by destruction of ideals there is going to be savagery, but whether ideals really help man to live completely, intelligently. Is there not savagery, chaos, misery, exploitation, war, in spite of your ideals, religions, and closed morality? So let us find out whether ideals are a help or a hindrance. To understand this, your mind must not be prejudiced or on the defensive.

When we talk about ideals, we mean those points of light by which we seek to guide ourselves across the confusion and mystery of life. That is what we mean by ideals: those future conceptions which will help man to direct himself across the chaos of present existence.

The subtle desire for ideals and their permanence indicates that you want to cross the ocean of life without suffering. As you do not fully comprehend the present, you desire to have guides in the form of ideals. So you say, "As life is such a conflict, as there is so much misery and suffering in it, ideals will give me encouragement, hope." Thus ideals become an escape from the present. Your mind and heart are crippled and burdened by them, giving you a subtle means of escape from the ever-living present, thus covering up and dodging the conflict and the suffering of the now. So gradually you come to live in theories and cannot understand the actuality.

Let me take an example which I hope will make my meaning clear. As Christians you profess to love your neighbors: that is the ideal. Now what is happening in actuality? Love doesn't exist, but we have fear, domination, cruelty, and all the horrors and absurdities of nationalism and war. In theory it is one thing, and in fact it is quite the opposite. But if you put aside for the moment your ideals and really confront the actual; if instead of living in a romantic future you face without illusion that which is ever taking place, giving your whole mind and heart to it, then you will act and know the movement of reality.

Now, you are confusing actuality with theories. You have to separate the actual from the theoretical, from hopes and longings. When you are confronted with the actual, there is action; but if you escape into ideals, into the security of illusion, then you will not act. The greater the ideal, the greater is its power to hold man in an illusion, in a prison. It is only in understanding life, with all its suffering, joy and deep movement, that the mind can free itself from illusions and ideals.

When the mind is crippled with hopes and longings which become ideals, it cannot understand the present. But when the mind begins to free itself from these future hopes and illusions, then action will awaken that intelligence which is life itself, the ever-becoming.

Question: I am deeply interested in your ideas, but I am opposed by my family and the priest. What should be my attitude towards them?

KRISHNAMURTI: If you desire to understand truth, life, then family as an influence, as a shelter, doesn't exist; and the priest, as an imposition with subtle exploitation, ceases to be a determining factor in life. So it is you yourself who have to answer this question. If you would understand the beauty of life and live deeply and ecstatically, without this continual creation of limitation, then you must be free from organized beliefs, as in religion with its exploitation, and from the possessiveness of family with its cunning and self-defensive shelters—which does not mean throwing away all things and becoming a licentious person. If you desire to understand profoundly and live intelligently with fulfillment, then family, priest, or public opinion cannot stand in the way.

What is public opinion, what are priests, what is family, when you really come to consider it? To discern, has not each one to stand alone, without support? This in no way means that you cannot love, that you cannot marry and have children. Because of your own desire for security and comfort, you begin to create an environment which influences, limits and dominates your mind and heart through fear. A man who would understand truth must be free from the desire for security and comfort.

Question: Some say you are the Christ, others that you are the Antichrist. What, in fact, are you?

KRISHNAMURTI: I don't think it matters very much what I am. What matters is whether you intelligently understand what I say. If you have a deep appreciation of beauty, it is of little importance to know who painted the picture or wrote the poem. (Applause and objections) Sirs, I am not evading the question, because I don't think it matters in the least who I am. For if I began to assert or deny, I should become an authority. But if you, through your own discernment, understand and live what is true and vital in that which I am saying, then there will be fulfillment. This, after all, is of the greatest importance: that you shall live fully, completely—and not what I am.

Question: Is there any difference between true religious feeling and religion as organized belief?

KRISHNAMURTI: Before I answer this question we must understand what we mean by organized belief. A structure of creeds, dogmas, and beliefs based on authority, with its pageantry, sensation, and exploitation—this I call organized religion, with its many vested interests. And there are those personal feelings and reactions which one calls religious experiences. You may not belong to an organized religion with all its subtle influences of authority, imposition, and fear, but you may have personal experiences which you call religious feeling. I need not again explain how organized belief, that is, religion, fundamentally cripples thought and love, for I have already gone into that fairly thoroughly.

Those experiences which we call religious may be the outcome of an illusion; so we have to understand how they come into being. If there is conflict, suffering, the mind naturally seeks comfort. In search of comfort away from suffering, the mind creates illusions from which it derives certain experiences and feelings which it calls religious, or by some other term. In understanding and freeing itself from the cause of suffering, the mind shall realize, not an objective experience which acts on a limited and subjective mind, but that movement of life itself, of reality, from which it is not separate. As most people suffer, and as most people have religious experiences of some kind, these experiences are merely an escape from the cause of suffering into an illusion which assumes, through constant contact and habit, a reality. You have to find out for yourself whether what you call your religious experience is an escape from suffering, or whether it is the freedom from the cause of suffering, and hence the movement of reality. If you seek religious experience, then it must

be false, because you are merely craving to escape from life and actuality; but when the mind frees itself from fear and its many limitations, then there is the flow of the ecstasy of life.

Question: How can I be free of fear?

KRISHNAMURTI: I think the questioner wants to know how to free himself from the deep and significant cause of fear.

To be truly free of fear, you must lose all sense of egotism; and that is a very difficult thing to do. Egotism is so subtle, it expresses itself in so many ways, that we are almost unconscious of it. It expresses itself through the search for security, whether in this world or in some other world which is called the hereafter. It craves to be secure, now and in the future, and thus hinders intelligence and fulfillment. As long as this desire for security exists, there must be fear. A mind that seeks immortality, the continuance of its own limited consciousness, must create fear, ignorance, and illusion. If the mind can free itself from the desire for security, then fear ceases; and to discover if the mind is pursuing security, it must become aware, fully conscious.

July 15, 1935

Third Talk in Buenos Aires

Friends,

If our actions are merely the outcome of some superficial reactions, then they must lead to confusion, misery, and to selfish individual expressions. If we can understand the fundamental cause of our action and free it from its limitations, then action will inevitably bring about intelligence and cooperation in the world.

Much of our action is born of compulsion, influence, domination, or fear, but there is an action which is the outcome of voluntary understanding. Each one of us is faced with the question: Are we capable of this voluntary action of intelligence, or must we be forced, directed, and controlled? To fulfill, to understand life completely, there must be voluntary action.

Action born out of some superficial reaction inevitably makes the mind shallow and limited. Take jealousy. By dealing superficially with it we hope to end it, be free of it. We try to control, sublimate, or forget it. This action is only dealing with a superficial symptom, without understanding the fundamental cause from which the reaction of jealousy is born. The cause is possessiveness. Action born of a reaction, of a symptom, without understanding the cause, must lead to greater conflict and suffering. When the mind is free from the cause, which is possessiveness, then the symptom, which is jealousy, disappears. It is utterly futile to deal with a symptom, with a reaction.

Again, we have to discover and understand for ourselves how we act towards the established system of exploitation; whether we are merely dealing with it superficially, and so increasing its problems; or whether our action is born out of freedom from acquisitiveness which causes exploitation. If we deeply consider the cause of exploitation, we shall discern it to be the outcome of acquisitiveness; and though we may sometimes solve superficial problems, until we are truly free of the cause, other problems and conflicts will continually arise.

To take an example. We go from one puzzling sect to another, large or small, with their dogmas, creeds, and with their organized authority and exploitation. We go from one teacher to another; from one cage of organized belief we fall into another. The fundamental cause of the existence of organized belief, which controls and dominates man, is fear; and until he is really free from it, his action must be limited, thus creating further suffering.

Each one of us is confronted with this problem: Are we to act superficially through reaction, or, through understanding the cause of exploitation, awaken intelligence? If we merely act through superficial reactions, we shall inevitably create greater divisions, conflicts and miseries; but if we truly understand the fundamental cause of all this chaos and act from that comprehension, then there will be true intelligence which alone can create the right environment for each individual to fulfill.

Question: If you have renounced possessions, money, properties, as you say you have, what do you think of the commission that organized your tour and is selling your books in the very theater where you give your lectures? Are you not also exploiting and exploited?

KRISHNAMURTI: Neither the commission nor I make any money out of these sales. The expense of hiring this theater is borne by some friends. Whatever money is received from the sale of these books is used to print further books and pamphlets. As some of us think that these ideas will be of great help to man, we desire to spread them, and to me this desire is not exploitation. You needn't buy the books, nor need you come to these talks. (Applause) You are not going to miss a spiritual opportunity by not coming here.

Exploitation exists where a person, or some unquestioned value or idea, dominates and urges you, subtly or grossly, towards a particular action. What we are trying to do is to help you to awaken your own intelligence so that you will discern for yourself the fundamental cause which creates suffering. If you do not discern for yourself and free yourself from all those limitations that crush your mind and heart, there cannot be true happiness or intelligence.

Question: To give up all authority, discipline, creed, and dogma, may be right for the educated man, but would it not be pernicious for the uneducated?

KRISHNAMURTI: Who is the uneducated and who is the educated is very difficult to determine. But what we can do is to find out for ourselves, individually, whether authority, with all its significance, is really beneficial. Please understand the deep significance of authority. One creates one's own authority when there is the desire to protect oneself or take shelter in a hope or in an ideal or in a certain set of values. This authority, this self-defensive system of thought, prevents one from living completely, from fulfilling. Out of the desire to be secure arise disciplines, beliefs, ideals, and dogmas. If you who are supposed to be educated are truly free from authority, with all its significance, then you will naturally create the right environment for those who are still held down by authority, by tradition, by fear.

So the question is not what will happen to the unfortunate man who is not educated, but whether you, as individuals, have understood the deep significance of authority, discipline, belief, and creed, and are truly free from all these. To consider what will happen to the uneducated man if he is not controlled is fundamentally a false way of seeking to help him. This attitude is the very spirit of exploitation. If you gave the opportunity for the so-called uneducated man to awaken his own intelligence and not be dominated by you or forced to follow your particular system or pattern of thought, then there would be fulfillment for all.

Question: Do you think that the exploited and unemployed should organize themselves and destroy capitalism?

KRISHNAMURTI: If you think that the capitalistic system is crushing and destroying individual intelligence and fulfillment, then you as individuals must free yourselves from it by truly understanding the causes which created it. It is, as I said, based on acquisitiveness, on individual security, both religious and economic. Now if you as individuals fully discern this and are free from it, then a true organization of intelligent cooperation will naturally come into existence. But if you merely create an organization without discernment, then you will become slaves to it. If each individual really tries to free himself from egotistic desires, ambitions, and success, then, whatever may be the expressions of that intelligence, they will not dominate and oppress man.

Question: What do you mean by morality and love?

KRISHNAMURTI: Let us examine the present-day morality in order to find out what should be the true morality. What is our whole system of morality, both the religious and the economic, based on? It is based on individual security, the search for one's own safety. The present-day morality is based on utter selfishness. There are happily a few who are outside this closed morality.

To find out what is true morality, we must individually begin to free ourselves, through comprehension, from this closed morality, which means that you must begin to doubt, to question the values of the present-day morality. You must discover according to what moral standards you are acting; whether your action is the result of compulsion, of tradition, or of your own desire to be safe, secure. Now if you are merely conforming to a morality of individual security, then there cannot be intelligence, nor can there be true human happiness. As individuals you must come intelligently into conflict with this selfish system of morality, because it is only through intelligent conflict, through suffering, that you discern the true significance of these moral standards. You cannot discover merely intellectually their true worth.

Now most of us are afraid to question, to doubt, because such questioning will bring about definite action, demanding definite alteration in our daily life. So we prefer to discuss merely intellectually what is true morality.

The questioner also wants to know what is love. To understand what true love is, we must understand our present attitude, thought and action towards love. If you truly thought about it you would see that our love is based on possessiveness, and our laws and ethics are founded on this desire to hold and to control. How can there be deep love when there is this desire to possess, to hold? When the mind is free from possessiveness, then there is that loveliness, the bliss of love.

Question: Should we give in to those who are against us, or avoid them?

KRISHNAMURTI: Neither. If you merely give in, surely in that there is no comprehension; and if you merely avoid them, in that there is fear. If your action is based, not on a reaction, but on the full understanding of fundamental causes, then there is no question of giving in or of running away. Then you are acting intelligently, truly.

Question: You are giving us chaotic theories and inciting us to useless revolt. I should like to have your answer to this statement.

KRISHNAMURTI: I am not giving you any theories or inciting you to revolt. If I am capable of urging you towards rebellion, and if you yield to it, then another will come and put you to sleep again. (Laughter) So the important thing is to find out whether you are suffering. Now, a man who is suffering doesn't need to be urged towards rebellion; but he must keep awake to understand the cause of suffering, and not be put to sleep by explanations and ideals. If you consider very carefully you will see that, when there is suffering, there is a desire to be comforted, to be put to sleep. When you suffer, your immediate reaction is to seek comfort; and those who give you comfort, consolation, become for you an authority whom you blindly follow. Through that authority your suffering is explained away. The function of real suffering, which is to awaken intelligence, is denied through the search for comfort.

Now you have to ask yourself whether you as an individual are satisfied with the religious, social, and economic conditions as they are, and if not, what your action is towards them. Not as a group or a mass, but as individuals. When you ask yourself this question, you must inevitably come into conflict with all those religious authorities and dogmas, with all those moralities based on selfish desires, and with that system which exploits the individual for the few. I am not inciting you to rebellion, or giving you new theories. I say that you can live with plenitude and intelligence when the mind frees itself from the stupidities of selfish, limited desires. When you begin to discover the true significance of the values that you have built about yourself, when the mind and heart free themselves from fear which has created doctrines, beliefs, ideals, which are continually impeding you, then there is fulfillment, the flow of reality.

Question: Is it natural that men should kill each other in war?

KRISHNAMURTI: To discover whether it is natural or not, you must find out whether war is essential, whether war is the most intelligent way of solving political or economic problems. You must question the whole system that leads up to war.

Now, as I said, nationalism is a disease. Nationalism is used as a means of exploiting the mass. It is the outcome of vested interest. Please think this over and act individually.

Nationalism, with its separative, sovereign governments which do not consider humanity as a whole, and which are based on class distinctions and vested interests—do you think that this nationalism is natural, human, intelligent? Is it not the outcome of exploitation and the instrument for inciting people to fight in order that a few may benefit? Also, we have built up a psychological necessity for wars, which is the grossest form of stupidity. As long as we are capable of being incited through patriotism, we shall inevitably yield to a false reaction; and from that arise innumerable problems. If you deeply question the whole idea of nationalism and acquisitiveness, you will never ask whether war is natural. There are some who are against what I am saying because they think that their vested interest is being disturbed; and others are delighted when I speak against nationalism, only because they have vested interests in other countries.

To live intelligently, without the distinctions of nationalities, classes, without the divisions that religions create between man and man, you as individuals must free yourselves from acquisitiveness. This demands great awareness, interest, and action on your part. As long as the individual is not free from the search for self-security there will be suffering, wars, and confusion.

Question: You promise us a new paradise on earth, but it is unreachable. Do you not think that we need immediate solutions, and not some far-off hopes? Would not universal communism be the immediate solution?

KRISHNAMURTI: I am not promising you a future paradise on earth, but I am telling you that you can make of this world a paradise by your own intelligent awakening and action, by your own questioning of those things about you that are false. No system is ever going to save man, but only his own voluntary intelligence. If you merely accept a system, you become a slave to it; but if, out of your own suffering, out of your own questioning of those values and traditions, you begin to awaken true intelligence, then you will create that which cannot exploit man.

Sirs, what is preventing each one of us from living intelligently, humanly, sacredly? Each one of us is seeking immortality, security in another world; so religions become a necessity, with all their exploitations, dominations, and fears. And, here in this world, we are seeking security of a different kind; so we have built a ruthless, competitive system of wars, class distinctions, and all the rest of it. You as individuals have created this agony of distinction and suffering, and you as individuals will have to alter it. But if you merely look to a group to alter the present conditions, then you will not realize that ecstasy of deep fulfillment.

So what will bring about in the world a happy, intelligent condition is your own awakening, your intense questioning of values, from which alone comes action. When you as individuals, through action, begin to understand the true significance of life, then there will be paradise on earth.

Question: Do you believe in the immortality of the soul?

KRISHNAMURTI: The idea of the soul is based on authority and hope. Please, before I go further into this, don't be on the defensive. We are trying to find out what is true, not what is traditional, not what you believe; so we must first inquire if there is such a thing as the soul. To discern, you must come without prejudice, either for or against it.

We have created through our desire for immortality, the idea of the soul. As we think that we cannot understand this world, with all its agonies, miseries, and exploitations, we want to live in another world more fully, more completely. We think that there must be some other entity which is more spiritual than this. The idea of the soul is based fundamentally on egotistic continuance.

Now reality or truth or God, or whatever name you like to give to it, is not egotistic, personal consciousness. When you seek security, continuance, you think of the soul as different from reality. Having created this separation you ask, "Is it immortal?" When the mind is free from its limited consciousness, with its desire for continuance, then there is immortality, not of personal, individual continuance, but of life.

Illusion can divide itself into many, but truth cannot. As the mind creates illusion, it divides itself into the permanent, which it calls the soul, and the impermanent, the transient existence. This division merely creates further illusion.

When the mind is free from all limitation, there is immortality. But you have to discern what are the limitations that prevent the mind from living completely. The very desire for continuance is the greatest of limitations. This desire is the outcome of memory which acts as a guide, as a warning of self-protection against life, experience. Out of this is born the force that makes you imitate, conform, submit yourself to authority, and so there is constant fear. All this goes to make up the idea of the 'I' which craves for continuance. When the

mind is free from this egotism, which expresses itself in many ways, then there is reality, or call it what you will. When there is that sense of Godhood, you do not belong to any religion, to any set of people, to any family. It is only when you have lost that sense of Godhood that you become religious, and submit yourself to all the absurdities and cruelties, to exploitation and suffering. As long as mind is not vulnerable to the movement, to the swift current of life, there cannot be reality. Mind must be utterly naked, unprotected, to follow the wanderings of truth.

July 19, 1935

Fourth Talk in Buenos Aires

Friends,

I have not come to Argentina to convert you to any particular creed or to urge you to join any particular society; but in understanding, through action, what I am going to say, you will realize that happiness which is born of intelligence, of fulfillment. If each one of you can live supremely, in deep fulfillment, then the world as a whole will be the richer, the happier; but the difficulty is to live profoundly. To live profoundly, you have to discover for yourself your own uniqueness, for in that alone is there fulfillment. It is only through our true fulfillment that we shall solve the innumerable social and economic problems. To rely on environment or on a religion to guide us is to create a dangerous hindrance to fulfillment.

During this brief talk before answering the questions, I want to speak of individuality and true fulfillment, and see whether existing social, moral, and religious conditions are a true help or a dangerous impediment. Before examining whether the conditions are dangerous or beneficial, we must understand what is individuality, what is the uniqueness of the individual, and in what manner he can fulfill.

Now I am going to put very succinctly what to me is individuality. I am not going to use psychological phrases or a complicated jargon. I shall use ordinary words with their ordinary meaning.

Individuality is the accumulated and conditioned memories of both the past and the present. That is, each individual is nothing but a series of conditioned memories, which impede complete and intelligent adjustment to the living, moving present. These memories give to each one the quality of separateness, and this is what you call the uniqueness of individuality.

Now, what are these memories based on, what are the conditioning causes that limit consciousness? If you examine you will see that these memories spring from defensive reactions against life, against suffering, against pain. Having cultivated these self-protective reactions, and calling them by high and pleasant-sounding names such as morality, virtues, ideals, the mind lives within this enclosure of safety, within this limited consciousness of self-created security. These memories, through the impact of experience, increase in their strength and resistance and thus create division from the living reality, until there is utter incompleteness; this causes fear with its many illusions, the fear of death and of the hereafter.

To put it differently, each one has the desire to be certain, secure, and with that desire approaches life, with that intention seeks experience. Thus one does not understand experience, life itself, completely. Whatever action is born of the desire for security must create incompleteness. Being incomplete, one is always guided by memories, which again further increase the emptiness, the isolation of our being. So this continued action of incompleteness prevents fulfillment, which is the full expression of life without the hindrance of conditioned memories, egotism. That is, when you approach life with all the memories based on security and the desire for safety, then whatever action proceeds from that must create an emptiness, an incompleteness; so there is no fulfillment, no comprehension. The significance of individuality is that the mind, through itself alone, through its own conditioned separateness, through deep comprehension of its own self-created limitation, must dissolve the impediments and barriers which create limited consciousness.

Please, you will have to think over this very deeply and not merely accept or reject it. The mind, being conditioned by memory based on security, by so-called virtues, self-protective moralities, is impeded in its fulfillment. Having understood this, we can find out whether society, morality, religion, help the individual to liberate himself and wholly fulfill.

Either the existing society, with its morality and religion, is fundamentally true and so helps the individual to fulfill; or, if it is not true, then we must completely revolutionize our thought and action. So the change depends on individual thought and action. You have to inquire whether your religions, moralities, are true. I say they are not; because society is based on acquisitiveness, moral values on self-protective security, and religion, which is organized belief, fundamentally on fear, though we try to cover this up by calling it love of God, love of truth. If there is to be true fulfillment, there cannot be this sense of possessiveness or acquisitiveness, nor these moral values based on defensive, egoistic security, nor these religions, with their promises of immortality which is but another form of selfishness and fear.

So you, the individual, will have to awaken to the prison in which you are held; and by becoming conscious, aware, you will begin to discover what is stupidity and what is intelligence. It is through your own intelligence that there can be fulfillment, not through acceptance of authority. So what is of importance is the individual, for only through his own intelligence is there fulfillment, the ecstasy of life. This does not mean that I am preaching individualism. Quite the contrary; it is the individualistic system of religious faith and belief, of moral values and acquisitive conduct, that is hindering true fulfillment. So you who are listening, you have to understand, you have to break away from this prison through your own intelligent discernment; and this demands continual alertness of mind. There cannot be the following of another, nor can there be the acceptance of authority, for in this there is fear; and fear destroys all discernment.

Question: I believe that I have no attachments whatsoever, and still I don't feel myself free. What is this painful feeling of being imprisoned, and what am I to do about it?

KRISHNAMURTI: One seeks detachment rather than the understanding of the cause of suffering. Now, when one suffers through possessiveness, one tries to develop the opposite, which is detachment. In other words, one becomes detached in order not to be hurt, and this opposite, one calls virtue. If one really discovered what is the cause of suffering, then in understanding it deeply, with one's whole being, the mind would be free to live fully and completely, and not fall into another prison, the prison of the opposite.

Question: Are you also against such organizations as railways, etc.?

KRISHNAMURTI: I have been referring to those organizations which we have created through self-protective fears. Now, most or-

ganizations in the world are based on exploitation, but I was referring especially to the organizations of religious belief throughout the world.

I maintain that these religious, sectarian organizations are real impediments to man. Those of you who belong to religious organizations, please don't be on the defensive when I say this, but try to find out if it is so or not. If you discover it is not so, then it is right to have them. But before saying that religious organizations are necessary, you must really impartially examine them. How are you going to examine them? To examine anything objectively, your mind must be completely impersonal. That means you must doubt every belief, every ideal that you have held so far or that these organizations offer. Through that questioning there comes a distinct conflict; and only when there is conflict can you begin to understand the right significance of organized beliefs. If you merely examine them intellectually, you will never understand their true significance. That is why most religions forbid their followers to doubt. Doubt has become a religious fetter, an impediment. You have, through your own fear, developed certain beliefs, ideals, illusions to which you have become enslaved, and it is only through your own suffering that you will understand their true significance.

Question: There are people who on the one hand exploit thousands of human beings, and on the other donate millions of dollars to religious institutions. Why? (Laughter)

KRISHNAMURTI: You laugh at this question, but you, also, are involved in it. We exploit, we amass wealth, and then we become philanthropists. Perhaps some of you have not the ruthless cleverness to amass wealth, but you do the same thing in another way, in pursuing virtue.

So what is behind this false charity of the philanthropist, and this false eagerness to accumulate virtue? The philanthropist, through fear, through many defensive reactions, wants to repay a little to the victim whom he has exploited. (Laughter) And you honor him, you say how wonderful he is. That is not charity. It is merely egotism.

And why do you pursue virtue and try to store it up? It is a defensive protection. It is a safeguard against suffering. Your virtue, if you really examine it, is based on the egotistic idea of warding off suffering. This self-protection is not virtue. By knowing what you are and not escaping from it, through so-called virtue, you will discover the beauty, the richness of life.

The philanthropist, through his desire for security, entrenches himself in the power that possessions give; and the man who pursues virtue builds about himself walls of protection against the movement of life. The virtuous man and the philanthropist are alike. Both are afraid of life. They are not in love with life.

Question: We are happy with our beliefs and traditions based on the doctrines of Jesus; whereas in your country, India, there are millions who are far from being happy. All that you are telling us, the Christ taught two thousand years ago. What is the use of your preaching to us instead of to your own countrymen?

KRISHNAMURTI: Thought does not belong to any nation or to any race. (Applause) Reality is not conditioned by religious or racial distinctions; and because the questioner has divided the world into Christian and Hindu, into India and Argentina, he has helped to create misery and suffering in the world. (Applause) When I talk in India about nationalism, they say to me, "Go to England and tell the people there that nationalism is stupid, because England is preventing us from living." (Laughter) And when I come here, you tell me, "Go somewhere else and leave us with our own belief and religion. Do not disturb us." (Laughter)

If your own beliefs and traditions satisfy you, then you will not listen to what I say, because your traditions and your beliefs are shelters under which you take cover in time of trouble. You don't want to face life, therefore you say, "I am satisfied; don't disturb me." If you would really understand truth, if you would know love, you must be free from beliefs and organized religions. There cannot be "your religion" and "the religion of another," your beliefs and doctrines as against another's. The world will be happy when there need be no preacher, when each individual is really fulfilling; and as he is not, I feel I can help him in his fulfillment.

If you feel that I am disturbing, creating sorrow, then you will naturally remain in the religion to which you belong, with its exploitations and illusions; but life will not leave you alone. In that lies the beauty of life. However much you have protected and enclosed yourself within certainties, securities, and beliefs, the wave of life breaks down all your structure. But the man who has no support, no security, shall know the bliss of life.

Question: What is that memory, created by incomplete action in the present, from which you say we must liberate ourselves?

KRISHNAMURTI: In the brief introduction to this talk, I tried to explain how memories as self-defenses are crippling our thought and action. Let me take an example.

If you have been brought up as a Christian, with certain beliefs, you approach life, experience, with that limited mentality. Naturally those prejudices and limitations prevent you from understanding experience fully. So there is incompleteness in your thought and action. Now this barrier which creates incompleteness is what I call memory. These memories act as a self-defensive warning, as a guide against life to help you avoid suffering. So most of our memories are self-protective reactions against intelligence, against life. When a mind is free from all these self-protective reactions, memories, then there is the full movement of life, of reality.

Or take another example: suppose you have been brought up in a certain social class, with all its snobbishness, restrictions, and traditions. With that hindrance, with that burden, you cannot understand or live the fullness of life. So these self-protective memories are the real cause of suffering; and if you would be free from suffering, there cannot be these self-protective values by which you seek to guide yourself.

If you will think over this, if your mind is aware of its own creations, then you will discern how you have established for yourself guides, values, which are but memories, as a protection against the incessant movement of life. A man who is enslaved to self-protective memories cannot understand life, nor be in love with life. His action towards life is the action of self-defense. His mind is so enclosed that the swift movements of life cannot enter it. He searches out eternity, immortality, away from life, the eternal, the immortal, and so he lives in a continual series of illusions. To such a man, whose consciousness is bound by memories, there can never be the eternal becoming of life.

Question: Is there no danger in seeking divinity or immortality? Cannot this become a limitation?

KRISHNAMURTI: It is a cruel limitation if you seek it, for your search is merely an escape from life; but if you do not escape from life, if through action you deeply understand its conflicts, agonies, and suffering, then the mind frees itself from its own limitations and there is immortality. Life itself is immortal. You are trying to find immortality, you do not let it happen. A man who is trying to fall in love shall never know love. This is what is happening to all those people who are seeking immortality, for to them immortality is a security, an egotistic continuance. If the mind is free of the search for security, which is very subtle, then there is the bliss of that life which is immortal.

Question: Why do you disregard the sexual problem?

KRISHNAMURTI: I do not; but if you would understand this question, do not try to solve it separately, away from the rest of the human problems. They are all one.

Sex becomes a problem when there is frustration. When work, which should be the true expression of our being, becomes merely mechanical, stupid and useless, then there is frustration; when our emotional lives, which should be rich and complete, are thwarted through fear, then there is frustration; when the mind, which should be alert, pliable, limitless, is weighted down by tradition, self-protective memories, ideals, beliefs, then there is frustration. So sex becomes an over-emphasized and unnatural problem. Where there is fulfillment, there are no problems. When you are in love, vulnerably, sex is not a problem. For the man to whom sex is mere sensation, it becomes an urgent problem, eating away his mind and heart. You will be free from this problem only when, through action, the mind frees itself from all self-imposed limitations, illusions and fears.

There are questions dealing with reincarnation, with death and with the hereafter, with spiritualism, mediumship, and with various other matters, which it would be impossible to answer, as my time is limited. But if you are interested, you can read some of the things I have already said. You seek explanations, but explanations are as dust to a man who is hungry. It is only action that awakens the mind, so that it begins to discern. Where there is discernment, explanations have no value.

Take this question, for example: "What is your conception of God?" If you are merely satisfied by an explanation, then it shows the poverty of your being; and I fear most people are thus satisfied. Your religions are based on explanations, on revelations, on the experiences of other people. So what is the use of my giving you another explanation, or giving you another belief to add to your museum of dead beliefs? If you deeply thought over this whole idea of seeking God, then you would see that you are subtly, cunningly escaping from the conflict of life. If you understand life, if you grasp the deep significance of living, then life itself is God, not some super-intelligence away from your life. But this demands great penetration of thought, not seeking satisfaction or explanation. In the very understanding of conflict and suffering, when all security and support have become useless, when you are face to face with life without any hindrances, there is God.

July 22, 1935

Talk at the National College, La Plata

Friends,

To most of us, profession is apart from our personal life. There is the world of profession and technique, and the life of subtle feelings, ideas, fears, and love. We are trained for a world of profession, and only occasionally across this training and compulsion, we hear the vague whisperings of reality. The world of profession has become gradually overpowering and exacting, taking almost all our time, so that there is little chance for deep thought and emotion. And so the life of reality, the life of happiness, becomes more and more vague and recedes into the distance. Thus we lead a double life: the life of profession, of work, and the life of subtle desires, feelings, and hopes.

This division into the world of profession and the world of sympathy, love, and deep wanderings of thought, is a fatal impediment to the fulfillment of man. As in the lives of most people this separation exists, let us inquire if we cannot bridge over this destructive gulf.

With rare exceptions, following any particular profession is not the natural expression of an individual. It is not the fulfillment or complete expression of one's whole being. If you examine this, you will see that it is but a careful training of the individual to adjust himself to a rigid, inflexible system. This system is based on fear, acquisitiveness, and exploitation. We have to discover by questioning deeply and sincerely, not superficially, whether this system to which individuals are forced to adjust themselves is really capable of liberating man's intelligence, and so bringing about his fulfillment. If this system is capable of truly freeing the individual to deep fulfillment, which is not mere egotistic self-expression, then we must give our entire support to it. So we must look at the whole basis of this system and not be carried away by its superficial effects.

For a man who is trained in a particular profession, it is very difficult to discern that this system is based on fear, acquisitiveness, and exploitation. His mind is already vested in self-interest, so he is incapable of true action with regard to this system of fear. Take, for example, a man who is trained for the army or the navy; he is incapable of perceiving that armies must inevitably create wars.

Or take a man whose mind is twisted by a particular religious belief; he is incapable of discerning that religion as organized belief must poison his whole being. So each profession creates a particular mentality, which prevents the complete understanding of the integrated man.

As most of us are being trained or have already been trained to twist and fit ourselves to a particular mold, we cannot see the tremendous importance of taking the many human problems as a whole and not dividing them up into various categories. As we have been trained and twisted, we must free ourselves from the mold and reconsider, act anew, in order to understand life as a whole. This demands of each individual that he shall, through suffering, liberate himself from fear. Though there are many forms of fear, social, economic, and religious, there is only one cause, which is the search for security. When we individually destroy the walls and forms that the mind has created in order to protect itself, thus engendering fear, then there comes true intelligence which will bring about order and happiness in this world of chaos and suffering.

On one side there is the mold of religion, impeding and frustrating the awakening of individual intelligence, and on the other the vested interest of society and profession. In these molds of vested interest the individual is being forcibly and cruelly trained, without regard for his individual fulfillment. Thus the individual is compelled to divide life into profession as a means of livelihood, with all its stupidities and exploitations; and subjective hopes, fears, and illusions, with all their complexities and frustrations. Out of this separation is born conflict, ever preventing individual fulfillment. The present chaotic condition is the result and expression of this continual conflict and compulsion of the individual.

The mind must disentangle itself from the various compulsions, authorities, which it has created for itself through fear, and thus awaken that intelligence which is unique and not individualistic. Only this intelligence can bring about the true fulfillment of man.

This intelligence is awakened through the continual questioning of those values to which the mind has become accustomed, to which it is constantly adjusting itself. For the awakening of this intelligence, individuality is of the greatest importance. If you blindly follow a pattern laid down, then you are no longer awakening intelligence, but merely conforming, adjusting yourself, through fear, to an ideal, to a system.

The awakening of this intelligence is a most difficult and arduous task, for the mind is so timorous that it is ever creating shelters to protect itself. A man who would awaken this intelligence must be supremely alert, ever aware, not to escape into an illusion; for when you begin to question these standards and values, there is conflict and suffering. To escape from that suffering, the mind begins to create another set of values, entering into the limitation of a new enclosure. So it moves from one prison to another, thinking that it is living, evolving.

The awakening of this intelligence destroys the false division of life into profession or outward necessity, and the inward retreat from frustration into illusion, and brings about the completeness of action. Thus through intelligence alone can there be true fulfillment and bliss for man.

Question: What is your attitude towards the university and official, organized teaching?

KRISHNAMURTI: For what is the individual being trained by the university? What does it call education? He is being trained to fight for himself, and thus fit himself into a system of exploitation. Such a training must inevitably create confusion and misery in the world. You are being trained for certain professions within a system of exploitation, whether you like the system or not. Now this system is fundamentally based on acquisitive fear, and so there must be the creation in each individual of those barriers which will separate and protect him from others.

Take, for example, the history of any country. In it you will find that the heroes, the warriors of that particular country, are praised. There you will find the stimulation of racial egotism, power, honor, and prestige; which but indicates stupid narrowness and limitation. So gradually the spirit of nationalism is instilled; through papers, through books, through waving of flags, we are being trained to accept nationalism as a reality, so that we can be exploited. (Applause) Then again, take religion. Because it is based on fear, it is destroying love, creating illusions, separating men. And to cover up that fear, you say that it is the love of God. (Applause)

So education has come to be merely conformity to a particular system; instead of awakening the individual's intelligence, it is merely compelling him to conform and so hinders his true morality and fulfillment.

Question: Do you think that the present laws and the present system, which are based on egotism and the desire for individual security, can ever help people towards a better and happier life?

KRISHNAMURTI: I wonder why I am asked this question? Does not the questioner himself realize that these things prevent human beings from living completely? If he does, what is his individual action towards this whole structure? To be merely in revolt is comparatively useless, but individually to free oneself through one's own action,

releases creative intelligence and so the bliss of life. This means that you yourself must be responsible, and not wait for some collective group to change the environment. If each one of you truly felt the necessity for individual fulfillment, you would be continually destroying the crystallization of authority and compulsion which man ever seeks and clings to for his comfort and security.

Question: It is said that you are against all kinds of authority. Do you mean to say that there is no need for some kind of authority in the family or at school?

KRISHNAMURTI: Whether authority should exist or not in a school or family will be answered when you yourself understand the whole significance of authority.

Now, what I mean by authority is conformity, through fear, to a particular pattern, whether of environment, of tradition and ideal or of memory. Take religion as it is. There you will see that, through faith and belief, man is being held in the prison of authority, because each one is seeking his own security through what he calls immortality. This is nothing but a craving for egotistic continuance; and a man who says there is immortality, gives a guarantee to his security. (Laughter) So gradually, through fear, he comes to accept authority, the authority of religious threats, fears, superstitions, hopes, and beliefs. Or he rejects the outer authorities and develops his own personal ideals, which become his authorities, clinging to them in the hope of not being hurt by life. So authority becomes the means of self-defense against life, against intelligence.

When you understand this deep significance of authority, there is not chaos but the awakening of intelligence. As long as there is fear, there must be subtle forms of authority and ideals to which each one submits, to avoid suffering. Thus, through fear, each one creates exploiters. Where there is authority, compulsion, there cannot be intelligence, which alone can bring about true co-operation.

Question: How could the liberty of the Occidental world be organized according to the sensibility of the Oriental?

KRISHNAMURTI: I am afraid I don't quite understand the question. To most people, the Orient is something mysterious and spiritual. But the Orientals are people just like yourselves; like yourselves they suffer, they exploit, they have fears, they have spiritual longings and many illusions. The Orient has different superficial customs and habits, but fundamentally we are all alike, whether of the West or of the East. Some rare people of the East have given thought to self-culture, to the discovery of the true significance of life and death, to illusion and reality. Most people have a romantic idea of India, but I am not going to give a talk about that country. Don't, please, seek to adjust yourselves to a supposedly spiritual land, like the East, but become aware of the prison in which you are held. In understanding how it is created, and in discerning its true significance, the mind will liberate itself from fear and illusion.

Question: What should be the attitude of society towards criminals?

KRISHNAMURTI: It all depends on whom you call criminals. (Laughter, applause) A man who steals because he cannot help it, must be looked after and treated as a kleptomaniac. The man who steals because he is hungry, we also call a criminal, because he is taking something away from those who have. It is the system that makes him go hungry, to be in want, and it is the system that turns him into a criminal. Instead of altering the system, we force the so-called criminal into a prison. Then there is the man who, with his ideas, disturbs the vested interest of religion or of worldly power. You call him also a dangerous criminal and get rid of him.

Now, it depends on the way you look at life, as to whom you call a criminal. If you are acquisitive, possessive, and another says that acquisition leads to exploitation, to sorrow and cruelty, you call that person a criminal, or an idealist. Because you cannot see the greatness and the practicality of non-acquisition, of not being attached, you think he is a disturber of the peace. I say you can live in the world, where there is this continual acquisitiveness and exploitation, without being attached, possessive.

Question: Many of us are conscious of and take part in this corrupt life around us. What can we do to free ourselves from its suffocating effects?

KRISHNAMURTI: You can be intellectually aware, and so there will be no action; but if you are aware with your whole being, then there is action, which alone will free the mind from corruption. If you are merely aware intellectually, then you ask such a question as this. Then you say, "Tell me how to act," which means, "Give me a system, a method to follow, so that I can escape from that action which may necessitate suffering." Because of this demand, people have created exploiters throughout the world.

If you are really conscious with your whole being that a particular thing is a hindrance, a poison, then you will be completely free from it. If you are conscious of a snake in the room—and that consciousness is generally acute, for there is fear involved in it—you never ask another how to get rid of the snake. (Laughter) In the same way, if you are completely, deeply aware, for example, of nationalism, or any other limitation, you will then not ask how to get rid of it; you discern for yourself its utter stupidity. If you are wholly conscious that the acceptance of authority in religion and politics is destructive of intelligence, then you, the individual, will disentangle the mind from all the stupidities and pageantry of religion and politics. (Applause) If you truly felt all this, then you would not merely applaud, but individually you would act.

The mind has imposed upon itself many hindrances, through its own desire for security. These hindrances are preventing intelligence and hence the complete fulfillment of man. Were I to offer a new system, it would merely be a substitution, which would not make you think anew, from the beginning. But if you become aware of how through fear you are creating many limitations, and free yourself from them, then there will be for you the life of rich beauty, the life of eternal becoming.

It is very good of you, sirs, to have invited me, and I thank you for listening to me.

August 2, 1935

Talks in Rosario and Mendoza*

Friends,

When one hears something new, one is apt to brush it aside without thought; and as I come from India, people are inclined to imagine that I bring to them an oriental mysticism which is of no value in daily life. Please listen to this talk without prejudice, and do not brush it aside by calling me a mystic, an anarchist, a communist, or by any other name. If you will kindly listen without prejudice but critically, you will see that what I have to say has a fundamental value.

*Condensed from the report of the talks given on July 27 and 28, and on August 25 and 27, 1935.

It is most difficult to be truly critical, because one is so accustomed to examine ideas and experiences through the veil of opposition and prejudice, that one perverts the clarity of understanding. If you are Christians, as most of you are, you are bound to examine what I say through the particular bias that your religion has given you. Or if you happen to belong to some political party, you will naturally consider what I am going to say through the bias of that particular party. We cannot solve human problems through any bias, whether of a system, party, or religion.

Everywhere in the world there is constant suffering which seems to have no end. There is the exploitation of one class by another. We see imperialism with all its stupidities, with its wars, and the cruelties of vested interest, whether in ideas, beliefs, or power. Then there is the problem of death and the search for happiness and certainty in another world. One of the fundamental reasons why you belong to a religion or to a religious sect is that it promises you a safe abode in the hereafter.

We see all this, those of us who are actively, intelligently interested in life; and desirous of a fundamental change, we think that there ought to be a mass movement. Now to create a truly collective movement, there must be the awakening of the individual. I am concerned with that awakening. If each individual awakens in himself that true intelligence, then he will bring about collective welfare, without exploitation and cruelty. As long as the intelligent fulfillment of the individual is hindered, there must be chaos, sorrow, and cruelty. If you are driven to cooperate through fear, there can never be individual fulfillment. So I am not concerned with creating a new organization or party, or offering a new substitution, but with awakening that intelligence which alone can solve the many human miseries and sorrows.

Now most of us are not individuals, but merely the expression of a collective system of traditions, fears, and ideals. There can be true individuality only when each one, through conflict and suffering, discerns the deep significance of the environment in which he is held. If you are merely the expression of the collective, you are no longer an individual; but if you understand the whole significance of the collective consciousness which now dominates the world, then you will begin to awaken that intelligence which becomes the true expression and fulfillment of the individual.

We are now but the expression, the result of past and present environment. We are the result of compulsion and imposition, molded into a particular pattern, the pattern of tradition, of certain values and beliefs, of fear and authority. For convenience we will divide this mold that is holding us, as the inner and the outer, the religious and the economic, but in reality such a division does not exist.

Religion is but an organized system of belief, based on fear and on the desire for security. Where there is self-interest, the desire for security, there must be fear; and through religion you seek what is called immortality, a security in the hereafter, and those who assure and promise you that immortality become your guides, your teachers and authorities. So out of your own desire for egotistic continuance, you create exploiters.

When the mind seeks security through immortality, it must create authority, and that authority becomes the constant cause of fear and of oppression. So to guide and to hold you, there are ideals, beliefs, dogmas, and creeds, out of which is born what is called religion. To minister to your illusory needs, brought about through fear, there are

priests, who become your exploiters. So you have religions with their vested interest, fear, oppression, and exploitation, holding man and thwarting the true, intelligent awakening and fulfillment of the individual. Religions also separate man from man. In that mold each individual is held consciously or unconsciously, subtly or crudely.

Outwardly we have created a system of individual security based on exploitation. Through acquisitiveness and the system of family, we have created the distinction of classes, cultivated the disease of nationalism, imperialism, and that great stupidity, war.

You have this mold, this environment of which almost all of us are unconscious, for it is part of us; it is the very expression of our desires, fears, and hopes. While you conform consciously or thoughtlessly to this system, you are not individuals. True individuality can come into being only when you begin to question this mold of tradition, values, ideals. You can understand its true significance only when you are in conflict, not otherwise. With your whole being you must turn upon the environment, which then creates conflict, suffering, and from that there comes the clarity of understanding.

How can there be individual fulfillment if you are unconscious of this machine, this mold that is holding you, shaping you, guiding you? How can there be completeness, bliss, when these unquestioned values are continually thwarting, perverting your full comprehension? When you as individuals become fully conscious of this prison and are free from it, only then can there be true fulfillment. Intelligence alone can solve human misery and sorrow.

Question: Is it possible to live without some kind of prejudice? Are you yourself not prejudiced against religious and spiritual organizations?

KRISHNAMURTI: I do not think I am prejudiced against religious or spiritual organizations. I have belonged to them, and I have seen their utter stupidity and their ways of exploitation. There is no illusion with regard to them, and so there is no prejudice.

Now that leads us to a further point, which is: Can man live without any illusion? In a world where there is so much suffering, so much mental and emotional anguish, where there is such ruthless cruelty and exploitation, can one live without some means of escape from this horror? Where there is a desire to escape, there must be the creation of illusion in which one takes shelter. If in your work, in your life, there is no fulfillment, then there must be an escape into some romantic idea or into an illusion. So where there is conflict between yourself and life, there must be prejudice and illusion which offer you an escape. It may be an escape through religion, through mere activity, or through sensation.

If you deeply understand the hindrances that cause conflict between yourself and life, and thus are free from them, then the mind does not need illusions. Your concern is with finding out for yourself whether you are escaping from life, not with judging me or another. Escape destroys the intelligent functioning of the mind. Illusion, prejudice, ceases when through conflict the mind frees itself from all the subtle escapes it has established in search of self-defense.

Question: Most of the discussions around your ideas are being provoked by your frequent use of the word exploitation. *Can you tell us exactly what you mean by exploitation?*

KRISHNAMURTI: Where there is fear, which is the result of seeking security, there must be exploitation. Now to free the mind of fear is one of the most difficult things to do. People say so very readily that they are not afraid; but if they really want to find out whether they are free from fear, they have to test themselves in action. They have to understand the whole structure of tradition and values, and in separating themselves from these they will create conflict, and in that conflict they will discover whether they are free. Now most of us are acting in conformity with certain established values. We do not know their true significance. If you want to discover the consistency of your being, step out of that rut and you will then discern the many subtle fears that enslave your mind. When the mind liberates itself from fear, then there will not be exploitation, cruelty, and sorrow.

Question: What advice can you give to those of us who are eager to understand your teachings?

KRISHNAMURTI: If you begin to live and so understand life, then you cannot help grasping the significance of what I am teaching. Don't you see, sirs, if you follow anybody, it does not matter who it is, you are creating further compulsion, further limitation, and so destroying intelligence, true fulfillment. Truth is of no person. If in action the mind frees itself from the limitation of fear and so of authority, compulsion, then there is the understanding of that which is truth.

Question: You say that ideals are a barrier to the understanding of life. How is this possible? Surely a man without ideals is little more than a savage.

KRISHNAMURTI: Let us not consider who is and who is not a savage, for in this world that is difficult to determine. (Laughter) Rather let us consider whether ideals are necessary for plenitude and rich understanding. I say that ideals, beliefs, fundamentally prevent man from living fully.

Ideals seem necessary when life is chaotic, sorrow laden, and cruel. Caught in this turmoil you cling to ideals as a way of escape, as a necessity for crossing the sea of confusion, and so they are false and deceptive. When you do not understand the present suffering and agony, you escape into an ideal. When you do not love your neighbor, you talk about the ideal of brotherhood. In the same way, when you talk about the ideal of peace, then you are not truly discerning the cause that creates separation, war, with all its brutalities and stupidities. Our minds are so crippled, so burdened with ideals, that we cannot see clearly the actual. So free the mind from your ideals, which are but frustrated hopes; then only will it be capable of discerning the present with all its significance. Instead of escaping, act in the present. That action uncovers beauty which no ideal can reveal.

Question: What do you mean exactly by "incomplete action?" Can you give us examples of such action?

KRISHNAMURTI: Each one of us is brought up with a certain background. That background is but memory. These memories are continually impeding the completeness of action. That is, if you have been brought up in a certain tradition, that memory prevents the complete understanding of experience or of action; it grows and becomes an increasing limitation, hindrance, separating itself from the movement of life. Where there is incompleteness of action, there is no fulfillment, which engenders fear. From this there arises the search for security in the hereafter. Completeness of action is the continual movement or the flow of life, reality, without the limitation of self-protective memory.

Question: Occasionally, some wealthy individual who loses his money commits suicide. Since wealth does not seem to confer lasting happiness, what must one do in order to be really happy?

KRISHNAMURTI: The people who accumulate wealth depend for their happiness on the power which money gives. When that power is removed, they come face to face with their own utter emptiness. As long as one is looking for power, either through money or through virtue, there must be emptiness, and for that emptiness there is no remedy, because power in itself is an illusion, born of egotistic limitation, fear. Understanding can come only in discerning the falseness of power itself, and this demands a constant alertness of mind, not a renunciation after accumulation. If there is that sense of acquisitiveness which destroys love, charity, then there is an emptiness, a shallowness, a frustration of life. In that there is no fulfillment.

Question: Some of your followers say that you are the new Messiah. I should like to know whether you are an impostor, living on the reputation established for you by others, or whether you really have the interest of humanity at heart and are capable of making a constructive contribution to human thought.

KRISHNAMURTI: I don't think it matters very much what others say or do not say concerning me. If you are merely followers, you cannot know the rich plenitude of life. What matters is that you, without being imposed upon by authority, by opinion, discover for yourself whether what I say has any deep significance. Some, by merely saying that it has, help to create the empty cage of opinion which limits the thoughtless; and others can easily create an opposite opinion by declaring that what I say is false, impractical, and so catch the unconscious in a net of words.

The questioner asks whether I am living on the reputation established for me by others. Please be assured that I am not. This idea of living on the past is destructive of intelligence. Most people, after achieving a certain height, rest on their laurels and thus slowly decay; and as they have that fatal habit, they try to draw me into their own illusion.

To me, living is completeness of action, which is its own beauty, and which neither seeks rewards nor avoids suffering. To find out the truth of what I say, you, as an individual, will have to experiment and discover for yourself, and not rely on opinion.

Whether I am an impostor or not is for me to find out, not for you to judge. How can you judge whether I am an impostor or not? You can measure only by a standard, and all standards are limiting. To judge another is fundamentally wrong. I know, without any fear, illusion, or self-deception, that what I am saying and living is born of life. Not through the desire to judge but only through conflict can you awaken intelligence. It is only in the state of conflict and suffering that you can understand what is true. But when you begin to suffer, you must keep intensely aware, otherwise you will create an escape into an illusion. Now the vicious circle of suffering and escape will continue until you begin to realize the futility of escape. Only then will there be intelligence, which alone can solve the many human problems.

Question: You say that all those who belong to a religion or who hold a belief are enslaved by fear. Is one free of fear by the mere fact of belonging to no religion? Are you yourself, who belong to no religion, really free of fear, or are you preaching a theory?

KRISHNAMURTI: I am not preaching mere theory. I am talking out of the fullness of understanding. Not belonging to any religion certainly does not indicate that one is free from fear. Fear is so subtle, so swift, so cunning, that it hides itself in many places. To trace fear down the lane of its own retreat there must be the intense and burning desire to uncover fear, which means that you must be willing to lose completely all self-interest. But you want to be secure, both here and in the hereafter. So, desiring security you cultivate fear; and being afraid, you try to escape through the illusion of religion, ideals, sensation, and activity. As long as there is fear, which is born of self-protective desires, mind will be caught in the net of many illusions. A man who really desires to discover the root of fear and so liberate himself from it, must become aware of the motive and purpose of his action. This awareness, if it is intense, will destroy the cause of fear.

Question: What are the characteristics of nationalism, which you call stupidity? Are all forms of nationalism bad, or only some? Isn't it wonderful that your country is striving to free itself from the yoke of England? Why are you not fighting for the independence of your country?

KRISHNAMURTI: To love anything beautiful in a country is normal and natural, but when that love is used by exploiters in their own interest, it is called nationalism. Nationalism is fanned into imperialism, and then the stronger people divide and exploit the weaker, with the Bible in one hand and a bayonet in the other. The world is dominated by the spirit of cunning, ruthless exploitation, from which war must ensue. This spirit of nationalism is the greatest stupidity.

Every individual should be free to live fully, completely. As long as one tries to liberate one's own particular country and not man, there must be racial hatreds, the divisions of people and classes. The problems of man must be solved as a whole, not as confined to countries or peoples.

Question: What do you think of your enemies, the priests, and the vested interests which in Argentina have prevented the broadcasting of your lectures?

KRISHNAMURTI: To regard anyone as an enemy is a great folly. Either one understands and so helps, or one does not understand and so hinders. The diffusion of that which is intelligent can only be hindered by stupidity. Each one of you has vested interests to which you are clinging, and which by continual thought and action you are increasing. If one attacks your particular vested interest, your immediate response is to be on the defensive and to retaliate. A man who has something to guard, something to protect, is ever in fear, and so acts most cruelly and thoughtlessly; but a man who has really nothing to lose, because he has accumulated nothing, has no fear; he lives completely, truly fulfilling.

Question: Has experience any value?

KRISHNAMURTI: What happens when there is experience? It leaves a mark on the mind, which we call memory. With that scar, with that memory, we meet the next experience, and from that experience we gather further memory, increasing the scar. Each experience leaves its mark on the mind. Now these collective layers of memories are essentially based on the desire to protect yourself against suffering. That is, you come to experience already prepared, already protected by your past memories. You are not really living completely in that experience, but you are merely learning how to protect yourself

against it, against life. Experience becomes valueless to a man who merely uses it as a means of further self-defense against life. But if you live in an experience wholly, integrally, without this desire for self-protection, then it does not destroy discernment; then it reveals the great heights and depths of life.

Now, to use experience as a means of advancing, that is, increasing the walls of self-protection, is generally called evolution. You think that through time this memory, this self-protective record, can reach truth or perfection or God. It cannot. True experience is the breaking down of those self-protective walls and freeing the mind, consciousness, from those scars that prevent discernment, fulfillment.

Question: What kind of action do you think would be most useful for the world?

KRISHNAMURTI: An action that is born without fear, and therefore of intelligence, is inherently true. If your action is based on fear, on authority, then such action must create chaos and confusion. In freeing action of all fear, there is love, intelligence.

Question: Isn't the sexual problem a real slavery for man?

KRISHNAMURTI: If we merely deal with this problem superficially, we cannot find a solution for it. Emotionally and mentally we are most of the time being frustrated by authority and fear. Our work, which should be the expression of our fulfillment, has become mechanical and weary. We are merely trained to fit into a system, and so there is frustration, emptiness. We are forced to take up a particular profession because of economic necessity, so we are thwarted in our true expression. Through fear we force ourselves to accept the many superstitions and illusions of religion. Our desires, thwarted and limited, try to express themselves through sex, which thus becomes a consuming problem. Because we try to solve it exclusively, apart from the rest of the human problems, we can find no solution for it. Because we have destroyed love through possessiveness, through mere sensation, sex has become a problem. Where there is love, without the sense of possessiveness or attachment, sex cannot become a problem.

Question: Why are there oppressors and oppressed, rich and poor, good people and bad?

KRISHNAMURTI: They exist because you allow them. The oppressor exists because you are willing to submit yourself to oppression, and because you also are eager to oppress another. You think that by becoming rich you will be happy, and so you create the poor. By your action you are creating the oppressor and the oppressed, the rich and the poor, and supporting those conditions which produce the so-called bad, the criminal. If you as individuals are tormented by all this hideous suffering in you and about you, then you will know how to act voluntarily, without fear, without seeking reward.

Question: Which has to be assured first, collective or individual well-being?

KRISHNAMURTI: We have to consider, not which of these shall come first, but what is the true fulfillment of man. I say you will know what this is when the mind is free from those limitations which it has placed about itself in its search for security. Following a system or imitating another does not lead to fulfillment.

What are the impediments? The desire to protect oneself, both here and in the hereafter. Where there is the desire to protect oneself, there must be fear which creates many illusions. One of the illusions is the authority or compulsion of an ideal, belief, or tradition, the authority of self-protective memories against the movement of life. Fear creates many limitations. When the mind becomes aware of one of its limitations, then in freeing itself from that, the real creator of illusions and limitations is revealed to be those self-protective memories called the 'I'. The liberation from this limited consciousness is true fulfillment. The awakening of intelligence is the assurance of the well-being of the individual, and therefore of the whole.

Question: I have heard that you are against love. Are you?

KRISHNAMURTI: If I were, it would be very stupid. Possessiveness destroys love, and against that I am. To help you to possess, you have laws which are called moral, and which the state and religion support. Love is hedged about by fear which destroys its beauty.

Question: Are we responsible for our actions?

KRISHNAMURTI: The majority of people would prefer not to be responsible for their actions. After all, who is responsible if you are not? The chaos in the world is brought about by the irresponsible action of the individual; but it is through individual, conscious action alone that the oppression, exploitation, and suffering can be swept away. We do not desire to act deeply, for that would involve conflict and suffering for ourselves, and so we try to evade full responsibility. Those who are in sorrow must awaken to the fullness of their own action.

Question: Your ideas, although destructive, greatly appeal to me, and I accept them and have been practicing them for some time. I have abandoned the ideas of religion, nationalism and possession; but I must frankly confess that I am tormented with doubt and feel that I may merely have exchanged one cage for another. Can you help me?

KRISHNAMURTI: Anyone who tells you exactly what to do, and gives you a method to follow, seems to you to be positive. He is but helping you to imitate, to follow, and so he is really destructive to intelligence and brings about negation. If you have merely given up religion, nationalism, and possession, without understanding their deep and intrinsic significance, then you will surely fall into another cage, because you hope to gain something in return. You are really looking for an exchange, and so there is no deep understanding which alone can destroy all cages and limitations. If you truly understood that religion, nationalism, possessiveness, with their full significance, are poisons in themselves, then there would be intelligence, which is ever free from all sense of reward.

Question: Are you the founder of a new universal religion?

KRISHNAMURTI: If by religion you mean new dogmas, creeds, another prison to hold man and create further fear in him, then certainly I am not. When you lose the sense of Godhood, the sense of beauty, then you become religious or join a religious sect. I desire to awaken that intelligence which alone can help man to fulfill, to live happily, without sorrow. But it depends on you whether there shall be mere followers and so destroyers, or whether there shall be love and human unity.

Question: Can you give us your idea of God and the immortality of the soul, or are these things merely stupidities invented by clever men in order to exploit millions of human beings?

KRISHNAMURTI: Millions are exploited because they seek in the hereafter their own egotistic continuance, which they call immortality. They want security in the hereafter, and so they create the exploiter. You are used to the idea that the ego, the 'I', is something that endures and lasts forever. The ego is nothing but a series of memories. What are you? A form, a name, with certain prejudices, qualities, hopes and fears. (Laughter) And through it all, through these limitations, there is a something which is not yours and mine, which is eternal, that is ever becoming, that is true. You cannot measure it by words or know it through explanations. That is to be realized through the liberating process of action. The mere inquiry into God, life, truth or whatever name you may give to it, indicates the desire to escape from the present, from the conflict of ignorance. Ignorance exists when the mind is but the storehouse of accumulative, self-protective memories, which is the 'I' consciousness. This limited consciousness hinders the perception, the realization of that eternal becoming, the movement of life.

July 27 and 28,
August 25 and 28, 1935

Santiago, Chile, 1935

✳

First Talk in Santiago

Friends,

Our human problems demand clear, simple, and direct thinking. Some of you may imagine that by merely listening to a few of the talks which I am going to give, your problems will be solved. You desire immediate remedies for the many aches and sorrows, and superficial alterations which will revolutionize your thoughts, your whole being. There is only one way to find intelligent happiness, and that is through your own perception, discernment; and through action alone you can dissolve the many impediments that stand in the way of fulfillment. If you can perceive for yourself simply and directly the limitations that prevent deep and complete living, and how they have been created, then you yourself will be able to dissolve them.

I would beg of you, in listening to me, to pass beyond the convenient and satisfactory illusion which has divided thought as Oriental and Occidental. Truth is beyond all climes, peoples, and systems. Though I come from India, what I say is not conditioned by the thought of that country. I am concerned with human suffering which exists all over the world. And please do not put aside what I say by thinking that it is not practical but merely some form of oriental mysticism. I

would beg of you not to think in terms of formulas, systems, catch-phrases, but to free the mind from the background of many generations, and think anew, directly and simply. Please do not think that by calling me an anarchist or communist, or by giving to me some other convenient name, you have understood what I have said. We must think anew and understand the human problem as a whole, and then only can we live harmoniously and intelligently. Where there is true individual fulfillment, there will also be the true well-being of the whole, the collective.

If each one of you can fulfill, live in complete harmony—which demands great intelligence and not the pursuit of egotistic desires—then there will be the well-being of the whole. Though we must have a complete revolution of thought and desire, it must be the outcome of voluntary comprehension on the part of the individual, and not of compulsion.

As most of you are deeply interested in happiness and in fulfillment, and have not come here merely out of curiosity, if you will carefully understand what I say, and act, then there will be the true ecstasy of life.

There is intense suffering throughout the world. There is hunger amidst plenty. There is exploitation of class by class, of women by men, and of men by women. There is the absurdity of nationalism which is only the collective expression of egotistic search for security.

This chaos is the objective expression of that inward suffering of man. Subjectively there is uncertainty, the agonizing fear of death, of incompleteness, of emptiness. Our action in the subjective and objective world is but the expression of egotistic desire for security. So the mind has created many impediments, limitations, and until we completely and thoroughly understand these impediments and voluntarily liberate ourselves from them, there cannot be fulfillment.

By individually understanding and liberating ourselves from these limitations, we can create true and necessary action, and thereby change the environment. A great many people think that there must be a mass movement in order to bring about individual fulfillment. But to create a true mass movement, there must first be a complete revolution of thought and desire in the individual, in you. That, to me, is true revolution, this individual and voluntary change. It must begin with you, with the individual, and not with a vague, collective mass. Don't be hypnotized by the phrase *mass movement.* Each individual who is caught up in suffering must change, he must understand the cause of his own sorrow and the hindrances he has created around himself. It is no use merely seeking a substitution, for that will in no way solve our human problems and agonies. That is merely a false adjustment to a false condition. Most of us in searching for a substitution are merely clinging to our own egotistic pursuits.

Do not, please, at the end of the talk, say that I have not given you a positive system. I am going to try to explain how our sorrows have been created; and when you discern the cause for yourself, then there will be a direct action which alone will be positive. This ac-

tion born of comprehension, of intelligence, is not the imitation of a system.

Each individual is seeking security, both subjectively and objectively. His subjective search is for certainty, so that the mind can cling to it, undisturbed. And his objective search is for security, power, and well-being.

Now what happens when you seek security, certainty? There must be fear; and if you are conscious of your thought, you will discern that it has its root in fear. Morality, religion, and objective conditions are based fundamentally on fear, for they are the outcome of the desire on the part of the individual to be secure. Though you may not have any religious belief, yet you have the desire to be subjectively secure, which is but the religious spirit. Let us understand the structure of what we call religion.

As I said, when one seeks security there must be fear; to be subjectively certain, you seek what you call immortality. In search of that security, you accept teachers who promise this immortality, and you come to regard them as authorities, to be feared, to be worshipped. And where there is this fear, there must be dogmas, creeds, beliefs, ideals, and traditions to hold the mind.

What you call religion is nothing but an organized form of individual self-protection for subjective security. To administer this authority based on fear, there must be priests, who become your exploiters. You are the creators of exploiters, for through fear you have created the cause for exploitation. Religion has become an organized belief, a crystallized form of thought, of morality, of oppression, domination. Religion, whose God is fear—though we use such words as love, kindliness, brotherhood to cover up that deep fear—is nothing but a subjective submission to a system which assures us security. I am not talking of an ideal religion. I am talking of religion as it is throughout the world, the religion of exploitation, of vested interest.

Then there is the objective search for security through egotistic power essentially based on fear and so on exploitation. If you look at our present system, you will see that it is nothing but a series of cunning exploitations of man by man. Family becomes the very center of exploitation. Please do not misunderstand what I mean by family. I mean the center which makes you feel secure, which demands the exploitation of your neighbor. Family, which should be the true expression of love, not of exclusiveness, becomes the means of egotistic self-perpetuation. From this there develop classes, the superior and the inferior; and the means of acquiring wealth accumulate in the hands of the few. Then there follows the disease of nationalism, nationalism as a means of exploitation, of oppression. This dangerous disease of nationalism is dividing people, as religions are doing. From this there arise sovereign governments, whose business it is to prepare for war. Wars are not a necessity; to kill another human being is not a necessity.

Thus, seeking your own security, you have created many impediments of which you are entirely unconscious; and these impediments are not only turning you into a machine, but are preventing you from being a true individual. In becoming conscious of these limitations there arises conflict. You do not want conflict, you merely desire satisfaction, security, and so these hindrances continue to create sorrow and turmoil. But you will find true happiness, fulfillment, reality, only when you come into conflict with the values that now oppress and limit the mind. Examining these values intellectually does not reveal their true significance. Mere intellectual examination will not create conflict, and only through suffering do you begin to understand their deep, concealed meaning.

Most people are acting mechanically in a system; so it is essential that they come face to face with those values and impediments of which they are unconscious. In this there is the awakening of true intelligence, which alone can bring about fulfillment. This intelligence, which is unique, will reveal the eternal. As the sun comes out clear and bright through the dark clouds, so through your own discernment and in the purity of your own action comes the realization of that life which is ever renewing.

Question: You are preaching revolutionary ideas, but how can any real good come from it unless you organize a group of followers who will bring about a revolution in fact? If you are against organization, how can you ever achieve any result?

KRISHNAMURTI: You cannot follow anyone, including myself. Out of your own voluntary comprehension you will create whatever organization is necessary. But if an organization were imposed on you, you would become merely slaves of that organization and be exploited. As there are so many organizations which are already exploiting you, what is the good of adding another to them? But what is important is that each one of you fundamentally understands, and out of that comprehension will come the true organization which will not impede individual fulfillment. I am not against all organizations. I am against those organizations which prevent individual fulfillment, and especially that organization which is called religion, with its fears, beliefs and vested interests. It is supposed to help man, but in fact it deeply hinders his fulfillment.

Question: Would there not be trouble, chaos and immorality in society if there were not priests to uphold and preach morality?

KRISHNAMURTI: Surely there is now in the world utter chaos, exploitation, and misery. Can you add more to it? We must consider what we mean by priests and what we mean by immorality.

I mean by a priest, one whose action is based on vested interest and so furthers fear. He may not be of any religious organization, but may belong to a particular system of thought and so create dogmas, creeds, and fears. A priest is one who forces another, subtly or crudely, to fit himself into a particular mold.

To understand what is true morality, we must first understand what morality is now. If we can discern how it has grown about us and liberate ourselves from its many stupidities and cruelties, then there will be intelligence, whose action will be truly moral, for it will not be based on fear.

If you observe dispassionately, you will see that our present-day morality is based on deep egotism, the search for security, not only here, but in the hereafter. Out of acquisitiveness, the desire to possess, you have established certain laws, certain opinions which you call moral. If you are voluntarily free from possessiveness, acquisitiveness, which needs deep discernment, then there is intelligence, which is the guardian of true morality.

You will say, "It is all right for us, who are educated, we need no one to support us in this morality; but what about the people, the mass?" When you regard others as not being cultured, then you yourself are not; for out of this so-called consideration for others, exploitation is born. What you are really concerned with when you ask about another is your own fear of conflict and disturbance. If you understood the present false morality, with its subtle cruelty, then there would be true intelligence. That alone is the assurance of kindly morality, inclusive and without fear.

Question: Is character another name for limitation?

KRISHNAMURTI: Character becomes a limitation if it is merely egotistic defense against life. This development of resistance against the movement of life becomes the means of self-protection. In this there can be no intelligence, and action then only creates further limitation and sorrow. We have developed a system in which, to live at all, we must possess what is known as character, which is but a carefully cultivated resistance, a self-defense against life.

A man who would live, fulfill, must have intelligence. Character is in opposition to intelligence. Character is merely a hindrance, a limitation, and in its development there cannot be fulfillment.

Question: Do you really believe everything you say?

KRISHNAMURTI: Now I am telling you what to me is truth, not belief. It is the fruition of my own living. It is not the pursuit of some ideal, which is but imitation. Where there is imitation, there is belief. But if you are fulfilling, which is not to achieve something or to become something, then there is the living reality.

Belief is born of illusion, and reality is free from all illusions. You cannot judge whether I am living what I am saying. I am the only person who can know about that, but you have to discover for yourself whether what I say has any deep significance for you. To judge, you must have a measure, a standard. Now that standard, as it generally happens, is the result of some prejudice or frustration.

Please examine what I have to say, for in the very examination you will begin to understand the true significance of living. When there is judgment, there is either condemnation or approval, and this division, this breaking up of thought and emotion does not bring about comprehension.

September 1, 1935

Talk in Valparaiso

Friends,

Before I enter into the subject of my talk, I should like to say that I belong to no organization, and that I have come to Chile at the invitation of some kind friends. To belong to any particular organization is not very helpful to clear thinking; and as in the newspapers and elsewhere it has been said that I am a Theosophist, and as I have also been called by other labels, I think it would be well to state that I do not belong to any sect or society, and that I hold it is detrimental to force thought into a particular groove.

Thought does not belong to any nationality; it is neither of the Orient nor of the Occident. What is true does not exclusively belong to any particular type of race. Please do not brush aside what I say as being communistic or anarchistic, or by saying that it has no particular significance for present-day problems. What I say has to be understood for its own intrinsic value, and not regarded as a new system. Also, please do not think that I am merely destructive. What one generally calls constructive is the offer of a system, so that you can follow it mechanically, without much thought.

We all say that there must be a complete change in the world. We see so much exploitation of one race by another, of one class by another, of followers by their religions; so much poverty, misery, and at the same time abundance. We see the disease of nationalism, imperialism, spreading everywhere with its wars, destroying human life, your life, life which should be sacred.

So we see all about us utter chaos and intense suffering. There must be a dynamic, universal change in human thought and feeling. Some say, "Leave it to the experts, let them think out a suitable system, and we will follow." Others say that there must be a mass movement to change the environment completely.

Now if you merely leave the whole of the human problem to the expert, then you, the individual, will become a machine, shallow, empty.

When you speak of a mass movement, what is meant by the mass? How can there be a mass movement miraculously born? It can come only through careful understanding and action on the part of the individual. To grasp this human problem, without superficial reactions, we must think directly and simply. In understanding truth, our problems will be solved. Individuals must fundamentally change. To bring about a true mass movement, which does not exploit the individual, each one of you must be responsible for your actions. You cannot be thoughtless and machinelike. Most of us are afraid to think deeply, because it involves a great effort, and also we sense in it a vague danger. But we must understand the limitations in which our minds are held, and in liberating ourselves from them, there will be true fulfillment.

Each individual, subtly or grossly, is seeking constantly his own security. Where there is the objective or subjective search for security, there must be fear. Through fear he has developed objectively one kind of system, and through fear, subjectively, he has submitted himself to another. So let us understand the significance of these systems which he has created.

This objective system is based essentially on exploitation. As the individual is seeking his own security, family becomes the very beginning and center of exploitation. Family has come to mean self-perpetuation. Though we may say that we love our family, that word is misused, for such love is but the expression of possessiveness. From that possessive attachment are developed class distinction, and the means of acquiring wealth is protected in the hands of the few. From that there arise different nationalities, again dividing people. Think how absurd it is to divide the world into classes, nationalities, religions, and sects. The love of country is turned into a means of exploitation, leading to imperialism; and the next step is war, killing man. Objectively, the individual's mind is held in a system of exploitation, which creates constant conflict, suffering, and war. This objective expression is but the outcome of the desire and search for one's own security.

Subjectively, man has created a system which he calls religion. Now religions, though they profess love, are fundamentally based on fear. Where there is fear, there must be authority. Authority creates dogmas, creeds, and ideals. Religions are but crystallized, dead forms of belief. To administer these there exist priests, who become your exploiters. (Applause)

I fear you agree too easily, but you are the creators of exploiters; you crave to be secure and cling to the assurance of your own continuance. Merely escaping from this desire into some activity does not mean that you are liberated from this subtle, egotistic longing.

So you have, in the objective world, a system which is ruthlessly preventing the fulfillment of each individual, and in the subjective world, an organized system which, through authority, dogmas, belief, and fear, is destroying the individual discernment of reality, truth. Action born of this subjective and objective search for security is continually creating limitation, bringing about frustration. There is no completeness, fulfillment.

There can be the welfare of mankind only when each individual truly fulfills. To realize individual fulfillment, you who are now but so many repetitive reactions, cogs in a social and religious machine, have to become individuals by questioning all the values, moral, social, religious, and discover for yourselves, without following any particular person or system, their true significance. Then you will discern that these values are fundamentally based on egotism, selfishness. The mere imitation of values, whose deep significance you have not understood, must lead to frustration. Instead of waiting for a miraculous change, a mass movement, you the individual must awaken; you have to come into conflict with those values which you have established through your craving for security.

You do this only when there is suffering. Now most of you desire to avoid conflict, suffering; so you would rather examine values intellectually, sitting at ease. You say there must be a mass awakening, a mass movement in order to change the environment. So you throw the responsibility of action on this vague thing called the mass, and man goes on suffering. You secure for yourself a safe corner, deceitfully, cunningly call it moral, and thus add to the chaos and suffering. In this there is no happiness, intelligence, or fulfillment, but only fear and sorrow. Awaken to all this, each one of you, and change the course of your thought and action.

Question: Do you think the League of Nations will succeed in preventing a new world war?

KRISHNAMURTI: How can there be the cessation of war so long as there are the divisions of nationalities and sovereign governments? How can war be prevented when there are class divisions, when there is exploitation, when each one is seeking his own individual security and creating fear? There cannot be peace in the world if subjectively each one of you is at war. To bring about true peace in the world so that man is not slaughtered for an ideal called national prestige, honor, which is nothing but vested interest, you the individual must liberate yourself from acquisitiveness. As long as this exists, there must be conflict and misery. So do not merely look to a system to solve human sorrow, but become intelligent. Throw away all the stupidities that now crush the mind, and think anew, simply and directly, about war, exploitation and acquisitiveness. Then you do not have to wait for governments which at present are but the expressions of vested interest, to alter the absurd, cruel conditions in the world.

Question: May divorce be a solution for the sex problem?

KRISHNAMURTI: To understand this problem, we must not deal with it by itself. If we desire to understand any problem, we must consider it comprehensively, as a whole, not a part, exclusively.

Why should there be this problem at all? If you deeply examine it, you will see that your creative energy, through fear, is frustrated, limited by authority, compulsion. The mind and heart are hindered from living deeply, through fear, through what one calls morality, which is based on egotistic security. So sex has become a consuming problem, because it is only sensation, without love. If you would release the creative energy of thought and emotion and so solve this problem of sex, then the mind must disentangle itself from self-imposed hindrances and illusions. To live happily, intelligently, mind must be free of fear. Out of this awakening there comes the bliss of love, in which there is no possessiveness. This problem of sex comes into being when love is

destroyed through fear, jealousy, possessiveness.

Question: Are not churches useful for the moral uplift of man?

KRISHNAMURTI: Now what is the present-day morality? When you deeply understand the significance of existing morality and liberate yourself from its selfish, egotistic limitations, then there is intelligence which is truly moral. True morality is not based on fear, and so is free of compulsion. Existing morality, though it professes love and noble sentiment, is based on selfish security and acquisitiveness. Do you want that morality to be maintained? Churches are built through your own fear, through the desire for your own egotistic continuance. The morality of religion and of business is born out of deep egotistic security, and so it is not moral. You must radically change your own attitude towards morality. Churches and other organizations cannot help you, for they themselves are founded on man's stupidity and acquisitiveness.

How can there be true morality if the governments throughout the world, and also the churches, honor those people who are the supreme expressions of acquisitiveness? This whole structure of morality is supported by you, and so by your own thought and action you alone can radically alter it and bring about true morality, true intelligence.

Question: Is there life beyond the grave? What significance has death for you?

KRISHNAMURTI: Why are you concerned about the hereafter? Because living here has lost its deep significance; there is no fulfillment in this world, no lasting love, but only conflict and sorrow. So you hope for a world, the hereafter, in which to live happily, fully. Because you have not had an opportunity of fulfillment here, you hope that in another life you can realize. Or you want to meet again those whom you have lost by death, which but indicates your own emptiness. If I say there is life in the hereafter, and another says there *is* not, you will choose the one that gives you the greater satisfaction, and thus become a slave to authority. So the problem is not whether there is a hereafter, but to understand here the fullness of life which is eternal, to liberate action from creating limitation.

For the man who fulfills, who has not separated himself from the movement of reality, for him there is no death. How can one live so that action is fulfillment? How can one be in love with life? To be in love with life, to fulfill, mind must be free, through deep understanding, from those limitations that thwart and frustrate it; you must become aware, conscious of all the impediments that dwell in the background of the mind. There is within each one the unconscious, which is continually hindering, perverting intelligence; that unconscious is making life incomplete. Through action, through living, through suffering, you must drag out all those things that are hidden, concealed. When the mind is not occupied, through fear, with the hereafter, but is fully conscious, aware of the present with its deep significance, then there is the movement of reality, of life which is not yours or mine.

Question: What you say may be useful for the educated man, but will it not lead the uneducated to chaos?

KRISHNAMURTI: Now is it very difficult to decide who is the educated and who is the uneducated. (Laughter) You may read many books, have many companions, belong to different clubs, have plenty of money, and yet be the most ignorant.

When you are concerned about the uneducated, it usually indicates that there is fear, that you do not wish to be disturbed or dislodged from your achievements. So you say there will be disorder and chaos; as though there were not chaos and suffering in the world now. Do not concern yourself about the uneducated, but see whether your actions are intelligent and fearless, which alone will create right environment. But if, without understanding, you merely concern yourself about the uneducated, you become a priest and an exploiter. If you who are supposed to be educated, who have leisure, do not take the full responsibility of your actions, then there will be greater chaos, misery, and suffering.

Question: In moments of great emptiness, when one thinks of the uselessness of one's own existence, one looks for the opposite, that is, being serviceable to others. Isn't that an escape from conflict? What must I do in such moments? They generally occur after hearing your talks, and come as a feeling of remorse. What do you think of all this?

KRISHNAMURTI: If you merely react to my talks and do not deeply understand what I say through action, through life, then you are conscious only of your own emptiness, shallowness, and so you think that you ought to develop the opposite, which is but an escape. Through action, which is not escape through activity, this emptiness gives way to fulfillment. Do not be concerned about this unhappiness, shallowness, but when the mind liberates itself from its self-imposed limitations, then there is rich completeness.

September 4, 1935

Second Talk in Santiago

Friends,

I want to talk briefly this afternoon about action and fulfillment. We realize the frustration and limitation which appear through our action. By one act we seem to create many problems, and our life becomes one endless series of them, with their conflict and misery. The mind in its movement seems to increase its own limitation, and action which should be liberating, merely intensifies its own frustration.

To understand this question of action and fulfillment, mind must be free from the idea of vested interest. Where there is vested interest, whether in an ideal, in a belief, in a hope, or in any other thing, there must be fear; and any action born of fear must bring about frustration, limitation.

I will try to explain what are the hindrances that really stand in the way of fulfillment. I am not going to describe what is fulfillment, because the mere explanation of that cannot indicate to us the limitations and the manner of liberating the mind from them. Please see why it is necessary to understand what are the hindrances, and how they are created, and not what is fulfillment. If I were to define what it is, the mind would make of that a rigid system and merely imitate it. The very desire for fulfillment becomes a great hindrance. Instead of imitating, if we can discover for ourselves what are the limitations that cripple the mind and free it from them, then in that very freedom is fulfillment.

Fulfillment, then, is not the search for security. Where there is a search for certainty, safety, comfort, that very search must engender fear. Most people, subtly or grossly, are craving for this security and by their acts create fear. So where there is fear, there is a deep longing for certainty. This desire creates its own limitations, and authority or compulsion is one of them.

There are many subtle expressions of authority. It is expressed through the desire to follow an ideal, a person, or a system. Why do we want to follow an ideal? Life is chaotic, conflicting, full of pain, and we think that, if we can find an ideal, then we shall be able to guide ourselves across this aching turmoil. But in reality, what is it that we are doing? We are creating what we call an ideal as a means of escape from conflict, from suffering. By following and submitting ourselves to an ideal, we think we shall be able to understand our contradictory and sorrowful life. Instead of liberating ourselves from those causes which are preventing us from living humanly, with love, with consideration, we try to escape into the illusion of an ideal. We hope by molding our minds and hearts through discipline, through the imitation of certain ideals and beliefs, to achieve that intelligent human state. This imitation creates a hypocritical attitude towards life. With a desire to escape from the movement of life, which is ever of the present, we seek to know the purpose of life. With a desire to escape from actuality, the mind submits itself to the compulsion of ideals which are but self-protective memories against life.

There is, then, this compulsion which is imposed through self-defensive memories. Most of us think that through a continual series of experiences, the mind can free itself from all its many limitations. But this is not so. What happens is that each experience leaves on the mind certain scars, memories of self-protection which are used as a means of defense against a new experience. That is, you have an experience, and you think you have learned something from it. What you have learned is to be careful, not to be caught in sorrow again. So through each experience you develop certain layers of memories which act as barriers between the mind and the movement of life.

Ideals and memories, with all their significance, prevent each one from living completely in action, in experience. Instead of living with experience completely, with your whole being, you bring forward all your prejudices of ideals, self-protective moralities and memories, and those prevent fulfillment. Where there is no fulfillment, there is ever the fear of death, and the thought of the hereafter. So gradually the present, the living movement of life, loses all its beauty and significance, and there is only emptiness and fear.

If there is to be true fulfillment, mind must be free from ideals and memories, with all their significance. Through the desire for security, these memories and ideals become the means of compulsion. Where there is security there cannot be fulfillment.

Question: You have often said, "Perceive and understand the full significance of environment." Does this necessarily mean action coming into conflict with environment? Or is it mere perception, without any dynamic expression in action?

KRISHNAMURTI: How can one truly discern if there is not action? There cannot be an intellectual discernment. There is either deep understanding or the creation of mere theory. If you desire to understand environment, not only the objective but the subjective which is so infinitely subtle, then you must individually come into conflict with it. It is only in conflict, in suffering, that you, the individual, begin to discern the true significance of values; and as most people are afraid to come into contact with suffering, they would rather intellectually perceive their significance. So they leave the responsibility of action to the mass, that vague and unreal entity, which they hope will miraculously alter their environment, and so bring happiness to them.

To understand deeply the subtle significance of environment, you, the individual, must become conscious and break away from those limiting conditions, whether they are social, religious, or traditional. Truth, the beauty of reality, can be discerned only when the mind is fearless; not with the fearlessness of intellectuality, but of utter insecurity. You can know of this only through action.

Question: Is it of any value to pray to the great intelligences for help in our daily life?

KRISHNAMURTI: None whatever. I will explain what I mean. What causes misery, conflict, suffering in our daily life? Traditions, selfish moral values, impositions of vested interest, attachment, acquisitiveness: these create conditions which prevent human happiness. And what is the use of praying to someone when you, through your own intelligence, can alter all this awful mess? Being unwilling to face suffering, we try to escape through prayer. You may escape momentarily, but the strength of your desire asserts itself again, plunging the mind into misery and confusion. So what matters is, not whether it is of value to pray, but to awaken that intelligence which alone will solve our human miseries. A mind and a heart that are hardened, that have limited themselves through their egotistic fears, pray. But if there were love, then you would free the mind from its own egotistic fears, and this alone can bring about intelligence and happy order.

Question: Doesn't love, freed from possessiveness, lead to the cessation of reproduction and therefore to the extinction of mankind? As this seems to be unintelligent, is it not the outcome of a belief?

KRISHNAMURTI: Before we can say it is the outcome of belief and so unintelligent we must understand what our present love is. It is nothing but possessiveness, except in those rare moments when the perfume of love is known. To control, to possess, we have certain laws which we call moral. To me, where there is possessiveness there cannot be love. Without being aware of all its subtle impositions and cruelties, you say, "If we freed ourselves from possessiveness, wouldn't we get rid altogether of love?" To find out if you would, you must experiment, you cannot merely assert. Let the mind wholly free itself from attachment, possessiveness; then you will know.

It is when we have lost love through possessiveness that we have sexual problems; we want to solve them separately, apart from the rest of man's problems and difficulties. You cannot isolate a human problem and solve it singly, exclusively. To understand deeply the problem of sex and dissolve its difficulties, we must know where we are being frustrated, dominated. Through economic conditions the individual is turned into a machine, and his work is not fulfillment but compulsion. Where there should be the release of self-expression through work, there is frustration; and where there should be deep, complete thought, there is fear, imposition, imitation. So the problem of sex becomes all-consuming and intricate. We think we can solve it exclusively, but this is not possible. When work becomes true expression and when there is no longer the desire, through fear, to cling to beliefs, traditions, ideals, and religions, then there is the exquisite reality of love. Where there is love there is no sense of possession; attachment indicates deep frustration.

Question: Have we to better the order of things created by God himself?

KRISHNAMURTI: That is the attitude of an exploiter. He wants to let things remain as they are, finding himself on the safe side. But ask the man who is in suffering, ask the man who lives in tattered clothes in a hovel; then you will know whether things should be left as they are. Both the poor and the rich want things to remain as they are; the poor are afraid of losing the little that they have, and the rich of losing all that they have. So when there is the fear of loss, of being made uncertain, there comes the desire not to interfere with the order of things which God or nature has created.

To bring about happy, human order, there must be within each one of you a deep, fundamental change. Where there is a continual adaptation to the movement of life, truth, there is never fear. Each one of you must feel the poison of compulsion, authority, and imitation. Each one must feel the immense necessity, through his own suffering, for a complete and radical change of thought and desire, free from the subtle search for substitution. Then there will be the true fulfillment of man.

Question: If sorrow is necessary for the purification of our souls, why do away with sorrow through the understanding of its cause?

KRISHNAMURTI: Sorrow does not purify. Why is there sorrow? When the mind is stagnant, drugged to sleep by beliefs, crippled by limitations, and is awakened by the movement of life, that awakening we call suffering. Where there is the disturbance of our security through the action of life, that we call suffering. Instead of seeing that suffering is a hindrance, we try to utilize it to get some other result. Through an illusion you cannot come to reality.

Now sorrow is but the indication of limitation, of incompleteness. When one discerns the impediment of sorrow, one cannot make of it a means of purification. You must be rid of its limitation. You must understand the cause and its effects. If you use it as a means of purification, you are subtly deriving from it security, comfort. This only creates further hindrances, impeding the awakening of intelligence. Out of these many hindrances, these self-defensive memories, is born the limited consciousness, the 'I', which is the true cause of suffering.

Question: Don't you think it is practically impossible for your lofty ideas and conceptions to germinate in brains degenerated by vices and disease?

KRISHNAMURTI: Of course, that is obvious. But vice is a cultivated habit, a means of escape, generally, from life, from intelligence.

Take the question of drink. The vested interest sells liquor, and the governments support it. Then you form temperance societies and religious organizations to awaken man to the cruelty and stupidity of alcoholism. On one side you have the vested interest, and on the other the reformer; and the victim becomes the plaything of both. If you want to help man, which is yourself, then you will see to it that you are not exploited through your own stupidity. This demands discernment of existing values and perceiving their true significance. Because of illusion, stupidity, man is exploited by man. After surrounding ourselves with so many limitations which prevent human happiness, kindliness, love, we think that we are going to be rid of them by seeking further substitutions. Through your acquisitiveness, through your fear, you are creating illusions, and in that net you are entangling your neighbor also.

Question: What is to be understood by God? Is he a personal Being who guides the universe, or is God a cosmic principle?

KRISHNAMURTI: May I ask why you want to know? Either you desire to be strengthened further in your beliefs, or you are seeking from me a means of escape from sorrow and conflict. If you are asking for confirmation, then there is doubt, which must not be allayed. You never ask another whether you are in love. And if anyone were to describe reality, it would no longer be real. How can you describe to one who has not known it, what it is to be in love?

Now I say there is a reality; it cannot be measured by words. You cannot be aware of that reality if there is fear, if there are limitations that destroy the delicate pliability of the mind and heart. So instead of inquiring what God is, find out whether your mind and heart are enslaved by fear which creates illusion and limitation. When the mind and heart free themselves from those self-imposed protections, then in fulfillment there is the understanding of that which is.

Question: In some of your earlier talks, you have said that conflict exists only between the false and the false, never between the real and the false. Will you please explain this?

KRISHNAMURTI: There cannot be a struggle between light and darkness. Illusion gives rise to conflict, not between itself and reality, but with its own creations. There is never conflict between intelligence and stupidity.

Question: Please explain the meaning of pure action. Does it come about when life expresses itself through the liberated individual?

KRISHNAMURTI: Let us for a moment leave aside the liberated individual, and understand what we call action.

With certain limitations and prejudices the mind-heart meets life or experience. In this contact between the dead and the living, there is action. Desire is seeking fulfillment. In its realization, in its action there is pain and pleasure, and the mind records them. In the expression of other desires there is again pain and pleasure, and again the mind stores them. Thus the mind becomes the storehouse of memories. These memories are acting as warnings. So action becomes more and more controlled and directed by these memories, based on pain and pleasure, on self-defense. Action, because it is born out of self-protective memories and desires, is continually creating restrictions, limitations. There is the action of self-defensive memories, and an action which is free from this center of self-imposed limitation.

Question: Do you hold back from the public something of what you know?

KRISHNAMURTI: There is in most people a desire to be exclusive, to separate themselves from others through knowledge, through titles, through possessions. This form of seclusion gives strength to their self-importance, to their small vanities. Our society, both the temporal and the so-called spiritual, is based on this hierarchical exclusiveness. To yield to this separativeness creates the many gross and subtle forms of exploitation.

I have no secret teachings for the few. Naturally there are those who desire to go more deeply into what I say; but if they become exclusive and create a secret body, they are being encouraged to do so by their own desire to be exclusive.

Question: Do you believe in God?

KRISHNAMURTI: Either you put this question out of curiosity to find out what I think,

or you want to discover if there is God. If you are merely curious, naturally there is no answer; but if you want to find out for yourself if there is God, then you must approach this inquiry without prejudice; you must come to it with a fresh mind, neither believing nor disbelieving. If I said there is, you would accept it as a belief, and you would add that belief to the already existing dead beliefs. Or, if I said no, it would merely become a convenient support to the unbeliever.

If a man is truly desirous to know, let him not seek reality, life, God, which will only be an escape from sorrow, from conflict; but let him understand the very cause of sorrow, conflict, and when the mind is liberated from it, he shall know. When the mind is vulnerable, when it has lost all support, explanations, when it is naked, then it shall know the bliss of truth.

September 7, 1935

Third Talk in Santiago

Question: What have you to say about the treatment of criminals?

KRISHNAMURTI: Now it all depends upon whom you call a criminal. A pathological person is not a criminal, and it is folly to put him in a prison. He needs medical attention and care. A person who deliberately steals is generally called a criminal. Unless he is a pathological case, he steals because there is for him an insufficiency of the necessities of life. So what is the sense of turning him into a criminal by throwing him into prison? He is the result of cruel, absurd, and exploiting economic conditions. He is not the real culprit, but the whole system of acquisitiveness which creates the exploiter.

There is yet another type of man who also is called a criminal; his ideas, being true, become dangerous, and you get rid of him by sending him to prison or by killing him.

Through one's own action one either creates conditions which produce the so-called criminal, or destroys those limitations which create sorrow.

Question: It is being said that you are an agent of the British government, and that your talk against nationalism is part of a vast plan of propaganda directed towards keeping India within and subject to the British Empire. Is this true?

KRISHNAMURTI: I am afraid this is not true. It is rather absurd to be told, when one says what one thinks, that one is an agent for some cause or country. (Laughter) To me, nationalism, whether in Chile, England, or India, is destructive. It separates human beings, causes many evils. Nationalism is an ugly disease; and when I say this, those people from other countries who have vested interest here or in any country not their own are very much in agreement with it; and those for whom nationalism is a means of exploiting their own people are very much opposed to it. Nationalism is, after all, a false sentiment, stimulated by vested interests and used for imperialism and war.

Question: Is not what you say against nationalism detrimental to the welfare of the smaller nations? How can we in Chile hope to uphold our national integrity and well-being unless we feel intensely nationalistic and defend ourselves against the larger nations who seek to control and dominate us?

KRISHNAMURTI: When you talk about upholding your national integrity and well-being, you mean developing your own particular class of exploiters. (Laughter) Do not

think in terms of Chile or any other country, but think of humanity as a whole.

Yesterday I was walking in the country, and there was a lovely sunset. The mountains and the snow were aglow, clear, beautiful. A laborer, literally in rags, passed by. Some have money to live comfortably and enjoy the luxury and the beauty of life; others have to work from morning until night, from a tender age until they die, without leisure, without hope. We allow in every country all this cruelty and horror. We have lost our delicate feelings, we are frustrated and are destroying ourselves through fear and acquisitiveness.

Surely, to abolish poverty, you must think as human beings, not as nationals. There can only be humanity, and not the cruel division of races and the childish absurdity of nationalism. Why cannot this happy and intelligent state be brought about? Who is preventing it? Each one of you, because you think in terms of Chile, England, India, or some other country. As beliefs divide people, so you have let frontiers destroy the unity of man. It rests with you, not with a vague thing called the mass, to bring about human unity and happiness.

Question: You apparently believe that all priests are scoundrels. (Laughter) In the Catholic church there are many great and saintly men. Do you call these also exploiters?

KRISHNAMURTI: Through fear one creates authority; and yielding to it must bring about exploitation. So each one, through fear, creates exploiters. By your own desires and fears you have created religions, with their dogmas, creeds, and all their pageantry and show. Religions as organized beliefs, with their vested interest, do not lead man to reality. They have become engines of exploitation. (Applause) But you are responsible for their existence. Mind must be free from those illusions which fear has created, those illusions that now appear as reality; and when the mind is simple, direct, capable of thinking truly, then it will not create exploiters.

Question: Your teaching concerning the family seems to me heartless and cold. Is not the family a most natural outcome of affection between human beings? Why then are you against it?

KRISHNAMURTI: What is the family now? It is based on possessiveness, which destroys love. Where there is a sense of possession, there must be exploitation. Where there is love, there is no imposition or possessiveness. But if you consider our present morality, you will see that it is based on maintaining this possessive attitude towards life. By our egotistic craving we are destroying the perfume and the beauty of life. Where there is love, family does not become a center of exploitation.

Question: If one lives free of such vices as the use of alcohol and tobacco and follows a strictly vegetarian diet, can this not be a great factor in helping one to understand your teachings?

KRISHNAMURTI: Please, it is not what you put into your mouth that gives you understanding. (Laughter) What gives you understanding is facing life directly, simply, and truly. But by merely giving up meat, alcohol, or tobacco you are not going to understand reality. A great many people have given up these things, hoping for happiness. Fulfillment lies not in giving up but in understanding. Mind cannot be a slave to fear and to illusions. Discover first the impediments, the limitations which cripple the mind and

heart, and when you liberate yourself from them, then there will be intelligent and natural existence.

Question: How can there possibly be individual well-being until there is a mass movement to remove the capitalistic exploiters from power? Surely the mass movement must come first in order to clear the way for the underdog, and only then will there be an equal opportunity for all.

KRISHNAMURTI: Now to put one or the other first, individual well-being or collective action, must ultimately hinder man's fulfillment. True fulfillment brings about the welfare of the whole as well as of the individual. What is it that we call the mass? It is you. There cannot be true collective action without individual comprehension. The mass movement is really the result of clear thought and action on the part of every individual. If each one of you merely says that there ought to be collective action, then such action will never take place, because you are merely avoiding your individual responsibility of action. When a man relies on the action of the mass, he himself is truly afraid to act.

If there is to be a radical, complete change, you, the individual, must awaken to the limitations that now cripple your mind and heart. In liberating yourself from those egotistic, illusory hopes, ambitions, and cruelties, there will be intelligent cooperation and not compulsion and exploitation.

Question: I have a friend who is mediumistic. When she goes into a trance, many great spirits talk through her, including Napoleon, Plato, and Jesus, and their advice is very helpful in the spiritual life. Why do you not speak about the value of spiritualism and mediumship?

KRISHNAMURTI: I have been talking about authority and its destructive influence upon intelligence, whether it be the authority of the living or of the dead. It does not become any the holier because it is of the past or of the dead. Authority, compulsion, destroys fulfillment, whether it is exercised by religion, by society, or by mediums. What is behind this desire for guidance? One is afraid that by one's own act one will be caught up in suffering; so, in order to avoid it—in fact, not to live—one says, "I must follow, I must be guided." There is the movement of truth only when the mind is no longer held by fear, with all its illusions, when it is no longer seeking guidance or being guided. This aloneness is not exclusiveness; it comes into being when there is the discernment of the false.

Question: You say that spiritual organizations are useless. Is this true for all people, or only for those persons who have gone beyond the spiritual level of mankind in general?

KRISHNAMURTI: When you think that what I say is applicable only to the few, you make of me an exploiter. You think that another needs the falseness, the illusions of organized belief. If it is false, if it is unspiritual for you, then it is unspiritual and false for all. There is no relative stupidity. Because we do not desire to think directly and clearly, we pacify ourselves by saying that intelligence is a matter of slow growth. For example, acquisitiveness, if you really think about it profoundly, is a poison in itself. But if you thought about it deeply, it would involve action and suffering, so you say that freedom from acquisitiveness is progressive, relative, to be realized by degrees. In other words, you are not at all sure that acquisitiveness is a poison. In the same way, you are not at all sure that religions, sects are inherently stupid. If a thing is false, it is false for everyone, under all circumstances.

Question: If the idea of individual immortality is false, what is the purpose of individual existence?

KRISHNAMURTI: To understand this problem of individual immortality you must come to it without any bias. The very craving for immortality prevents its deep comprehension. To understand this deeply, mind must have the power of complete discernment, not choice based on identification. Our cravings are so strong, our egotistic self-protective impulses are so vital, that our very want blinds us. Where there is craving there cannot be discernment. True culture is action for its own beauty, without seeking reward.

When you say 'I', what do you mean by that? You mean the form, the name, certain unfulfilled desires, qualities, and defensive reactions which you call virtue; all these make up that limited consciousness which we call the 'I'. The mind has enclosed itself within the many walls of illusion and limitation, and the many layers of memories cause frustration. What you are trying to do is to immortalize this frustration which is the 'I'. There cannot be immortality for illusion. Life is eternal, ever becoming. To discern this deeply, mind must liberate itself from all the impediments that cause frustration. By being fully aware, all the hidden, secret desires, fears, and pursuits come into consciousness; then only can there be true freedom from them. Then there is reality.

Question: I have a daughter who was formerly very studious and loved her music, but now she does nothing but read your books. What do you advise her mother to do? (Laughter)

KRISHNAMURTI: I wonder why your daughter has given up her music? It may be because she has discovered that it was not her deep fulfillment, and she is trying to find her true expression. But if she merely reads what I have said, without the fullness of action, then my words will become a hindrance.

We often think that living according to a certain idea will awaken intelligence. What really awakens intelligence is action without the fear of not adjusting oneself to a standard or an ideal. This demands great awareness and pliability of mind.

Question: Have you attained to what you are in this life, through a series of past lives?

KRISHNAMURTI: You are asking me if one can understand truth, life, or God through accumulation of experience.

Experience has merely taught us to be cunningly self-protective, to create defenses against the movement of life. In this enclosure the mind takes shelter, guarding itself more and more against the continual becoming of life. These defensive barriers divide the movement of life into the past, the present, and the future. It is this division that destroys the continuity of life as a whole. From this there arises fear, which is covered over by illusions, hopes. So long as the mind-heart is caught up in this division there cannot be the understanding of truth; for then experience merely becomes a source of conflict and sorrow, whereas it should wear down these self-protective barriers and so liberate the mind and heart to the movement of life.

September 8, 1935

Mexico City, Mexico, 1935

---- ✳ ----

First Talk in Mexico City

Friends,

As many incorrect statements have been made in the newspapers concerning me, I wish to correct them before I proceed with my talk. I am not a Theosophist. I do not belong to any sect or party or to any particular religion, for religion is a distinct hindrance to man's fulfillment. Nor do I desire to convert you to some fantastic theories and conclusions.

Now you may ask, "What is it that you want to do? If you don't want us to join any society or accept certain theories, what is it then that you want to do?"

What I want to do is to help you, the individual, to cross the stream of suffering, confusion, and conflict, through deep and complete fulfillment. This fulfillment does not lie through egotistic self-expression, nor through compulsion and imitation. Not through some fantastic sentiment and conclusions, but through clear thinking, through intelligent action, we shall cross this stream of pain and sorrow. There is a reality which can be understood only through deep and true fulfillment.

Before we can understand the richness and the beauty of fulfillment, mind must free itself from the background of tradition, habit, and prejudice. For example, if you belong to a particular political party, you naturally regard all your political considerations from the narrow, limited point of view of that party. If you have been brought up, nursed, conditioned in a certain religion, you look at life through its veil of prejudice and darkness. That background of tradition prevents the complete understanding of life, and so causes confusion and suffering.

I would beg of you to listen to what I have to say, freeing yourself for this hour at least from the background in which you have been brought up, with its traditions and prejudices, and think simply and directly about the many human problems.

To be truly critical is not to be in opposition. Most of us have been trained to oppose and not to criticize. When a man merely opposes, it generally indicates that he has some vested interest which he desires to protect, and that is not deep penetration through critical examination. True criticism lies in trying to understand the full significance of values without the hindrance of defensive reactions.

We see throughout the world extremes of poverty and riches, abundance and at the same time starvation; we have class distinction and racial hatred, the stupidity of nationalism and the appalling cruelty of war. There is exploitation of man by man; religions with their vested interests have become the means of exploitation, also dividing man from man. There is anxiety, confusion, hopelessness, frustration.

We see all this. It is part of our daily life. Caught up in the wheel of suffering, if you are at all thoughtful you must have asked yourself how these human problems can be solved. Either you are conscious of the chaotic state of the world, or you are completely asleep, living in a fantastic world, in an illusion. If you are aware, you must be grappling with these problems. In trying to solve them, some turn to experts for their solution, and follow their ideas and theories. Gradually they form themselves into an exclusive body, and thus they come into conflict with other experts and their parties; and the individual merely becomes a tool in the hands of the group or of the expert. Or you try to solve these problems by following a particular system, which, if you carefully examine it, becomes merely another means of exploiting the individual. Or you think that to change all this cruelty and horror, there must be a mass movement, a collective action.

Now the idea of a mass movement becomes merely a catchword if you, the individual, who are part of the mass, do not understand your true function. True collective action can take place only when you, the individual, who are also the mass, are awake and take the full responsibility for your action without compulsion.

Please bear in mind that I am not giving you a system of philosophy which you can follow blindly, but I am trying to awaken the desire for true and intelligent fulfillment, which alone can bring about happy order and peace in the world.

There can be fundamental and lasting change in the world, there can be love and intelligent fulfillment, only when you wake up and begin to free yourself from the net of illusions, the many illusions which you have created about yourself through fear. When the mind frees itself from these hindrances,

when there is that deep, inward, voluntary change, then only can there be true, lasting, collective action, in which there can be no compulsion.

Please understand that I am talking to you as an individual, not to a collective group or to a particular party. If you do not awaken to your full responsibility, to your fulfillment, then your function as a human being in society must be frustrated, limited, and in that lies sorrow.

So the question is: How can there be this profound individual revolution? If there is true, voluntary revolution on the part of the individual, then you will create the right environment for all without the distinction of class or race. Then the world will be a single human unit.

How are you going to awaken as individuals to this profound revolution? Now what I am going to say is not complicated, it is simple; and because of its very simplicity, I am afraid you will reject it as not being positive. What you call positive is to be given a definite plan, to be told exactly what to do. But if you can understand for yourself what are the hindrances that are preventing your deep and true fulfillment, then you will not become a mere follower and be exploited. All following is detrimental to completeness.

To have this profound revolution, you must become fully conscious of the structure which you have created about yourself and in which you are now caught. That is, we have now certain values, ideals, beliefs, which act as a net to hold the mind, and by questioning and understanding all their significance, we shall realize how they have come into existence. Before you can act fully and truly, you must know the prison in which you are living, how it has been created; and in examining it without any self-defense, you will find out for yourself its true significance, which no other can convey to you. Through your own awakening of intelligence, through your own suffering you will discover the manner of true fulfillment.

Each one of us is seeking security, certainty, through egotistic thought and action, objectively and subjectively. If you are conscious of your own thought, you will see that you are pursuing your own egotistic certainty and security, both outwardly and inwardly. In reality, there is no such absolute division of life as the objective and the subjective world. I make this division only for convenience.

Objectively, this search for egotistic security and certainty expresses itself through family, which becomes a center of exploitation, based on acquisitiveness. If you examine it, you will see that what you call the love of family is nothing but possessiveness.

That search for security again expresses itself through class divisions which develop into the stupidity of nationalism and imperialism, breeding hatred, racial antagonism, and the ultimate cruelty of war.

So through our own egotistic desires we have created a world of nationalities and conflicting sovereign governments, whose function is to prepare for war and force man against man.

Then there is the search for egotistic security, certainty, through what we call religion. You like fondly to believe that divine beings have created these organized forms of belief which we call religions. You yourself have created them for your own convenience; through ages they have become sanctified, and you have now become enslaved to them. There can never be ideal religions, so let us not waste our time discussing them. They can exist only in theory, not in reality. Let us examine how we have created religions and in what manner we are enslaved to them. If you deeply examine them as they are, you will see that they are nothing but the vested interest of organized belief, holding, separating, and exploiting man.

As you are objectively seeking security, so also you are seeking subjectively a different kind of security, certainty, which you call immortality. You crave for egotistic continuance in the hereafter, calling it immortality. Later in my talks I will explain what to me is true immortality.

In your search for that security, fear is born, and so you submit yourself to another who promises you that immortality. Through fear you create a spiritual authority, and to administer that authority there are priests who exploit you through belief, dogma, and creed, through show, pomp, and pageantry, which throughout the world is called religion. It is essentially based on fear, though you may call it the love of God or truth; it is, if you examine it intelligently, nothing but the result of fear, and therefore it must become one of the means of exploiting man. Through your own desire for immortality, for selfish continuance, you have built this illusion which you call religion, and you are unconsciously or consciously caught in it. Or you may not belong to any particular religion, but you may belong to some sect which subtly promises a reward, a subtle inflation of the ego in the hereafter. Or you may not belong to any society or sect, but there may be an inward desire, hidden and concealed, to seek your own immortality. So long as there is a desire for self-continuance in any form, there must be fear, which but creates authority, and from this there comes the subtle cruelty and stupidity of submitting oneself to exploitation. This exploitation is so subtle, so refined that one becomes enamored of it, calling it spiritual progress and advancement toward perfection.

Now you, the individual, must become conscious of all this intricate structure, conscious of the source of fear, and be willing to eradicate it, whatever be the consequence.

This means coming into conflict individually with the existing ideals and values; and when the mind frees itself from the false, there can be the creation of right environment for the whole.

Your first concern is to become conscious of the prison; then you will see that your own thought is continually trying to avoid coming into conflict with the values of the prison. This escape creates ideals which, however beautiful, are but illusions. It is one of the tricks of the mind to escape into an ideal, because if it does not escape, it must come directly into conflict with the prison, with the environment. That is, the mind wants to escape into an illusion rather than face the suffering which will inevitably arise when it begins to question the values, the morality, the religion of the prison.

So what matters is to come into conflict with the traditions and values of the society and religion in which you are caught, and not intellectually escape through an ideal. When you begin to question these values, you begin to awaken that true intelligence which alone can solve the many human problems.

As long as the mind is caught up in false values, there cannot be fulfillment. Completeness alone will reveal truth, the movement of eternal life.

October 20, 1935

Second Talk in Mexico City

Friends,

Everyone desires to be happy, to be complete, and to fulfill; to fulfill in order that there may be no emptiness, no void, but a deep richness of continual sufficiency. One calls this the search for truth or God, or gives some other name to it to convey the deep desire for reality. Now this desire, for most people, becomes merely an escape, a flight from the actuality of conflict. There is so much suffering and confusion in and about us that we seek a supposed reality as a means of flight from the present. For most people, what they call reality or God, or happiness is merely an escape from suffering, from this continual tension between action and understanding. Each one tries to find an escape from this conflict through some kind of illusion which is offered by religions or by various so-called spiritual societies and sects; or he seeks to lose himself in some kind of activity.

Now if you carefully examine what these societies offer—organized, as they are, around a belief, as are all religions and sects—you will find that they give security, comfort, through a saviour or a Master, through guides, through following certain systems of thought, ideals and modes of conduct. All these modes of conduct, systems, assure a subtle form of egotistic security, self-defense against life, against the confusion created by thoughtlessness. As we cannot understand life with its swift movement, we look to systems to help us out, and these we call modes of conduct or patterns of behavior. So, being afraid of confusion and sorrow, you create for yourselves an authority that assures you of safety and security against the flow of reality.

Take, for example, the desire to follow an ideal or a mode of conduct. Now why is there the need to follow an ideal, a principle, or a pattern of behavior? You say that you need an ideal because there is so much confusion in and about you; that this ideal will act as a guide, as a directive force to help you across this confusion, uncertainty, and turmoil. In order not to be caught in this suffering, you subtly escape through an ideal, which you call living nobly. That is, you do not want to confront and understand the confusion itself, and you do not desire to comprehend the causes of conflict; your only concern is to avoid sorrow. So ideals, modes of conduct, offer a convenient escape from actuality. In the same way, if you examine your search for guides and saviors, there is in it a subtle and hidden desire to run away from suffering. When you talk about seeking truth, reality, you are really seeking complete self-protection, either here or in the hereafter. You are molding yourself after a pattern that guarantees you against suffering. This pattern, this mold, you call morality, creed, belief.

Now all this indicates that there is a deep, hidden fear of life, which must naturally create authority. So where there is authority in the form of an ideal, a mode of conduct, or a person, there must be egotistic craving for protection and security. In this there is not a spark of reality. Thus your actions, shaped and controlled by ideals, are always made incomplete, for they are based upon defensive reaction against intelligence, life.

In following an ideal or a mode of conduct, or submitting oneself to a particular authority, either of religion, or a sect or of society, there cannot be true fulfillment; and only through fulfillment is there the bliss of truth.

As what we call our morality and ideals is based on self-defensive reactions against life, we are unconscious of them as impediments, as barriers which separate us from the movement of life. Complete fulfillment exists only when these self-protective barriers have been wholly dissipated by our own effort and intelligence.

If you would know the bliss of truth, you must become fully aware of these self-defensive barriers, and dissipate them through your own voluntary decision. This demands steady and continuous effort. Most people are not willing to make that effort. They would rather be told exactly what to do, they would rather be like machines, acting in the grooves of religious superstition and habit. You must examine these defensive barriers of ideals and morality and come

directly into conflict with them. Until you as an individual voluntarily free yourself from these illusions, there cannot be the comprehension of truth. In dissolving these illusions of self-protection, the mind awakens to reality and its ecstasy.

Question: Is it possible to know God?

KRISHNAMURTI: To speculate and intellectually draw conclusions as to whether God exists or not, has to me no deep significance. You can know whether there is God or not, only with your whole being, not with one part of your being, the intellect. You have already a fixed belief, either that there is God, or that there is not. If you approach this question either with a belief or with non-belief, you cannot discover reality, for your mind is already prejudiced.

You can discover whether there is or there is not God only by destroying these self-protective barriers and being completely vulnerable to life, wholly naked. This involves suffering, which alone can awaken intelligence, from which is born true discernment. So what value has it if I tell you that there is or that there is not God? The various religions and sects throughout the world are filled with dead beliefs; and when you ask me whether I believe in God or not, you only want me to add another dead belief to the museum. To discover, you must come into conflict with the various illusions of which you are now unconscious; and in that conflict, without any escape through an ideal, through authority or the worship of another, there will be born the discernment of reality.

Question: Are you or are you not a member of the Theosophical Society?

KRISHNAMURTI: I do not belong to any society or sect or party. I do not belong to any religion, for organized belief is a great impediment, dividing man against man and destroying his intelligence. These societies and religions are fundamentally based on vested interest and exploitation.

Question: How can I be free of sexual desire, which prevents me from leading the spiritual life?

KRISHNAMURTI: For most people, life is not fulfillment but continued frustration. Our occupation is merely a means of earning a livelihood. In it there is no love, but only compulsion and frustration. So your work, which should be your true expression, is merely an adjustment to a pattern, and in this there is incompleteness. Your thoughts and emotions are limited and thwarted by fear, and so action brings about its own frustration. If you really observe your own life, you will see that society on the one hand, and the whole religious structure on the other, is forcing, compelling you to shape your thoughts and actions after a pattern based on self-protection and fear. So where there is continual frustration, naturally the problem of sex becomes overwhelming. Until the mind and heart are no longer slaves to environment, that is, until they have discerned the false in it through action, sex will be an increasing and overpowering problem. To treat it as unspiritual is absurd.

Most people are caught up in this problem, and to solve it truly, you must disentangle your creative thought and emotion from the impositions of religion and the stupid morality of society. (Applause) Through its own effort the mind must disentangle itself from the net of false values which society and religion have imposed upon it. Then there is true fulfillment, in which there are no problems.

Question: Will you tell us how to communicate with the spirits of the dead? How can we be sure that we are not deceived?

KRISHNAMURTI: You know, it is becoming throughout the world a craze to communicate with the dead. It is a new kind of sensation, a new toy. Why do you want to communicate with the dead? Is it not because you want to be guided? Again you want to defend yourself against life, and you think a person being dead has become more wise and so able to guide you. To you the dead are more important than the living. What matters is, not whether you can communicate with the dead, but that you shall fulfill, without fear, completely and intelligently.

To understand life deeply and fully, there must be no fear either of the present or of the hereafter. If you do not penetrate the present environment through your own capacity and intelligence, you will naturally escape into the hereafter or seek guidance and so avoid the beauty of life. Because this environment is restrictive, exploiting, cruel, you find a release in the hereafter, in the search for guides, Masters, and saviors. Until you act completely with regard to all the human problems, you will have various fears and subtle escapes. Where there is fear there must be illusion and ignorance. Fear can be eradicated only through your own effort and intelligence.

Question: I gather that you are preaching the exaltation of the individual and that you are against the mass. How can individualism be conducive to cooperation and brotherhood?

KRISHNAMURTI: I am not doing anything of the kind. I am not preaching individualism at all. I am saying that there can be true cooperation only when there is intelligence; but to awaken that intelligence, every individual must be responsible for his effort and action. There cannot be a true mass movement if each one of you is still held in the prison of selfish defenses. How can there be collective action for the welfare of the whole if each one of you is secretly acquisitive, defending himself and so fearing his neighbor, classifying himself as belonging to a particular religion or belief, or smitten with the disease of nationalism? How can there be intelligent cooperation when you have these secret prejudices and desires? To bring about intelligent action, it must begin with you, individually. Merely to create a mass movement involves exploitation and cruelty. When you, the individual, realize the stupidity and the cruelty of the interrelated social and religious environment, then through your intelligence will it be possible to create collective action without exploitation. So the important thing is not the exaltation of the individual or the mass, but the awakening of that intelligence which alone can bring about the true welfare of man.

Question: Will I reincarnate on earth in a future life?

KRISHNAMURTI: I will explain briefly what is generally meant by reincarnation. The idea is that there is a gap, a division between man and reality, and this division is one of time and of understanding. To arrive at perfection, God, or truth, you must go through various experiences until you have accumulated sufficient knowledge, equivalent to reality. This division between ignorance and wisdom is to be bridged only through constant accumulation, learning, which goes on life after life until you arrive at perfection. You who are imperfect now, shall become perfect; for that you must have time and opportunity, which necessitates rebirth. This, briefly, is the theory of reincarnation.

When you talk about the 'I', what do you mean by it? You mean the name, the form, certain virtues, idiosyncrasies, prejudices, memories. In other words, the 'I' is nothing but many layers of memories, the result of frustration, the limitation of action by environment, which cause incompleteness and sorrow. These many layers of memories, frustrations, become the limited consciousness which you call the 'I'. So you think that the 'I' is to go on through time, becoming more and more perfect. But since that 'I' is merely the result of frustration, how can it become perfect? The 'I', being a limitation, cannot become perfect. It must ever remain a limitation. The mind must free itself from the cause of frustration now, for wisdom lies ever in the present. Understanding is not to be gained in a future.

Please, this needs careful thought. You want me to give you an assurance that you will live another life, but in that there is no happiness or wisdom. The search for immortality through reincarnation is essentially egotistic, and therefore not true. Your search for immortality is only another form of the desire for the continuance of self-defensive reactions against life and intelligence. Such a craving can only lead to illusion. So what matters is not whether there is reincarnation, but to realize complete fulfillment in the present. And you can do that only when your mind and heart are no longer protecting themselves against life. The mind is cunning and subtle in its self-defense, and it must discern for itself the illusory nature of self-protection. This means that you must think and act completely anew. You must liberate yourself from the net of false values which environment has imposed upon you. There must be utter nakedness. Then there is immortality, reality.

October 27, 1935

Third Talk in Mexico City

Friends,

Most people have accepted the idea that man is something more than the mere result of environment. I mean by environment, not only the social and religious background, but also the past. That man is something more than this is especially accepted by those who call themselves religious, spiritual people. The majority of you have accepted this idea, if you carefully examine it, on the authority of another; or it is dictated to you by your own hope or longing, which you call intuition. You have not discovered for yourselves whether you are something more than merely social entities. Seeing that life around you is stifling, sorrowful, you crave for happiness and submit yourselves to a particular mode of conduct which is based on self-protection. You believe that man is more than mere matter because teachers have proclaimed it and many religions and sects have maintained it throughout the ages. But if you strip your mind of these authorities and illusions created through hope, you will inevitably come to the conclusion that there is no deep certainty within you concerning this matter.

Then there are those who say that man is nothing but the result of environment. They say that to change man, environment must be wholly controlled and man must be subjugated to it, so that there can be the certainty of his happiness.

There is the religious idea which conceives of lasting happiness only in the hereafter, which says that you can never find happiness here. From this there are developed beliefs, creeds, dogmas, saviors, and Masters, to lead you to that lasting happiness. Thus we have innumerable escapes through which man is exploited.

So you have two diametrically opposed ideas concerning man, at least they seem to be, but fundamentally they are not. One maintains that man is mere clay to be conditioned by intelligent environment, and the other, that he can be truly intelligent only in the hereafter by conditioning himself through certain beliefs. Some maintain that man can be made intelligent through law, by controlling environment; and religions, through threat and fear, promise divine happiness in the hereafter if man conditions himself to certain beliefs and dogmas. If you examine both ideas, they have common attitudes towards man: one says that he must be controlled by the law of the state, and the other that he must be dominated through punishment and reward in the hereafter. The religious and the nonreligious, though they hate each other, are fundamentally alike, for they both believe in conditioning and controlling man. This is what has happened and what is now taking place. In both there is this fundamental idea of dominating, compelling, forcing man to a certain pattern.

With this compulsion there can be no true fulfillment. There can be creative intelligence and happiness only when there is no compulsion, when you act voluntarily, without fear. To know creative action, without this continual, limiting compulsion, you must become conscious of the innumerable impositions that are placed upon you, and which you have created in search of your own egotistic security through society and religion. In voluntarily freeing yourself from these egotistic compulsions, there is fulfillment.

How can there be fulfillment if there is compulsion and so fear? Fear and compulsion will exist as long as action is based on egotistic expression. When your mind and heart free themselves from those values based on exploitation and religious egotism, then there can be true and intelligent fulfillment. It is only voluntary action that will ever keep society pure and man intelligent.

Question: If man is life and life is eternally perfect, why must man pass through experience and sorrow?

KRISHNAMURTI: Again this is one of our religious prejudices, that life is eternally perfect. You know nothing about it. All that you know is that life is a continual struggle and pain, and occasionally there is a spark of happiness, beauty, and love. The real question is: Must there be continual suffering and what significance has experience?

Sorrow is but the indication of a mind and heart held in limitation; the mere escape from sorrow and the search for a remedy does not liberate the mind, does not awaken it to intelligence. Experience becomes limitation and hindrance if the mind uses it as a means of further self-protection. We learn from experiences to protect ourselves, be more cunning, so as not to suffer. The avoidance of sorrow is called knowledge gained from experience. We learn from experiences to guard ourselves against the movement of life. So each experience leaves a self-defensive memory, and with that limitation we live through another experience, adding further walls of self-protection. Thus there is an ever-increasing barrier and limitation, and when this comes into contact with the movement of life, there is suffering. When the mind voluntarily frees itself, through understanding, from these self-protective barriers, then there is the flow of reality.

Question: What should be the ultimate goal of the individual?

KRISHNAMURTI: There can never be a goal, a finality, because life is a continual becoming, and that becoming is immortality. But the desire of man is to have something definite and certain to which he can cling and by which he can guide himself. He is continually seeking this through many subtle forms, for he is afraid of being insecure. So he says, "There must be an ultimate objective or goal." There cannot be. You want an ideal to follow because life is so confusing, conflicting, sorrowful, and you say, "I must have something by which I can guide myself, so as not to suffer." If you examine it, this is only a deep desire to escape into an illusion. So your ideal, your goal, your perfection, is simply a means of escape from this turmoil and pain.

Question: Is the law of karma, or cause and effect, a fact in nature?

KRISHNAMURTI: The Sanskrit word *karma* signifies action. You can act deeply, fully, only when the mind and heart are not held in limitation. Where there is fear, there must be the creation of illusion, limitation. This limitation creates incompleteness of action and causes suffering. From this suffering the mind seeks an escape through some illusion, ideal, belief, which only creates greater limitation in action and so further sorrow. In this vicious circle the mind is caught.

As long as action springs from fear, born of egotism, there must be incompleteness. All action born of a closed mind and heart must create conflict and suffering. As our minds are filled with many frustrations, caused through fear, it is necessary to awaken to those limitations, and the mind must voluntarily free itself from them through action. Then there is completeness of action, fulfillment.

Question: What is your opinion of spiritualism?

KRISHNAMURTI: There are many things involved in this desire to know if there is life in the hereafter. Because we have lost someone whom we love greatly, in our sorrow we desire to find out if that person continues to live. But suppose you know that life continues in the hereafter, the question of sorrow is in no way solved. The emptiness, the void is still there, but the momentary happiness of some assurance cannot lastingly cover up our agony. This constant search for consolation makes our life more and more empty, shallow, worthless.

Also there is a desire to find what is called a guide, an authority. You want to be guided because you are afraid of life, and so you create exploiters, as in organized religions.

So in your search for comfort, consolation, you are destroying yourself, creating emptiness in your mind and heart. Where there is a desire to follow, there is an indication of fear and the creation of self-defenses against intelligence, against life, reality.

October 30, 1935

Fourth Talk in Mexico City

Question: How can we educate a child to best fit him to attain the fulfillment of which you speak?

KRISHNAMURTI: Education is given either to make a child fit into a particular system, pattern, or to awaken intelligence in him so that his life shall be full and complete. If you desire to mold him to a definite system, you must first inquire into its real nature. Boys and girls are being trained to conform to a particular form of thought and action, essentially based on acquisitiveness and fear. Now do you desire your child to fit into this particular mold? If you do not, then you must look at this problem quite differently. That is, you must consider whether a human being is to be forever shaped, controlled, dominated by environment, whether he is to be forever conditioned, limited by fear; or whether, by awakening his intelligence, he is to be helped to break through this environmental limitation to deep fulfillment.

If human beings are to fulfill, there must be intense, steady thought and action on your part, because your minds are so influenced, so dominated by authority, that you think children must be imposed upon, must be shaped to fit into a particular pattern of society. When you desire a person to fit into a particular mode of conduct it indicates fear, on which your religions and social morality are based. In this frame there is no fulfillment. Please understand what I mean by individual fulfillment. I do not mean egotistic expression in any form. True fulfillment comes when the mind and heart voluntarily free themselves from those self-defensive values imposed by religion and society.

So if you would really help the child to fulfill, you must understand individual fulfillment in society. I cannot now go into details or explain the many subtle ideas that are connected with it; but as long as the mind and heart are forcing themselves to conform to a particular mode of conduct, to a pattern of egotistic self-defense, there must ever be fear, which denies true fulfillment and makes of man an imitative machine. You who are grown up, you have to awaken to the limitations of these self-defensive values, and create the true revolution, not the mere antithesis of authority.

Question: Is it your intention to create a world revolution against the existing order?

KRISHNAMURTI: Where there is the exercise of authority, there cannot be intelligence. Where there is compulsion, imposition, there must be revolt. Revolution is the result of oppression and of authority. Where there is compulsion, domination in any form, there must be revolt, revolution. After revolution has taken place, there is again established authority, the crystallization of thought and morality. From the imposition of authority to revolution, and from revolution to compulsion once again—this is the vicious circle in which the mind is continually caught. What will break this circle is the understanding of the deep significance of authority itself.

We create authority through the desire for comfort and security, for enrichment and protection, not only here but also in the hereafter. Based on this desire there is established a social and religious structure which must oppress and exploit others; and against this, there is the reaction of revolt. If you who are creating compulsion and hence misery for others and for yourself become deeply aware of its poison, then there would not be fear expressing itself through attachment to an ideal, to a belief, to a family, as a means of security. There would then be that constant becoming, that living movement of life, the everlasting.

Mere revolution, without the fundamental inquiry into authority, creates a new prison in which your mind and heart will again be caught. A revolution is created by a group, and that group has come into being through individual thought and action. But if the individual is only seeking, consciously or unconsciously, his own security, then there will arise but another group of compulsions and impositions. What truly matters is this constant awareness to free the mind and heart from their own desire to be secure. When the mind is truly free from craving for security, when the mind is truly insecure, then there is the ecstasy of the movement of life, which cannot be known through a mere revolt, a reaction against authority.

Question: What is the significance of death?

KRISHNAMURTI: We will discover the significance of death by understanding the unhappiness and the agony caused by death. When there is a death, there is an intense shock which we call suffering. You have lost someone whom you love greatly, on whom you have relied, who enriched you. When there is suffering, the indication of poverty of being, we seek a remedy, the remedy which religions offer, the final unity of all human beings, with the many theories concerning it. Then there is the spiritualistic drug, and the comfortable remedy in the idea of reincarnation. We seek innumerable escapes from the agony caused by the death of someone whom we love greatly. These escapes are but subtle ways to lose and forget ourselves. Our concern is not with the dead, but with our own suffering. Only we call it the love of the dead.

Now if you do not seek consolation, however subtle it may be, then that very suffering will awaken your true intelligence, which alone will reveal the flow of reality. I am not theorizing; I am telling you what really does take place. Through death you become conscious of your own emptiness, void, loneliness, and this causes pain; and to be free of this agony, you seek remedies, consolations. You are merely seeking opiates to drug your mind. So the mind becomes a slave to ideals, beliefs, and the inquiry into the idea of reincarnation, into the spirit world, only leads to further enslavement. All this indicates poverty of being. To cover it up you seek guides, modes of conduct, systems of thought. But you can never cover it up. However much the mind may try to avoid it or try to escape from that shallowness, it continues to express itself in many ways. It is important that the mind does not escape through any remedy, that it faces wholly its own emptiness. As most of you have not faced it completely, you cannot say that there will be nothingness, further emptiness. You will find out what takes place only after experimenting, living in this manner. In becoming fully conscious you will observe how the mind is ever trying to avoid the deep understanding of the cause of sorrow, and in that full awareness you will truly dissolve the cause.

In carefully covering up the cause of emptiness, the subtle and deep egotism, you think that you have solved the problem of death. Suffering is but the indication of a stagnant and attached mind, and instead of realizing this you merely seek another form of drug to put it to sleep again. So our life is a continual awakening, called sorrow, and being put to sleep again.

When there is suffering, beware of being put to sleep by comforters with their remedies. When the mind has lost its own egotistic limitation, then there is that movement of life, ever becoming, in which there is no shadow of death.

Question: It is clear that organized religion cannot make man perfect, but does it not bring him nearer to God through encouraging a life of virtue and unselfishness?

KRISHNAMURTI: Let us be very clear what we mean by religion. For me, organized religions have nothing to do with the sayings of the great teachers. The teachers have said do not kill, love your neighbor, but religions of vested interest encourage and support the slaughter of humanity. (Applause) By encouraging nationalism, supporting a special class, with all its organized belief, religion participates in the killing of man. Religions throughout the world not only exploit through fear, but also separate man from man. Such organized religions cannot in any way aid man in the realization of truth.

Now this organized belief which we call religion has been created by us, it hasn't miraculously come into being. We have created it through our desire for security and as a means of self-defense. As we have brought it into being through our fear, we must through our thought and action free ourselves from its false ideals and values; but if we merely seek further security, it will become another prison to hold the mind and heart. Where there is a search for security, self-protection, here or in the hereafter, there can never be the understanding of truth, which alone shall set man free.

When you say that you must be unselfish in order to realize God, you are really being egotistic in a subtle form. That is, you say, "I shall love my neighbor in order to find happiness, God." Then you do not know love; you are merely looking for a reward; the mentality of one seeking an exchange cannot understand truth. You do not perceive beauty in action itself, but you are really interested in what reward action will bring you. You develop virtue as a means of self-protection. The so-called virtuous shall not know the beauty of truth. Man can understand it only when his mind and heart are completely naked and vulnerable. Most people are afraid of being vulnerable to life, so they develop protective walls which they call virtue. When there is no longer the desire nor the necessity to protect oneself, then there is bliss.

Question: Is God just and good? If so, why does he permit evil in the world?

KRISHNAMURTI: Let us leave God out of this question, because you don't know, really, whether God is good or evil. You have been told that God is love, that he is just and good. And if you really, profoundly believed it, your whole life would be different. As it is not, do not concern yourself about God.

You want to know how and why evils, miserable conditions, exploitation exist in the world. We have created them. Each individual, through his intense desire to be secure, to be safe, to be certain, has created a society, a religion, in whose shelter he takes comfort. So we as individuals have created this system, and as individuals we will have to awaken to our creation and destroy all the things that are false in it; then in that freedom there will be love, truth.

Instead of escaping from the objective world of confusion and misery into the subjective, in which you hope to find God, let there be harmony between the subjective and the objective. Begin to discover this harmony; do not crave for it, but become aware of the cause of disharmony. By understanding how this disharmony comes into being through the many forms of egotistic expression, you will naturally come to that harmony which is enduring, living.

Question: Does consciousness evolve?

KRISHNAMURTI: Many people think that there is a universal or cosmic consciousness, or whatever they call it, and a particular, individualistic consciousness. What we intimately know is the individualistic, limited consciousness, and you are asking me if this consciousness is progressive, evolving.

Now what do you mean by individual consciousness? This limited consciousness is the result of conflict between desire and environment, that is, the present and the past; this consciousness is the result of the various impositions, compulsions, to which the mind has submitted itself in its search for security; it is also the many scars of incomplete action. The 'I' or egotistic consciousness is made up of these conflicts, compulsions, and the many layers of self-defensive memories. With this background the mind lives through an experience and learns from it only further means of self-protection. When you say you are learning through experience, you fundamentally mean you are erecting greater and more cunning walls of self-defense. So each

experience is creating further defenses, barriers against life.

You ask me if this limited consciousness, having its roots in self-protection, evolves and perfects itself. How can it? It cannot. However much it may seem to evolve, it must ever remain a center of limitation and frustration. A consciousness based on self-protective memories must lead to illusion, not to reality.

Question: You speak of a truth which is at present beyond the reach of our minds and hearts. Since we know of its existence only through you, how can we strive for it unless we accept it on your authority?

KRISHNAMURTI: As I explained, we accept authority when we seek security, comfort, certainty. If you seek truth in order to shelter yourself against the storm and confusion of life, then you will find authorities that will give you comfort. But I am not offering you comfort. I say that there is the bliss of reality when the mind is free from compulsion and illusion. Where there is a search for comfort there must be egotism, which in its subtlest form is sometimes called the search for truth. The following of another cannot awaken your mind to reality. Instead of escaping to an ideal, to the truth of another, discover how confusion and sorrow have been created in and about you. In piercing through the false values in which the mind takes shelter there comes the perception of reality.

We think that intelligent fulfillment lies in following a method, a discipline, and so we look to another, which makes our action incomplete and limited. We try to escape from this shallowness, frustration, by creating new authorities, and so increase our limitations. They are caused by our own actions based on reward, recompense, on fear and compulsion. Instead of trying to become complete, discover the cause of frustration, which is

egotism in its many subtle forms. As long as
you are living in a set of false values, there
must be incompleteness and suffering. None
can lead you out of it except you yourself
through your own effort and understanding.

November 3, 1935

Questions

Auckland, 1934

41. Without wishing to exploit the speaker, I look upon him as one of the greatest of all exemplifiers of philosophic altruism, but I would much like him to tell his audience here this afternoon what belief he has in the ultimate millennium, that no doubt he and the whole of the human race seek.   52

Ojai, 1934

1. You say that the 'I' is the product of environment. Do you mean that a perfect environment could be created which would not develop the 'I' consciousness? If so, the perfect freedom of which you speak is a matter of creating the right environment. Is this correct?   59

2. When I see vice rampant in the world, I feel an intense desire to fight against that vice and against all the suffering it creates in the lives of my fellow human beings. This means great conflict, for when I try to help I am often viciously opposed. How then can you say that there is no conflict between the false and the true?   60

3. In your talk yesterday, you spoke of environment as the movement of the false. Do you include in environment all the creations of nature, including human forms?   61

4. It is perfectly clear to me that the 'I' consciousness is the result of environment, but do you not see that the 'I' did not originate for the first time in this life? From what you say it is obvious that the 'I' consciousness, being the result of environment, must have begun in the distant past and will continue in the future.   61

5. What is the difference between self-discipline and suppression?   62

6. Granted that the 'I' is made up of reactions from environment, by what method can one escape its limitations?   64

7. You speak of the necessity of a drastic revolution in the life of the individual. If he does not want to revolutionize his outward personal environment because of the suffering it would cause to his family and friends, will inward revolution lead him to the freedom from all conflict?   65

8. Can you explain why environment started being false instead of true? What is the origin of all this mess and trouble?   65

9. Do you consider that karma is the interaction between the false environment and the false 'I'?   66

10. Does intuition include past experience and something else, or only past experience?   67

11. How can I act freely and without self-repression when I know that my action must hurt those that I love? In such a case, what is the test of right action?   67

12. Am I right in believing that all conditions and environment become right to a really intelligent mind? Is it not a question of seeing the art in the pattern?   68

13. There seems to be the idea that liberation is a goal, a culmination. What is the difference in this case between striving for liberation and striving for any other culmination?   69

14. Some people say your idea is that we should become liberated now, while we have the opportunity, and that we can become Masters later on, at some other time. But if we are to become Masters at all, why is it not good for us to begin to set our feet on that way now?   69

New York City, 1935

Brazil, 1935

Montevideo, 1935

Argentina, 1935

Chile, 1935

Mexico City, 1935

Index